1st ed
1750

The Letters of Alexander Woollcott

Also by Alexander Woollcott

LONG, LONG AGO

WHILE ROME BURNS

Anthologies

AS YOU WERE · WOOLLCOTT'S SECOND READER

THE WOOLLCOTT READER

The Letters of
Alexander Woollcott

Edited by
Beatrice Kaufman and Joseph Hennessey

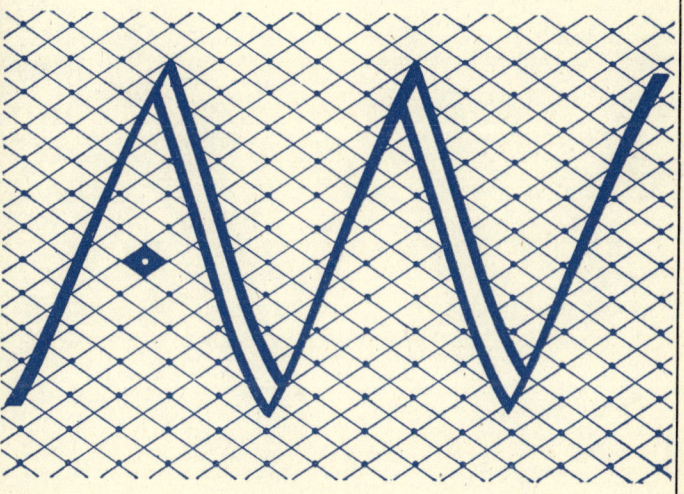

NEW YORK
The Viking Press
1944

THIS EDITION IS PRODUCED IN FULL COMPLIANCE WITH
ALL WAR PRODUCTION BOARD CONSERVATION ORDERS

COPYRIGHT 1944 BY THE VIKING PRESS, INC.

PUBLISHED BY THE VIKING PRESS IN JULY 1944
PUBLISHED ON THE SAME DAY IN THE DOMINION OF CANADA BY
THE MACMILLAN COMPANY OF CANADA LIMITED

PRINTED IN U. S. A. BY THE HADDON CRAFTSMEN, INC., SCRANTON, PA.

Contents

A portrait of Alexander Woollcott and reproductions of three letters precede page 1

BIOGRAPHICAL INTRODUCTION   vii
A NOTE ON THE LETTERS   xxiii

THE LETTERS

I	CHILDHOOD TO 1910	1
II	WORLD WAR AND POSTWAR, 1917-1919	21
III	THE 1920's	75
IV	1930-1932	85
V	1933-1935	117
VI	1936-1937	157
VII	1938-1939	199
VIII	1940	225
IX	1941	268
X	1942	289
XI	1943	388

INDEX   403

Biographical Introduction

Alexander Woollcott's letters, even on business matters, were always personal, and in a personal correspondence a great deal of knowledge before the fact is taken for granted. We will not attempt to give a detailed biography of Woollcott, or any appraisal of him, but only to supply the reader with a factual backdrop for the letters. Through them, the man speaks for himself.

Alexander Woollcott, the youngest of the five children of Walter and Frances Bucklin Woollcott, was born on January 19, 1887, in Phalanx, New Jersey. The settlement itself, known as "the Phalanx," was the seat of a co-operative society derivative, together with the better known Brook Farm, of the eighteenth-century social philosophy of Charles Fourier. It was an experiment in communal living combining agriculture and industry, and, like all these early experiments, it failed to provide a living for its members. Within a few years of its inception, the Phalanx was taken over by Woollcott's maternal grandfather, and from then on became the Bucklin family seat.

The house was a large, rambling, eighty-five-room structure which was continually swarming with near and distant relatives of all ages who came and went continually. In the years to follow, the Woollcott branch often found it a valuable refuge in times of financial stress.

Woollcott's first two years were lived at the Phalanx. But Walter Woollcott had an errant nature; he seems to have spent a great deal of his life migrating from one side of the country to the other, often accompanied by his family, and in 1889 he took his brood to Kansas City. There Woollcott first went to school. (Half a century later his first teacher, Miss Sophie Rosenberger, sent him one of his compositions she had carefully saved.) His friendship with Lucy Christie (Drage) began there, and his first interest in the theatre was aroused when Roswell Field (Eugene's brother) took him to see *Sinbad the Sailor*. There, also, he made his first public appearance when he took the part of Puck in a Shakespearean pageant at the age of four—and was made ineffably happy forty years later by the discovery of a photograph of himself in the role.

In 1896 the family moved to Germantown, Pennsylvania, and their summers were again spent at the Phalanx. Woollcott went to public school, and it was to his teacher, Miss Sorber, that he wrote the first letter which we have been able to obtain. At this time his friendship with his schoolmate and neighbor, George Smyser Agnew, began—a friendship which went on until his death.

Although the Woollcotts were on the poor side, financially speaking, they were intellectually affluent. During the summers at the Phalanx, music and art were part of the daily life, and Dickens and Thackeray were read aloud to the family by Mr. Woollcott. Woollcott's mother and his sister Julie were definitely of bookish tastes; an evening's diversion often consisted of the reading of Shakespeare, with each member of the family assigned roles. Julie and he spent long hours together; despite the fact that she was considerably his senior, the bond between them was always exceptionally strong, and she had a great influence in directing his early literary tastes. Amateur theatricals were his favorite diversion.

By the time Woollcott was ready for high school the family

had installed themselves more or less permanently at the Phalanx, leaving him to board out during the four years he attended Central High School in Philadelphia. He helped support himself during this period by writing book reviews which his cousin, Miss Helen Sears, helped him to place in the *Evening Telegraph* and the *Record*. Whenever he had any extra money he betook himself to the gallery of a Philadelphia theatre, where for the first time he saw such stars as Otis Skinner and Minnie Maddern Fiske, who later became friends to whom he was devoted.

Autumn of 1905 found Woollcott climbing the hill to the Hamilton campus overlooking the Mohawk Valley. Edwin Root, a distant relative and an alumnus of Hamilton, was responsible for this choice of college, a choice which had an enormous influence on his whole life.

He was a good student. He won his Phi Beta Kappa key during his junior year; he took an immediate interest in the college paper, and was editor of the *Lit* in his junior and senior years; he founded the first dramatic club, Charlatans. Woollcott was a poor boy who went to a college which, at that time, was also poor. His love for Hamilton was the love of a son who felt the need of caring for his mother, like him in need. When the news that the Carnegie Fund had made the college a gift of a hundred thousand dollars was announced, Woollcott wrote an ecstatic editorial for the *Lit* called "Surely Our Cup Runneth Over."

He became the ideal alumnus; Hamilton always occupied a large place in his heart and he planned for it with love and care. Besides helping innumerable boys pay their tuition at his Alma Mater, he worked assiduously for the Hamilton Choir, which he transported to New York for yearly concerts to fill their coffers; he also founded and contributed to a yearly literary prize; he sent hundreds of books to fill the library shelves. He made substantial contributions to the college itself and served on the board of trustees for several years. His ashes are buried in the college cemetery next to the campus he loved so well.

In 1909 Woollcott came to New York with his diploma in his hand and got a $15 a week job as a clerk in the Chemical National Bank, but this was quickly terminated by a particularly virulent attack of the mumps. Upon his recovery he armed himself with a letter from Samuel Hopkins Adams, another Hamilton alumnus, and went to see Carr Van Anda, managing editor of the *New York Times*, who put him to work as a reporter. He seems to have been only a fair reporter; although he loved newspaper work, the limitations imposed by cold, impersonal facts were not well suited to a style of writing which was already showing the earmarks later to become so characteristic. He was therefore delighted when, in 1914, at the resignation of Adolph Klauber, he was appointed the *Times* dramatic critic.

In those days the *New York Times* obviously considered the theatre of minor importance. Dramatic criticism was relegated to a small and inconspicuously placed space in the daily paper, and Woollcott's pay was $60 a week. It served, however, to allow him greater latitude in which to develop his own particular style, and Woollcott the phrase-maker began to emerge. By the time of the war he had become a well-known figure on Broadway and an influential critic.

When America entered the World War in 1917, Woollcott was unable to get into combatant service because of his bad eyesight. He enlisted in the New York Post-Graduate Hospital Unit, afterwards officially known as Base Hospital No. 8, and went with them to France, where he was promoted to Sergeant. In the hospital he performed the usual duties of an orderly, and he did his unpleasant job well. In 1918 he was transferred to the *Stars and Stripes*, the weekly newspaper of the AEF. His job as its star reporter took him often to the front. On the *Stars and Stripes* were many men who afterwards made conspicuous places for themselves: Harold Ross, founder and editor of *The*

New Yorker; Franklin P. Adams (F. P. A.); John T. Winterich (now Colonel); Stephen Early, Mark Watson, A. A. Wallgren. Woollcott stayed in France until six months after the armistice, still working on the paper.

In the summer of 1919 he returned to this country. He resumed his job as dramatic critic of the *New York Times,* and his first book was published, *The Command Is Forward,* a collection of stories, most of which had appeared in the *Stars and Stripes.*

His vitality at this time was enormous, as was his love for the theatre, and he bellowed his praise and condemnation so violently that he became the most influential critic of his day. Now his reviews were signed, and his eccentric appearance made him a conspicuous first-night figure. He affected a flowing cape, an opera hat, and a cane, and he was definitely the cynosure as he swept down the aisle into his front seat in a theatre. The poses which he adopted at this time were gradually assimilated into the picture of him which remained in the minds of the public, a picture which he deliberately encouraged and which afforded him amused satisfaction.

The next nine years of Woollcott's life were spent primarily in the theatre; he left the *Times* in 1922 for a brief sojourn as critic of the *Sun,* but he was not happy on an evening paper, as he felt that his potency in that position was diminished. When Munsey sold the *Sun* he was switched to the *Herald,* another Munsey paper. In 1925 he went to the *World,* then under the aegis of Herbert Bayard Swope. Here, along with Walter Lippmann, F. P. A., Heywood Broun, Deems Taylor, Frank Sullivan, and others, he helped to make that paper the most exciting of its day.

Woollcott's personality made it inevitable that he should develop both great loves and great hates in the people who made up the world of the theatre. His enthusiasms ran away with him, and his praise often was enough to start a long line at the box office. His condemnation, sometimes considered injudiciously bestowed, was often a death knell. Woollcott's extraordinary skill in using words obviously gave him power to inflict great pain; people of the theatre were chagrined and resentful at some of the phrases relating to their performances. Many of his warmest friendships, however, were begun because of his praise of hitherto unrecognized talents. In 1924 the Marx brothers, who had played in vaudeville for years, came to New York in a musical comedy (*I'll Say She Is*) which, because its opening was during a particularly busy week, was comparatively unnoticed by the critics. By chance Woollcott attended a matinee, and was so captivated by the antics of Harpo Marx that he re-reviewed the play (a brief notice had already been written by a second-string critic), and his enthusiasm dragooned all the other first-line critics into seeing the show. This made the play an instant success and established the Marxes. Woollcott not only recognized the rare comedy spirit of the four brothers, but discovered in Harpo a quality and charm which made them the closest of friends during the rest of his life.

Woollcott was now living in a reconditioned house on West Forty-Seventh Street, where he approximated, perhaps unconsciously, his earlier communal life at the Phalanx. The other apartments were occupied by Harold Ross and his wife, Jane Grant, Hawley Truax, Kate Oglebay, an old friend originally from Kansas City, and another friend, William Powell. There was a dining-room shared by all and a great deal of informal entertaining. His days were a happy combination of work and people. He lunched daily at the Algonquin Round Table with a group of men and women, still young, who were to become extraordinarily successful in various creative fields. The Round Table in its day was the informal meeting place for F. P. A., Heywood Broun, Brock and Murdock Pemberton, John Peter Toohey, Peggy Wood, Margaret Leech, George Kaufman, Marc Connelly, Deems Taylor, Robert Benchley, Dorothy Parker,

Donald Ogden Stewart, Jane Grant and Harold Ross, to mention some of them. This group knew each other intimately; their humor was frequently barbed, and Woollcott took great advantage of his skill in riposte. When his remarks were particularly sharp, it was not unusual for angry words to pass back and forth, with Woollcott likely to be the victor. Many people thought him rude; but it was a rudeness of manner rather than intent. The comedy of insult was quite the order of the day. This did not, however, excuse him in the eyes of many whose feelings were hurt.

The other great social event which occurred with regularity was the weekly meeting of the Thanatopsis Inside Straight and Literary Club, a poker game played each week at the home of a member. Its personnel was drawn from the Algonquin Round Table, and was entirely masculine, with an occasional woman permitted as both dinner companion and kibitzer.

Woollcott's life was full now—the theatre was flourishing and there were often as many as ten new plays to be reviewed in a week when the season was at its height. In addition to his newspaper work, he had become a frequent contributor to magazines such as *The Saturday Evening Post*, *Vanity Fair*, *Cosmopolitan*, *Collier's*, and he had begun his weekly column, "Shouts and Murmurs," for *The New Yorker*. This informal column concerned itself with a criticism of a current play, a note about an interesting murder (a subject which fascinated him all his life), caustic or favorable comment on contemporary fiction, or just a recounting of an amusing story about one of his favorites. He also found time during these years to do more sustained pieces of writing: *The Story of Irving Berlin* was published; a book about Mrs. Fiske; *Mr. Dickens Goes to the Play*; *Enchanted Aisles*. None of these earlier books had wide circulation.

Woollcott's life had assumed a pattern, adapted to the hours of a newspaper man. His day began at noon at the Algonquin; the afternoons he spent at the newspaper; an early dinner, the theatre, and then to write his review. Later he would take up again with his guest of the evening; he had supper or joined a group of friends, where there might be a game of bridge, hearts, cribbage, backgammon, or anagrams, any one of which he would play passionately till early in the morning. He loved to gamble; but he played all games with a competitive zest that had no relation to the size of the stakes. Obviously such a schedule left him little time for letter writing and accounts for the dearth of letters from this period.

About this time Woollcott began to feel that dramatic criticism was no longer a satisfactory medium. He had to write too quickly; his style was at its best when it had time to be seasoned; both his truculences and his enthusiasms needed tempering, and he was aware of it. In 1928 he resigned from the *World* with no very definite idea of what he wanted to do.

In the next few years he wandered both here and abroad; twice he took houses in the south of France with friends; he made many trips to England and went to both Japan and China.

On his return he moved from the house on West Forty-Seventh Street and took an apartment next to Alice Duer Miller, on Fifty-Second Street at the East River. Here he thought he would have greater privacy. That this turned out not to be so was, of course, no accident; by this time the pattern of his social life was firmly fixed, and he allotted people small parcels of minutes with the exquisite timing of a busy doctor. A large calendar hung on the wall right above his desk; he could see at a glance what he would be doing every hour of the day for months ahead.

In the summer of 1929 he wrote his first play, in collaboration with George S. Kaufman. *The Channel Road*, an adaptation of the Maupassant story, "Boule de Suif," had a run of exactly fifty performances. Woollcott was not discouraged, but turned to still another field—radio. His first appearance on the air was on an isolated fifteen-minute sustaining program which he called "The Town Crier." It got a sponsor quickly and went on twice a week; from there it was just a brief time until he appeared on a national network on a program known as "The Early Bookworm," and his voice saying "This is Woollcott speaking" soon became familiar to millions of people. He loved the radio; it opened up a wide and responsive audience, and one with which he felt he was in immediate contact. Fan mail delighted him; his pockets were continually bulging with comments from his listeners, which, like a schoolboy, he read to all who would listen.

Throughout his life Woollcott had a reluctance to see himself tied up too far ahead, and he never allowed even his radio life to interfere with his summers. In 1923, with some friends, he founded a little club on Neshobe Island, Lake Bomoseen, Vermont. In the beginning the clubhouse itself was a summer camp of the simplest kind, with kerosene lamps and life reduced to the essentials. The wooded island covered seven acres and guaranteed complete privacy; the lake water had a balmy quality which made swimming delightful. The club membership, which did not change much during the years, was composed of such friends as Neysa McMein, Alice Duer Miller, Harpo Marx, the Raymond Iveses, Beatrice Kaufman, Raoul Fleischmann, Grace Eustis, Harold Guinzburg, and Howard Dietz. Its pastimes were swimming, sailing, badminton, croquet, and in the evening all sorts of games from anagrams to bridge. Woollcott considered Lake Bomoseen the most beautiful spot in the world at all seasons of the year. He never tired of it and never felt restless; gradually he came to spend more time there each summer, until soon he was living there six months of the year.

But the theatre bug was still in his system. In 1931 his friend S. N. Behrman, author of such comedies as *The Second Man* and *Rain from Heaven*, offered him a part in his play, *Brief Moment*. Woollcott was delighted from every point of view; the character was a mild caricature of himself who lay supine on a couch throughout the play, occasionally exploding into typical Woollcottian invective, and he was continually on the stage from the beginning to the final curtain. He loved every moment of it.

After the play closed, in 1932, he went to Russia, where his old friend Walter Duranty, then Russian correspondent for the *New York Times*, served as guide. He saw everything there was to see in the Russian theatre, to the detriment, perhaps, of more attention he might have paid the Communist experiment; but he met all the leaders in the contemporary political picture and returned to the United States full of admiration and respect for things Russian.

In 1933 Woollcott again collaborated with George Kaufman, this time in a mystery play entitled *The Dark Tower*, which was also doomed to fail. This was his last attempt at playwriting and he again turned his attention to radio, in which he functioned continually and successfully until his death. By this time his services were in great demand, and he was one of the highly paid stars of the air. His subject matter varied greatly; sometimes he reviewed a play or a book (his enthusiastic praise of James Hilton's *Good-bye, Mr. Chips*, for example, made it a national best-seller overnight); sometimes he gave a surprise serenade to some well-known figure (such as Jerome Kern or Walt Disney) with a large orchestra and such guest stars as Noel Coward, Ethel Barrymore, or the Lunts; or he talked of some organization like the Seeing Eye, which was close to his heart. It was part of a self-imposed mission to try to stimulate the public into reading a book or seeing a play he thought worthwhile.

He was also popular as a lecturer, but was never willing to commit himself to a national tour. He chose instead to speak occasionally at universities, where he might, perhaps, influence the minds of the young. In 1933 he gave a series of lectures on journalism at Columbia University, and a little later another series at the New School for Social Research. In 1934 his first best-seller was published, *While Rome Burns*, a potpourri of his magazine writing.

Woollcott's life had by now changed completely from that of his newspaper days. He arose at eight, read his mail, which had become voluminous by this time, while he drank cup after cup of black coffee. If he did not have to dictate a radio broadcast or a magazine article to his secretary, the first visitor would be shown in promptly by nine o'clock. The procession of guests was steady until he went to dine. He was extraordinarily gregarious. A Sunday morning breakfast went on steadily from nine o'clock in the morning until four in the afternoon. When Woollcott's apartment became overcrowded, the guests often spread out over Alice Duer Miller's more spacious quarters adjoining. They shared so many mutual friends that it became a habit for him and Mrs. Miller to entertain together, formally as well as informally. In the evenings he wandered among his friends, and went occasionally to the theatre. It still held its interests for him and, now that he was no longer a dramatic critic, he was able to pick his fare more discriminatingly. He loved it now mostly for the friendships he had made in it, and he often went to out-of-town openings to see such friends as Ruth Gordon, the Lunts, Katharine Cornell, Helen Hayes, or the first performance of a play by Thornton Wilder, whom he admired above all American dramatists.

In 1936, after eight or nine years of a frantically busy life in New York, Woollcott decided that his Vermont island offered him a much more restful and agreeable routine. He wanted a house for all-year-round use, and Joe Hennessey, who had been running the club for several years, undertook to build it for him. A site was chosen on a ridge overlooking the lake on all sides, and a low, rambling, stone house was built which became his permanent home until his death.

With Woollcott established in his own home in 1937, he became the dominant force on the island to an even greater extent than he had been before. Even here his innate gregariousness, however, forced him to approximate his New York routine as closely as possible. He ran the island as a benevolent monarchy, and he summoned both club members and other friends to appear at all seasons of the year; he turned the island into a crowded vacation ground where reservations must be made weeks in advance; the routine of life was completely remade to suit his wishes. He decided which guests were to sleep where; late risers were assigned rooms in his own house where the early morning activities of the clubhouse would not awaken them. Others were summarily called for a seven o'clock pre-breakfast dip regardless of temperature.

Breakfast went on all morning, with Woollcott presiding at the table in a dressing gown. Around eleven o'clock there was a croquet game if possible; it was always his favorite form of exercise both physically and in terms of the peculiar competitive quality which this game, above all others, is able to arouse in its players. The Woollcott version of croquet is played with long-handled, heavy English mallets and composition balls which barely pass through the narrow wickets, and to play it well requires skill at a complicated strategy. The course on the island is a tiny plot of rough ground surrounded by woods dipping sharply to the lake, so that balls sent into the woods often required three strokes to get them back into the clear. It was nothing for one game of croquet to last three hours. Passions ran high, including Woollcott's, even when the game was played for nothing.

A secretary was in constant residence, and Woollcott generally worked a few hours each day. In 1935 he had edited an anthology called *The Woollcott Reader* which quickly reached a very large audience. Now he followed this with *Woollcott's Second Reader*. These were, in reality, an evangelistic enterprise designed to make people read his favorites. He did an occasional series of broadcasts, was a frequent contributor to magazines, and he lectured here and there at his pleasure. In the Fall of 1938 he again returned to the theatre as an actor, this time in another play by S. N. Behrman called *Wine of Choice*, and in a part not too dissimilar to the one he played in *Brief Moment*. The play stayed on the road for three months and had a brief run in New York. It then quietly folded in time for Woollcott to return to the island for the summer.

By now, however, his appetite for acting had been considerably whetted by his two experiences, and when Moss Hart visited the island in 1939 Woollcott suggested that he and George Kaufman write a part for him in their next play. The two playwrights were delighted with this idea, but in the course of their planning *The Man Who Came to Dinner*, it turned out to be not only a play for Woollcott but one about him. He was ecstatic, but cool afterthought made him feel that it was in questionable taste for him to appear in a play in which he himself was the protagonist. In the eyes of most of its audience, the portrait of the self-centered prima donna riding roughshod over ordinary people's feelings was far from flattering. The fact that he, himself, liked it and longed to play it is evidence that he was not unaware of his faults as others saw them. Subsequently, after the play had become a New York success, the temptation became too great and he happily volunteered to appear in the Pacific Coast company. He used the early Fall months for a lecture tour which took him from New York to Seattle and left him in Hollywood in January 1940, in time for rehearsals. He learned the enormous part of Sheridan Whiteside with great ease. He now had his wish so far as his career in the theatre was concerned; he was not only playing a leading part, but the play itself was a big success. And he was in Los Angeles, the home of many of his friends. Harpo Marx was there, Walt Disney, Frank Craven, Charlie Chaplin.

He took a bungalow at a hotel; he had his valet and his secretary with him, and Joe Hennessey was there also. In near-by bungalows were George Kaufman and Moss Hart, Charles Laughton, Robert Benchley, Dorothy Parker and her husband,

Alan Campbell; between them all and the demanding role he was acting every night, his life would have been a taxing one even for a man with more vitality than his. When the play finally settled for a run in San Francisco in March, the same life continued, with, of course, the list of friends changed. The average actor spends his mornings in bed, but Woollcott continued with outside activities at the same tempo as though he had not the extra strain of his nightly role on his shoulders. He still arose at eight in the morning to read his mail and his papers, he still dictated letters and articles till noon, and his late afternoons and late nights were taken up by his friends.

Late in April Woollcott had a severe heart attack, his first serious illness since the mumps in 1909. It necessitated his immediate withdrawal from *The Man Who Came to Dinner*, and the show was forced to close. After several weeks in bed he was able to return to Lake Bomoseen for a long period of complete inactivity. From this time on his health was a matter of great concern to everyone who cared for him; he never completely recovered from the serious damage done to his heart. The attacks were recurrent; the curtain had begun its final descent and he knew it. Each convalescence found him attempting to return to at least a modified form of his old routine; in the Fall of 1940 he went on the air electioneering for Roosevelt and early in 1941 he was back on the road again in *The Man Who Came to Dinner*. By this time he had been forced to realize that there were definite limitations to what his body could stand, but the curtailment of his activities was a constant sorrow to him. The hot breath of war could already be felt and he longed to contribute something for the causes in which he believed so strongly.

In the Fall of 1941, against all medical advice, he went to England, and did a spirited series of broadcasts which the English seemed to find heartening. On his return he gave some lectures in the Middle West in the form of a report on English morale in a section of our country which he thought needed it. This activity brought on another series of heart attacks which were followed by an operation and a long convalescence, but the Fall of 1942 found him feeling greatly bettered and functioning with all his zest of ten years ago.

He came to New York for the winter and established himself at the Hotel Gotham. He broadcast several times for commercial programs, he was on "Information Pleace" a couple of times, he wrote a monthly article for the *Reader's Digest,* and he also edited a pocket anthology called *As You Were,* selected to please the men in the armed forces, from which he turned over all earnings to the United Seamen's Fund.

On January 23, 1943, he had a fatal heart attack while broadcasting on a program called "The People's Forum." He died that same night.

To the average man a life devoid of the family relationships which make up the usual human experience would necessarily be an unhappy one; Woollcott found work and friendship, which he inextricably combined, a satisfactory substitute.

His letters show how much his work meant to him. Woollcott loved to work; he sat down to the actual job of transferring his thoughts to paper with infinite pleasure, and if the finished article satisfied him, he rose exhilarated. He was a meticulous worker who painstakingly searched for the perfect phrase. His work did not always measure up to his hopes; he knew it was uneven, but when it was good he was like a small boy who has just found a full jar of cookies. He entered on each job with anticipation, as he always felt that his best work was still ahead of him. He received both critical praise and condemnation. This, we feel, is not the place for either.

His letters also show how much people meant to him. He was unusually sociable and had many more close friends of all ages than the average person: a boy at college, a neighbor in Vermont, a young girl who wanted to write, an agreeable companion on a train, as well as important figures of the theatrical and literary worlds in which he moved. He entered eagerly and with infinite curiosity into the lives of each and every one of them; each was an unfinished serial and he looked forward to every meeting for the next installment. His incredible memory enabled him to follow these lives intimately and with unflagging interest. Retold and embellished with the Woollcottian touch, their stories often acquired romance and adventure to such a degree that the protagonists would hardly recognize themselves.

Friendship with Woollcott was precarious, but this seemed never to serve as a deterrent. He was capricious, wilful, spoiled, and at times moody. He was impatient with the obvious and the trite. These characteristics inevitably brought quarrels. He wrote angry, cutting, and sometimes cruel letters; none of them is included in this collection for the reason that the editors did not receive any. Certainly they exist, but they were withheld by their recipients either because the fundamental relationship with Woollcott was good enough to blot out whatever emotion the letters had originally aroused, or because the attack was so vitriolic that they were unwilling to see it published. Most of Woollcott's quarrels, however, were quickly reconciled. He accepted criticism cheerfully and was never reluctant to admit it when he was in the wrong. He was essentially a sentimental person. He was warm, affectionate, and generous to those he loved. He liked his friends to like each other, just as he wanted them to share his enthusiasm for a favorite play or book.

Woollcott's friends found him gay, tender, stimulating, and steadfastly loyal. These letters are the token of his great gift for friendship.

Beatrice Kaufman
Joseph Hennessey

A Note on the Letters

This book is only a small representation of the thousands of letters which Alexander Woollcott wrote. His correspondence was enormously far-flung; he wrote with no idea that his letters would ever be published; and he kept no copies. To prepare this book, we wrote to his known friends and published notes in the literary journals, asking that his letters be sent to us. It is, therefore, quite possible that some whole groups of letters have escaped us. Some we know are war casualties—close friends such as Walter Duranty and Eleanora von Mendelssohn had left them tucked away in various parts of Europe. Still other friends, Ethel Barrymore and Dr. Logan Clendening, for example, did not save their letters. And correspondence with the friends he saw most frequently consisted largely of notes arranging meetings. Yet we received a generous collection—perhaps one thousand—to select from, and of these we have chosen those which seemed of the greatest general interest.

Letters from the period of the Twenties are scarcest; then he was seeing most of his close friends daily around New York and consequently not writing many letters. The preponderance of his correspondence came from the last few years of his life, when his illness precluded his usual activity and enforced a greater leisure. Still, it has been a satisfaction to us that we have been able to represent in considerable detail the interests, activities, and associates of the most important periods in Woollcott's life. We are grateful to all the friends who sent us letters, whether we could use them here or not.

We have done as little editing as possible. Deletions were largely of material that was repetitious or too personal for inclusion. We have briefly identified people and explained the circumstances of a letter only when we felt that the point might otherwise be lost. In deciding when to supply these notes, we had to remember that what will seem obvious to Woollcott's friends may be unfamiliar to his larger audience. As notes could not be repeated, the reference is usually given only on the first appearance of the name. Readers who do not go through the book consecutively can refer to the index, where the pages on which notes appear are indicated with an asterisk. Similarly, first names or last names used alone in the letters have usually been completed by us only on their first appearance or when they might be confusing. Material in [brackets] has been supplied by us; (parentheses) are Woollcott's.

Woollcott wrote occasionally in longhand, but most of his letters were dictated. We have retained his salutations and signatures, which often followed a personal whim. Sometimes he did not like a friend's given name and arbitrarily assigned him another which pleased him more; other times the names were literary allusions or were used as part of some private game. We have followed chronological order; the groupings by years is arbitrary, for the convenience of the reader.

B.K.
J.H.

ALEXANDER WOOLLCOTT

Neshobe Island
May 31

Beatrice:

You must come here some part of this and every summer. It is my favorite place in all the world. I am simply exhausted from buttering so many griddle cakes and can write no more

A.W.

FOUR HUNDRED AND FIFTY EAST FIFTY SECOND STREET

ALEXANDER WOOLLCOTT
Hotel Carlton
London
April 26th

My blossom:

    Noel is the only gamester I ever knew with my own whole-heartedness. We played backgammon or Russian Bank all the way over. I had never before crossed the Atlantic without once laying eyes on the darned thing. The other passengers were mysteriously angered by this singleness of purpose. They would stop by and say:"Dont you two ever tire of that game" or "Still at it?" or, in the case of the German passengers, they would merely say"Immer!"to each other in passing. We finally devised an effective rejoinder,merely singing in duet:
    We hope you fry in hell
    We hope you fry in hell
        Heigho
        The-merry-o
    We hope you fry in hell.

    I did not have much luck. Paid for my passage but not much over. "Cavalcade" last night. Noel's party in the royal box. A convenient arrangement,with a salon behind it for coffee and liqueurs and an adjacent room for the occasional relief of the royal kidney.

THE CREAM OF WHEAT
Broadcasts

Office of
Alexander Woollcott

485 Madison Avenue
New York City

March 1, 1935

Dear David:

These are the facts:

1: Departing for Chicago on the night of March 3rd.
2: Address until March 20th Hotel Blackstone.
3: Lecture at the Convocation at the University of Minnesota, Minneapolis, on the morning of March 7th.
4: Broadcast from Chicago Sunday evening, March 10th. Later the same evening, Thornton Wilder, Gertrude Stein and I will be the guests of some undergraduate honor society for several hours of continuous high discourse.
5: March 12th, lecture Northwestern University.
6: March 14th, lecture Toledo.
7: March 15th, lecture Detroit.
8: March 17th, broadcast from Chicago.
9: March 18th, lecture Indianapolis.
10: March 19th, visiting with the Tarkingtons and inspecting Foster Hall.
11: March 20th, lecture Chicago University.
12: March 23rd, Signet Club dinner, Harvard.
13: March 24th, broadcast from New York City.
14: March 26th, visit to Laura E. Richards, Gardiner, Maine.
15: March 27th, lecture Bowdoin College, Brunswick, Maine.
16: March 31st, broadcast from New York City.
17: April 1st, death of Mr. Woollcott, as thousands cheer.
18: April 2nd, dancing in the streets; half-holiday in all the schools; bank moratorium.
19: Burial at sea April 3rd.

Alexander Woollcott

I

Childhood to 1910

To MISS K. R. SORBER

[Woollcott was ten years old when he wrote these letters to his public school teacher.]

Phalanx, Red Bank, N. J.
August, 1897

My dear Miss Sorber,
        The Phalanx is just as beautiful as it always was and everything is so very free here.

I just got here last night and then I was so happy.

You know I spent the night in Jersy City. That is a very beautiful place. Parts of course are very busy and like any other city but then of course it has its' pretty spots. A great many in fact.

The catalpa tree's are blooming and makes the front of the house very beautiful.

It has been to hot to go on the hill this afternoon but I expect to spend tomorrow morning there.

I will take the spy glass and then I can see what changes have taken place around the country.

My Aunt Annie has a beautiful dog called Don. He is very intelligent.

I hope you are having a pleasant time. I am.

                              Your sincere pupil,
                                  Aleck Woollcott

To *MISS K. R. SORBER*

Red Bank, N. J.
August, 1897

Dear Miss Sorber,
   Please don't detest me for not answering your lovely letter. Well I flatter myself I did answer it but I lost it and somehow I let the days slip by.
   Do you remember, on the last day of school you read us about the Indian chief, Pontiac and you spoke of Evangeline. Well the other day I got it out and read it and I entirely agree, with you as to it's being fine.
   I have just finished the fourth of seven pincushions I am emboidering (dont consider spelling.
   I have just had an old tooth out. When I had gone through with the terrible ordeal I laughed.
   I have hauled out a basket of St. Nicholass and have been reading them.
   We have a lot of company now so I want to go out.

Yours truly
A. H. Woollcott

To *GEORGE SMYSER AGNEW*

[The correspondence with his boyhood best friend began when Woollcott was twelve. Their friendship continued all his life.]

Red Bank, N. J.
August 21, 1899

Dear Smyser:
   I got your little note from York and I answer it promptly.
   My brother Phil and cousin Tod have started to print old plates of people and landscape of the Phalanx. They are very

[2]

dear to all of us and so the boys have sold quantities. I have bought several so you will be glad to see them.

The other day three boys, of which I am the oldest, went on our wheels to Highland Beach, fifteen miles. We went the ocean and the river.

I am coming home on September the seventh, I think. I am very anxious to hear what you are going to say to me when I come home. I have a presentiment that it is something about Harriet Pauline. Is it?

I have *nothing* to say.

Aleck Woollcott

To GEORGE SMYSER AGNEW

Philadelphia, Pa.
June 25, 1900

Dear Smyser,

I rode up to Courtland's house today and he says he is coming tomorrow and says he will go to the Gymnasium with you. He received your note. Of course I would not have mentioned the subject to him had I not known beforehand that you had asked him yourself.

My dear Mrs. Aleshine are you going in the pool tomorrow. If you dont it will be exceedidingly malocious and i should not admire it in the extreme.

My dear mrs. Aleshine the following is a sample of the ALESHINE and LECKS UNPRONOUNCEABLE and unheard of vocabulary dictionary.

malocious .... unmusical and noisy
delupititude . weariness and utyritoyjgheirua745n ness
galavonishaw .... carthinghetreskellness

Mrs. lecks and Mrs. Aleshine are not responsible for the mean-

[3]

ing or the spelling of their vocabulary but the above is the most authorized edition of the words and their soul perspirin meanings.

Farewell Farewell
Mrs. Lecks

P.S. It is sweet to be remembered

[The boys had been reading Frank S. Stockton's *The Casting Away of Mrs. Lecks and Mrs. Aleshine*.]

To GEORGE SMYSER AGNEW

Red Bank, N. J.
July 18, 1900

Dear Smyser:
It was very wicked of you not to write to me before. It was a snipy short letter when it did come but still it is sweet to be remembered. You spoke of a Bert in your letters. Was it H.P.D. From the tune of your letter you seem to be having a good time. I know I am. I have played over three hundred games of croquet since I have been here. I am in a high temper just now having been robbed of my swimming.

When we went there today there were two bulls and about twenty cows bathing. I tried to chase them off but the bulls looked so *feee*rocious I decided not to.

I am going off crabbing tomorrow with five other boys about my age. We will be gone from about 8 A.M. till 8 P.M.

When I woke up this morning I was hopping mad to find she had skipped off to Philadelphia for a few days.

I have only been to the ocean once so far but I will pretty soon. I have malaria pretty often so I shall proceed to take a pill. We take the pill, We take the pill etc.

Oh—Matilda this place is simply littered up with a huge painting which I know would make your mouth water.

Eleanor. She brought me a little purse from Paris, with a coin from each country through which she traveled. Olive, Julie [A. W.'s sister], and Mr. Sumner (young Mr. Swigger's brother-in-law) departed on Monday, bag and baggage, mid weeping, and lamentations. (N.B. Mr. Sumner's bag and baggage consisted of a valise 1 inch by 3 inches.) We enjoyed our straw-ride very much. I ate a bag of candy, a bag of peanuts, 2 bars of popcorn, a glass of Huyler's ice-cream soda, a chocolate Milk-Shake, and a hot Frankfurter. We had a lovely ride and the moon was glorious. We sang all the way. We reached home at half past one Sunday morning. I slept all Sunday morning.

Frank Swigger and Mr. Barker went Saturday. We had a frightful thunder storm yesterday. It struck just across the road. I have written to Berry, Waldie, Mamma, and Justus but have had no answers. I don't know what would happen to Phil S. if we had a serious battle because I have to blow out his light and tie his tie. Yesterday evening he went to bed before me but staid in his mother's room because he was afraid to go into his house alone. Have just had some lovely huckle-berry-roly-poly. It certainly is handsome.

Very truly yours
Aleck. H. Woollcott

To GEORGE SMYSER AGNEW

Philadelphia, Pa.
May 3, 1903

Dear S—

We will appear tomorrow night (Monday). I am writing as you told me to warn you when the evil was to fall upon you.

I have discovered a new way to discover B's. Give this sum in mental arith. to a person whose B you want. For instance

Lyde. Tell her to think of the number of the month in which she was born, to double it, add 5, multiply by 50, add the day of the month on which she was born, subtract 365, add 115, and then ask her the result, which in her case would be 720, that is seventh month, twentieth day, July 20th, and thus you can find a persons B without their knowing it.

As in case of Mrs. Murphy this would be convenient.

Adieu
A. H. W.

What gorgeous writing.

To GEORGE SMYSER AGNEW

Theta Delta Chi House, Hamilton College,
Clinton, N. Y.
October 2, 1905

Dear Smyser,

I hope you will pardon the use of the machine but it belongs to my room-mate and as it is a new kind to me I practice on it all I can in order to get the hang of it. Arthur [Richdale] tells me that you were surprised to hear that I had come up here and I realize that I still owe you a letter. But things have gone so swiftly since I have been here that I have only scribbled off a line here and there when I had something special to communicate. Here it is after midnight and I am starting in on a letter to you.

Arthur perhaps told you that I had been chosen as one of the four freshmen to enter Theta Delta Chi this year and I am still trying to realize my good fortune. Until you have actually entered college you can have no conception of what the word fraternity means and I myself am just beginning to understand. Prior to the invitation to join there were box parties, dinner parties and card parties to give the fellows and me time to look each other over and once I accepted the pledge I moved down the hill and started in my life at the frat house. There are sixteen of us who live here together, four from each class. These live the most intimate kind of lives month in and month out, always together in each other's rooms and partaking in the same amusements. The house is a large one with fine porches and grounds and it is half way up the hill on which the campus stands.

Two ladies act as housekeepers and we all eat together a senior presiding and he always says grace. It is one of the principles of the frat to make it as much of a home life as possible and the house is furnished throughout as a large and fine residence would be. I hope you don't get tired of hearing about these details as I am very enthusiastic and think of nothing else.

We all go to chapel every morning at 8:30 and have a short, opening service. Then every Sunday we have a regular service that is supposed to be non-denominational but the leanings are decidedly Presbyterian. One of the seniors plays the organ, a big beauty that covers the entire front wall of the chapel. For voluntaries he always gives some good music instead of hymns. For instance last Sunday we had the War-march of the Priests before the service and the third movement of the *Tannhäuser* overture afterwards. There is a choir of the eight best voices in the college and we all open by singing a chant. Then there is the responsive reading which is followed by singing the "Doxology" and then the "Lord's Prayer" is given and then the sermon. I don't think much of Dr. Stryker as a teacher but he certainly is the most eloquent preacher I ever heard and he gets his ten thousand a year for that very reason.

We have gymnasium twice a week and do all the stunts to music which makes it partake something of the joys of dancing school.

Here is a coincidence for you. My chief friend here in the senior class is Selden Talcott Kinney of Easton, Pa. and it was at his father's sanitarium that your very dear friend John Bentley was staying when he was taking the cure that summer they were all at the Phalanx.

I hope you liked the picture of the Victor party. We had them very frequently and Mr. W. always distinguished himself by referring to the nocturne as "Choppins Nocterine."

I will close by telling you about the Roots' house where I stayed the first week I was on the hill. It was built in 1790 for an inn and is altogether the quaintest house I was ever in. Every room is on a different level and there are little alcoves and short flights of stairs everywhere you happen to step. But the thing that would appeal to you is the furniture which is almost entirely colonial from the pictures to the china. Room after room without a single stick of modern furniture in it and I never ceased raving over it.

Tell me all the news and the health reports of the family.

Aleck Woollcott

[The Root family, including Oren and his brother Elihu, was intimately connected with Hamilton affairs.]

To *GEORGE SMYSER AGNEW*

Clinton, N. Y.
November 24, 1905

Dear Smyser,

Excuse the letter on a typewriter, but I have fallen into the habit of using one, and I manipulate it with speed and ease.

I enjoyed your letter very much indeed: it was the first account I had of your meeting with Helen and Maymie though since then each of the dames has written me a long and detailed account of the whole teekish affair. Maymie is in Georgia much the same as usual, and Helen is still wandering around the old town.

[10]

It is beginning to settle down to a good old-fashioned winter as they have it here with 20 below as a common thing and three months of sleighing as a regular occurrence. Our house is about three quarters of a mile from the chapel and is supplied with a set of sleds each marked with the Greek letters of the fraternity. These are taken up in the morning and the boys come down to the house in about one minute. You can slide for a mile and a half without stopping to the bottom of the hill and so far only two broken bones have resulted this year, which is a much better record than usual.

I continue to love it here with all my heart and everything is just ideal. I have several very close friends in my own and the upper classes, and there is always so much to do. We gave a small informal dance here to about fifty people and I was so tired when I crept into bed at five in the morning that I slept until three the next day. The boys invite their damsels from all over the state and girls pack up and come all the way from New York just to attend the Theta Delta opening dance. In February is dance week when the whole week is used in gayety, and our crowd gives a house party, each boy bringing a girl for the week and sleeping in the dormitory to leave the house clear for the girls and their chaperones. There are dances every night and sleighing parties in the daytime and it costs all the boys who entertain damsels just about fifty dollars. So yours truly will go stag.

This sounds as if we never did any work but the course is a stiff one and no shirks ever get past the first term.

Your mother will expire when she learns that I am still sporting my entire summer outfit of summer garb with no idea of donning anything heavier for some time to come. I shall have to buy some winter underwear, tell her, as I thoughtlessly neglected to save the remnants of my last year's stock and the safety pins.

I have made great friends with the old man who owns a

great estate opposite us and has ten dogs and eight cats. I am invited there for dinner Sunday, which is provoking as he is a vegetarian, though happy thought—he may have buns and apple sauce.

I have no particular Phalanx news: Mrs. Root is to have a play go on before Christmas. I have neglected to answer Celia's three impassioned postals that arrived all in one mail. But I really cannot undertake another correspondent when I have so many unanswered letters on hand.

Write me all the news

Aleck

To *GEORGE SMYSER AGNEW*

Utica, N. Y.
June 22, 1907

Dear Smyser:
      I suppose you received my postal and now I've found an opportunity to write sooner than I had expected. My friend Hawley Truax, who, if you remember, I said was exactly like you, has a motor here at college and it has broken down leaving me in Utica, stranded on a hot June afternoon. So I am writing to you.

Mother forwarded your letter and I was much interested in all the news, and also much conscience stricken at my long neglect of my correspondence. I don't see why I don't take a brace. I certainly can't afford to seemingly ignore all my friends, yet there isn't half enough time to do all I want to do, and so it's only natural dozens of letters go unwritten.

First of all I've had the play to distract my attention. Since Easter we have been at work on the Sophomore play in which I took the leading girl's part. It was a howling success and we took in a mint of money. I'll send you the special supplement to "Life" the college newspaper, which was issued in honor of the play with pictures of the cast in it. Since the play I have had four large dances and three teas, beastly hot, but Utica society just wakes up in June when the men and girls are back from college. Yesterday I went to a tea and sweated like a June bride for a half hour and solemnly swore I'll never go to another. Yesterday noon there was a dear little wedding in Clinton into which I butted and besides all this exam week is in full blast. It is hard to shine both in your studies and in gay society.

It's stupid for me to ramble on in this aimless fashion about my gadding here which can hardly interest you. Yet you would love it here, I'm sure. The work takes a lot of time but generally I do my studying on the grounds of the Root House, lying on the grass, two of us, smoking and looking out across the valley, where you can see the tips of the Adirondacks, forty miles away.

I have formed a number of close friends here. I am the only poor guy in the crowd so they take me motoring, to dinners and theatres and I roll around as if my pockets were bulging. My best girl friend is the daughter of the big Grace Church in Utica, and I dine at the Rectory quite often tho I'm sure the rector loathes me as a rank heathen, tho he is nice to me and tells most unrectorish stories when the ladies are not around. But woe is me the fair Katherine sails for Iceland on Wednesday to be in Europe indefinitely, so no more dinners for me at the Rectory for some time to come.

Commencement week begins Monday and will leave me dead as a rag. The larks go on day and night till Friday morning. Monday night there are three dances, Tuesday night there are three dances, Wednesday the Alumni Banquet and Thursday commencement day, Thursday night the Ball which lasts till six in the morning, and then they scatter. I shall cut the ball because of the expense and because I start work at Chautauqua for the summer on Friday.

Do you know Chautauqua, the big summer school on Chautauqua Lake about ten miles from Erie? Well I have some sort of a job there for the summer and haven't the vaguest notion what I am to do. Still the place is beautiful, the lake great and the chances for hearing fine music and big speakers is continuous.

I wish I could have joined the Jamestown [Va.] party which starts from here on the first of July. About a dozen Hamilton Freshmen are going down there to roll chairs on the midway; they get a quarter of what they take in, which will cover most of their expenses. Still the carfare down there will be considerable, and I fancy the chair rolling will be hot work.

I suppose Mother wrote to you and told you what news there is, that Ella Richdale and John Bucklin each have children, only Ella's is born and I don't think John's is yet, that the Woollcotts have done nothing in this line at all yet, that Mrs. Oliver is dead, that Nancy Root is still at the Phalanx growing big and pretty, and always under the firm conviction that there is no one in the world like Bam [the family's pet name for A. W.'s mother], who, as she confided to Aunt Ann, is a fine old girl.

Guy Richdale and June are both in the Standard Oil Company now and both doing well. They'll probably marry in no time.

Tomorrow night the Dramatic Club have a box party at the theatre in Utica to celebrate our success. The play is "Big Hearted Jim" which sounds pretty rotten and I guess it will be.

If you will write me I'll try to answer more promptly.

Aleck Woollcott

To *GEORGE SMYSER AGNEW*

Chautauqua, N. Y.
July 21, 1907

Dear Smyser:
  Your letter was so duly appreciated that here I am answering within a reasonable time which is quite remarkable. I don't know where Mamma got the idea that I was coming to Phalanx in September. It would be entirely too expensive a trip and so, between the week that College opens and the time my work ends here I shall visit my room-mate Len Watson in his home in Westfield, about ten miles from here on Lake Erie. From there we shall probably go to Hamilton together. At any rate I shall take in Niagara on the way which is near here.

  So I guess I don't see the Phalanx before Xmas at the earliest and unless I have some unexpected expenses this year, maybe I can save up enough to go down to Philadelphia Xmas week if you people would put me up for a day or two. I hate to think of not seeing the place again for another year so I shall make a desperate effort to come then.

  You needn't sniff at my occupation for the summer. Almost all the waiters at Chautauqua are college men and we get board and room for our pains. All we have to do is to come at meal times, serve our table and clear it away. Then we all select a table and eat our own meal—generally a table in the tents which surround the St. Elmo. There are four boys and three girls and we have a very good time.

  My other job, as janitor, requires about a half hour's sweeping every day and I have to take tickets for the occasional lectures and concerts given in the hall—so you see I have most of my time to myself. I have read a whole library since I've been here, wrote twenty-two letters the first week, and go swimming and rowing when it's warm enough.

  I suppose that last sounds queer—for I've read how rotten hot it's been in Philadelphia at the time of the Elk's parade.

But it's cool enough here for Chautauqua sits some 1300 ft. above sea-level. It's a great old place with six or eight entertainments every day all free. They have the finest music in Chautauqua of any resort in the country. This is music week and all the big authorities are to lecture on different subjects. There is to be a course on the life of the great composers, and every night they give an oratorio. This being Sunday they give Haydn's "Creation" in the amphitheatre—a choir of four hundred—the quartet and orchestra. You would enjoy it no end.

Last week they had the Prize Spelling Match. New York against the rest of the world. I went in for New Jersey and covered her with glory by missing the first word they gave me.

Write again when you have time and give my love to all your people.

Aleck H. Woollcott

To *GEORGE SMYSER AGNEW*

Clinton, N. Y.
November 4, 1908

My dear Smyser,
I have probably lost your good opinion permanently by my erratic ideas about correspondence, but it is really very hard for me to find much to write about, when Mother tells you all the Phalanx news and the accounts of my own doings would be filled with names that are utterly unfamiliar to you. Howsumever I think of every one I know there in Philadelphia, probably far oftener than they think of me, and unless something unforseen comes up to interfere, I shall most certainly accept your invitation for the holidays, coming down sometime between Christmas and New Year's.

We are to have eighteen days vacation and that will leave me time to gad about New York a bit, and some time for the

Phalanx and Philadelphia. Marian [Stoll] as you probably know is in Germany, which is too bad as I should like very much to see her. I came very near to going over myself last spring and indeed I threaten to go every once in a while but it doesn't seem very likely just now. Phil Welch wants me to go in January with him, but it would certainly be foolish to have gone this far with college and then throw it up just for a chance to see Europe.

I was in Utica Election night, taking dinner with the mother of the girl whom I hope to marry some day, and she played "Hearts and Flowers" for me. It started me thinking of your mother, and the horror you used to express when she tried that old favorite of yours. Out of this started a train of thought that led to this letter.

I have been doing very little of interest this Fall. Senior year is one of few studies and beyond the editorship of the college magazine I have very little on my mind. Phil Welch and I are very apt to spend the large part of every day together, and that means Utica and the theatres when his pockets are full and my room in the dormitory when they are empty.

I have a great fireplace in my room, with woodboxes which the Freshmen are supposed to keep full, only they don't. Last night the snow was so thick and the wind so noisy that we darkened the room, and lay all evening in two Morris chairs in front of the fire. It is a harmless way to spend a few hours. About ten we sent a Freshman over to Commons for some eggs on toast, candy and cigarettes, with the result that I have a rather sour stomach this morning. It is still snowing and the sleds are out in full force, which will give you a hint as to the climate here.

I don't know what started me thinking of it, but there came into my mind the other day the recollection of Courtland Baker playing priest on the third floor of our house on Walnut Lane. I can see him now, and smell that ghastly odor of incense that he managed to stir up somehow. That house wasn't half bad and we used to have some pretty good times there. Ask your mother if she remembers how she used to prophesy that it wouldn't be long before we were back in it again, which is rather pathetic now that you come to think of it. As far as I am concerned everything has gone beautifully. I never have had four such wonderful years and I never expect to have again.

I think it is high time that I came back, however, and refreshed my mind a little. I picked up my old birthday book a few weeks ago and for the life of me I couldn't remember more than half of the names in it. I hope I shall have a chance to run out to Germantown and see Miss Wilcox and Miss Montgomery. But it will be vacation time and they are always queer and out of their element when you visit them in their homes.

I don't think there is any recent Phalanx news that would interest you particularly. I am pretty rusty on it for I'm there only once a year at Christmas, and for the life of me I can't remember where all the people are.

You must tell me when the time comes what part of the vacation would be most convenient for you to have me, so that I can make my plans accordingly.

Excuse the typewriter but I use it almost all the time.

Yours as ever
Aleck

To GEORGE SMYSER AGNEW

Red Bank, N. J.
July 29, 1909

Dear Smyser:

You would have heard from me before this but I have been sick and unable to write. Two weeks ago I was at Lillian's and woke to find a swelling behind my ears. That suggested mumps. It took me about two minutes to fly into my clothes and start for the Phalanx. Frances was here for the week and Julie.

I was pretty sick and got worse. By Saturday I couldn't move and had to be lifted from the bed—and then that beastly complication set in and I am still here tho better. Sunday was the worst. Julie in one room undergoing a slight operation and I in my room where three injections and several doses of morphine brought small relief. Mother was flying around in a fine state.

Julie has gone back to New York and I expect to go by Monday.

Your letter reached me all right but my address is 34 W. 12th St. where Phil Welch and Julie and I are all rooming. I'd be glad to see an occasional *Record*.

Affairs here are by no means settled but I think Aunt Julie and Mother will descend into their graves from this place and no other.

Aleck

To *GEORGE SMYSER AGNEW*

THE NEW YORK TIMES
September 24, 1909

Dear Smyser,

It is too bad that most of my plans for coming to Philadelphia never amount to anything. As you see by the above heading, I am located here as a young and hopeful reporter, instead of being on the Philadelphia *Record*, but I nonetheless appreciate your sending me the paper.

I am sorry that you avoided me so carefully when you were in the city. Julie must have seemed a little dopy, though I doubt if you realized that she was so sick that she could hardly stagger. She collapsed that night with a horrible attack of indigestion. I am glad to be here on her account, not that she isn't far better able to take care of me than I of her. She gads around something fierce, as your friend Bert would say. I did four theatres myself last week: a number of the fellows were in town on their way back to college and I took my last fling before starting work. Miss Atherton was here too on her way to Vassar. She stopped at the Martha Washington and I got passes to go up on the roof where we had several barn dances before we were stopped by the authorities.

It is great up here in the *Times*: we are in the tower of the Times Building and can see all over the city on all four sides. It's great at night and will be fine as an observation ground during the coming week.

I can't tell you how much I enjoy my newspaper work. It will never bring me any money but I love it and that's enough. There have been some gay times this winter. I see very little of Julie who has her friends, interests and work while I have mine. We do meet at breakfast.

There is no news from the Phalanx. Julie, Frances, Uncle Will, and I went down for Labor Day and saw the Monmouth County fair. My first and last Mrs. Giles had resurrected an antique quilt of hers which won a five dollar prize, to her great delight. The plans of the family as a whole will take more definite shape after the first of October and I will let you know the news whenever there is any.

I don't expect to get away for Xmas: it will be the first spent away from the Phalanx since that memorable one in 1907, when I gave a few readings at the Mennonite after the comic opera was given up.

Give my best to the family and let me know how Mrs. Deaney fares. I think she is a greater favorite with Mother than anyone she met in Philadelphia. Oh by the way, Helen Sears [A. W.'s cousin] is to be in New York hereafter. I tell you that you'd better come over. The rats are leaving the old ship.

Yours sincerely,
Aleck W.

II

World War and Postwar
1917-1919

To MRS. ALICE HAWLEY TRUAX

[During his early days in New York, Woollcott made the Truax house his home. Hawley Truax had been one of his best friends at college. Mrs. Truax was Hawley's mother; his sister Katharine married Lloyd Stryker, another college friend; and his brother was Chauncey Truax.]

New York City
June 9, 1917

Dear Mrs. Truax,

I have not written because I had nothing to add to the news Katharine [Truax Stryker] was able to carry with her to Blue Hill. I do not yet know when or where we are going; the entire unit is a pawn in the war department's game. We think we are going to France and we think we will be there before the first of July. But we don't know and one of us doesn't care. I haven't any idea what I will do—different work at different times, I imagine. As a tentative preparation, I am brushing up my French, arranging to have it spoken to me several hours a day. Roche, whom you met, and Alphonse of the Metropolitan Opera, are helping and I have put an ad in the *Courier* for the services of "un Français bavard ou une Française sérieuse. C'est amusant, n'est-ce pas?"

I feel like a pig to go away leaving my things strewn all over your apartment. I think much of my raiment, shoes, shirts, etc. might well be bestowed on the City Mission or Salvation Army. Of the books, only those on the lowest shelf are greatly treasured. The rest can go to Malkans if there is not room for them in the celebrated Chest. When the time comes for you to move or whenever they are in the way, will you consult with Julie about their storage, either in a warehouse or at the Phalanx? As for our financial entanglements, I will turn over a lump sum to Hawley on the eve of departure.

If we do not sail next week, I shall try to go to Commencement and to take Hawley with me.

I have bought a rubber life-preserving suit, quite a structure. It fits over me like a baby's crawling-suit, very rubbery and very bulky, so that I somewhat resemble the gods in *The Gods of the Mountain*. It keeps one warm, upright and afloat for days, with a whistle to summon help and a pouch for food, stimulants and light reading matter—*The Atlantic Monthly*, I presume. I tested mine in the Howard plunge and it worked like a charm. Heywood Broun wanted me to stay in the tank for four days as a true test but I declined. He was interested because he was to sail today and I suppose he has. He ordered two suits, one for himself and one for Ruth Hale—now, and since Wednesday, Mrs. Heywood Broun. He goes as correspondent for the *Tribune*.

I will complain to the *Times* about the subscription.

Aleck

To *LAWRENCE GILMAN*

Governor's Island
June, 1917

My dear Brother Gilman,

The only cloud on the memory of a most delightful evening is the fact that I found no trace of my watch next morning. I remember looking at it in Delmonico's and it occurs to me as possible it may have slipped to the floor instead of into one of the many new pockets with which I am not yet on intimate terms. It is open-face—an old watch with a back-case of beaten gold. Will you inquire after it in Delmonico's and if, by any wild chance, it is in the pound there, send it to me here and forever oblige

Yr obt. servant
George Washington

[Before Woollcott sailed for France, the New York critics gave him a farewell dinner. As music critic of the *North American Review*, Mr. Gilman was one of the party.]

To MRS. ALICE HAWLEY TRUAX

Governor's Island
1917

Dear Mrs. Truax,

When you get this, you will know that my days on the land—in this land—are numbered. Thereafter my address will be as follows:

PRIVATE ALEXANDER WOOLLCOTT
AMERICAN EXPEDITIONARY FORCE
AMERICAN EMBASSY
PARIS
FRANCE
U. S. BASE HOSPITAL #8
FRANCE

It sounds rather formidable, doesn't it?

Everything here on the island has been outrageously agreeable—the men, the food, the equipment, even the drill, strangely enough. I have just come in from an hour of marching and feel as fresh as a daisy.

I shall never cease to be grateful to you for my home of the last two years. I wish I could say it in some way to make it sound more than a mere formal acknowledgment. If it had not been

[23]

there, ready and hospitable and sympathetic, when I came back from Baltimore last Christmas, I do not know what would have become of me. You and Hawley will be always in my thoughts and of course I shall write whenever I can. Love to Katharine. Au revoir,

Aleck

To *JULIE WOOLLCOTT TABER*

[Woollcott's close relationship with his older sister, Mrs. Charles Taber, is brought out in the letter to Lucy Drage, on page 79.]

On Board an American Transport
[*Received September 11, 1917*]

Dear Julie,

On what ought to be the last day of our voyage, I have dug my writing case out of the bowels of my barrack bag and brought it up on the forecastle deck in the hope of writing a few letters to be mailed after we reached the land that should come over the horizon before sundown. There is really not much I can say except that I am feeling serene and uncommonly well. I am assuming you will have received official word of our arrival long before this letter reaches you.

I acquired a new typewriter just before we set sail and when—if ever—we are finally settled, I know I shall feel more like writing you. If ever a letter arrives that is full of odds and ends of our doings over here, please pass it on to Mrs. Truax for there isn't going to be an awful lot of time for writing.

We were all so displeased by the unsavory old transport that originally bore us from shore, that everyone grinned from ear to ear when we were rammed and had to be taken off. Our present craft is an immeasurable improvement, and though the huddled sleeping quarters and the unimaginative meals have staggered those who have never roughed it at all, I have emerged quite unruffled after a curious voyage that has really been mighty enjoyable. You know I haven't a decent minimum of fastidiousness and I have enjoyed every day.

I don't know where we are going or how soon we are to be at work and—as far as I personally am concerned—do not know for sure what that work will be. But I do know that whatever the work, the co-workers will be congenial and everything thus far has been much, much pleasanter than I had any right to expect.

I got the typewriter in the hope that from time to time I might be able to write pieces for publication. It will be some time before I'll know how much if any time I will have for writing and how much if any of what I write will get through. By way of an experiment I wrote a piece for the *Times* yesterday and if, after a while, you should encounter a little sketch on life aboard a transport, you will know more of our trip than I have written here.

Our officers are an agreeable lot with no disposition whatever to lord it over us. Among the enlisted men, there is every variety—a nice miscellany. I have made new friends and encountered old ones. When we were on the old *Saratoga*, I slept my one night on deck and about four in the morning, a captain of artillery went along waking everyone up and sending them below because the ship was about to move out. I came to in time to hear him say "What the hell are you doing here?" and found it was Fritz Burrows who was in college with me. Again, when we came aboard this transport, the first person I met was Bob Hull who was a Theta Delt of my time at Hamilton. He is crossing with another hospital unit.

The crossing has been as calm as Hop Brook—and we have been able to spend practically all our time on deck. We have eaten on deck, bathed on deck and slept on deck—or some of us have. It's rather fun to roll up in army blankets and poncho and go to sleep on the forecastle deck under the stars and it's not half bad to come shivering up at four and stand in front of a hose to get your bath.

This morning I sang in the choir at morning services to the great amusement of the ungodly and now we are all polishing our boots and side-arms and mending up generally to look neat and pretty for the French. This letter will be mailed from France.

With love
Aleck

Next day

P.S. Just a line to say that after as wildly exciting a morning as I can recall, we are all smiling at the land which seems not more than a stone's throw from the bow. I wanted to add too, as a message to Aunt Julie, that Nelson Sackett* is an exceptionally fine fellow, much liked and already designated a corporal. We are the best of friends.

A.W.

* Nelson Sackett is Anna Benson's boy—a Princeton undergraduate.

To MRS. ALICE HAWLEY TRUAX

With the American Expeditionary Force
September 2, 1917

My dear Mrs. Truax,

I am sitting as I write in the garden behind a house taken over by the YMCA, seizing a free hour for a letter to you. The chief burden of the letter is that I am well and busy and cheeful. If I do not write much more than that, it is not because I have anything painful or sensational to conceal but because a long list of censorship rules makes me falter and I *do* want this note to get through with my greetings. I think the very fact of a censorship cramps one's style, no matter how innocent one's prattle, so I have attempted nothing but postal cards. Besides, I keep my mind off America and all the folks as much as I can. There is no use being riven by homesickness all the time. But you mustn't forget me.

Some day, when it's all over, I'll take an evening off to tell you of our unforgettable crossing: that should have a chapter all to itself. It seemed pretty good at last to get the first sight of the red sails of the fishing crafts, to see people waving to us from the fields and catch a glimpse of an American flag flying from some housetop. We were an old story to the gamins of the quai when we finally reached our moorings but they were all ready with fruit to throw on board and our first greeting and tribute was a well-meant pear which hit one of our men in the eye.

We were pretty glad, too, to reach what appears to be our quarters for some time to come—*a* quainter and more picturesque town than ever I saw when I was in Europe before, unbelievably remote in spirit from this war and this century. When we had leave, we would clatter over the cobble-stones to some seamy little buvette for dinner. I remember one dinner that consisted of bread and butter, fried eggs innumerable, salad, plenty of red wine and milk, cheese, preserved cherries and coffee, and the check for the four of us was only six francs. I remember, too, the evening when I disrupted the whole town buying some stuff—très pratique—and engaging an old woman to make it into laundry bags for a procession that formed as soon as my enterprise was discovered. And I remember the excitement in a tiny, old imprimerie when I discovered a story in French by O. Henry, author of "Le Chou et le Roi." I was so agitated at this souvenir d'enfance that the shopkeeper was much affected and kept exclaiming, "Comme vous étes sensibles!"

Everything was so serene and agreeable there and our hikes along the blackberry lined roads were such picnicky jaunts that I've no doubt it was good for our immortal souls that some of us were transferred to another post for some hard though temporary duty. This detached band (of which I am one) knows not the day nor the hour where (if ever) it will rejoin its unit and we are too busy to think much about it one way or the other. We had all become such good friends that the splitting up, even if only for a short time, was quite gloomy.

My French has served me well and I can even negotiate messages over the telephone. One of my first assignments was to find, borrow and bear off a frightful old harmonium for the Chaplain, and the French that was shattered on that occasion was shocking to contemplate. I find it flows easily enough and that I can understand even the most voluble.

I have seen few people I knew though just as I sat down to write this letter, a young YMCA secretary blew up and introduced himself as Whitcombe, Hamilton '17. He tells me he saw Tom Orr two months ago in Paris and that Tom was as fat as butter and fully determined to go to the French school for artillery after he had served his time in the ambulance.

I am afraid all this is pretty idle chatter but I'm not moved or encouraged to send you any searching revelations. I'll just add that I'm glad I came and am already satisfied I did the best and most I could. Will you ship this note on to Julie instead of tearing it up. My best to Hawley and Lloyd [Stryker—Katharine's husband] and Katharine. Think of me once in a while and when the war is over, watch out for my knock at the door.

Alexander Woollcott

To *JULIE WOOLLCOTT TABER*

Base Hospital #8, AEF, France
September 23, 1917

Dear Julie:

I have had several letters and enclosures from you, and a letter from Aunt Julie—the last dated August 27th—and, since then, no word at all from the other side of the Atlantic. Our mail comes in bunches, and I am getting hungry for another bunch. I have it in mind to drop you a postal every week, so that you can keep track of me even when I have no chance or mood to write.

I have always hated to write letters until all was tranquil and settled and completed for an indefinite period, but, if I wait for such intervals here, you will not hear from me until the end of the war. If I were to try to tell you what a day is like, I might —with discreet omissions—get away with it, but, by the time the letters reached you, as like as not I would be doing something else, and living a totally different existence. It cramps my style.

I *can* say that, so far, everything has been varied, interesting and satisfying, and I cannot imagine anything happening which would make me regret for one moment that I had come across. Most of the time, I am busy at the desk of the receiving office in the hospital to which a group of us were sent some weeks ago for temporary duty. But I also go out on the ambulances a lot, and have all manner of miscellaneous work—all the way from carrying a coffin for an officer's funeral, to bringing milk and chickens from the farms for miles around, and trying vainly to persuade the old Frenchwomen to gather the wild raspberries that are so thick along the roadside, but which they have scorned for so many years that they don't propose to pick them at this late date.

In the evenings, if we are free, we gambol downtown, to pick up the latest gossip from the front; to talk with men who have been to Paris; to buy chocolate and other less innocent beverages, and to pick up all the rumors concerning the arrival of newcomers from home. The air is full of rumors. Soldiers in transit sit around the little terrace café tables, and tell stories of the death of kings. Paris editions of the Chicago *Tribune,* the New York *Herald* and the London *Daily Mail* are to be had, but there is nothing in them, and the New York *Times*, by which we all swear, is, at least, two weeks late. You all know much more about the war than we do, and I'm sure you talk about it much more.

Once in a while, we meet old friends as the stream passes our way. The other day, for example, one of the ambulance drivers from a near-by camp dropped in on me with an invitation to a small, but select, Hamilton dinner of five. It was great fun as one of the crowd was a Theta Delt. We sent a post card to Dr. Stryker, and signed our names somewhat unsteadily upon it.

I think I have relished nothing more than my excursion with the mess-sergeant into the country to teach the natives how to clean the chickens we buy from them twice a week. We needed a chicken and some boiling water. The chicken was obtained after we had convinced little François that we would not take the gray one which he was fattening for his father, due back from the front the next Sunday. Then we went into the kitchen of the old house—a very old house that had been a fine château before the Revolution. We sat around the smoky hearth, waiting for the water to boil in the kettle swinging over the twigs, while the old woman brought out her red wine, and the old man poured it out. I wanted to explore upstairs, but I was given to understand that it was scarcely clean enough for inspection, and I guess that was true.

These little excursions break in pleasantly enough on our days, which run from 5.15 ("daylight saving" schedule) to 6. We all work hard enough. If you are driving an ambulance or running the operating room, you are happy, and if you are working in the kitchen, or holding raving spinal meningitis patients in bed all night, you are not so happy, but, in the long run, I guess it doesn't matter much.

I am afraid this is all very disjointed, but I write a paragraph every once in a while—between ambulance calls and other interruptions—and the result is confusion. I see by the mail bags that pass our way that there is some method of addressing old magazines vaguely to the soldiers and sailors in France for general distribution. Any magazines and books—especially books—you may address to me, will reach far and wide. I yearn for *The New Republic*, but I am scarcely settled enough now to subscribe for it. Do mail me a copy now and then.

We hear the Red Cross notice of our safe arrival reached our folks after a week and more of delay. I shall be curious to know when and how the news reached you.

I am very well. I haven't had an hour's sickness since I saw you. The day we landed, I fell on the deck and wrenched my ankle badly enough to tear a ligament, so I rode in state over the ground covered by our first hike, and then got on well enough with the aid of a Sayre bandage.

Goodbye.

Aleck

To *JULIE WOOLLCOTT TABER*

Base Hospital #8, AEF, France
October 2, 1917

Dear Julie:

Not your first letter, but your first answer, reached me yesterday, and I promptly acknowledged it with a serial post card. I have now laid hold upon this simple but tasteful stationery to write you a letter, which I shall begin today and finish when I can.

I do not remember whether I wrote and told you that Heywood Broun and Ruth Hale tracked me to my lair, and demanded that I either report at once for a week-end in Paris, or clear the decks for their descent upon me at the hospital; I have fended them off until I can see a little way ahead. A week-end in Paris! That, of course, is impossible. I know how Mrs.

Fiske feels when her friends urge her that it is too rainy for her to bother going down to the theatre. Ruth is toiling on the Paris Army Edition of the Chicago *Tribune*, and they are happily domiciled on the Boulevard Raspail, and she still insists on being known as Ruth Hale. I found her note tremendously heart-warming.

The other day, while we were in the throes of receiving ambulance-loads of patients, I discovered that Lieutenant Lincoln—a much-admired man hereabouts, and, I imagine, an exceedingly competent physician—was from Worcester, and knew the Tabers well.

We are all the time running across traces of home that way. I found one of the ex-members of the *Times* staff, the other evening, embracing the buxom proprietress of a little chocolate shop in town, and learned from him—between embraces—that Phil Hoyt is a captain in the National Army. Think of that!

You must tip me off as to whether my letters come to you in a mutilated condition. So far, none of mine have been scornfully returned by the censor—and no wonder, for I have been insipidly discreet, and evaded trouble by saying nothing at all. You must tell me, too, whether, on receiving the letters which I confide to the post without postage, you have to pay anything. As Bam used to say, "Don't forget to answer that question." Also this one: Was there a postcript about the last day of our voyage on the letter sent you from the ship? [The next line of writing was deleted by the Censor.]

I am afraid that by this time you are quite bewildered by the myriad addresses I have given you. The latest official address is at the head of this letter, and my intuition tells me it will be a fixed address for some little time to come. You must not imagine that I have skipped about France for every change of address. Usually, I have remained stubbornly stationary, while the address changed over my head. As a matter of fact, our crowd is just now scattered to the four corners of the earth, various groups on detached service doing every conceivable kind of work. I do not know when all will come together again, but I am under the impression that those of us who have been working here at one of the emergency points will be replaced before the week is gone, and so be free to journey back to our own headquarters.

This is really an eventful week. We are ingenuously expecting to be paid off tomorrow. They have a little song here which (to the tune of "Glory, Glory, Hallelujah") runs something like this:

> Every day we sign the payroll,
> Every day we sign the payroll,
> Every day we sign the payroll,
> But we never get a G—D— cent!

This is spirited but untruthful: We do get paid in sufficient abundance, but we know neither the day nor the hour.

Also, this week, we recover the stolen hour. We rise every day, except Sunday, at 4.15. The clocks say 5.15, but they don't deceive us. Next Saturday, this hour will be formally returned to us while we sleep, and (as we always have an extra thirty minutes sleep by way of keeping Sunday holy) we shall luxuriate in an hour and a half extra sleep that night. These little blessings are much appreciated.

However, you would not think our life very vigorous, I am afraid, if you could share one of the chicken-and-sweet-potato dinners they serve to our detachment (however differently others may fare), or if you could see the dozen Roger & Gallet tubes of shaving cream at present under my bunk, or if you could go to Victorine's with us for chocolate and crème-au-beurres of a pleasant October evening when the work is done.

I got this far with my letter on the 2nd, and here it is the night of the 6th. That impression of mine was fulfilled. I am back at headquarters after an absence of five long, toilsome weeks. The return was accomplished after as fitful a series of starts as that which ushered us from the States. You may remember we were forever starting. Well, the last two days on detached service were spent in the same way. We were all packed up, even unto our soap and tooth-brushes, for forty-eight hours before the relief arrived, and, in the dark of the moon, we set forth in a train of ambulances for our own post. There is no describing the serenity of this ancient spot with the unbelievable sunsets, and the music of the angelus coming through the twilight. I am mighty glad to be back.

I had a fearful shock, however. An American mail had arrived just before we reached here—sack after sack of it, and not so much as a card for me. I think some letters must be delayed —not gone astray for good, but delayed. One of the boys who is betrothed to a dazzling vision of a girl, has heard from every one else in the world, but never a word from her! I have had letters from many people in France—newspaper guys and other men on service at various stations—but, from America, no one has been true to me but you. I suggest that you number your letters so I shall know if they are all reaching me. Here it is the 6th of October, just two months since we sailed, and not a letter have I had save yours and those you have forwarded to me.

Every man here has, apparently, come from a family which reads the *Times*, for they have all had clippings from that excellent journal for the 11th.

Au revoir—tout va bien.
Aleck

To *JULIE WOOLLCOTT TABER*

Base Hospital #8, AEF, France
Late October, 1917

Dear Julie:

I find the only way to get a letter written in these parts is to start valiantly forth upon it and take it up from time to time until you think the hour has come for it to be signed and entrusted to the Censor. I have started such a letter to you several times of late, but whenever I have come back to it it would seem so dull and peevish. Peevish, because it is difficult to take one's pen in hand without mentioning the uncertainty of our mails, and that it is a subject for sulks. The mail that blew in here last Sunday after a three weeks silence, brought me your letter of October 2nd, a request from the Farmers Loan and Trust that I subscribe to the second Liberty Loan, and a note from Myra Holmes, wanting to know who this John Corbin was. I was afflicted because I had signed, have been in olive drab for three months—been away from America for almost three months, with never a word from the old crowd in town, from Mrs. Fiske and the stage folks, from the Truaxes and the Hamilton bunch. I was enraged because the Farmers Loan and Trust, after cheerfully professing ignorance of the enormous sum I transferred to the Paris Bank, had the nerve to circularize me for a loan to which I had already subscribed over here as handsomely as I could under the circumstances. However I realized that I need not think myself quite forgotten, for I can never feel sure all these far-away friends have not written me again and again. Perhaps some of the letters will show up some day. Those who keep tab on such things by having their letters numbered serially, will get the first, second and then the seventh, in the most disconcerting way. Some who know that many a letter must have been written, will get none at all, or perhaps just a note asking why *they* have not written, when, as a matter of fact, they have written often and laboriously ever since their arrival. I know one boy who is frantic because his mother has not heard a word from him—or had not on October 6th. I know a young father who is pretty worried because the last letter said the baby was sick, and there hasn't been another letter for six weeks. Then, on the other hand, some are lucky and emerge from the mail distributing with a dozen or so of letters and as many packages. I found one embarrassed young man with enough sweaters to keep the entire AEF comfortably warm all winter. So it goes—all very puzzling and depressing. I would wash my hands of the whole matter, and bend my attention entirely on the absorbing work and the likable crowd around me, if it were not for you and a few others I really cannot banish from my thoughts. All this I started to say yesterday, but it sounded so ungracious to roar with rage about a mail that had, after all, brought me a welcome letter from you. However, you understand.

Anyway, I feel amiable today. I have just received word from the Farmers Loan and Trust that, after all, they did have authority to cash my checks, from the Paris branch, or from another branch in a certain town just an hour's drive from where I now sit. At first they had disowned me utterly, and this gave me a forlorn feeling of being without any outside resources at all—nothing to fall back on in case I should have the bad luck to break my glasses often, or something like that. It was the more of a blow because I am not yet rid of all my "chip-of-the-old block," spendthrift habits of civil life. For instance, I casually order a rather costly edition of *Les Misérables* to be sent from Paris to the funny little book shop in the town here, and then too, I sent to Paris for the score of *Pierrot the Prodigal* which a young chap who is an exceptional musician plays for me once in a while—those dear melodies which produce an exquisite nostalgia, as you can imagine. I can pay for all these little flights, —never worry—but it reduces me to scant funds, so it is a comfort to know that money is within reach, if an emergency should arise. Then too, I am feeling especially amiable because this morning's post brought me another expansive, warm-hearted letter from Ruth Hale, together with the news that she and Heywood are meditating a descent upon me here this coming Sunday. I will put them up at one of the comic old hotels in this dear old town, and I shall get old Madame Lefeuvre to prepare one of her extraordinary dinners with omelette au kirsch (blazing), with veal, perhaps, cooked with mushrooms and chestnuts, most appetizing. "Très, très bon, M'sieur" as she always roars from the doorway while we eat her dinners.

They are making great plans for a Christmas Eve in Paris. I get plans of the apartment on the Rue Raspail with my room all marked with a cross to show where the body will fall in a stupor from overeating; and they swear they have the seats to the opera already reserved. I laugh ironically at such didoes, but, whereas I can't say it will be Christmas week, I *can* say I hope and expect to spend five days in Paris before the winter is over. Our party is already made up, and we shall go to my little old Cornille in the Latin Quarter, and I shall see Wythe Williams and Walter Duranty, and Ruth and Heywood and it will be a real reunion.

I must rush away now, for the mess hall has been cleared for the dress-rehearsal of a vaudeville bill to be given there tomorrow night in honor of Hallowe'en, and for the general amusement of the patients, the personnel, and stray neighbors and other AEF folk who happen to be with us for the moment. I have a one act play in it which I wrote one night last week, and which we have been rehearsing in the x-ray laboratory whenever we had a chance. Schuyler Ladd is playing the leading part. It is called "And Ye Took Me In"—tell Hawley, who will understand and be ever so scornful.

Two days later.

Well, the show is over and was a real success. We encountered our troubles when we brought the scenery into the mess hall, intending to make a stage out of the mess tables and plant the set on top of it. There wasn't room and we hated to cut down the scenery because it was a remarkably workmanlike set made by an engineer corporal who is serving in France as a carpenter, and who had been a stagehand for twenty-five years. We were in a quandary when the engineers came gallantly to the rescue, offered us their new barracks as a theatre, knocked out the end of it, built a stage in a few minutes, roofed it over, put in the scenery, knocked out a stage entrance, ran up headlights and footlights, strung a curtain, and really gave us as perfect a theatre as you could ask, with perfect acoustics. The Unit is large enough to provide all sorts of talent. One of the men is a costumer in civil life, and the ravishing creation he made out of nothing was unforgettable. Another is an organist of repute and he led the orchestra, recruited generally, and expert enough to step into the breach without rehearsal. The play—my play that is—employed two of the boys and three nurses, and was devised so that the men could appropriately appear in their own uniforms, and was so loaded with local humor that it could not very well help going over. Schuyler was splendid and patiently developed all the others. He is a marvel of good humor, consideration and dignity—one in a thousand, and the least actory actor I have ever known—bar none. Our audience was in high good humor, with the Colonel and the Major in the seats of the Mighty, with a mass of minor officers, with the nurses and secretaries and non-coms filling a good portion of the hall, to say nothing of all the patients who could be trundled down from the wards, and a few favorites from the village, including a hero of the Marne, who was wounded three years ago, and lives now in our town.

 I am afraid this letter conveys the impression that we have come over here on a spree, but you should see me unloading freight cars in the pouring rain, or presiding at night as wardmaster in a syphilis ward, or measuring dead darkies for their coffins. I put these in because they sound impressive but I must admit I had the time of my life in the syphilis ward. Then of course the grim work really lies ahead of us, except for those who—or rather some of those who—have gone forward on detached service, much as we did a few weeks back, to be gone we know not how long.

Five days later.

It is just as well I didn't sign this letter, and consign it to the Censor, for in the interval since I wrote the last paragraphs, we have had a flood of letters—one from you, and one from Aunt Julie (very melancholy) and one from Mrs. Truax, and one from Mrs. Fiske—a great rush of letters, entirely restoring our good humor. Then too Sunday morning before the first mess, and while I was racing in extremely fatigue uniform across the courtyard of the Hospital, Nelson Sackett, who was corporal on guard at the moment, came with the news that a lady and gentleman were inquiring for me and in the faint light of dawn, I discovered Ruth and Heywood waiting for me at the gate. They spent Sunday with me and are staying over until tonight. They went to mess with me at noon, went out with us on an ambulance call during the afternoon, dined with me en ville in the evening, and altogether made it a full rich day. It demoralizes me to mix my old self with the new this way, but I enjoyed it just the same. I enjoyed it hugely, and I look forward to seeing them at Christmas time, which is now fairly certain.

All the letters speak of Brother Corbin, but I never read his stuff, not from spleen, but because I would rather not read the *Times* at all. I have no news from the old set around Times Square, except the tidbits Ruth passes on from Paris. There has been a terrific row between Arnold Daly and John Williams, in the course of which, I hear, Daly sent John five closely typewritten pages of insults. He then sent carbon copies of the letter around among the managers, and one of them is on its way to Ruth in Paris. It is to be passed around here and we are all to initial it and forward it solemnly on its way in the most military manner possible.

Heywood is sending back a story about our play. Keep your eye out for it. *Read the Tribune.*

Much love always.
Aleck

[John Corbin took Woollcott's place as dramatic critic of the New York *Times*.]

To MRS. ALICE HAWLEY TRUAX

Base Hospital #8, AEF, France
December 4, 1917

Dear Mrs. Truax,

Your letter which you began to write me on the 4th of last month and wound up several days later found me here yesterday. It came along with many other letters—a real treasure of a mail which I carry around with me inside my blouse and re-devour every time I get a chance. Our letters come all at once after days and weeks of silence. We hang on to them for days, snatching odd moments to read and reread them. I take mine to bed with me and go through them in the last half hour before taps.

Here was this letter from you and a letter from Hawley sent on from the camp at Allentown. There was a letter from Tom Smith, the agent who handled my stuff for the *Century* and who writes to tell me he is now managing editor of that moribund publication so that he can just slam in any of my stuff he wants without having to ballyhoo for it. A convenient arrangement. Then a brisk little note from Walter Duranty—my old pal of the Paris *Times* office—hailing my advent there at Christmas time.

Then a dear letter from Prof. [William P.] Shepard, two long letters from Julie, two very comforting letters from the Farmers Loan and Trust—who had previously agitated me by mislaying my money—letters from the *Times* office and bit of a Christmas card from Greta and her mother.

This letter of mine to you must serve as a Christmas greeting—not, I hope, the only one to reach you through me for, if fortune is kind, you will receive a modest Christmas gift, an old card case, of no conceivable use in this day and generation but something to leave lying around to prod an occasional memory of one who thinks of you often with the greatest affection and gratitude.

It is true that my letters must necessarily be an uneventful chronicle but, whereas there are hundreds and hundreds of things I might say but would not be allowed to say, still none of those is really of vital importance. I know nothing big and significant about the war that you yourself do not know. The censorship is vexing but it is not really choking back anything worth mentioning from me. Indeed, I am not sure you have not a far clearer view of things from the vantage point of West Fifty-Seventh Street. I think we in our corner see the war less clearly, talk of it less often and think of it far, far less. You have no idea how isolated is each little bit of the Allied armies—how entirely concerned with its own community tasks, pleasures, hardships and intrigues. I remember, when I was back home, that I was amused at the comfort the British correspondents drew from the woe and discouragement of the prisoners they took at Messines Ridge. Naturally enough the prisoners at Messines Ridge felt that the end of the war was at hand. They didn't know anything about it, but from their point of view, it seemed as if the thing couldn't continue another twenty-four hours. And I imagine that a great hospital, splendidly run far back of the Riga front, would feel as if everything were going wonderfully well, even in the midst of a complete Russian rout. So if I were running some small office in some small hospital on the Western front, all would seem well if that office went well and we would seem pretty badly off if that office ran badly. I can imagine that Hawley's notion of the war will, at any given time, depend on how well his car runs. It really is that way.

I am well and busy—fairly busy with the ordinary coming and going of the hospital and especially busy during the past month with our preparations for the Thanksgiving show which fell to me this time—each of us at all inclined that way must take charge of one of them. The unit is full of talent so that if it were ever possible to count on a rehearsal, the thing would be easy enough. As the major number of the bill, I did a hasty dramatization of Leacock's "Behind the Beyond" with Mr. and Mrs. Audience and a dramatic critic sitting in a box and keeping up a chorus of remarks on the play. It went fairly well and would be fun to do really some time.

We gave the show Thanksgiving Eve in the new convalescent barracks across the road, before a miscellaneous audience of patients (some crazy), visiting colonels and majors, engineers, marines, our own men, our own nurses, French guests of honor and the washwomen from the village. I made an opening address in French that would have agonized Hawley and then stage-managed the rest of the evening, with Schuyler Ladd—you remember the Daffodil in *The Yellow Jacket*—as one of my stars and Bobby Burlen, a side-partner of Walter Wanger's at Dartmouth, as the other. The show made enough of a hit for us to have to give a command performance at the big camp eighteen miles away. That was pulled off last evening. Late in the afternoon I assembled my troupe and we trundled off in ambulances to the next town, where we were dined in state at the Officers Club there and then went out to camp to play in the YMCA before an audience of a thousand men—mostly enlisted men, very keen, very cordial and simply starved for something to laugh at. They gave us a royal reception and things really went with a bang. I shall always remember the departure of the players by moonlight, when, after gulping down some hot chocolate and gathering our props and costumes together, we piled into the ambulances and drove singing home along the country lanes, arriving long after taps. I enclose an all but invisible snapshot of the dress-rehearsal where I can be faintly seen standing in the box. I write all this with the slight uneasiness that it will seem to you we are all frivoling over here, but you needn't worry about that. Not that there have been any hardships. I haven't experienced anything that could possibly be called a hardship since I landed in France. I have at times had to work very hard and have had tribulations of the spirit—mostly self-made of which I would rather not speak or write till I can see them in some sort of perspective. But life has been far more comfortable than any of us expected and it may continue so for a long time to come. The food has, for the most part, been good— quite good enough. Now and then sugar is lacking or butter but we have plenty to eat and the spreads we can buy for very little in town are simply luxurious. Dinners of partridge and rabbit, beef-steaks and perfect omelettes, patisserie worth going miles to eat and plenty of hot chocolate. At least so it has been with us in our out-of-the-way corner of France and that is all I know about.

I may see more at Christmas time for I am planning to go to Paris to spend my five days leave with Heywood Broun and Ruth Hale. I am dashed by the news that they plan to leave for America shortly after the holidays as his job is done here. He came over to cover the arrival of our troops and that story has pretty well written itself out by this time.

Very likely Ruth will be back in New York before the end of January. I shall ask her to call you up or write to you with an eye to seeing you. She will be able to describe our life here more vividly than I can do by mail. She and Heywood came in upon me one Sunday morning just as I was racing across the courtyard to mess and they stayed for two days, exploring everything and making friends on all sides. I want Ruth to call on you and on Julie and to tell you anything you want to know. She herself has been far nearer the front than I and can tell you many things I have never seen and may never see. We never know.

Will you give my love to Katharine. Give my best to Hawley and to Lloyd. And to Alethea [Rudd]. I shall try to write each of them before another week is past. Remember me to Mary, if, as I hope, she is still with you. I often think of her and her heavenly puddings. I often think of her with contrition when I make my bed and tidy up my barracks box. Tell her I lie so still in bed that I never take the covers off more than once a week and tell her that I never throw anything down anywhere. If ever I come back, you will find that, whatever else it has done, the army has produced a house-broken Alexander.

This letter has run long enough. I am sending it out pretty close to the anniversary of a very desolate time. I shall never forget how kind and comforting you were this time a year ago and I look forward always to a time when I may come back to you and Hawley.

Alexander Woollcott

To *JULIE WOOLLCOTT TABER*

Base Hospital #8, AEF, France
December 10, 1917

Dear Julie,

I have postponed writing this for so many days that now I am pretty sure it will not reach you in time for Christmas. I will be lucky if it arrives in time for your birthday. Merry Christmas, Happy New Year, many happy returns of the day.

Even if this letter is late for Christmas, I hope at least one of the two Christmas gifts I have planned for you will arrive before that day. One of them is a useless sort of bag, made from an ancient altar-piece and dispatched to you long since, via Paris. The other will come to you from New York thanks to the machinations of that Carolyn Talcott.

I have a miscellany of small things to say to you. First I must answer your question about Nelson Sackett, who tells me, by the way, that his mother is sending me a book. I don't know what book nor why. Of course I see him daily. The day your letter arrived, I remembered having seen him that morning with painful clearness for he conducted morning exercise in the bright moonlight a little way down the road from the hospital and quite·upset me by his solemnity on that occasion. He is in great fettle today for he has gone on the pleasant detail of visiting one of the several debarkation ports and camping there on the lookout for Christmas packages due this unit. I trust some of mine will arrive, for several people have written me from back home telling of things dispatched in my direction and I am hopefully on the lookout. Nelson is an uncommonly nice fellow and very devoted to his mother of whom he speaks in the most homesick accents I ever heard. For a long time he had no luck in getting letters from her and he was terribly low about it but they started to arrive at last and I take it from his manner that they have been coming steadily ever since.

I must send you this extract from a letter from Walter Wanger. You remember Walter was the Dartmouth prodigy who managed Nazimova and was a great pal of mine. He has turned up somewhere in Italy and I have a note from him which says:

"I was sitting in my room today after our first American mail came in—one of my fellow birdmen asked me if I knew by any chance a wayward cousin of his that lived in NY and lately had departed for France. When he said 'Alexander Woollcott' I sneered and admitted that I once had a press agent by that name and no sooner had I said those words of confession than, opening a letter from my sister, I found the pleasant surprise—your note. In short, what John Corbin would call a coincidence; someone with the original spirit of Roi Cooper Megrue capped the climax by remarking, 'What a small world it is after all.'

(Curtain)

Next morning
    Trite, theatrical but effective.

Alexander Woollcott, NY Times
Note. The realism of the story is that your cousin Walter Woollcott's son of Raleigh, N. C., is bunked in the room here—a delightful and nice boy with no weak tendencies toward that evil thing—the theatre!"

I thought this would interest you.

Long discouraging interruption at this point. Letter resumed two hours later.

I was delighted to get Lucy's [Drage] letter which came trailing along some time after the first announcements of it. I fell to thinking of how wonderful she is and what a gift she has for holding on to people no matter how many years and how many miles and how many new interests come between. She puts so much of herself into a letter and herself is so extraordinarily vital that I feel all warmed and thrilled even by a letter months old which reaches me second-hand. She is one of the wonder-people of our life, isn't she? What do time and space matter to such spirits as hers? Send her my love.

I am still hoping to get to Paris Christmas though all manner of things, such as quarantine or a sudden inundation of patients or whatnot might abruptly put an end to our giddy series of Paris leaves. If I go I shall stay with Ruth and Heywood in their apartment while the others of our party go on to the University Union. Ruth has planned all manner of festivities. She has a tree and Christmas gifts waiting for me, she has a room prepared, she has guests invited for a series of dinners,

Walter Duranty, of course, and Wythe Williams and Viola [Williams] and others who are in Paris now. I am desolated by the probability that they will sail for America in January and leave me alone. However, if that befalls as I think it will, I shall ask Ruth to get into touch with you and with Mrs. Truax and tell each of you all it is proper for her to tell of my adventures in the past four months. She can tell you it in an interesting way because she is a gorgeous lady with a heart as big as the AEF. I imagine, by the way, from something she said, that she has written you of her visit to my peaceful haunts.

The other day I snatched a twenty-four hour leave and, in company with a boy I like enormously, I visited the cathedral town near here—I have been there before. In the afternoon, after lunch with Schuyler Ladd and one or two others, I went a-shopping to buy gifts for some of the men to send to their folks and searching all the antique shops for a present for Ruth. I found a most extraordinary Louis XVI fan of ivory and point d'Alençon but it cost 300 francs and I am not as rich as once I was so I left it in the shop. I found some old seventeenth century chessmen of ivory but they seemed purposeless and in the end I went to dinner empty-handed. That night we went to hear Offenbach's *Barbe-Bleue* sung by the local opera company—very passably by the principals with the aid of a chorus of women who resembled nothing so much as the old crones in the illustrations of a W. W. Jacobs story. After a luxurious hot bath we went to our luxurious and virtuous beds and came home next day in the rain. I blush to admit that we caught the train by the skin of our teeth without time to buy tickets and that the ticket-taker accepted our pass as some mysterious authority for traveling free on his road. I imagine the French, in their polite and silent way, are secretly disgusted with the extravagance of the American soldier. It must be hard for them to understand his luxurious way. He may be the merest of buck privates like myself but he has a way of taking the best room in the best hotel and of preempting the best seats at the opera. We ought not to do it—but there you are.

I never finish a letter like this without an uneasy feeling that you will gain the impression we are all here on a spree. You little know if that is what you think. I tell you the incidents of my hours of ease, but even now I have to work darn hard—had to work sometimes to the point of absolute exhaustion and we are only just beginning. The program at our particular point in the line is a staggering one and the imagination reels before the work that lies ahead of us—just a little way ahead.

I have written giddily to avoid getting on the subject of Bam and the anniversary which tomorrow will bring. But I do want to say that as I think of how enormously sympathetic and hospitable her heart was and when I think of how she shared everyone's sorrow, that it is well she left the world last winter, well she has been spared a time so full of heartache for so many people and sure to be full of woe before the business is through. I find life indescribably poorer because she is not living but I am glad she is out of a troubled world which would have saddened her last years beyond even your great power to comfort and cheer.

And now no more for a time. Don't mind being forty-five and never doubt I will come back to you and spend the rest of my days close to you.

Aleck

To *RUTH HALE*

Base Hospital #8, AEF, France
January 12, 1918

Dear Ruth:
This is an arrow shot into the dark for I know not whether you two have set sail for home. I came back from Paris only to be engulfed in such a quadrupling of our work as makes me think the days of comparative leisure are over for good and

all. It left me not a minute for writing—even to you—and then, when I planned to make amends by telegram, I got caught up myself for a few days as a patient in the hospital and never had the chance to send my farewell message to you.

I think after all, I won't try to thank you for your amazing creation of a Christmas, I'll just send my love and my blessings. I think a special providence watched over our party: it would not listen to any of the things that tried to interfere. And let me tell you this last shining evidence. On the very morning I left you and started back to work, word went forth that the pleasant custom of Paris leaves was thereby suspended throughout the AEF for all and sundry—I was only just in time.

I came back to find my bunk buried completely under a stack of accumulated Christmas boxes, and still they come. I came back to find that the ever astonishing David Belasco had started sending me magazines in such droves that I can supply the whole hospital. I came back to find our work piling up to staggering heights (for us) and no end in sight. Heywood's simply execrable story on our little hospital dramatics has begun to arrive from various sources and when I saw to what rank he had magnificently appointed me, I understood in a flash why he had looked so enormously guilty and contrite throughout those halcyon days in Paris long ago. Tell him I don't mind at all.

This doesn't pretend to be a letter and I don't promise ever to write a real one again to anyone till this business is over. But I wanted to report present and I'll do *that* every once in a while. I shan't pretend to be full of jollity and glee when I'm not nor to be bursting with health if I have spinal meningitis. As a matter of fact my present brief hospitalization is traceable to eye-strain and Dr. Devol is in charge of a moody, fractious patient who has nothing much amiss with him and who has not earned the extra sleep and egg-nogs he is getting. You will be thrilled to learn that I have not smoked for two days—the first recess in ten years—and that I'm not finding it particularly hard. Above all, dear Ruth, I shan't dissect myself again and again to show you the progressive corruption I know is under way in my soul in this ignobling enterprise. Maybe it'll be because I am realizing—a little late—that it really doesn't matter so very much what happens to my dirty little soul.

My love to Heywood and Arthur Hopkins and my best in the world to you. Here's to our next meeting.

Alexander Woollcott

[Note on letter, from Dr. Devol to Miss Hale.]

Dear dear Miss Hale—I want very much to see you. I wish you might be here at "Alex's" bedside—in Ward 3—of course you would have to wait your turn as there is a constant line. He is much better you will be happy to know. With much love.

Faithfully
Edmund Devol

To JULIE WOOLLCOTT TABER

Base Hospital #8, AEF, France
January 26, 1918

Dear Julie:

This is another scrappy note written as a stop-gap between my last long letter to you and the next. It will be a few pages full of nothing, for I have no eventful things to relate, and no typewriter within reach, and without one it is so hard for me to be garrulous.

Yesterday came your letter of January 3rd, and Aunt Julie's as well, and many others—one from Arthur Hopkins telling me he had sent me the script of *Madame Sand* which I would most tremendously like to see, and one (a very charming one) from Mr. Van Anda telling me the [*Times*] office had sent me a Christmas box. It is one of two Christmas boxes that have failed to reach me yet—the other sent by the [Brock] Pembertons and that set. The first Christmas of the AEF was bountiful beyond anyone's imaginings—such heaps and mounds of packages, truckloads of packages, something for everybody, boxes from mothers and fathers, boxes from schools and clubs and offices, and boxes for no one in particular. My two boxes from the Phalanx were among the first to appear. They were held, as most of the Christmas mail, at the nearest port, and delivered here on Christmas Eve, so that I got my hands on them only after my return from Paris. It reminded me of that first Christmas at the Phalanx I remember—the one in '95, when we were all very poor and Bam warned me not to expect much, and then was quite overcome because everyone on the place—literally everyone—contributed something to the Christmas of the youngest. You must thank everyone for me. You see Charles' paper before you, and of course you spotted your envelopes.

I am so thankful it was neither of the Phalanx boxes which went astray, and if any of mine are lost to me for good, I hope some other soldier has them rather than the fishes of the deep. There has been a good deal of that I imagine, although each organization had its man stationed for a fortnight in advance at each of the big ports. That was what Nelson Sackett was doing, by the way. Mrs. Sackett sent me a book of essays by Crothers, of whom I heard Brother Burton [Dr. Richard Burton] sing the praises more than ten years ago. Very charming stuff, but I know now what book I would want if I were cast away on the proverbial desert island with the just one book for company. It would be *The Golden Age,* by Kenneth Grahame. I sent to Paris for it shortly after my arrival, and have read and reread it since, and it is the only thing I have been able to read with any pleasure or with any attention for several months past. It is one of the perfect things in our imperfect world.

On my birthday—very timely—came a sumptuous box from Professor Shepard with so much in it that it was evidently intended for distribution—a dozen pencil-sharpeners, a dozen trench mirrors, etc., etc. I made the acute medical ward and the mastoid ward perfectly happy the night of its arrival.

I think I told you I had been in hospital myself for several days. I escaped as soon as possible, but as I was forbidden any close use of my eyes for several weeks, I elected night ward work as a substitute for my regular job, and have been enjoying it immensely—enjoying the night hours, the escape from the crowd, the sleeping in a squadroom of eight instead of a squadroom of fifty, and, above all, the chance to slip downtown every afternoon for a walk and a dinner. The night men go on duty at 6.30 P.M. and work till 7.30 A.M.—the rest of the day is generously bestowed on them by a grateful government.

Those dinners in the village are unforgettable. I particularly like Mère Cocaud's, an inconspicuous little buvette I stumbled on our first night here back in August. Since then, it has been almost too popular, particularly with some of the draft boys who are doing their dirty, noisy best to make it uninhabitable. But the night workers, dropping in at 4.30 of a winter's afternoon, can get the sole table in the kitchen, right beside the open hearth where, with a single frying-pan held over the crackling twigs, Mère Cocaud can make the most extraordinary dinners of sausage, omelettes, French pancakes and honey, coffee, etc., etc. No matter how many come in of an evening for dinner, they must wait their turn, for Mère Cocaud will not add a stove or even another frying-pan to her stock. Nor can she be induced to make a profit out of us, but keeps her prices way, way down, as in the days before the war. She was a very sad little woman when we first came, talking all day long of her brilliant young son who was killed in the second autumn of the war. There were always a few furtive tears when we tried to talk with her, but the boys have become her great solace, and she is all smiles these days, and never so happy as when every table is full, and she is flip-flopping the crêpes in the frying-pan. A dinner there of sausages and strawberry jam, crêpes and honey, bread and butter, coffee and milk, will cost anywhere from 3 to 4 francs, and be worth going miles to eat.

Tell Aunt Julie I *should* enjoy an occasional glance at *The Bookman,* and tell Charles I have no photograph in uniform for his collection, and would violently decline to appear in such a gallery. I have not seen much of the war, but I *have* seen a good deal of the AEF, and if I could describe it faithfully, if I could give you a cross-section of the men's thoughts, if I could show you the motives that control, if I could suggest the Sammy's real feelings about France and the French, and the French emotion on the subject of the AEF—why, it would be hard to prevent any previously cherished sentiment about our expedition from dying, or languishing at least, for lack of nourishment. In all events, let's don't celebrate it until it has done something.

(I don't know why this sour outburst at this point.)

I am glad the things came through safely from Paris to you. With Ruth as adviser and purchasing agent, I got some little offerings for you and Mrs. Truax and Mrs. Fiske and Alethea. It was back in November we did it and my memory is a little vague, but I am under the impression that the enamel box was added by Ruth on her own hook to the altar-piece I got for you. Maybe by this time, or rather by the time you get this, you will have seen Ruth. She and Heywood sailed on the 19th. She will have so much to tell you. I wish she and Heywood could come down and visit you for a few days. I wish you could get to know her. She is a most tremendously fine person, and he, of course, is a dear.

I am hating to think of the hard winter you are having and of the hard winters to come. I'm glad I'm over here. I may have my glooms from time to time, but I'm always glad I'm here.

Aleck

To JULIE WOOLLCOTT TABER

Base Hospital #8, AEF, France
February 14, 1918

Dear Julie:

I imagine it must be a relief to receive another letter from me written on a typewriter, for I have been out of touch of one these last few weeks, and my hand-writing has been abominable for several years past. I have used a pen so seldom.

Of course I am fierce homesick. I think anyone who goes around the AEF with a long face ought to be shot at sunrise, but on the other hand, anyone who is here in this year of grace, and does not feel sad and homesick, must be an insensible clod. There is none such that I have found. Of late, and almost for the first time, I have taken to dreaming myself back in America, but I am no Gogo Pasquier, and I cannot dream dreams worth while, not see the people and the places to which I would rush the first chance I had. The other night I dreamed I was making an uninteresting call at the Agnews. Again I was back in Rittenhouse Street trying on two costly but horrible-looking sack coats that Father had bought in days of greater prosperity, and which Bam was sneaking to me on the q.t. The climax came when I spent one whole dream driving along Grand Street on the surface car, and going to Broadway Rouse's wholesale store (which I never entered in my life) and there purchasing a bolt of foulard silk to be cut up into waist lengths for Christmas presents for my friends. What a dreary business—what a waste of dream power.

You must tell Mrs. Holt that I was amused to see our friend Miss Sergeant in the court of the hospital the other day. She was visiting here with Mrs. J. Borden Harriman who bounced through our otherwise peaceful midst for several days. I don't mind her coming to look us over, but I do mind her preempting the kitchen of Madame Cocaud's so that one night it was impossible to get anything to eat there. Miss Sergeant is the writer who lunched with Mrs. Holt one day at the Cosmopolitan Club

[54]

when I was there. The other man at the luncheon was named Stork Younf or Stock Young, or something like that—an Amherst man, who, by-the-way, has dashed me off several business notes under the delusion that I am still at the *Times*. Every now and again, I get a note or letter from someone singularly oblivious of my present state, asking me to review a book or speak this good word for so-and-so I can-do nowadays.

So Miss Sergeant can tell Mrs. Holt many things about our world but not so much as Ruth Hale can tell you. Mrs. Truax, in her last letter, intimates that she can tell pretty exactly where I am, but she never gleaned it, I imagine, from any letter of mine. I have never tried to intimate anything contraband in my letters, partly because I am naturally a law-abider, and partly because I think it is rather sinister practice. However, the news must be pretty well disseminated by this time. I imagine they know in America, and I am sure they know in Germany. One of our village women, whose son is a prisoner in Germany, and has been there these two years past, writes her to advise her to make a lot of money out of the Americans at the hospital, and how he found out we were here the good lady is at a loss to explain.

There is one thing that all our family must keep in mind, and that is that we are a very mobile force, and that a man who enlisted in Base Hospital #8 back in the States may be far, far from it now. The changes have already begun, and I think they will continue soon and rapidly. I doubt if our little group of serious enlisters will hold together long, and both Mrs. Truax and Eva McAdoo will be interested to know (if they have not heard it long since) that even Dr. Lloyd, who established the original Post-Graduate Unit, and came over as its Director, that even Dr. Lloyd and Base Hospital #8 have parted company. Several other men have been transferred to other fields. Three have been commissioned. Others have gone and will go on detached service of various kinds. Many, I think, will get close to the front, and I think most of them are itching to do that.

I am. I would never have believed when I left that I would have been so eager to get up and mix with it. I wish to heaven I were as well equipped for field work as Hawley will be when he gets here. As far as that goes, I don't know a single bit more than when we last met.

I hope to see Hawley when he passes this way, as he is more than likely to do. It will be a great meeting. There are many such—some of them unforgettable. Do you remember my telling you, or rather did I tell you, of seeing Tommy Lee, a Hamilton Theta Delt, 1914, last September, and dining with him in company with several other Hamilton men?

It gave me quite a pang and quite a thrill yesterday to stand down in the hold of a ship bound for home. I had toiled down the companionway to the second hold (oh, memories of our own trip) to help down an awfully nice young Brooklyn boy who is going back minus an arm he had when he came over.

I wonder if you ever saw that paltry account Heywood Broun wrote of our Hallowe'en Show. I got the clipping some time ago, and was much irritated to see he had called me a sergeant. It was this way: He was here back in early November at a time when Colonel Siler named a number of sergeants in our midst, which was nice of him, only the promotions were none of them approved from Paris. Not a personal disapproval, you understand, but a sweeping disapproval of promotions in general at that time. I had been much too canny to mention it myself until it was sealed and approved from on high, but Heywood was not so canny, and he spilled the beans, with the result that Jane Grant addressed me letters with the rank to which I was not entitled. It doesn't matter now, as I was made a sergeant late in January, and still hold that rank at this writing. This is a pleasant distinction, and it has its advantages, but it has its drawbacks as well.

The length of the war might be almost anything you can

name, and we can tell better in the summer. Personally, I feel as if the next few months will see great upheavals, as if everything anyone said or thought or planned or hoped in February would have to be revised and redeclared in June, as if the day of change was at hand, and the world we know on the edge of a maelstrom. This is not from evidence I see, but from things I hear, and, more particularly, things I read, things written back home, for heaven knows we get little or nothing from the appalling journals they publish in English for us in Paris.

I suppose there is enough general information here for this letter to go on to Mrs. Truax of whom I think often and wistfully these days. She writes me letters packed to the brim with the things I want to know, and I am in pretty close touch with all our little set in Fifty-Seventh Street. I feel as if, in order to ensure my getting another such letter one of these days, I would best write her at great length, but when I write such a letter as this to you, my time and writing mood are spent, and if she will realize that I am writing to you both perhaps she will let me off and still write from time to time.

Good night and my love to all of you.

Aleck

To MRS. ALICE HAWLEY TRUAX

THE STARS AND STRIPES
Paris, Spring 1918

Dear Mrs. Truax,

I am afraid it is a long, long time since I last wrote you and I am afraid this won't be a very interesting letter for it can be nothing but the chatter of one who, for the time being, is leading as unsoldierly existence as you could imagine. I am working these days on the army newspaper and eking out a pleasant but impecunious existence under the skyline of an old hotel in the Rue d'Antin, just ~~south~~ of the boulevards.

The *Stars and Stripes* suddenly burst into print in February, and from time to time a newspaper man here and a newspaper man there is detached from his command and shipped up to its staff. I had heard there was such a sheet but had never seen a copy when I was requisitioned for the job. As far as I can make out, everyone I ever knew suggested my name but I rather think I owe the somewhat doubtful service done me to an exceedingly decent and energetic officer in the intelligence section whom I met at the Brouns at Christmas time. I say doubtful, for no one can work far behind the lines without feeling restless and dissatisfied and if, as seems tremendously probable to me, we drop back eventually into our organizations, I shall find myself just as inexpert and unequipped as when I first staggered Governor's Island with my unmilitary appearance.

Shortly after I arrived, the door of the restaurant where I was gorging myself swung open, and thinly camouflaged in an officer's uniform, in walked F.P.A. [Franklin P. Adams]. I saluted and fell ~~on his neck~~ and we have had a good many parties since then, one at the Grand Guignol when the few seats occupied were largely occupied by Broadwayites so that it seemed like a first night once more. Où sont les neiges? F.P.A. has his colyum on the paper, of course.

The staff has some pretty good men on it, those first rate men whom the provincial papers produce and who remain little known and underpaid simply because they are not in New York. There is an engineer from the Frisco Park Row, a first rate poet and copy-reader from the Springfield *Republican*, a professional humorist from the *Sun* and Hartford *Times*, etc., etc. One was laying rails, the other keeping the books of an aero detachment and a third wriggling along the ground as machine-gun messenger when uprooted for this detail.

As each number of the *Stars and Stripes* carries our names up in the corner as comprising the editorial staff, I am occasionally run to earth by an old friend and so the weeks have their little reunions. Don Stone and I ran into each other and had a quite unforgettable evening together. I mean I won't forget it. Then today, in blew Baba Engs. You know. Russell's lovely sister. She is a Red Cross woman. I believe orphans are her specialty. She has a party all planned for tonight and perhaps I can go. I have seen and played about with Jack Calder, who is in fine fettle these days and fairly thriving on army life and I hear quite often from Walter Wanger who is an aviation cadet and who will be a first lieutenant in a day or so. Walter is impending on ~~Paris~~ and I shall be glad to see him.

We have occasional days off and spend them frugally. One day we wandered through Père-Lachaise and I think you would have smiled at the sight of a bare-headed marine standing with downcast eyes and placing an onion on the tomb of ~~Oscar Wilde.~~ Last Saturday, the chill was out of the air for the first time this spring and we ate on a little restaurant terrace across the way from St. Germain des Près. I love St. Germain and have my best times on that side of the river. That afternoon, we loafed interminably in the Luxembourg gardens and acquired great merit by treating all the refugee children to a ride on the most ricketty carousel extant.

I would live on that side of the river if the air raids did not make it impossible. If you are caught out in one there is simply no getting back. That shrieking siren and the sound of the distant barrage has no sooner started than every light in the city goes out as if a single hand had turned a single switch. You hear and half feel the panicky scamper around you on the streets as people make for the abris and there's simply no groping your way all the distance to the Odéon. The night of my arrival was the occasion of the worst air raid—the most thunderous and the most spectacular, a great sight if you will stay out of the cellar and keep your eye ~~on the heavens.~~ There have been fewer of them of late and they have been mild and inconsequential. All Paris goes underground when they begin and it's a nuisance if the warning sounds just after you have climbed into bed but no one thinks much about them and the boys are quite taken aback when they get letters from home and find the folks are worrying about them.

Then came the gun but that, too, seems to have lost ~~some~~ of its first fine enthusiasm. The steady blasts from it are no more. We hear it only occasionally and no one even stops what he is doing. "Ah, there, Bertha," or some such greeting is enough of a response. Of course it was very much in everyone's mind at first, particularly after its extraordinary shot on Good Friday. The memory of that overhung Paris on Easter Day and I shall never forget the morning services at Notre Dame with the thought of that slaughter in every bowed head.

We eat in abundance. As far as I can see, everyone in France has all he wants to eat. Butter is rare, bread is rationed and they talk of meatless days, but I am terribly fat. We have to use the bread tickets but that doesn't mean there is any lack of it or any serious inconvenience. The allowance provides a good deal more bread than you want and there you are. Once a month, you must step in at the nearest mairie and get your supply of tickets and that is all there is to it.

If I am due for a long stretch of service on this detail, I trust devoutly that I can work up front. I have applied to be attached to a mobile, field hospital and combine the functions of medical sergeant and *Stars and Stripes* correspondent. Good-bye and much, ~~much~~ love. I cannot tell you how often I think myself back to the apartment in ~~West Fifty-Seventh Street.~~ I am always looking up toward the ~~Great Northern,~~ always hearing you stepping about in your room, and hearing Mary's step in the dining-room. (Please note F.P.A.'s censoring throughout this letter.)

Oh, yes, and now and then a letter thanking Mrs. Fiske for a box. Her Christmas box, which was a screaming mixture of Huneker, soap, dice, cigarettes, ~~Bibles,~~ etc., arrived in perfect condition on April 4. Once she wrote and insisted on knowing what I lacked. I replied, truthfully enough, that I had all the heart could desire except America and tooth-paste. She sent me the tooth-paste—enough to polish a regiment for five years. I hope some of us will get home before that.

Much love
Aleck

(*Passed as censored*)

Franklin P. Adams, Capt., N. A.

[Cartoon was drawn on the letter by A. A. Wallgren of the *Stars and Stripes*.]

To MRS. ALICE HAWLEY TRUAX

Paris
July 6, 1918

Dear Mrs. Truax,
 I have had two days off in the last two months and this is one of them, so you may know I am busy, preoccupied, and therefore—for the moment—not actively discontented, in the sense that we used to say actively ill.

I am becoming, week by week, a passionate enthusiast on the subject of America, something I never was before. I was ever so much more interested in the total cause, and not so very deep in my heart, there were doubts about the record America would make. I used to listen to the boys on the boat and in camp prattling away their easy optimism to the effect that the American would make the best soldier in the world, that an American could beat the life out of any German, that there was something essentially strong and brave about an American, etc. etc. And I used to shudder because it seemed provincial, because I thought there was nothing in history to justify it, because I thought it would sound offensive in the ears of the French and the English, etc. Well, I have been living at the front with the infantry, getting to know the American under fire, getting to know whole rafts of men from all corners of America as I never knew them before, and I do believe with all my heart, there never were braver, gentler, finer, more chivalrous soldiers since the world began. I think I first came to know mine own people in the woods near Château-Thierry.

Of course, it is impossible not to feel all this in the air. I cannot tell you how important, how fine, and how telling was the work done by the men who raced across France and jumped into that battle just north of the Marne—literally did that, leaping from the big camions as they slowed up and fairly running into the fray without stopping to stretch their legs. I can think of nothing I would rather be just now than a private in the Marines. Not that they were all Marines and not that the most remote and untested of us are not sharing in the exhilarating American popularity which is in the very air these days, so that you felt the tingle of it as you hiked through French villages and caught an expression of it in every wave of the hand from a French window and every smile from an old French soldier.

I drove in from a town beyond the Marne to be in Paris for the Fourth and I shall always be glad to remember I was here for the Fourth. I shall never forget it. You must think of me standing weeping on a chair in the Champs Elysées, too choked to cheer as the bunch went by, some of whom I knew in camp, with the sun on their helmets and a grin on their faces. They marched through a very rain of rose petals. When the poilus came next, with the hortensias showering all about them and a little American flag fluttering from every bayonet, there was no containing us. And all the while, a band either ahead or behind was playing "Swords and Lances"—that march we have heard pilot so many parades around the corner from Fifth Avenue into Fifty-Seventh Street. And all the while overhead, circled and swooped the aviators, dropping roses as they flew, now looping the loop till we were dizzy from watching them, now dropping so low they grazed the tree-tops.

Of late—since May some time, I have been going every week to some part of the front, sometimes dropping off with my pack and living with a company in the ravine, now sticking to a car and covering a great deal of ground. It is fairly easy to get along. France is small, a country of short distances. If you are at the front and must gravitate slowly toward Paris it is no great undertaking. You sleep with the Infantry, hook a ride with an ambulance, mess with some field hospitals, hike a while, make the railhead by nightfall and come on in that way. More often, the staff has a car of its own and scoots all over the country in it.

Recently three of us found ourselves late at night at a French village which is headquarters of one division. We had not had any sleep worth mentioning and had driven a hundred miles. Besides, the artist who was with me—[C. Leroy] Baldridge and a Lamb of God if ever there was one—was running a fever which worried me a little. The driver—who is French—volunteered some real beds. He went to the town mayor and declared we must have a house to ourselves. The town was, of course, evacuated. He produced a bunch of keys, large enough to open the Louvre, I should have thought, but they merely gave us entry to a morsel of a French cottage on the edge of the town. We each picked a bed—throwing dice for choice—and settled down rather like the three bears. I pried open the shutters of my ground-floor room, and pushed them wide so I could go to sleep watching the roses in the little garden and watching the moon come up over the edge of the woods just beyond. And so I dozed off, only to be awakened by the painful discovery that on the edge of that woods was a French 145, an enormous gun every flash of which lighted up my room and every shot shook me in my bed like corn in a popper. It was a comic sequel to a wild day. I have got used to sleeping through the droning boom boom of a barrage and I can sleep under the steady bang of the Soixante-Quinzes, but this monstrous thing was more than I could bear.

The next day was full of things to remember, including a chance encounter with the Commander-in-Chief who had come unheralded to decorate some men with the Distinguished Service Crosses—seven of them. It was the first ceremony of American Field Decoration and we just strayed into it. The rehearsal of the battalion parade in the green meadow, with an airplane duel going on overhead that ended in a German machine coming down in flames, the music of the regimental band from the edge of the woods and the boom, boom, boom of the cannons, then the arrival of the general and the fine pomp and circumstance of the decoration—I was fairly uplifted and would have been quite happy, except for the misadventure of having eaten some bad meat at the cavalry mess down the road, so that I maintained military bearing with some difficulty and vomited at every hedge between Montdidier and Paris.

Usually when my friends blow into France, they get hold of a copy of this unprecedented newspaper, see my connection with it and write me or drop in and go out to dinner with me. I have not heard from Lloyd [Stryker] but the other day Max Foster came in and then in blew Phil Hoyt and Roy Durstine, so we have had some parties on the tip top of Montmartre, the part of Paris I love best. I took Baba Engs up there for supper last night and was somewhat embarrassed to have the patronne of the little restaurant where we eat confide to me that one of my friends had been in the other day to breakfast—with a girl.

Give my love to Katharine and Eva and tell Mary to save some bread pudding for me.

Alexander Woollcott

(Censored by) Charles P. Cushing

To RUTH HALE

Paris
September 5, 1918

Dear Ruth,

This is a rainy day in Paris and nothing could be nicer than that.

I have been luxuriating in it through a week's permission, which I was much too discerning to spend at any official leave area. So I am soaked in it just now. This afternoon, on my way from déjeuner, I have been playing with my friend, the sacristan of St. Germain l'Auxerrois, who, as a great treat, took me up the old Norman Tower and showed me his twelfth century psalters, his sixth—no, seventh century chests, his old altar carvings. He told me how once an American had gone off in disgust because

[65]

he didn't believe such tales. The sacristan thinks it must be hard for people from so young a country to realize how old things can be. I guess it is. While we were climbing down, we heard the innocent old bell in the clocher that had given the signal for the massacre of St. Bartholomew's eve.

I must say, we fare pretty well in Paris. You can get anything in the world you want to eat except pudding. Sugar, butter, cream, all the little forbidden things are easy enough to get if you know where to go. If you know enough to go to Montmartre—the very tip—so high up that the rules and regulations never reach there. Or to M. Jacques, who has a discreet back room. Or to my petit déjeuner place behind St. Germain l'Auxerrois (a stone's throw from the hotel of the musketeers) where all these contraband things and others (such as café cognac) may be had boldly on the sidewalk. I never knew why this was so brazen till I discovered that the police station was across the way and the place itself the police restaurant.

M. Jacques, who used to run the big hotel in Rouen before the war, is devoted to his clients fidèles from the *Stars and Stripes* and when, in early June, it looked as though all Paris would have to—or might have to—move out, he wanted to go along with us and reopen wherever we set up our presses again. Recently, he has been a bit flustered due to his wife, in Switzerland, having presented him with twin boys—and very triste for three weeks because the closing of the frontier shut off all news from them. I was there the other evening when, at last, the postman brought a letter. Such excitement! Of course, the old postman had to be treated to a drink then and there. The news was good. I was interested because the elder twin is—formally and officially —my godson. I have sent him a spoon of gold and silver from his parrain. His name is Marcel Benoît Dick—le petit lapin. And then Montmartre—Do you know la butte? Gimalac's, or Nini's or Freddie's?—better far any of them than the Coucou where the approval of Julian Street is announced in English by a sign out front. Such good things to eat and such leisurely service as if there were all the time in the world! Such absurd dogs as gather about your table and ogle you for scraps! At Nini's, if you will keep quiet, you can stay till midnight, playing poker. At Freddie's, there are apt to be songs and recitations. Quite as though the quaint notion had just occurred to him, Freddie will ask the old, long-haired poet to sing Musette's song or a slatternly female, much impaired by opium, to recite something impassioned from Baudelaire. As they have come for the purpose they are not hard to persuade. Afterwards, Freddie, with equal spontaneity, passes the hat for them. Once the place was full of American officers who all fled after the Baudelaire. Freddie consulted me about it. Didn't Americans like Baudelaire? Not American officers, I told him. A great light dawned. "Ah," he exclaimed, "then it is with you as it is with us. All your officers were drawn from the grocer class." Once Freddie announced, with great empressement, that a young American was present who would sing in American and French. We all applauded and shouted "Bravo" and in the midst of this uproar, I discovered that the young American in question was I. I tell you, cryptically, that I rose to the occasion.

We sing a good deal, I'm afraid. The favorite song with all our French friends is

 Qu'est-ce-qu'arrive lundi? Lundi Bolles
 Oh vous salle Boches, je vous souhaite de même,

a free translation of "Oh you dirty Germans," the soldiers' song which Elsie [Janis] has been singing hereabouts. Then there is the new song the poilus have—of which the refrain is

  Two testaments
  The old and the new
  But there's only one hair
  On the head of Matthew.

The verses are all outrageous puns on the numerals. Par example:

> On dit qu-y-en-a dix
> Distance au front
> Neuf à la coque
> Huitres-d'Ostend
> C'est épatant
> System metrique
> Saint Sebastien
> Katherine de Medicis
> Troyes-en-Champagne
> Deux testaments
> L'ancien et le nouveau
> Mais il n'y-a qu'un Cheveux
> Sur la tête de Mathieu.

Elsie loved Montmartre. I have guided so many footsteps there. F.P.A., Grantland Rice, Lee Dodd, etc., etc.—I was led there by Wythe Williams. Paul West usually haunts the Place du Tertre, you know—the place staged in *Louise*. Did I tell you that after looking at my picture, caught by the camera in full war paint with mask and helmet, he said, "Ah, the daughter of the regiment!" I was on Montmartre not long ago with my dear Walter Duranty, than whom no one can have a warmer spot in my foolish heart. As we were skating home in midnight darkness, a polite young lady (who was out shopping, I suppose) linked arms with us and walked bantering all the way to the opera. Walter urged her on me as one passionate as a lion. I whispered to her that he was passionate as a rabbit, which is much more to the point. On leaving, she confided to the stars her private opinion that we were both as passionate as two plates of noodles.

I haven't had much chance at the theatre. Brieux's *Robe Rouge* wasn't bad at the Odéon and *The Cricket on the Hearth* with exquisite oboe music by Massenet. There's an English stock company that has been packing the Théâtre Albert Premier with

Aussies and Canadians on leave—a mighty good stock company with *Smith, The Mollusc, The Tyranny of Tears, Billeted* and *Wanted a Husband*—the last was much mauled about and spoiled to make a play for Marie Tempest as *A Lady's Name*. Nous avons changé tous cela. We were very hilarious during the first performance of *Billeted* when the lovely ingenue dropped her lighted cigarette down the bosom of her gown. It was an agonizing moment and no time for false delicacy. You should have seen her go after it.

The theatres are packed now. So is Paris. There never was any repining all through the anxious spring. No bells were rung when the tide turned, even when the boches were no longer at Noyon. But everyone smiles, everyone walks with a gayer step and all's well.

It seems to me there are twice as many people on the boulevards as there were in June, twice as many people sipping apéritifs at the green hour, twice as many puttering over the bookstalls on the quais. It takes me an hour to walk a block along the quai that starts here below my window. I revel in fearful translations. "M. Britling commence à voir clair." Do you recognize that? I found a French *Trilby*, with delightful French illustrations which, unlike the author's own, were of the period. Also a French *Alice in Wonderland*—would you detect "a bright idea popped into Alice's head" under the disguise of "Une ideé lumineuse traversait l'esprit d'Alice"? Dear, dear.

There are some darned good books on Paris which you'd enjoy if you haven't found them long since. The one in the Mediaeval Towns series is the best. E. V. Lucas's *A Wanderer in Paris* is for beginners but it has nice chapters and enchanting pictures. I enjoyed Belloc's *Paris*.

Poor Rufie is to be laden this Fall with business for me. If I have any luck, I'll get a Liberty Bond sent you to dispose of and buy Christmas things for me. Also, before long, I'll send you money to pay my civilian insurance for 1919. Also, I might send you something to sell for me, all with an eye to raising Christmas funds.

I must copy out for you a Tommy's will, of which I have seen a transcript. It read:

"In the event of my death (cheers!) I leave all my estate (loud cheers!) to my older brother Charles (loud and prolonged cheers!)."

It was probated—of course.

I never intended to write you such another long letter and never set out to fill it to the brim with Paris. But I have been spending a week's leave in the place. I have been working in and out of it for six months and I love it above all places in the world. The river that flows past my window now is gleaming in the sunset that has followed the rain, and the bridges fade away mysterious in the distance—and no German foot shall ever cross them.

Alexander Woollcott

P.S. I forgot to tell you that on the night I sang at Freddie's—his place looks like a Belasco gesture indicating Bohemianism—I noticed on my way out that the long-haired poet and the opium queen were busy dividing the gate. I burst in indignantly and demanded my third and while they were still uncertain as to whether or not I was facetious, I let them buy me off with a glass of something.

P.P.S. Notre Dame is having a bath. They are scrubbing the old lady from base to gargoyles. Her ancient stone emerges unexpectedly white and embarrassed—like Heywood found nude on Fifth Avenue.

A. W.

(Censored by) Charles P. Cushing

To DR. EDMUND DEVOL

Bar-le-Duc
le 12 Novembre, 1918

My dear Major,

I was glad to hear from Dr. Trexler and have confirmation of Capt. Pease's report that you had been made a major and I want you to feel sure I will not let it make any difference between us.

I wish everyone at the hospital could have shared some of my recent experiences. I was at the front—isn't it a wonderful place?—till the last shot was fired but I do not mean that.

For instance, not long ago, being out at elbow and thinly clad, with winter coming on, I drove to the commissary at St. Dizier and appealed to the old corporal in charge there for a little raiment. Instead of demanding this and that of me and tossing a salvaged coat out to cover my nakedness, he assigned two darkies to me as fitters and held up the whole line for an hour while he fussed about, getting me oilskin capes, his best quality of leggings, his finest whipcord breeches, etc., etc. I dared hardly question this benevolence lest it would break some spell—but finally he grinned and said, "I guess you don't remember me." I admitted I didn't. "Why," he said, "don't you remember old Cherry, who threw the chocolate pot at the orderly down at Savenay? I was one of your patients down there and you were mighty nice to me."

Now the point of this story, Major, is this—that, as you well know, I was never remarkably nice to anyone and I gather from this and other cases that the least kindness, the least little human touch, warms the heart of these soldiers when they are—as the service records say—"Sk in hosp." I wish, when I was there, I had realized this as I realize it now. But I did not get religion till that great morning in June when I saw the Marines tearing up the road on the way to Château-Thierry.

I have met our old patients again and again. They hail me

from passing trucks. I run into them on the edge of Sedan. Once, I remember, when a kitchen capsized on the first day of the St.-Mihiel attack, it could serve only cold coffee and this was almost gone when I came toiling up the road. The cook stood guard over the last cup. "I am saving it for that fat medical sergeant with the specs," he said, "he took care of me at Base last Fall."

I shall always remember Ward 3 very vividly and the sight of a fashionable New York doctor giving old sickly fretful darkies just as much care as if each and every one were Gertrude Atherton. By the way, do you remember that wretched fellow, Miss Ward's pet patient, with the loud voice and the mitral insufficiency? It seems he called at the *Times* office and regaled my old confrères there with the most startling stories about me and certain very lovely nurses, leaving them with the impression that France had transformed me into something of a blade.

Well, I hope and expect to visit Savenay before the winter is gone and I hope and expect to dine with you in New York before I set forth on the journey around the world that I am now planning.

I have time to write you this long letter because I am waiting at Bar-le-Duc for the arrival from Paris tonight of my new automobile. In it, I am going to the Rhine.

My love to Dr. Trexler, Schuyler Ladd, Red Moore and yourself—these four and no one else.

Alexander Woollcott

P. S. Don't you think the *Stars and Stripes* has been darned good? We have slaved to make it so.

A. W.

To JULIE WOOLLCOTT TABER

Paris
December, 1918

From: Alexander Woollcott
To: Mrs. Charles Taber
Subject: Alexander Woollcott

I clip a little editorial I wrote for the *Stars and Stripes* for the issue of December 6th—wrote it just about the same time you were expressing exactly the same thought in a letter to me.

Last Saturday I decided the time had come to go to Paris so off I set, driving as far as Nancy. We had to put up at a little town in Alsace-Lorraine for the night and were most royally served at the inn there by one who spoke pretty good English considering he had been a waiter in New York for eighteen years. We trailed through Metz in the dismal morning rain and made Paris at midnight.

I had come in, expecting to straighten out a lot of little things and start back immediately for my beloved Rhineland and for my still more beloved Army of Occupation. But I find they want me here for no end of things—so there will be the old round of editorial conferences and this and that. Still I don't pretend it will not be pleasant to be in Paris—especially to be here through the Christmas holidays—just as I was last year.

Immediately, the business of life accumulates. There are reams of letters, there are cablegrams. Old friends are in town. Telephone messages and this person and that popping up in the mob. Here are two boys from my old tent squad on Governor's Island, up from Savenay to buy glass eyes for the hospital—a pleasant errand. I hear my dear Major Devol (my doctor when I was sick at Savenay) is in town and has been in to see me. Then a most embarrassing letter from Mrs. Truax, congratulating me on the acceptance of my play—which, malheureusement, has not even been written. It was all a joke—or partly so. One night at Bar-le-Duc when an air raid on the town shut out all but candlelight and precluded more sustained literary effort, I whiled away the time by dashing off some post cards. One was to Arthur Hopkins, the producer in New York, with whom both Ruth Hale and Brock Pemberton are associated and who, I believe, is the best producer in America. I idly told him that after the war I was minded to set forth on a tramp-steamer for a long year at sea—that when I got off I would have a play for him called "World without End" and that then he *would* be ruined. I was highly amused at Coblenz to receive a cable from him saying "Accept play and ruination," which I thought was a pleasant though expensive jest. You can imagine I was startled to receive a clipping announcing that Mr. Hopkins had accepted the play without reading it, but I rather imagine Ruth started that story going just to be facetious. I think I will have to spoil the joke by writing the play after all. It is all in my mind.

Tomorrow night, nine of the staff will go to Nini's little restaurant on Montmartre and dine there en famille, with something witful for each as a gift from each of the others. [John T.] Winterich, I know, has already bought a YMCA pin for a foul-mouthed little varlet and he has purchased a second-lieutenant's bars for the most aggressively private private on the staff.

Next day, M. Jacques—proprietor of the restaurant where we usually eat—will give us a dinner.

I am mailing you today, a copy of the current issue which has a letter to America from me in it and also my story of the Rhine crossing. There is one paragraph in that story at which, I am pained to say, Mr. Wilson is said to have laughed uproariously.

You can imagine how content I am to have Mr. Wilson here and how relieved to feel the undercurrents of intrigue and unrest subside at his coming. I believe he will blow away all the obstructions in the path of a decent peace.

Aleck

III

The 1920's

To A. A. WALLGREN

New York City
November 15, 1920

Dear Wally,

I am passing the hat for Marie Louise Patriarche—I hope for the last time, certainly for the next few years. I want to catch her by Christmas time with the news that her bank account will see her through indefinitely. Please send me a check for any amount between one and one hundred dollars.

I hear you've been married several times since we last met. Why don't you ever write me or draw me or call me up? You remember Chesterton's slogan—"My mother, drunk or sober!" Well, them's my sentiments toward you, old thing.

The other day a girl blew in with a letter of introduction from F.P.A. which puzzled me a little until I discovered that he had given it to her when we were still in Paris two years gone by. It bade me introduce the girl to "everyone in the office, including the Scandinavian." Yet she was a very nice girl.

A. W.

P.S. Saw Father Brady the other night. He asked after you. I told him you were married. He fainted.

A. W.

[Marie Louise was a little French orphan adopted by the *Stars and Stripes* staff, on which Mr. Wallgren was a cartoonist.]

To EDNA FERBER

Paris
July 21, 1922

Dear Ferber,
         I never got your telegrams and probably you never got my letter written to Frankfort. However, I cannot remember that it was important. It described my huge 19-cent room at the Hotel Traube and my unbelievable breakfasts of fruit, eggs, toast, echt coffee und cream for 12 cents—all served on a table overlooking the Rhine. It told how I would probably stay in Coblenz until I had caught up with my work—which I did.

         I enclose several items for your entertainment. The letter from Deems Taylor (isn't "living like Swopes" a perfect phrase?) will amuse you. The squanderous $15 referred to is a check I sent Mary in the hope that she could get one of those bags for me—or two.

         Speaking of Swopes, I eventually called on them. It was high noon at the Ritz. Margaret was in bed, garbed in pink and altogether too beautiful. Herb was receiving correspondents, being shaved by an imported coiffeur and describing London hotel prices. There were silk stockings and fragments of toast and huge bunches of roses in pleasant profusion, but nothing much to do, so Margaret and I shot craps while Herb talked.

         Your note from Carlsbad awaited me at the Hotel when I returned from Carcassonne. When you suggest that anything that befell in Berlin "puzzled" me, you don't know your good old "she-ancient," as the low [Marc] Connelly once called

Your affectionate
A. Woollcott

[Herbert Bayard Swope and Woollcott were both young reporters on the New York scene before the war. Later, when Mr. Swope was managing editor of the *World*, Woollcott became its dramatic critic.]

To JEROME KERN

Bomoseen, Vt.
July, 1924

Dear Kern,

Confidentially, I am puttering about at present with a biography of Irving Berlin whose story has a strong appeal to my foolish and romantic heart. I need hardly say that I have no notion of trying to turn learned in the midst of it nor do I think that grave musical criticism has any place in the project. But I would, when the thing reaches book form, like to see one chapter that says something intelligible about him as a composer, his place in the history of ragtime, his melodic gift, his place as a maker of folk song, etc.—not gushy, not untrue, not a floral wreath. I think the thing for me to do is to call a witness and I am wondering if you would care to be the witness. If it could take the form of a letter from you to me, the trick would be done.

This is just a tentative inquiry which I will follow up, if encouraged, by coming out to see you when I am back in town late this month.

Yours
A. W.

To EDNA FERBER

Bord S.S. France
le 10th June, 1926

Dear Ferber,

I am debarking tomorrow at Plymouth, reinforced by a wireless from Irving [Berlin], confirming my reservations at the Carlton and inviting me to dine with him on the night of arrival—carefully ascertaining first, I suppose, that I could not possibly land in London before midnight.

But what I really wrote to tell you was about the shocking revelations into the character of Nancy Woollcott.

She is the twelve-year-old eldest of that Baltimore bevy—the exquisite flower of the flock, the perfect one. I suppose her sisters and cousins have always rather resented her. Now they are getting out a magazine and thus far all of Nancy's contributions in prose and verse have been returned to her without comment. Finally, in desperation, she asked bitterly if she might be permitted to insert an advertisement, and was assured (probably after a hasty investigation of her assets) that she might take a page on payment of 6 cents. Her dignified announcement read as follows:

> MISS NANCY B. WOOLLCOTT
> *The Most Charming*
> *Woman in the*
> *World*
> Call between 2:30 and 3

Well, that's that, and I have no news beyond the fact that [Charles] MacArthur who is with me says he can't get over the notion that he's on a boat and that [Robert] Benchley, wishing to get us something we couldn't get in Europe, brought us a plate of wheatcakes and left it in the cabin.

I don't know when I will reach Paris but I hope to find there a letter telling me when you are to arrive from the South. My elegant motor trip to St. Jean was crushed by the Fleischmann mishap. The kid came out of the operation (double mastoid) all right but their European trip had to be called off.

I have no plans beyond a few vague dates at Antibes for the end of June.

I am going to Scotland in July.

Woollcott

To *HUDSON HAWLEY*

New York City
May 15, 1928

Dear Hawley,

I am sailing on May 19 aboard the *Roma*, bound for Naples where I will be lodged for a day or so, at least, at the Hotel de Vesuve. My party, which consists of Alice Duer Miller, Harpo Marx and Mrs. George S. Kaufman [Beatrice Kaufman], will then motor up through Rome, Perugia, Siena, Florence and probably Milan and Maggiore, settling eventually at Antibes for the summer.

I am writing to warn you that you may get a telephone message of greeting as I dash through Rome, and to tell you that if you were half a man (admittedly a matter for nice and anxious calculation), you would persuade the Commendatore Oro, or whoever is in charge of the Department of Tours, to put a handsome automobile at the service of so influential a cluster of American journalists for the trip from Naples to the Lakes.

A. W.

To *LUCY CHRISTIE DRAGE*

[Lucy Christie Drage and Julie Woollcott Taber became close friends when the Woollcotts lived in Kansas City. After the death of Julie, Lucy's memories of her served as an unbroken bond with Woollcott.]

Antibes
June, 1928

Dear Lucy,

When Julie died, I had a strong impulse to jump on a train and go to you as the only person left in the world to whom I could really talk about her. There seemed to be too much to do. The day she died, Billy [A. W.'s brother] himself was taken to a hospital in Baltimore and hung between life and death for weeks of anxiety. Then I think I invented things to preoccupy me, made a great pother about work to be done, ran round and round in busy little circles, anything rather than sit down and face the fact that there was no Julie any more and never would be again.

I wired you that day that I would write you a letter and here I am at last, in this corner of the Riviera where I have bestowed myself for the next few weeks, sitting down before the portable I have toted across the world, batting out a letter that should be full of the things I would have told you had I really hopped on that train and gone out to see you. I wish now I had done it.

I am glad you did not see her in those agonizing summer months when her sickness first took hold of her, when we were dragging experts to see her and she was trying to walk but couldn't, unable to speak clearly but trying to all the time, shaking so that she could hardly guide a cigarette to her lips. It was cruel business. The experts had some elaborate explanation of the inexplicable phenomenon—a progressive degeneration of the nerve tissue which defeats medicine and eludes surgery. But the ways of the spirit are mysterious and I know that she had just invented a way of getting out of a world that was too intolerably lonely for her without Charles. You could tell that from the peace and satisfaction which settled on her when the invention worked at last, for in the final six weeks at the hospital, there was no pain or distress or trouble. She just lay there at rest in a room that somehow began to look like her, with the yellow roses on the table and the blue silk shawl thrown across the foot of her bed. Day by day the years seemed to fall away from her, cast off like garments she no longer needed. She did not know even me, but she was pleased when it was Paul Robeson's voice on the phonograph and pleased when the nurse would put a gardenia on the pillow beside her. If you bent close, you could hear her say "Sweet, sweet." The lines went out of her face, the gray out of her hair, the pain out of her eyes. Her hair, braided and tied with little blue ribbons, lay tossed upon the pillow and framed so prettily a face that was the one you saw when she first came out to Kansas City nearly forty years ago.

Toward the end, while she was still talking, all her thoughts ran back to those years and the ones between were forgotten. She talked of the day I was born and of the trip west and of Aldine Place, with Rose Field calling up to your window and making all manner of fun of her because she was so excited over the fact that Frank and Mailie [Sauerwen] were coming. One of the last things she said was that she must find out where Rose Field was living and go to him and offer to keep house for him. One of her last commissions to me was to write you the birthday letter for which she could no longer hold a pen.

She told me all about the day in January when I was born —how, after breakfast, Mother told her not to bother to clear away the things but to go up to the old house and ask Grandma to send one of the teamsters to fetch the doctor. It was snowing and old Dr. Kimball came the seven miles in his cutter. The other youngsters on the place were not told what was up and went to their lessons in Mailie's room as usual. While they were bent over their books, Mailie slipped out and found her father taking a surreptitious drink in honor of so agitating an occasion. She came back with the news and imparted it cryptically by scribbling a line on a piece of paper and smuggling it unseen into Julie's hand. It was a line from *Bleak House* which they were all reading then. It ran something like this: "A young gentleman has arrived whose name is Mr. Guppy." So they always called me Mr. Guppy. I made a stab at it myself but got no nearer than Guffy. Mailie called me Guffy always. The advent of the newcomer was regarded as a family calamity. Aunt Julie told me once that she spent that day crying in her room as the least she could do.

It was of those days Julie talked toward the last. It is then I wish you could have come. I wish you could have seen her when the sentries we all post to warn us that the world is looking could no longer do their duty. I am sick at the thought of what swinishness and poltroonery and malice the spectators would find if ever *my* guards were dismissed and I could no longer edit myself for my neighbors' inspection. But the Julie that was turned toward you and toward me was the same all the way through—a gentle and gracious and gallant person in the very core of her. There was nothing base in her.

There are just a few of us left to whom it matters. In September Dr. Humphreys died. You remember I was named after him. He was a person of circumstance and Trinity was so crowded for his funeral that I had to stand in the back of the church. In the shadow of the pillar there I watched the procession following the coffin out into the afternoon sunlight—Aunt Eva, bent and old but able to make the journey, and behind her young Eva and her husband and a swarm of grandchildren. And I knew that there were great-grandchildren stowed away in sundry nurseries. And I knew, too, that I could stand in the shadow of that pillar for a hundred years without seeing the end of the procession, without seeing the end of the chapter written by that full and fruitful life. It is so different when a childless woman dies. Julie's chapter is ended. She was perfume, scattered now on the ground. And there is just a small company of us —you, dear Lucy, and a few others, for whom the fragrance of her lingers in the air.

The Phalanx is ghostly now. There are strangers in the little cottage, so that what Aunt Anne used to call the Julie light can once more be seen through the trees. But the big house is mostly dark. When I used to come home at Christmas time from school, I could see it from a great way off through the bare branches of the trees, warm lamplight shining from each of the twelve French windows that looked out across the lawn. Now only two or three windows are lighted.

The last to go was Uncle Will. He had been born there and

did his first toddling in that pretty ravine of which he painted the beech trees all his days. Even when he had to go into exile as an old man and was supposed to be painting landscapes in Florida and California, it was the beech trees he saw with the eyes of his heart and the beech trees that kept showing up in those pictures of his. Aunt Anne took his ashes down into the ravine and buried them at the roots of one of those trees. Then she just carved his initials in the bark of the trunk. That was only a month ago.

So one by one the lights go out. I have had to write you about them. It is because Julie loved you with a surpassing loyalty and tenderness. The miles and the years between made no difference to her at all—none at all. I think you knew that there was always that lamp in her window for you, always that loving kindness in her heart.

Something stops me from trying to say anything of the impoverishment I feel. What a world this would be—what a morning light would shine across it—if all people were like her. I think of that and of many things and I send you her love and mine. I wish I could stand beside you at some window today and look out into the twilight and say nothing.

Aleck

To *EDNA FERBER*

Antibes
June 2, 1928

Dear Ferber,

I am here leading the life of a rosy, middle-aged dolphin—here alone, though this coast swarms with people I know. Why don't you motor here en route to Grenoble? I think you'd love it.

Love to Julia— A. W.

P.S. I attended the strike debate in the House disguised as a Liberal Expert and I had tea with Philip Guedalla who looks a little like Channing Pollock. And I won a pound playing croquet with the English at the Duke of Manchester's.

A. W.

To *PETER HACKETT*

New York City
July 15, 1929

My dear young man:
    Some decayed old gentlemen whose poker games in happier days used to be enlivened by the occasional presence of your sainted mother before she found something better to do, have, out of an institution known as the kitty, purchased you the enclosed present being under the impression that when you got around to it, you would find it more pleasing than a bassinet or even a gold safety pin.

In behalf of the Thanatopsis Inside Straight and Literary Club, I beg to remain your obedient servant,

Alexander Woollcott

[The gift that was presented to Peter Hackett a few days after his birth, and a few months before the market crashed, was one share of U. S. Steel.]

IV

1930-1932

To *BEATRICE KAUFMAN*

London
April 26, 1930

My blossom:
   Noel [Coward] is the only gamester I ever knew with my own whole-heartedness. We played backgammon or Russian Bank all the way over. I had never before crossed the Atlantic without once laying eyes on the darned thing. The other passengers were mysteriously angered by this singleness of purpose. They would stop by and say: "Don't you two ever tire of that game" or "Still at it?" or, in the case of the German passengers they would merely say "Immer!" to each other in passing. We finally devised an effective rejoinder, merely singing in duet:

We hope you fry in hell
We hope you fry in hell
Heigho
The-merry-o
We hope you fry in hell.

   I did not have much luck. Paid for my passage but not much over.
   Cavalcade last night. Noel's party in the royal box. A convenient arrangement, with a salon behind it for coffee and

[85]

liqueurs and an adjacent room for the occasional relief of the royal kidney.

Adele Astaire and Lord Cavendish in the next box and the Duke of Bedford in his. In fact, everyone on hand with the possible exception of Frances Wellman. The audience gala, much cheering at Noel's entrance, a speech afterwards from the stage. The show very moving. Also a good play. No one had ever told me it was that.

I am lunching today with Jeffrey Amherst, dining tonight with the incomparable Rebecca [West], lunching tomorrow with Mrs. Belloc Lowndes. Tomorrow afternoon, Lilly [Bonner] arrives by plane from France. Program from then on a blank, but probably a week-end at Noel's, which is near Dover and might be taken in en route to Paris.

I must make clear a curious illusion of which I am conscious. If I write a note to either you or George Backer, I feel as if I were writing it to both of you. This note, for instance, will leave me with a feeling of having just communicated with him. I am dimly aware that any message for him I have in mind might reach him more immediately if I were to send it care of Kuhn, Loeb but I cannot be bothered with his endless fluctuations of address and I prefer looking upon you as the nearest thing to a permanent address he will ever have.

As a matter of fact, I have a message for him. Tell him to read Van Wyck Brooks' *Life of Emerson*. I don't think it's a very good book—watery and general. But Backer should read it and when he does he will see why I think so just as clearly as if I were to mark the significant passage for him.

Joyce [Barbour] and Dickie [Bird] are immensely bucked up. He is rehearsing the leading part in the new Priestley play and she is rehearsing for the new Joe Cook show and after ten weeks in that she will go into the new Coward revue. This hasn't a title yet. I suggested calling it "Here's to Mr. Woollcott" or "Here's to Mr. Woollcott, God bless him" but Noel is curiously inhospitable to suggestions from others and he does make the good point that in England it would not mean so much as in the States.

Both Dickie and Joyce look uncommonly well. Joyce has a figure like Lilly's. It makes me wonder if a year of complete destitution would not be good for baby.

A. W.

[The friendship which began when George Backer was in his early twenties continued through the period when Mr. Backer was publisher and editor of the New York *Post*.]

To BEATRICE KAUFMAN

Kyoto
April 22, 1931

Light of my Life:

I cannot tell you how often I have rejoiced that you were not with me on this curious expedition. I could not have gone through with the necessary ceremonies—dropping repeatedly to my knees, scraping the floor with this old forehead, ch-eh, with your unamiable eye upon me. It is difficult enough, God knows, for me to eat with chopsticks. Inevitably a few bamboo-shoots fall off onto my long-suffering lapels. But with your eye on me, they would have *all* fallen off. Then you would have been so disagreeable about my arrival at the Imperial Hotel—me getting at once into pajamas and receiving deputations in the Campanile manner, with no conspicuous difference except that I take tea now instead of coffee and the Gideon Bible in the room was in Japanese. When Mr. Hyashi came and bowed low and said he trusted I would find equally enchanted aisles in Japan, I just thanked my stars that none of you crude people was within earshot. When finally I went into dinner and the orchestra struck up the "Dance of the Hours" (on my word of honor) I had a dreadful moment of feeling that you at least had a spy on the job.

I have had such a swell time since I started and, in this one week in Japan, gone through such eye-filling and beguiling hours that I keep thinking it can't last. Today I've been trundling around Kyoto in a rickshaw, fairly beaming with contentment. Perhaps the misadventures and misgivings will set in when I go down to Kobe on Saturday and embark in a noxious and unseaworthy little Japanese boat for a four days' sail across the Yellow Sea to Tientsin where Yuan will meet me. Something will have to go wrong soon or I will get apprehensive. My luck has been holding so long.

I sat down here tonight with the notion that I would recount my various adventures, some charming, some hilarious. I had it in mind to describe the entrancing supper that Kikugoro, the great Tokyo actor, gave me at his house the night I left Toyko (the Lunts will really have to do better by me from now on) and the speech I made to two hundred girls at a school and the arrival here in Kyoto in time for the cherry-blossom festival. But instead I'll save it all up until I get back and then find everyone walking out on me after the first five minutes. I'm already a little sore when I think how nobody's going to listen quietly to my relentless travelogue.

Your parting gift, which must have involved the denuding of several orchards, was gratefully received at Seattle. And that about clears matters up except for an impulse to report how fond of you I am. From time to time my heart dwells on that fact. Occasionally it will occur to me when I am dropping off to sleep on the other side of the world. Then it smites me with such intensity that I should think it might easily light a lamp in your room—thereby, I am afraid, catching you at all manner of mischief.

I'm off to Osaka now to see the marionettes and a few

good temples. Yesterday I saw a fervent Japanese gentleman standing, in the frosty twilight, under a sacred waterfall. He wore a suit of tasteful underwear and prayed aloud with chattering teeth for the good of his immortal soul.

Hoping you will soon take similar measures I remain
Yours respectfully
A. Woollcott

[Henry Yuan is the son of Yuan Shih-kai, the first President of China. He was sent to the United States to be educated, and went to Hamilton College, where he and Woollcott became acquainted.]

To *HERBERT BAYARD SWOPE, JR.*

[Herbert Bayard Swope, Jr., was a schoolboy of sixteen when Woollcott wrote this letter to him.]

Kyoto
April 22, 1931

Son of Heaven:

I would address this to the school at Riverdale but I suppose you are seldom there. It is intended as a line of thanks for those expensive groceries with which you so agreeably showered me on the eve of my departure. They sustained me all the way to Seattle where the business of speeding me on my way was taken over by your aunt Phyllis's father [Mr. Blake]. He is a tall and imposing creature of whom I could catch only glimpses in the flurry of my final arrangements, which included everything from buying some garters to a brief dash to the local chiropodist. He (the chiropodist, not Mr. Blake) was from Oneonta, N. Y., and makes shoes for Babe Ruth, whose bunions, I was credibly informed, are just like spurs.

Well after that, there were a dozen days on the boat, devoted to much reading, some writing and the minimum of typhoid injections. I enjoyed the voyage so much that I felt outraged when we lost a day en route. I am aware that this was no special bit of fraud. Indeed, it's quite the usual thing. I had merely forgotten about it.

We had a rather interesting murder on board. An Indian traveler in the steerage dropped dead fifteen minutes after buying some soda pop. As he weighed 300 pounds, it was a little difficult getting him up the companionway in order to drop him overboard—feet weighted—into the deep. His bride was inconsolable for as much as half an hour but thereafter perked up and flirted around hopefully. Her charm for me was somewhat impaired by the circumstance that, in her front teeth, a gold spade and a gold heart had been skillfully inlaid. Of course no one breathed an official suspicion of murder, as it would have meant inquests for the next ten years.

I have never enjoyed traveling in a country so much as in Japan. The meals in the Japanese homes and restaurants, rather than in the foreign hotels, delight me continuously. I am afraid they would revolt one who has been brought up to look at every edible twice and then spit it out. I have particularly relished two dinners I have had here in Kyoto, sitting up at a little counter of spotless, new unpolished wood and taking my food direct from the hands of the chef, an expert who is tastefully attired in a suit of durable underwear and who works with an immense gravity, occasionally interspersed with sudden shrieks of falsetto laughter, usually inspired by my maladroitness with the chopsticks. And even your sainted mother would relish the custom of starting the meal with a face-wipe with a soft, moist, perfumed, hot face-cloth, brought by a pretty girl who kneels beside you while you tidy up for dinner. And certainly she would approve the gargle which was supplied—pitcher, cup, spittoon and all—as the final course of my dinner last night at Osaka, where I had gone to see the famous puppet theatre.

As for your sainted grandmother, I don't like to say anything or to inquire what Oriental colony there may have been in

Far Rockaway, but it is extraordinary that about one out of every three young Japs I meet are the living image of your uncle Bruce.

I bid you au revoir.

A. Woollcott

To *LILLY BONNER*

[The Bonner family consists of Lilly Stehli Bonner, her husband Paul, and their four sons; Woollcott's long friendship with them was unusual for him because it embraced the whole family. He spent much time at their home in Locust Valley, Long Island, and later visited them during their long sojourns in Europe.]

Nara, Japan
April 24, 1931

My dear Lilly

You have had your sweet revenge. Never had I thought to see the day when I would long for those splendid, capacious, substantial two-tined forks of yours. But it has come to pass. When I am crouched on a silken cushion beside a lacquered tabouret, trying (while the little waitress kneeling beside me titters with ecstasy at my efforts) to convey to my lips a morsel of bamboo-shoot dipped in gravy and mashed radishes and have only chopsticks to do the trick with, then I eat my words—the bamboo-shoots having fallen by the wayside. And there can be other difficulties. For instance, the little waitress will lift the sake bottle with a pretty inquiring gesture and I bow and say thank you at which, with a regretful sigh, she puts the bottle away. It's like the equivocal French merci and I must get the intonation wrong. But the real hardship is these damned chopsticks. I have abandoned my diet as a work of supererogation. I can lose weight just by the process of elimination which my lack of dexterity forces upon me.

But I've never seen so enthralling a country. Every waking

minute entertains the eye. For sheer delight, I offer you this ancient and quiet town—so quiet that I hear all the bird-calls in the countryside and the rattle of a distant cart somewhere and the occasional boom of the gong at the Temple where some pilgrim must have paid 5 sen for the luxury of calling Buddha's attention to his prayers. I practically spent the day feeding rice-cakes to the sacred deer who drift by thousands through Nara and whose attentions, when they suspect you of concealing rice-cakes on your person, are even moister than Paddy's. It was a benign spring day and it seemed as if all the school children in Japan were out on the highways on a picnic. Sometimes I saw them trudging along through a very snowstorm of cherry-blossoms. I invaded one Temple at a time when about two hundred girls were at prayer. Their shoes were ranged outside and how they ever get back into the right ones, is beyond me. Perhaps they don't. They were all about six years old each. Henry Bonner would, I am sure, have risen to the occasion and asked for more.

Tomorrow I am going over to Kobe for a four-day sail across the Yellow Sea to Tientsin in what will probably be a horrid little boat. But Yuan and [John] Thomason have been wiring greetings and I look forward to Peking where I should be well established a week from now.

I found it hard to believe it was only four weeks ago last night that I heard Toscanini conduct the Ravel music, I listening from a vantage point which gave me a superb view of your back in that black dress. If memory serves, you were wearing what I hope (in case we ever have to hock them) were emeralds. I trust you do not mind if I drift around the Far East with a pleasant memory of the nape of your neck etched on my heart.

Tell Paul that getting only one drink of sake is rather a hardship because it is served in a cup so tiny that compared with it the offerings of eye-dropper Bonner seemed like the gigantesque libations of a medieval baron.

Au revoir. I'll see you around the end of June if the fates are kind—to me, that is.

A. W.

To *LILLY BONNER*

New York City
July 2, 1931

My dear Lilly:

Here I am, safe home and feeling singularly bereft. I know now exactly how Stefansson must have felt when he came out of the Arctic regions at the end of 1915 and heard for the first time that the world had been at war for more than a year. The news that you have departed these shores greeted me at San Francisco and in Hollywood I caught up with George Backer who told me it was all true. I do not think until then I had stopped to realize how inextricably the Bonners—root and branch—had grown into the fabric of my life. I had been looking forward all the way back across the Pacific to the moment when I would reappear on your horizon and had been getting down to brass tacks on my old and then still unrelinquished idea of taking a house in Locust Valley. Well—that's that. Or, at least, for the present, that is that.

As to coming over to Saint-Cloud, I have every intention of doing so between now and the end of the year. The exact time would be determined by the schedule of my work. After three fallow months, I am due just now for some weeks of steady writing. By the middle of August I should know what if any radio work I must do in the Fall and whether I would have time, before starting in, to take a quick trip across the Atlantic. I would really like to do none at all for then I could come over in October which would be perfect.

From everyone I hear only regret at your absence and

admiration for the way you managed the exit. It seems to me among the probabilities that you will live to look back on that departure as the beginning of a better existence but the whole chapter is one too involved and too abundant for me to dabble in it. I move we postpone the subject until I have a free afternoon and can settle down to it.

My adventures in China were soul-satisfying and one of the rare treats you cannot escape by trans-Atlantic flights is the evening when I sit down and tell you all about it. Also the elegant keepsake I brought you from Peking must wait a while, although I might find someone going your way to deliver it for me. I know that the Fatios are leaving this evening but they will land in Naples, go to Switzerland and Sweden and not reach Paris until September.

Aleck

Next Day.

P.S. F.P.A. has been muttering over the telephone about a letter from Paul I was to read, and I held this open on the chance that I would find it in this morning's mail. It hasn't come yet, so I will wind this up without having read it. Tell him I know how unsettling it is to give up any job which has become a habit, and which had, through many years, absolved one from the anxious burden of choice. But tell him that the task of picking up each day and making it with his own hands is a good job, too, though more exacting. I know very few people equipped with the rare talents needed for leisure, but Paul does happen, I think, to be one of them. I include some snapshots taken of an oblivious backgammon game, which was staged at the [Kathleen and Charles] Norrises beautiful ranch, to which I transported Harpo [Marx] and [Harold] Ross when they met me at the boat in San Francisco.

Miss Ryan tells me that I owe Paul $5.50 on silk sheets made up to complete an order, but as he owes me $25 for recklessly betting against me in the matter of the sex of an impending baby, I will thank him to send me his check for the balance at once. All of which sounds very light-hearted and jolly, and it ought to, for that is exactly the way I feel. I have no sense of separation, but rather a strong belief that somehow, somewhere, I will see much of you in the next forty years. If you were not practically illiterate, I could rely on you to know that the last paragraph of *Great Expectations* runs as follows:

> *I took her hand in mine, and we went out of the ruined place; and, as the morning mists had risen long ago when I first left the forge, so, the evening mists were rising now, and in all the broad expanse of tranquil light they showed to me, I saw no shadow of another parting from her.*

A. W.

To *LILLY BONNER*

New York City
July 22, 1931

Dear Lilly:

As I suppose you already know, it's a girl at the F.P.A.'s. Esther came into the hospital Monday and attended to the matter within two hours. The whole thing makes a sucker out of me, but there were no bets. Incidentally, Paul is a menteur and pouilleux bâtard when he says he didn't bet me that little Miss Stehli would be a boy. Frank was here till all hours last night watching [Harold] Guinzburg and me play backgammon, and trying to screw up his courage to the point of calling his daughter Persephone. I pointed out that she would be known as Phony, and am myself recommending Rachel.

Broun's revue was staged last night, but it so smelled of failure in advance that I couldn't make up my mind to attend it. The reviews this morning are written with a kind of crushing kindliness.

I am having Holliday send you Wells's *The Science of Life*. This impulse has been forming ever since I vanished for five days in the Yellow Sea into the enchantment of its fifteen hundred pages. I thought then how simple, everyday biology had been left out of not only my own education, but that of pretty much everyone I know. I think that's because we are brought up by schoolmasters, and schoolmasters are classicists. I doubt, for instance, if either Reache or Manfred knew any biology worth imparting. I then progressed to the point of thinking it would be a grand idea to present your spawn with a first-rate microscope, and that you could get some biology teacher in one of the Long Island schools to come for two hours once a week and start the kids off on a little laboratory work for which the material abounded all over the place. I wish to God someone had done something like this for me. Then I would have gone into high school and college with the ground to some extent prepared for the very meagre amount of planting such institutions usually give. What I had in mind was the liberal application of a corrective to the still strong monkish influence in our schools and tutorial systems, something to give a boy the rounded mental equipment that a man like Wells has. Well, I don't know whether the great migration has shot this plan all to hell, but anyway, I think you will get a good deal of pleasure out of *The Science of Life*. Everything except the section on genetics I found easy enough reading, and my only fear is that you already have the damned book. In that case, I shall be too irritated!

Life at Sands Point seems to be much as usual. I find it pleasant, distracting, and singularly unnourishing. It is no way to live.

On the way back, the boat put in at Honolulu for twelve hours. I thought a good deal of Sibyl [Lady Colefax], noted that the beach at Waikiki was not any larger than the Stehli riparian rights (or wrongs) on Oyster Bay, and bought a copy of *Time*, in which I read with mixed emotions the story of Ralph Barton's suicide.

Well, I was gone only three months, but in that time you had migrated, and Belasco had died, and Ralph had killed himself, and everyone had taken up Culbertson.

A. W.

To *LILLY BONNER*

August 26, 1931

Dear Lilly:

I am trusting this to the mails with what I can remember of your address, for I am writing from Hawley Truax's place in the Berkshires and I left my address book behind me in New York. I am on my way by motor to the Tarkingtons in Maine.

There is to be one final expedition before I settle down at the Campanile—a house party at the island, consisting of Beatrice, Backer, Harpo, the Guinzburgs, and, I hope, the Dietzes. I plan to herd them there on September 11th, and stay three or four days, it being part of an old notion to see what a Vermont September was really like. A pretty successful island party was wound up without casualties a week ago—the Ives, the Fleischmanns, Neysa [McMein], George Abbott (we now call Neysa's place in Port Washington the Abbottoir), Alice [Duer Miller], Harpo, and myself. It was a part-time arrangement for the Fleischmanns, who kept making disastrous trips to Saratoga, but as Charlie Brackett would rush over from Saratoga, this evened matters up. Ruth [Fleischmann] stayed on the island only long enough to complain a good deal about the beds.

As for my plans, I shall have to confess a secret shame. I

am resuming the Shouts and Murmurs in *The New Yorker* with some September issue, but with radio people and the like I have been arch and hard to please because it now seems likely that I will go on the stage—just once and get it over with. It seems that Katharine Cornell has leased the Belasco Theatre for three years, and will inaugurate her management by producing there, in October, a comedy by S. N. Behrman called *Brief Moment*, in which Francine Larrimore will star, and in which there is a part Behrman wrote with me in mind. This character is a stout, indolent and unamiable creature who spends a large part of the play lying on a chaise-longue and making an occasional insulting remark. After a good deal of palaver, it looks now as if I would surely go into rehearsal with this, and even get as far as the week's tryout in Washington on October 12th without being fired. I suppose that if I were still in the cast when the play opened in New York, I would have to play it for at least four weeks. Perhaps it would work out so that I could come over and spend Christmas with you. All this is so uncertain, even now, that I have not spoken of it to anyone around here, but having sworn to announce my plans to you, I can at least confide to you what's afoot.

The new Marx picture is to open next week, and Harpo has taken a penthouse in East Fifty-First Street for six months. The brothers (or rather, three of them at least) jumped into Heywood's show for two nights, ensuring a profitable week for that somewhat anxious venture. They did it for nothing, and were solemnly presented with three of Heywood's paintings in full view of the audience. Groucho said it was bad enough playing for nothing.

Alexander W.

P.S. Speaking of beds at the island, they have found a new name for the big double-bed in the front room on the ground floor. It is comfortable but noisy, and lets out a tell-tale groan if you move in it. We now call it the informative double.

A. W.

To A. A. WALLGREN

Washington, D. C.
November 6, 1931

Dear Wally,

Your amiable letter soothed and assuaged the tedium of my recent exile in Detroit. It makes me proud to think that you sit in your little suburban home reading from my works. I can almost picture you in your arm-chair with your feet up and your lips moving. What embarrasses me is a secret conviction that you then turn to the other communicants of Old Swedes' and say: "There's a man who has a lovely prose style and once in Paris, during an air raid, he got drunk and took off my shoes for me."

A. Woollcott

To LILLY BONNER

New York City
November 20, 1931

Dear Lilly:

Well, I'm just a fool. Here I am sold down the river in so many different directions that I practically have no private life. If you could see me dictating breathless* prose while brushing my teeth in the morning, and correcting proof while applying grease-paint in the dressing-room, you would have some rough idea of my present demented state. After the opening at the Belasco ten days ago, I had reason to believe that you were getting reports from Neysa, Miss Ryan, et al. I don't know how I can supplement these, except by letting you know that we seem

[99]

to be something in the nature of a hit. At least we are doing a lively business—uncommonly good business in a season when most of the plays are dying like flies. Next, it has occurred to me that it might amuse you to see the script, accompanied by a complete set of the photographs of the production. These will go forward to you within a day or so. I had thought by this time to know what I, myself, would be doing. But I think it will need another two weeks before we can make an estimate on how long the play is likely to run, and when I know that, I can come to some conclusion about how necessary I am to it, if at all, and whether I want to go on playing it for months. My sense of freedom in the matter is somewhat tinged by the circumstance that I own a small but tender fraction of the production, and would a little prefer that it should not lose money. Of course, I'm having a robustly amusing time, and am really quite good in the play, thanks to the fact that it is an actor-proof part which fits me better than any suit I ever had did.

One advantage of my present visible preoccupation is that I don't have to go to any parties at all. The only exception in the past two months was that annual birthday party of the Krock-Kaufman-Fleischmann aggregation which brings together, by the arbitrary accident of birth, people who would not normally go within ten miles of one another. I moved from the demi-tasse right into a car and drove back to town, but the occasion did have its compensations.

It is barely possible that before the winter is out, you will get an invitation to dine with Elsie DeWolfe (Lady Mendl to you). I am very fond of her, and enjoy her company enormously. She is a really fabulous creature. She fed me before the play on Wednesday night with Lanson 1914 thrown (or rather poured) in for good measure. But she is leaving for Paris in another fortnight, and I have filled her head with the importance of getting you and Paul to come and see her. You will probably hear from her. Paul can play around with Sir Charles.

Well, dear, the call boy (who happens to be a girl, by the way) is announcing the overture, and I must go down and conceal my breaking heart under the eternal mask of the clown. In another two weeks I will be full of information about this business of my visiting Vaucresson. I hear rumors of the suggestion that I accompany the Duer-McMeins on their projected exploration of the Nile. I must impart to your private ear a resolution made several years ago never to travel anywhere with anybody except my dear George Backer, who is incapable of minding my acerbities because, in his vagueness, he doesn't even know I'm present. He is, incidentally, so ill as to alarm me. They wanted to operate on him for appendicitis, and found that a six-weeks course of treatments to reduce an enlarged liver, etc., would be necessary first. I suppose he will be operated on early in December. Much love.

A. W.

* I dictated "deathless," by the way.

To *LILLY BONNER*

New York City
December 4, 1931

Dear Lilly:

Elsie Mendl is sailing back home to Versailles this Saturday, and she carries with her (unless she has forgotten) a small gift from me to you. I cannot make up my mind whether it is a Christmas present or just something in between times. Perhaps if you really get it, and I don't happen to come to life in time to send something else, you would better call it a Christmas present. You can tell Paul that I felt fairly bitter when I examined his catalogue at Dutton's the other day and saw that he was offering for sale the first edition of *The Whilomville Stories* which I had given him for Christmas two or three years ago. As I had paid two dollars and he is asking thirty-five, I feel that its sale at this price will involve an unearned increment in which I ought to share. The whole episode gave me a good idea. I am having that rug you gave me for Christmas last year exhibited in Sloane's window as part of the Alexander Woollcott Collection of objets d'art. I am asking a thousand for it and will give you half of what I get.

I have been busy as hell, and have had time for nothing except one hurried trip to Newark to see Maude Adams play Portia, and to become involved in a local squabble which has, I think, left none of the Swopes except Ottie speaking to me.
A. W.

To *ALFRED LUNT*

New York City
December 14, 1931

Dear Alfred:

There was such a mob backstage last night, and I was so trampled under foot by the *Mourning Becomes Electra* company, that I had no time for the civilities beyond telling Henry Travers what I have been telling him for years—that he's just about my favorite actor, who never fails me whate'er betide. In the confusion I found myself out on the street again without attending to one matter that was on my mind. I wanted to hunt up this man [Eduardo] Ciannelli, whom I do not know, and tell him how beautiful I thought his performance was—especially in the last act.

When your grandchildren (on whom you have not yet made a really effective start) gather at your rheumatic knees and ask you what you did during the great depression, you can tell them that you played *Reunion in Vienna* to crowded houses, and enjoyed the whole depression enormously.
A. Woollcott

To *PAUL BONNER*

New York City
December 30, 1931

Dear Paul:

I was delighted beyond measure with my Christmas present. I think that, after all, I must own up to something I have always thought myself free of—the lust of possession. I know that when you had this book it created a mild flicker of interest in me, but certainly nothing comparable to the one I began to feel as soon as it was lodged here under my own roof. By the way, without any intention on my part to accumulate a library that is anything except a work-shop, mine is growing insensibly in value. This Fall Constance Collier gave me the first English edition of *Plays Pleasant and Unpleasant* inscribed by the author "to Ellen Ellen Ellen Ellen Ellen Terry." The copy has a certain evidential value just now when Gordon Craig is setting up a tiny clamor to the effect that Shaw had not, as a matter of fact, made much impression on Ellen. I would have to testify she thought so little of this brain-child of his that she casually bestowed it, inscription and all, upon a boy friend. And as Constance Collier carried the boy friend off from under her nose, the book, in the whirligig of time, came into my possession.

Life hereabouts seems very congested. I myself cannot get to see the few plays that are worth seeing, and would not have seen the one big hit in town, *Reunion in Vienna,* if they had not given a Sunday night benefit for the unemployed. It is a good comedy made enchanting by its performance, particularly, I think, by Lynn [Fontanne], who plays with a kind of exquisite delicacy that can't even be described. I don't know whether you've heard anything about the play, but it is a reunion of an exiled Hapsburg who returns from driving his taxi in Nice, and after an interval of ten years sees once again the safely ensconced matron who had once been his mistress. The meeting is electric. He sees her in a mirror, turns slowly around, scorches her from head to foot with his eyes, circles silently around her, comes close, lets his hand play over her bosom and buttocks, then slaps her in the face and gives her one long, exhausting kiss. All that time she never speaks, never moves a muscle, but when he straightens up again, you can see that she is swooning inside. Everything about her has wilted in the heat. The lady sitting in the seat behind me kept up a helpful causerie for the enlightenment of her companion. At this point she said, "You see, she ain't responsive."

There's another scene I think you might like to know about. It's the one where the returning Hapsburg has his first encounter with the old beldame (played, of course, by Helen Westley) who runs the restaurant where the reunion is effected. He can be heard speculating idly as to whether she still wears her old red flannel drawers, and at an opportune moment lifts the skirt to see. The glimpse of Helen's behind incarnadined in flannel is a nightly joy to the Guild subscribers. The other evening, unfortunately, even Helen knew by the gasp of the minor actors on the stage that she had forgotten to put them on. One saw the thing itself hung with shreds of old Jaeger like some Doré conception of the Inferno. Alfred came out of his catalepsy at last unable *not* to speak the line which was then due. It was, "Well, thank God there is one thing in Vienna that hasn't changed."

I have had it in the back of my mind all along that I would be able to crawl out from under the debris of my life along about the middle of March. If it should turn out that by then I would be well and solvent, I want to take ship for Europe, roughly dividing the next ten weeks between London, France and Spain, not necessarily in the order named. I'd like to motor in some part of France I've never seen—the Aveyron or the Dordogne. I'd like to have a look at Spain, which I have never seen, and I'd like to spend a week in London with Rebecca West, and Jeffrey Amherst, and Noel [Coward], if he is back by then, and Mrs. Belloc Lowndes, and Siegfried Sassoon, if I can break through his door. Recently Henry [Stehli] wrecked my peace of mind by suggesting that Lilly would bounce over to America after the flight from Egypt. I do hope that you or she will write me before she departs, telling me just what her plans are. It would be too sickening if we were to cross on the Atlantic. Also, tell Lilly that I am doing up a bundle of choice reading matter in a shawl-strap, and Alice [Duer Miller] has promised to transport it in return for the privilege of sampling it en route. I think you are all going to have an enchanting trip, but I am too involved in this venture at the Belasco to be able to get out in time to join you. Besides, the damn thing has so gutted my calendar that unfinished work is piled high around me in crushing quantities.

A. Woollcott

To *LAURA E. RICHARDS*

[Mrs. Richards, the daughter of Julia Ward Howe and Samuel Gridley Howe, was in her eighties when Woollcott began to correspond with her. He had recently read and reviewed her memoirs, *Stepping Westward*, and this was a reminder of the pleasure her early stories, including *Captain January*, had given him. This friendship continued until her death, at the age of ninety-three.]

New York City
February 9, 1932

My dear Mrs. Richards:
             I do not aspire to enrapture posterity with another Shaw-Terry correspondence, but I must write you once more if only to withdraw "paw." I am now quite sure that you do not paw, though perhaps you pounce occasionally.

Then if you don't mind, I should like to say something about the word "rubbish." I must tell you that it is an old trick of mine to snatch, when venting some great enthusiasm, at any chance of disparagement in order to lend credibility to the bouquets I am tossing. It is a kind of back-pedaling, I suppose. As a matter of fact, the other books are all vague to me. I suppose I avoided most of them because they were written for girls. They came along in that time of my life when I read ravenously. We lived in Germantown, outside Philadelphia, and in order to get enough reading matter to last me over Sunday, I had everyone in our household (including the cook) become a subscriber to the Germantown Library, which was the lovely eighteenth century Wister Mansion set in a park. This gave me jurisdiction over four cards. I used to set forth with a small hand-cart (actually) and come home heavy-laden except on the several occasions when, coming of absent-minded stock, I appeared at the library with the letters which my mother had given me to mail, and only then discovered that, in passing the box at the corner of our street, I had posted the library cards. This misfortune used to infuriate me to tears. I have no idea which of your books I gobbled in that period but after nearly thirty-five years, I seem to recall an impassioned young woman who was dedicated to the slogan, "Cuba Libre," and also a family group named Basil, Merton and Susan D.

I can report one thing to you. No. 8 Bond Street is still standing, but No. 23 is gone. However, it must have gone recently, for the passerby can see the traces of old rooms and stairways left like scars on the wall of the building still standing next door.

One thing I looked vainly for in *Stepping Westward* and that was some allusion to Kate Douglas Wiggin. I thought your paths would have crossed somewhere in Maine. She was a great and a dear lady, and we were neighbors for many years, and I think of her often. The first letter I got in response to the *Stepping Westward* review was from her sister, Nora Smith.

And you yourself tell me there is something else you left

out of the book. So you wish now that you had "put in another story" and then add: "No matter." No matter? I am livid.

Yours sincerely,
Alexander Woollcott

To LAURA E. RICHARDS

New York City
March 15, 1932

My dear Mrs. Richards:

I seem to have accumulated a number of things to tell you. As soon as I have reported my delight in your letters and my immense gratification at the valentine, I can settle down to the business of the day. To begin with, I take it that I need not spend too much time disposing of that somewhat blurred stencil comprised in the word "sophisticate." It is used as a classification stamp on the work of all of us who, through inertia, continue to function in New York. A fair analogy would be the comic-journal notion of yesteryear that all little boys in Boston had enormous, dome-like foreheads and wore spectacles. I am under the impression that it was Gertrude Atherton who first printed this label for wide distribution. Well, the tales I could tell you about Gertrude Atherton! She didn't live in a tree with an affinity. That would have struck her as too humdrum.

You see, I am not a book reviewer at all. For too many years I was a dramatic critic, a post nicely calculated to rot the mind. After my flight from Times Square, I invented this page in *The New Yorker* where, as a kind of town crier, I can say anything that is on my mind. The trouble is that there isn't often much on it. But every once in a while I have the satisfaction, which is the breath of the journalist's nostril, of hearing bells ring all over the country. Then I know that I have had the good fortune to say something which a lot of people had wanted to have said. Said *for* them, that is. This happens just often enough to keep me going. It happened in the case of the piece I wrote about *Stepping Westward*. At the risk of seeming vainglorious, I must (because, after all, they are your affair, not mine) report some of these reactions to you. I do not think there has been a day in the past two months when someone has not written me about that piece. More often than not the note takes the form of someone thanking me for reminding him or her of *Captain January*. I get descriptions of angry hunts through the bookcase until the mislaid copy is run to earth in the spareroom closet. Then follows a fond reunion with a few tears for the story's sake, and for the sake of days gone by. I have received several stern letters from followers of Hildegarde. The lovely Anne Parrish tells me that she still reads them for the peace they bring her. I never knew Hildegarde, but at least her wallpaper seems to have made a vivid impression on her contemporaries.

As for that small express wagon in which I used to trundle a five-foot shelf home from the Germantown Library, I have been trying to reconstruct its contents. I make out a list for myself and it sounds implausible. I suppose it is because it underwent such violent fluctuations in the years from nine to fourteen. But I think if I could go back and stop it on any one expedition, I would find incredible variations in a single wagonload. There would be candid juvenilia written for the slower-witted boys, sandwiched between books that I could and do read now for pleasure. But I think that even at the time, I knew there were those among my favorites which were good in a sense that the others were not. I think I knew, when first I read them, that I would always like *Huckleberry Finn*, and *Little Women*, and Kenneth Grahame's *The Golden Age*, and Howard Pyle's *Robin Hood*, and *Captain January*. Mixed in with such treasures, and pretty much at the same time, was a good deal of addiction to Harrison Ainsworth and to Charles Reade. But above all, and through all, and to this day, my dear Charles Dickens. My father started me when I was ten by reading *Great Expectations* to me. I still think it is the best of the lot. I had read all except *Bleak House* by the time I was twelve. Later I took on Jane Austen, and one of the reasons why I am not particularly well read today is because I have spent so large a part of the last twenty years rereading Dickens and Jane Austen. I remember Shaw admitting once to me that a concordance of his own writings would reveal the Dickens allusions as running four to one against any other writer. He told me it was a kind of shorthand, and I realized that that was what it had always been with us. If I had not known the people in Dickens as well as I knew the neighbors, I wouldn't have understood what the family were talking about half the time. My grandfather lived to be eighty-eight. Toward the end he relinquished all jurisdiction of his acres, but kept his eye on the hollyhocks, and we would know the chickens were at them by the sight of him hobbling down the steps, brandishing his cane and shouting, "Janet, donkeys!" I understand that I, myself, arrived on this scene when all the boys and girls in the family were at lessons. The tidings were clandestinely conveyed to my sister on a slip of paper which contained a sentence from *Bleak House,* the book in which they all happened to be immersed at the time. The sentence was: "A young gentleman has arrived whose name is Mr. Guppy." For some years thereafter, I was referred to in the family as Mr. Guppy.

Well, I must run now.

Alexander Woollcott

P.S. Since we're talking of favorites and the vice of rereading, I might add that the best of all biographies, to my notion, is Trevelyan's *The Early History of Charles James Fox.* I always keep a few copies on hand for distribution among the benighted. I have just been reading an advanced copy of the excellent memoir which the present Trevelyan has written about his father. In one of the letters printed in it I notice the old man referring to the time when he, too, "commenced author." I suppose I ought to know where that phrase came from, but I don't.

A. W.

To ROBERT BARNES RUDD

New York City
March 24, 1932

Dear Bob:

Your word reached me too late. I had already indignantly returned the drawings to him. Total strangers all over the country dump scripts of plays, novels, short stories, poems and the like on me all the time. The accompanying letter always asks if I would mind telling them whether it would be a good idea sending them to *The New Yorker*. I should think it would be so simple to send them direct and find out that way. When I sold "The Precipice" to *Young's Magazine* (or, perhaps, *The Black Cat*), I do not recall that I first mailed it to the editor's laundress to find out if she thought the editor would open the envelope when I sent it to him.

I can find no record that *Guy Domville* was ever published, but I have a notion that Thomas Beer would know if a manuscript copy were anywhere available, and I am writing to ask him. I remember reading in something of his an account of the disastrous first performance.

Speaking of John Aubrey, I have just been rereading the lovely Strachey piece about him in *Portraits in Miniature*. The realization that I will never have another book by Strachey to read gives me such a sense of impoverishment as I have never known before in reading the death notice of some writing fellow. There is a fine preface on Aubrey by his new editor, John Collier, the young man who wrote *His Monkey Wife*. Aubrey was new to me, but that is only because Bib was my last attempt at a teacher of English literature. I have been trying to find a diagnosis of the peculiar twinge of pleasure that I get from such a first-hand witness as Aubrey. Take this passage, for instance, in the profile of Ben Jonson:

In his later time he lived in Westminster, in the house under which you passe as you goe out of the churchyard into the old palace; where he dyed.

He lies buryed in the north aisle in the path of square stone (the rest is lozenge) opposite to the Scutcheon of Robertus de Ros, with this inscription only on him, in a pavment square of blew marble, about 14 inches square,

O RARE BEN JONSON

which was donne at the charge of Jack Young, afterwards knighted, who, walking there when the grave was covering, gave the Fellow eighteen pence to cutt it.

I suppose the twinge is a response to the evidence that anything so casual and unpretentious could have become, by the mellowing of time, so momentous. I know that kind of twinge keeps me in a constant state of pleasurable agitation when I read those somewhat kindred favorites, *The Fugger News-Letters,* and *Private Letters, Pagan and Christian,* edited by Lady Brook (or Brooke). There, if you like, are two absolute essentials for the browsing room. If they are not there, something must be done about it at once. If you do not know them, I cannot bear it. The best letters of the latter collection are the Christian ones, particularly those of the Bishop of Clermont, who was a seventh century fellow. You must read his account of a week-end at Arles, and of his dinner with Theodoric.

I was amused that you listed *Salvation Nell* only as an afterthought. I always associate it with you, and I am not sure we didn't see it together that Christmas vacation when I was lodged for the night at your house on my way home from college. I probably made you buy the tickets, but perhaps we both made Hawley buy them. However, the association derives from that action of the impressionable Alicia who, as you will recall, was so affected by the play that, between the acts, she tore the corsage of violets from her bosom and thrust it into the tambourine of the Salvation Army lassie in the lobby. Sheldon roared with delight when I told him about that years ago.

I last saw Mrs. Fiske in San Francisco in June—just for a few moments in her dressing-room. I found her playing there when my boat put in from Japan. Then we were both in Cleveland in October. It was the week *Brief Moment* opened, and I was a great local success due to the fact that, in the fearful acoustics of the Hanna Theatre, the critics could hear only me and the prompter. Arriving in town on that Saturday to resume her interrupted tour in some dreadful play, she sent a note around to the stage door saying: "Dear child, many, many congratulations." Then, at Christmas time, her maid sent a note to the Belasco Theatre saying that Mrs. Fiske was too ill to pick out a book for me this Christmas, and adding: "But she bids me tell you there will be another Christmas." But there will be no other. I feel inexpressibly poorer.

Of course I loathe Gordon Craig with intensity. I have never known anyone so overweeningly pretentious with so little to show for it. His book goaded me into two pieces in *The New Yorker* some months ago. One of them was reproduced in *The Era*, a London newspaper, under the simple heading: "New York Critic's Bad Lapse in Taste."

A. W.

P.S. Good God. What a long letter.

To CHARLES MACOMB FLANDRAU

[Flandrau's *Viva Mexico* and *Diary of a Freshman* were among Woollcott's favorite books, which he constantly urged others to read.]

New York City
March 31, 1932

My dear Mr. Flandrau:

By sending you the accompanying pamphlet (the printing house in the Middle West which published it without leave shut my mouth by giving me fifty copies), I have a chance to thank you for your letter and to report that Copey [Professor Charles Townsend Copeland] and I talked about you a few days ago when I made a pilgrimage to 15 Hollis. When I tried to find out from him why you wrote so infrequently, I discovered I was treading on difficult ground. You see, he hasn't written much either, and he would prefer that the subject should not be brought up.

I had a copy of *Viva Mexico* with me when I went to Japan a year ago this time. A young Japanese scholar named Osamu Yamada borrowed it from me with a promise to send it on to a young Swiss friend of mine in Basle. It has since been rapturously acknowledged. You will say I am like one of those women who come up to a lecturing author thinking to please the poor wretch by saying: "I cannot tell you how much I enjoyed your book. I have lent my copy to everyone I know." Poor Kate Douglas Wiggin used to lament with genuine emotion that she was the most *borrowed* author in the world.

However, this leads me at an ambling gait to the report that when I set sail from Kobe to Tientsin, I could not resist sending you a note. As the address had to be sketchy, it seemed doubtful, at the time, that you would ever get it. I merely felt obliged, for old times' sake, to exclaim at my first encounter with the Japanese: "What a wonderful little people they are!"

Then I could describe Harpo Marx's delight in the story of your old horse from *Loquacities*. But perhaps you know not Joseph and would not care that you had pleased him.

Alexander Woollcott

To *BEATRICE KAUFMAN*

London
December 8, 1932

Beloved friend: (that is the way my hurried notes from Mrs. Belloc Lowndes begin) It is all so confusing. I mosey over from Berlin and find the Bonners—the bankrupt Bonners—most exquisitely ensconced. A lovely house with a hair-raising butler and five maids and a Rolls Royce. And I dine there the first night and not far down the table sits your own personal George, immaculate in a white tie and wasting gems of small talk on a Mrs. Leslie. And I come back to my hotel and learn from my mail that you think there's a chance—just a bare chance—that George *may* come to London next week.

George, whom I encountered the next evening chez the [Raymond] Masseys and the evening after that at the Savoy grill, is in a mood so benign that I think you should be alarmed. I hear he not only took all Paul's plays to read but that he *volunteered* to. At this writing (11 A.M.) he is toying with the idea of casting Paul as the doctor [in *Dinner at Eight*]. This would please Lilly and annoy Dickie [Bird] a good deal. But George just beams in a saint-like manner.

I even hear that he has offered to buy into the American rights of the new Maugham play which Rebecca [West] and I went to see the night before last and which we considered (to put it conservatively) Godawful. Seeing Rebecca again is my great delight. She is now extraordinarily beautiful, having gone over to some doctor near Vienna or Dresden and lost eleven and a half pounds the first twenty-four hours. Address furnished on request.

My immediate calendar runs something like this:

Today: Lunch with Mrs. Belloc Lowndes.

Tonight: Dinner with Lilly, then *Words and Music* with Lilly, then all to supper afterwards at the Savoy with Jeffrey.

Tomorrow: Lunch at the House of Commons with Cazalet and a dinner party with Rebecca at the Bonners.

Day after: Lunch with Robert (*Brief Moment*) Douglas and dinner at Rebecca's with Clive Bell.

Next evening: Dinner at Lady Colefax's with George and, I suppose, Edna [Ferber].

Following evening: New play with Dickie (I mean I am to be with Dickie, not the play).

Following day: Lunch at the Jardin des Gourmets (dear, dear) with that Mr. Bailey who writes the Reginald Fortune stories and dinner later at the Bonners.

Etc. Etc.: Lunch with Lady Ravensdale Thursday, dinner that night with Mrs. Lowndes and the Charles Morgans, dinner on the 20th with Lady Iddesleigh.

So you see. The same old jig. And this is the odd thing about it. I allotted myself a month of the fleshpots in London as a kind of reward for all I would have to endure in Russia. The trouble is that I had a delightful and continuously satisfactory time in Russia, so that by rights I ought now to be undergoing something pretty grim in the penitential way. I don't quite know what to do about this. Maybe God will do something about it.

As for Russia, I don't think I want to chatter about it in this fashion. I will save it up and tell you all I know, which is a good deal.

When I come back, you can climb on my lap and go through my pockets to see what Nunkie has brought you. Some comfit or trinket, I'll be bound.

I love you, my dear.

A. W.

[See note about Lady Colefax on page 161.]

To CHARLES LEDERER

[Mr. Lederer, then a young protégé of Woollcott's, has since become a successful Hollywood writer.]

London
December 31, 1932

Son of Heaven:
          I am sailing home aboard the *Bremen* on the 15th. This will compel me to observe my own birthday alone on the high seas. I will be forty-six. Getting to be a big boy now.

    I think you might grace the occasion by writing me a letter of such date that I would find it waiting for me in New York—a letter telling me the news of your health, present plans and the state of your immortal soul, which last I consider, without much warrant, my peculiar care. Also news of Harpo. I do not even know what continent he is now adorning. Also news of Charlie MacArthur and family.

    I have seen so many earls and countesses lately that a glimpse of one so ignobly born as yourself would be refreshing. Have seen nothing of dear, dear Lady Cavendish, who once sat on this old knee. But that was when she was Adele Astaire. I understand she gets along famously with her mother-in-law, the Duchess of Devonshire. Has the Duchess saying "Oke" already. Then I suppose I should tell you about Lord Redding's recent marriage to a woman some forty years younger than himself. The London *Times* account of the wedding ended, unfortunately, with this sentence: "The bridegroom's gift to the bride was an antique pendant."

                                          A. Woollcott

V

1933-1935

To *JEROME KERN*

*Washington, D. C.
February 22, 1933*

Dear Jerry:

On New Year's Night I was finishing up a week-end in a superb old place in Kent, since closed by its defeated family for lack of cash to keep it open. The younger son of the house is an incredibly charming young country squire, who was married the other day to that lovely stepdaughter of Wodehouse—a marriage made in heaven, I should say, and likely to be blessed in Kent, for the young folks were moving into one of the farmhouses to go right on with the horses, the vegetables, and the orchids.

However, we were fiddling with the radio when we tuned in on the Holland station, and what should we hear but music pouring from the finest instrument fashioned by nature in our time. And what should he be singing but the lovely song you wrote with the notion that he should sing it!

But I am writing to assure you no jury would convict if you wanted to join me in murdering Eddy Duchin. At least, until further details are available, we might begin by murdering him. It is his orchestra that plays the Brunswick record of "Egern on the Tegernsee," and the idiot who sings that melting and lovely song never took time, even with the hint the rhyme gave

[117]

him, to learn how to pronounce Tegernsee; and then, just to make things harder, he gets another line of the song wrong. "One more light," he sings, instead of "One light more." As soon as I find out who this singer is, I am going to drag him out on a cement sidewalk, take him by the throat, kneel on his stomach, and pound his head on the hard surface until it cracks like a melon. Then it will be your turn.

My God, Jerry, what a time of years it seems since Julia Sanderson was singing "They Wouldn't Believe Me," and Marion Davies was just a nobody in *Oh Boy!* Things move so fast in this age that when they revived *Show Boat* last spring, and everyone spoke of it as such a dear old classic, I began to have you confused with Elgar. It was reassuring to have you bounce right back with a score I like even better. Or at least a show I like much better, because it is *all* of it good [Kern's *Music in the Air*]. Indeed, I never have seen a musical play so well acted. Never in my life. The casting and direction are miraculous. Irving [Berlin] tells me that should be your credit. Is he right? [Walter] Slezak's performance is Godgiven, but so is that of the old girl who sings "Egern on the Tegernsee." And the one who plays the prima donna's maid, and the young woman with the sweet voice who looks like Mrs. Gilbert Miller and plays the publisher's secretary. And [Harry] Mestayer is superb. Generations of the very blue blood of the theatre entitle him to make that magnificent speech, which he does to my heart's content. I do not even mind that he mispronounces his key word. Or, at least, I do not mind much. Do take him aside and tell him he is a magnificent actor but that it is *not* pronounced "ameeteurs."

And Al Shean, Jerry. Do you know about him? He and his sister were children of an old German musician named Lafey Schoenberg, who played the small towns of Hanover for fifty years, traveling from one to the other in a cart, and who died in Chicago at the age of one hundred and one. When they came to this country Al went to work as a pants-presser, and the sister made lace in a tenement. Al was known as the fastest presser south of Rivington Street, but he had a passion for singing swipes. He was always organizing quartets and being fired for practicing in the can during working hours. Once, when a whole quartet was fired it went right into vaudeville as the Manhattan Comedy Four. This success inflamed the sister. It was too late for her to go on the stage, what with her five children and all, so she decided *they* must, and then pushed them into the theatre, although they and the theatre both resisted strenuously. Of course you know they are the Marx brothers. When their star went into the ascendant in 1924 the Gallagher and Shean partnership had broken up, and Mrs. Marx was faithless enough to think Al had better go into the ginger ale business. And now look at him. Playing so legitimately. Playing so beautifully. She would have been so proud and happy.

Well, I guess I am just an old fool about *Music in the Air*. I haven't been a third time, but that is because circumstances have sequestered me here for several weeks. I did rush around again to see it the night before I left town. Several times I found tears pouring from these old ducts. Very likely it was from fatigue. Or perhaps I had a cold.

As I write this letter, I find myself working up into a mood that will not be satisfied until I have done a war dance on *Music in the Air* in *The New Yorker*. To assist me, will you rush me, if you can, the name of the criminal who sings the Brunswick record, so that I can put him on the spot? Also, if it is not too difficult, will you have someone at the office send me here a transcript of the speech Mestayer makes from the orchestra pit?

While I was in London, under the most engaging circumstances, I received as a gift from the relict of Alice Meynell a Dickens item which I have reason to think must be new to you, and which I shall be glad to let you see if you want it. I could send it to you by registered mail.

Well, God bless you and keep you. Keep you going, I mean. I would not go so far as to call you a sight for sore eyes, but I would call you a boon for sore hearts, and there is not your like in all the world today.

A. Woollcott

To *EDNA FERBER*

Washington, D. C.
February 23, 1933

Dear Ferber:
Speaking of [Jules] Bledsoe, did you ever hear of his misdeed in Lancaster, Pa.? He was in the cast of *Deep River*, an American opera which Arthur Hopkins produced in one of his more bemused interludes. Arthur was so absorbed in the task of trying to prevent the members of the cast from becoming operatic on him that other details escaped him—such as the fact that the music wasn't very good, and that the young romantical New Orleans hero was being played by an Italian Jew from Frankfort who spoke an English strangely resembling Sam Bernard's.

Anyway, Arthur was determined that none of the singers should attack their arias by turning head on to the audience and letting them rip. Perfect docility in this matter marked all the rehearsals, but when they opened in Lancaster, Bledsoe sniffed the audience. It was an old-fashioned stage with an apron. Turning, he walked forward to the footlights, squared his shoulders, threw back his head, and emitted his song. Arthur was embedded in a packed audience, oblivious of them, forgetful that the rehearsals were over. At Bledsoe's defiance, he half raised from his seat and ejaculated, "The son of a bitch!" A woman sitting in front of him turned around and muttered angrily, "If you don't like it you can get your money back." "I wish to God I could," said Arthur and stamped out. It seems the woman was wrong, by a margin of $120,000.

My meditative seclusion here is interrupted only by occasional debauches with Arthur Krock, Alice Longworth, Cissy Patterson, the Senate Finance Committee, the Senate and House Committees on Agriculture, Russell Owen, Pat Sturhahn, and a few relatives.

Be sure to order in advance a copy of *The Werewolf of Paris*, a magnificently monstrous book which that sinister ruffian, Johnny Farrar, is going to publish late in March.

Remember that your heart is God's little garden.

A. W.

To *THORNTON WILDER*

New York City
March 11, 1933

Dear Thornton:

I wish I already had the house in the country I'm going out to look for today. Will you come and stay a month some time? A winter month, I think. The point is that if you are reading *Great Expectations*, I ought to be in the next room so you could come in from time to time and report that you have just met Mr. Pumblechook and Herbert Pocket and Trabb's boy. And I could tell you how Shaw (mistakenly) points to Estella as proof that Dickens *could* paint a real heroine. Estella, he says, is Mrs. Patrick Campbell to the life. Which is the wildest nonsense, but shows what he thinks of Mrs. Patrick Campbell. Did Ruth [Gordon] ever tell you of that luncheon in our villa when Shaw talked about Stella Campbell for an hour and a half until Mrs. Shaw was driven to beating a tattoo with her salad fork as a way of warning him that she couldn't stand another word on the subject?

I think I am taking Ruth to see *The Cherry Orchard* Wednesday night. I would love taking you, too, if you wanted to come along. Anyway, send me back *Cosette* as it's my only copy.

A. W.

To *BEATRICE KAUFMAN*

Neshobe Island, Vt.
May 31, 1933

Beatrice:

You must come here some part of this and every summer. It is my favorite place in all the world. I am simply exhausted from buttering so many griddle cakes and can write no more.

A. W.

To *LILLY BONNER*

New York City
September 13, 1933

Dear Lilly:

It was to me highly exciting to hear your voice coming out of Surrey, that peculiar soprano chirp which you reserve for the telephone and "Au clair de la lune." I shall soon indulge myself again in the luxury of hearing it. It seemed to come from just around the corner, and I had a feeling that I ought to be hurrying to Locust Valley to sleep under the uproar of the play room and hear about your troubles with the oil burner and join with Frederick in idle speculation as to whether Mr. Backer would or would not come.

The play, at the moment of writing, is called *The Dark*

Tower, and should go into rehearsals on October 23rd with George [Kaufman] and me directing jointly. I do not know who will be in it, but there is talk of Margalo Gillmore, Louis Calhern, Ernest Lawford, Margaret Dale and others you wouldn't know. The leading part, which is as yet uncast, presents certain unusual requirements, and during the next six weeks I suppose we will try out a lot of people in it. My own candidate is Henry Clapp Smith, and on Saturday night he and George and I are meeting secretly at the Music Box and rehearsing one or two scenes as a sample. This is heavily confidential and should not be mentioned in any letter you may be dashing off to the folks at home.

It has taken me over two years to recover from the painful experience of having Locust Valley shot from under me. I have finally pulled myself together, and on October 5th will open a country estate, nominally my own, but really held in partnership by Beatrice, Sam Behrman and myself, and open to all our friends who feel like paying so much a night. Such a pity that you and Paul never thought of this. Joe Hennessey will be in charge and we shall have eight months to experiment. We have taken an enchanting house at Katonah until the first of June.

I enjoyed the week-end at the Backers. They are living for the present in the old Mortimer Schiff house in East Norwich—beautiful grounds and an interior of stupefying ugliness. I had Adele's room, a dainty boudoir about the size of the Pennsylvania Depot. There was a great coming and going of Berlins, Fatios and the like, and all passed off pleasantly.

I suppose you want to hear the latest Swope story. Burdened with Gerald Brooks as a croquet partner, he became so violent that Brooks agreed to do only what he was told and thereafter became a mute automaton, a condition which Swope enjoyed hugely. Brooks never moved his mallet or approached a ball without being told by Swope: "Now, Brooksy, you go through this wicket. That's fine. Now you shoot down to position. Perfect!" And so on. Finally, before an enthralled audience, Swope said: "Now you hit that ball up here in the road. That's right. Now you put your little foot on *your* ball and drive the other buckety-buckety off into the orchard. Perfect!" It was only then, from the shrieks of the onlookers, that Swope discovered it was his own ball which had been driven off.

The stream of passersby is unmoderated. Tell Sibyl [Lady Colefax] that Thornton Wilder came in last night all chuckles. The other day we heard an uproar under my window. It was Alice Longworth discovering that I lived here and dragging Wild Bill [Colonel William J.] Donovan up to see me. I am lunching tomorrow with William Gillette. The Lunts arrive from Genesee Depot tomorrow afternoon. They sail on the *Bremen* for Stockholm, Helsingfors and Moscow before returning to London in November. Then Egypt and then London again.

I vastly enjoyed a visit from Mrs. Pat Campbell last week. She came here to dinner, bringing with her a snow-white Pekinese named Moonbeam. In her little black velvet vanity bag, in addition to her powder-puff, lipstick, handkerchief, small change and letters from Shaw, she had a chicken bone with which to feed him after his performance in her play. We talked about her book of memoirs, which was published ten years ago, and I objected to it only on the ground that she had kept the reader in ignorance of her most salient characteristic—a disposition to make devastating remarks. She denied ever having made any in her life, but I would not hear any such nonsense. Why, I said, even in the book the cloven hoof shows occasionally. "Ah!" she said. "But that's on the foot that's in the grave now." At eight o'clock I put her in a taxi, and she and Moonbeam went off to the theatre. An hour later, when I was going out myself, the doorman told me apologetically that the taxi driver had come back in a state of considerable frenzy when he found she had paid him in what was not really legal tender. I made good the deficit by redeeming two shillings, which are on my desk as I write you.

Harpo calls from Hollywood to say that he will be here in two or three weeks, and after perhaps another two or three weeks, will go on to Europe, taking his harp with him and giving performances by himself in Vienna, Budapest and possibly Moscow. Recently he shaved off all his hair and is, I am told, a singularly repellent object. The other night Winchell announced that he was secretly married in January to a Miss Susan Fleming. Harpo denied this, but not, I thought, very vigorously.

I think you must arrange to come here in January. Let Paul take his safari, or his mufti, or wallah, or whatever it is called, to the Sudan. You hop on a boat and come here under an assumed name. I will give you my apartment, where you can hide from all the Stehlis and Bonners, and run in next door to Alice for meals.

Alexander W.

P.S. By the way, I am starting broadcasting tonight. Wednesdays and Fridays at 10.30, Columbia Network, national hook-up, sustaining program, topical broadcast. It's a thing I have been wanting to do for years, and now they are letting me try it. After a month of experiment, I ought to be pretty good. I am so frantically busy this week that I ought not be writing you at all. And I darkly suspect that I have dictated this letter over my breakfast coffee as a means of limbering up before tackling the broadcast.

A. W.

P.P.S. Alfred [Lunt] just rushed in and out—hysterical because he has lost his passport.

To *THORNTON WILDER*

New York City
September 18, 1933

Dear Thornton:

I am chiefly writing to tell you that the Ben Hechts have, on the Palisades at Nyack, one of the most unbelievably desirable houses I ever stepped into. The other night I lay in Ben's bed and wished him dead, and that his inconsolable widow would go to Cyprus for five years so that I might rent her house. It is vastly improved by the fact that the Hechts themselves are in Los Angeles and have given the place to Master Charles Lederer. I have decided to break it to him that you and Alice Miller and I are coming up on Saturday to spend the weekend with him. You could sit all day in the gazebo and look down the Hudson toward the sea. Twenty houses down the main street of Nyack dwell the MacArthurs. Charlie MacArthur will by then have arrived from Hollywood, Helen [Hayes—Mrs. Charles MacArthur] will be full of her rehearsals for *Mary of Scotland*, and we will see something of that somewhat different house-guest, Miss Ruth Gordon.

We can wrestle about the book over the week-end, but I should warn you you are likely to be thrown over the Palisades. I am inviting readers of *The New Yorker* to give me a title, but I suspect none of them will be as good as the one Lederer has just devised. He suggests "I Told You So." I am also running the letter I got from Nora Waln's daughter. I think I showed it to you. It is my guess it will escape from its present flimsy fetters and have a life of its own in the anthologies.

A. W.

[The final title, *While Rome Burns*, was suggested by one of the readers of *The New Yorker*. The note from Nora Waln's daughter, defending her from his strictures on *The House of Exile*, ended with this sentence which Woollcott often repeated: "My conclusion is that you are not a bad man but a too hasty one."]

To *FRODE JENSEN*

[The full story of Woollcott's relationship to Frode Jensen, a young Dane who became a doctor in America, is told on page 305.]

New York City
September 26, 1933

My dear Mr. Jensen:

Your nomination of a title is on file. It will be duly considered and doubtless rejected. What delights me far more than your knack for naming a book is the evidence in your letter that you are not going to Jefferson after all. My acquaintance with that medical school was both sketchy and out of date, but even so, I had an uneasy feeling you were heading in the wrong direction.

Both for Grace Root's sake and your own, I wish you would feel that this flat of mine on the East River is a place to which you can come any time you feel, as I know newcomers to New York must sometimes feel, that you need a neighbor. As a sign of good faith I hereby give you my private telephone number, which is Plaza 3-0199. If you will call any morning after nine o'clock, you will track me down. Since I am not making this offer as a matter of form, I hope you will have an unburdened feeling that you can make use of it whenever you want to. As I grow older, I become acutely aware that I have few privileges as valuable as the occasional privilege of being of service to people like you.

Yours respectfully,
A. Woollcott

To FRANK SULLIVAN

[The friendship with this fellow-columnist began on the New York *World*.]

New York City
December 14, 1933

Dear Frank:

I should like to dine with you Monday evening. I think that old room at the Plaza is closed evenings but the other room is pretty nearly as good. What do you say to meeting me there or at the chez Pulitzer, where a cocktail assemblage seems to be scheduled for that evening. Telephone here and leave word tomorrow. I shall be rushing around the Atlantic Littoral on sundry trains and boats, but don't envy me too much, for this life of ceaseless fame and adulation has its drawbacks just as your own obscure one has.

A. W.

To LYNN FONTANNE and ALFRED LUNT

New York City
February 1, 1934

My dear children:

I have started so many letters to you only to get interrupted by this treadmill which, with indefatigable energy, I seem to have constructed for myself. My life as a broadcaster, which completely enthralls me, also leaves me so little time that, except for an occasional trip to the water-closet, I do nothing else. I submit to this the more cheerfully because I know it will all end the first of June when I go off to Vermont for four months. Until then the radio will keep me on a short tether and anyway I start next week a series of fifteen lectures at Columbia University which would not let me get very far away.

I did have some thought (Noel may have told you) of writing Sibyl a letter beginning something like this:

"Dear, dear Sibyl:

It is hard on you, for I can imagine how they must be pestering you all the time, but it is a great relief to us to have the Lunts out of America. I don't mind Alfred having a touch of the tar-brush, or Lynn being seventy-six if she's a day, my dear, but their habit of lying in a stupor and clad in nothing but rather soiled loin-cloths in the middle of Fifth Avenue did play hob with the traffic. Their excuse for this rather degenerate fatigue was that exhausting season in Design for Living. I keep telling them they should have played a repertory of Macbeth, King Lear, Antony and Cleopatra *and* Le Cid. This would have left them feeling fresh and invigorated. Or possibly dead. In any event and etc., etc."

I say I thought of sending this to Sibyl (and enclosing a carbon for you) but it seemed upon reflection a laborious jest. And, anyway, that now famous incident still mystifies me. As it has come to me second- and third-hand, it just doesn't make sense. There is a missing piece in the puzzle.

Of *The Dark Tower* I can report only that it was a tremendous success except for the minor detail that people wouldn't come to see it. Yet it really was a kind of success at that. I mean that we enjoyed it enormously and it seemed to be attended with great relish by all of the people (without exception) whose good opinion I would respect and therefore want. Then, thanks to the movie rights, it brought me in rather more money than I am used to getting for the same amount of work. George Kaufman seems to think that Gilbert [Miller] is going to do it in London this spring. On this point I am skeptical but [Rudolf] Kommer is at work on the translation for Vienna and the Scandinavian rights have just been applied for and Random House has published the play and altogether the episode baffles me. If all this befalls one who writes a flop, what happens when one writes a success?

Since I seem to be reporting on my own activities I might

add that I bounced around the other day and wrote and played the leading role in a movie short. It was a speculative response to a man's suggestion that I make a great string of them. I am to go around and see it tomorrow but I go without much interest as I cannot imagine any offer sufficiently tempting to make me go through another such day. It was, I think, the dullest and most exhausting day I ever spent. I did think it would have the compensation of novelty and that I could at least extract some copy from it, but by noon I was so numb with fatigue and so indignant at my own stupidity in becoming involved in such nonsense that I never knew what happened during the rest of the day.

I have so much to tell you. If you will come to the island on your way home I will tell you about Harpo's return from Muscovy, about Lilly Bonner's birthday which we are celebrating tomorrow, about that hulking young prodigy [Orson Welles] who is off touring with Kit Cornell, about my ripe romance with Miss Cornelia Lunt, which is the delight of my declining years, about Bob Sherwood's expulsion of Mary [Sherwood] from his bed and board, about my pretty brawl with Edna Ferber, who has announced to the world at large that she is "weary of the tyranny of this New Jersey Nero," about certain overtures of forgiveness from Kathleen Norris which embarrass me because of my guilty knowledge that the offending article is already incorporated intact in the book I am publishing next month. I could tell you how Master Charles Lederer was evicted from the Warwick (Alas, poor Warwick!) for non-payment of room rent and how, when the manager went around to throw him out, he was peculiarly annoyed by a message that the defaulter was even then shopping at Cartier's. Oddly enough, this was true. He was designing a Christmas present for Alice Miller; a breast-pin in the form of a scarlet letter A.

The other evening when Lilly and I had succeeded in escaping from Paul, we both agreed that you two were the only people in the world we enjoyed as much together as apart. It's just as well perhaps. I enclose a few oddments from my mail. You might send them on to Romney [Brent]. I hear that you are a prodigious success and it must be fun for you both and I should like to know, please, when you are coming home.

Duckey Dee

To *ALFRED LUNT* and *LYNN FONTANNE*

New York City
June 7, 1934

My dear children:
    Well, it seems I didn't come over after all. My expectation of coming was always slight and I found as the time approached that I couldn't manage even a flying trip. You see, after letting myself get involved in an imbecile congestion of overwork I really cracked up rather badly and decided from the depth of my bed at the Medical Center to lead a new life. This involved four months of relaxed and serene existence in Vermont and I have been busy clearing the decks for that purpose. Taking off weight by a new and rather hazardous medication, which is part of the program, has already progressed so far that I am probably in better physical shape than you have ever found me. I have already lost more than thirty pounds and intend thus to dwindle with dignity until there shall be no other word for me but lissome. Lissome my children and you shall hear—

  In that entrancing letter you wrote me you spoke of coming direct to the island from the stage door of the Lyric Theatre and though I take it that was only a gesture, I shall at least go through the form of telling you that I shall stand for no such nonsense. The island is my favorite spot in the world but that is partly from habit and association and I would not think of allowing its charm to be subjected to the strain of having it visited by two people whose minds were all intent on getting to Genesee Depot as fast as their legs would carry them. I will not have you flopping around in my lake thinking all the while how much you would rather be in that new swimming pool of yours. It is my hope and expectation to stay at the island at least until the middle of October and it is my great hope that both of you will come and visit me there some time late in the summer or early in the Fall. Just now it is undergoing prodigies of renovation. I am putting in electric lights, refrigeration, new beds and a score of other things, and all out of my own pocket, to the great and unfeeling delight of the other members. But what of it, I say. Didn't I just get my share of the cool $100 paid down for the Czechoslovakian rights of *The Dark Tower*? While in this mood I bought me one of the new Chrysler cars. And Pip, my coal-black French poodle, has been taking lessons on the dirt roads of Westchester County on how to go motoring without throwing up on the upholstery. A kind Italian gentleman named Angelo undertook for a small consideration to take him out every day in the station wagon. Well, all this is a foreword to a series of casual excursions around Vermont during the summer whenever I get restless at the island or whenever it is visited by people I don't much like. There will only be three jobs I will really have to do. Those are three lectures on journalism I am going to give at Bread Loaf. Bread Loaf is the summer school of Middlebury College. It is on a small mountain top overlooking Lake Dunmore about fifteen minutes drive from the island. I think the notion of doing something equivalent to teaching in Vermont will appeal to my deep and unsatisfied neighborhood instinct which has been starved. The great excursion will come a little later when Lederer arrives from the coast (I mean Charles, not Francis) and with him at the wheel and Pip in the back seat we will repair to Kennebunkport for a visit to the Tarkingtons.

Helen [Hayes] has been replaced by Margalo [Gillmore]

in *Mary of Scotland* and will leave in another fortnight for the coast. Charlie [MacArthur] and Ben [Hecht] are in ecstasy as moving picture producers in Astoria (it is their naughty and admirable aim to destroy Hollywood). Ruth Gordon's son is now a feature of the American scene. Guthrie [McClintic] has just bought a play written by Beatrice Kaufman and Peggy Pulitzer. Edna Ferber has just unnerved Jack Wilson by renting his Connecticut house for the summer. Kit [Cornell] will shortly wind up an enormously successful tour which has made a pot of money and taken her to seventy-one different cities this season. The best current joke is an anonymous one by whatever person described *The Shining Hour* as the English *Tobacco Road*. When, as I wrote Noel, the *Times* inadvertently billed the new Arch Selwyn production " 'Cora Potts' *without* Francine Larrimore," it was Howard Dietz who exclaimed, "What a cast!"

I am not sure whether this story by a young Englishman named James Hilton [*Good-bye, Mr. Chips*], for which I have been lustily beating the drum, has yet been published in England. It comes out tomorrow as a small book and on the chance that you may not have seen it I am sending you a copy by the same mail. I feel it will take me a week of listening to catch up with you. After a lot of adding and subtracting I would be inclined to say that the past year has been the most generally satisfying one I have ever spent. The chief flaw in it was that you two who are both most dear to me were flourishing so far away.

Alexander W.

To *NOEL COWARD*

Bomoseen, Vt.
August 11, 1934

Dear Noel:

Your little pencilled scrawl filled me with a great and unexpected longing to see you. I had heard about your illness in the most belated and roundabout fashion. Your Mr. Lunt mentioned it in a hurried letter, breaking it to me gently by saying that you had almost died and then going on laughingly to matters of more real interest to him. As a friendly and endearing note from Temple in the same mail had failed to mention your indisposition at all, I was then at a loss to guess how serious it might have been.

I am considerably upset about this course of action pursued by the fourth and a half Earl. With the exception of Mrs. Stanley Baldwin and two or three articled clarks living near Liverpool, the entire citizenry of the British Empire has written me with great enthusiasm about *While Rome Burns*, all explaining that they had borrowed their copy from Earl Amherst. This would seem to indicate that thanks to his lordship's lavishness all sales of the book in England and the Dominions had been rendered unnecessary. I hope the little bleached son of a bitch fries in hell. As there now seems to be no hope of your buying a copy, I might as well send you one and will do so when I return to New York in October. In the interval I am happily ensconced on my island. I get news of the outside world in the form of telegrams which are telephoned from Rutland to a boatman living on the shore who takes them down in a firm Spencerian hand and gives them to his son to bring over to me in a motor boat. This makes my favorite occupation guessing what the sender really intended to say. Thus, when the Lunts recently threatened to visit me, I was thrown into an agreeable state of agitation by a distracted telegram from Alfred which said that Lynn was "too ill to take Johnny." Her condition seemed, indeed, desperate. I enclose a clipping which will show you that we here in the colonies keep up with your work.

By the way, put an order in at Hatchard's for a copy of a new novel by Charles Brackett called *Entirely Surrounded*. It is to be published by Knopf on August 27th. The scene is our island and all the characters will be painfully recognizable. Neysa [McMein] comes off best. The portrait of Dorothy Parker [Mrs. Alan Campbell] is the most astonishingly skillful and the owner of the island is a repulsive behemoth with elfin manners whom you would be the first to recognize. He is named Thaddeus Hulbert and makes his first appearance playing backgammon with an English actor at a party. He calls a passing redhead to his side. I quote:

"The fat man clapped a plump, well-molded hand, with dice in the palm, against Henry's copper-colored hair, rubbed it back and forth. 'Now I double; do you take it?' 'Uncle Thaddeus is in wine,' the fat man's opponent observed in clipped British accents. 'I take it, Duck.' Henry had seen the speaker's tired, eager, charm-furrowed face behind footlights: Nigel Farraday."

It is a charming book; and now, my blemish, au revoir.

A. Woollcott

To LYNN FONTANNE

Bomoseen, Vt.
September 25, 1934

Dear Lynn:
            Thanks for letting me see these Graham Robertson letters. Anything he puts down on paper, even when he seems to do it most casually, acquires at once an incomparable and unmistakable bouquet. Of course everything he said about the movies warmed the cockles of my heart, but even so I don't

think he goes to the bottom of the matter. I think that even if the scenes and furniture subsided the result would still be essentially dissatisfying. There is something false and ugly in the very idea of a talkie. There is something inherently and permanently outrageous in a talking photograph. It is like that exhibit which won the first prize in The Bad Taste Exhibition held in New York a few years ago. It was a Venus de Milo with a clock in her stomach—obviously offensive but undebatably so. It just was, that's all.

I am just back from a flying trip to New York but already my days here are numbered. I shall creep back to work more unwillingly than ever before in my life for this is the only place in the world I really like. I seem destined to return. When the club acquired the island a number of years ago, the original owner held out for himself a small plot in case he should ever want to build a house on it for himself. This summer, either as a threat or out of pique, he actually started to build the house and at least got the masonry done—it is a small stone cottage with a huge fireplace—before he paused dramatically for breath. In that pause I bought him out, so that now the month of October will be spent in finishing his job and when I come back next spring I will find a house of my own ready for occupancy. As long as the club continues to function happily I shall use it in the daytime as a studio where George Kaufman can write his plays and Alice Miller can type out her profitable serials for *The Saturday Evening Post*. There will be two bedrooms in it where we can tuck away at night those guests who peculiarly resent the island custom of getting up noisily about seven o'clock. Those of us who are hardy enough to favor the sunrise swim always emerge in the morning with a great deal of clatter and there has been some snarling about this from those who prefer to remain unconscious until noon.

Graham's letters have set me to thinking about him as I do a good deal. One of the games I play with myself as I lie in the sun is to select the five pictures which I would like to own and have in my own house. Even if there could be only five, one of them would certainly have to be the Sargent portrait of him when he was such a young man as I wish I might have known. He assures me that that young man and I would have got on together famously and I suppose he knows.

I start broadcasting on October 7th, sponsored by Cream of Wheat. I don't know how I shall enjoy being served out every Sunday night with a cereal as if I were so much cream and sugar. It is peculiarly ironic that I should thus be helping to sell a product which in my new austerity I may not indulge in. My net loss to date is fifty-five pounds. This alteration of contour has driven my tailor to the verge of madness. By a rather neat trick he is turning all my coats into double-breasted ones but out of each pair of trousers they are having to remove enough cloth to outfit half the unemployed.

I am going to be in Chicago on October 25th, a fleeting trip that will leave me no time to come up and see you.

Alexander Dee

To ROSALIND RICHARDS

New York City
October 20, 1934

My dear Miss Richards:

This is a secret and confidential communication which I am trusting you to answer on the sly. As I gather you know, I am doing a weekly fandango on the radio. I am of two minds how much I object to being served with Cream of Wheat but there is no other way to get a good hour on a nation-wide hook-up. In these broadcasts I am having considerable fun serenading my ten favorite Americans. I have done Mr. Tarkington already and next week we are going to do Irving Berlin and after him Walt Disney and Charles Chaplin. We get the victim's permission and ask him to tell us what song he would like to have sung under his hypothetical window. I am writing you to tell me, out of your knowledge of the lady in question, whether your mother would be more pleased than annoyed if I were to visit upon her one of these honest but conspicuous and reverberant attentions. Will you consult your own judgment and advise me privily at the address on this stationery?

I cannot begin to tell you how much I enjoyed my visit to Indian Point. I consider that all the years I never knew Mrs. Richards were just years wasted by one of destiny's monstrous mismanagements.

There is some palaver to and fro as to whether I should or should not lecture this winter at Bowdoin. I don't know how the matter stands at present but it does sound to me like a good chance to come up to Gardiner for a dish of tea.

Yours sincerely,
A. Woollcott

To IRA GERSHWIN

New York City
November 10, 1934

Ira Gershwin:

Listen, you contumacious rat, don't throw your dreary tomes at me. I'll give you an elegant dinner at a restaurant of your own choosing and sing to you between the courses if you can produce one writer or speaker, with an ear for the English language which you genuinely respect, who uses "disinterested" in the sense you are now trying to bolster up. I did look it up in my own vast Oxford dictionary a few years ago only to be told that it had been obsolete since the seventeenth century. I haven't looked up the indices in your letter because, after all, my own word in such matters is final. Indeed, current use of the word in the seventeenth century sense is a ghetto barbarism I had previously thought confined to the vocabularies of Ben Hecht and Jed Harris. Surely, my child, you must see that if "disinterested" is, in our time, intended to convey a special shade of the word "unselfish" it is a clumsy business to try to make it also serve another meaning. That would be like the nit-wit practice of the woman who uses her husband's razor to sharpen her pencil. The point of the pencil may emerge, but the razor is never good again for its peculiar purpose.

Hoping you fry in hell, I remain

Yours affectionately,
A. W.

To *ROSALIND RICHARDS*

New York City
November 19, 1934

My dear Miss Richards:

My plans are jelling beautifully. The Town Crier wants to serenade Mrs. Richards on the evening of Sunday, December 9th, and as I know precisely what she would like to have sung, I need not bother to ask and therefore need not even tell her she is going to be serenaded. We could make it a surprise party and I know just how to do it if you will trust me and act as a fellow conspirator. All I would need would be some kind of last minute telegraphic assurance from you that she would be listening at nine o'clock.

I had a most pleasant visit (and some good sherry) with your brother at St. Paul's. That is a lovely pencil portrait he has of Mrs. Richards on his wall. I besought him to have a photostat made of it so that I may have one. I hope that you will prod him about this in the course of time if he forgets.

And in the meanwhile, mum's the word.

Yours sincerely,
A. Woollcott

To *HAROLD K. GUINZBURG*

[From 1934 on, Woollcott's books were published by The Viking Press. Mr. Guinzburg is head of the firm.]

New York City
November 19, 1934

Dear David:

I suppose some statistican in advertising would be able to tell anyone how many households see both the New York *Times* and the *Herald Tribune* on Sundays. But even without any more evidence than that of my own senses, I would, were I a publisher, regard the use of the same page ad in both book sections as proof positive of somebody's laziness and lack of resource.

From time to time I will thus send you hints, for I am always glad to do anything I can to put the publishing business flat on its ass.

Yours with great affection,
A. Woollcott

To MALCOLM COWLEY

[Mr. Cowley was then, as he is again, one of the editors of *The New Republic*.]

New York City
December 7, 1934

My dear Mr. Cowley:

I was deeply interested in your informed and sagacious piece on Proust which you were good enough to send me. But I am puzzled beyond expression by the following sentence: "But Mr. Woollcott, being so eager to have the job well done, should have done it himself or come forward with a better translator." Quite aside from the fact that no public notice was served about the fearful dearth which led to Dr. Blossom's selection as translator, I am puzzled by your implied conception of a reviewer's function. It recalls the happy, far off days when, as a dramatic critic, I ventured to regret in print that a prima donna had, throughout the premiere of an operetta, sung firmly off key. Her ringing riposte was a public statement to the effect that she would have liked to hear *me* sing that role. Of course, she wouldn't have liked it at all. People are so inexact in moments of stress.

Yours sincerely,
Alexander Woollcott

To MISS K. R. SORBER

[The first two letters in this collection were written to Miss Sorber.]

New York City
January 4, 1935

My dear Miss Sorber:

Of course I remember you and most gratefully. In my first day at school I was clapped into Miss Montgomery's class and after the first recess lost my way and showed up in your room instead. This was a terrifying experience but you were so sympathetic in steering me to where I belonged that I looked forward to being in your class the following year. I remember when in one report you gave me excellent in every subject except penmanship, which you reported as "fair but improving." Later it deteriorated in so marked a manner that I now use the typewriter exclusively.

Since you already have a book of mine, I send you an inscription to paste on its flyleaf.

Alexander Woollcott

To DOROTHY PARKER

New York City
February 7, 1935

My dear Dorothy:

Your letter was a source of great delight to me, except in one particular. You say nothing about when you are coming back. Even if you continue to be the pet of Hollywood for years to come, won't there be intervals when you might visit us here?

I, too, have not been idle. I am working anonymously (hysterical laughter) in the new Hecht-MacArthur picture [*The Scoundrel*] of which Noel [Coward] is the star. My previous experiences under the Klieg lights had seemed to me unbearably tedious. Once in Brittany, for several weeks, I was ward master in a base hospital and carried bed pans to *and from* moribund Negro stevedores. I found my foolhardy attempts to act for the camera somehow more degrading. But it did seem likely that, with Charlie and Ben directing in their cockeyed fashion and Noel fluttering about the studio (his name in Astoria is "Czar of all the Rushes"), it might be fun. It seems I was wrong about this, but, as they won't need me more than four days all told, the damage is inconsiderable. At that, I did extract a wintry smile from one episode. Did I ever tell you about Owen Davis directing his first play, which was called *Through the Breakers?* He had asked an agency to send him over eleven actors but no one had told him he was at liberty to comment on their work during rehearsals, so when it grew unbearable he would dismiss the company for lunch and then gumshoe after the individual members on the street, whispering his criticisms to them singly. As a director Charlie is tempered by a similar diffidence. After I had said one line ninety-seven times and begun to forget what it was, he walked past me and ventured a criticism out of the corner of his mouth. What he said was that he thought my reading of the line was "just a bit too violet." But in consideration for my somewhat exaggerated sensitivity, he spoke so softly I thought he said my reading was "a bit too violent." In subsequent renditions therefore I tried to subdue somewhat my too virile manner and, as I watched him out of the corner of my eye, he did look a bit frustrated.

Professor [Robert Barnes] Rudd has just passed this way on his annual visit with a good story about one of his sophomores who, in an English exam, was asked to compare *Moll Flanders* with some contemporary novel. He elected to compare it with *Penrod* of which he thought more highly because the story of Penrod exhibited a more wholesome home life.

Alexander Woollcott

To *HAROLD K. GUINZBURG*

New York City
March 1, 1935

Dear David:

These are the facts:

1: Departing for Chicago on the night of March 3rd.
2: Address until March 20th Hotel Blackstone.
3: Lecture at the Convocation at the University of Minnesota, Minneapolis, on the morning of March 7th.
4: Broadcast from Chicago Sunday evening, March 10th. Later the same evening, Thornton Wilder, Gertrude Stein and I will be the guests of some undergraduate honor society for several hours of continuous high discourse.
5: March 12th, lecture Northwestern University.
6: March 14th, lecture Toledo.
7: March 15th, lecture Detroit.
8: March 17th, broadcast from Chicago.
9: March 18th, lecture Indianapolis.
10: March 19th, visiting with the Tarkingtons and inspecting Foster Hall.
11: March 20th, lecture Chicago University.
12: March 23rd, Signet Club dinner, Harvard.
13: March 24th, broadcast from New York City.
14: March 26th, visit to Laura E. Richards, Gardiner, Maine.
15: March 27th, lecture Bowdoin College, Brunswick, Maine.
16: March 31st, broadcast from New York City.
17: April 1st, death of Mr. Woollcott, as thousands cheer.
18: April 2nd, dancing in the streets; half-holiday in all the schools; bank moratorium.
19: Burial at sea April 3rd.

Alexander Woollcott

To *COLONEL WILLIAM J. DONOVAN*

["Wild Bill" Donovan, now a Brigadier General and head of the Office of Strategic Services, won his first claim to fame as Colonel of the famous Sixty-Ninth Regiment in the first World War.]

*New York City
May 1, 1935*

Dear Bill:

Incidentally, the editors of *Fortune* recently had what seems to me a brilliant editorial idea. Wishing to have a candid and detached profile of George the Fifth written for their magazine, they found it impossible to get one from any Englishman and in desperation sent Archibald MacLeish to London to get the material. It was part of their project that his manuscript should be annotated, however sarcastically, by some representative Englishman. And that these marginalia should be presented to the reader together with the original text. For this purpose Winston Churchill was enlisted but his word-rate for this patriotic service proved so ruinous that he was abandoned as a collaborator.

The idea, however, is still a good one. And often in reading a book I have wished I could absorb it with certain corrective annotations. Such a book is the one called *Road to War* by the same Walter Millis of the *Herald Tribune* staff who wrote *The Martial Spirit*. In *Road to War*, which is the May choice of the Book-of-the-Month Club, Millis writes a chronological history of the factors which, working between 1914 and 1917, involved this somewhat startled country in the Great War. It is an illuminating and disturbing book which I would like to read aloud to half a dozen men in order to elicit their instinctive comment on it. I would, for instance, like to have a copy annotated by Newton Baker and another copy annotated by you.

Perhaps some day after you have read the book, as you inevitably and reluctantly will, you may come to dinner with me and tell me over the coffee cups the thoughts it wrings from you.

In the meantime, I remain your humble if somewhat recalcitrant servant,

A. Woollcott

To W. GRAHAM ROBERTSON

[As a painter, scenic designer, writer, playwright, and collector, Mr. Robertson figured in the world of Ellen Terry and Sarah Bernhardt. Woollcott saw him on his last visit to London in 1941.]

Bomoseen, Vt.
August 1, 1935

Dear Graham Robertson,
From the wealth of data given above you may learn where I am spending the summer, as so often before, in a healing torpor. Ours is a pine-clad island a mile from shore. In summer it looks like a green tea-cosy, in winter like a birthday cake. We are always finding arrowheads on our island—left behind since the days when Vermont was so spunky a possession of the British Crown that it declared its independence fourteen years before the other colonies and so small a one that nobody—not even George the Third—noticed the defection.

My friend Pip [the black poodle] has always had a strong sense of private property. Last year any stranger was met at the dock by Pip and ordered to leave at once. But this year he even objects to rowboats and canoes from the mainland if they venture merely to encircle us. This keeps him pretty busy and he is exhausted by nightfall, but, singlehanded, he has created a valuable legend in this part of the country that we keep three bloodhounds to repel invaders.

All of my neighbors who cherish French poodles owe their interest in them to Booth Tarkington's various accounts of his dear Gamin, this many years dust in some such apple orchard as your own. Tarkington himself swore he would never own another—too much of an anxiety in these days when motor cars whiz past on every road. Then last Fall, when he found all his disciples so happy with their poodles, he weakened. Now a chic and engaging black clown named Figaro is the focus of the Tarkington household. I stopped off to see the two of them when I was lecturing in Indianapolis in March and already Figaro was so elegantly accomplished a gentleman as to make my Pip seem—by comparison—a country bumpkin who had never had any advantages.

All through luncheon Figaro sat in his cushioned window seat looking pensively at the leafless trees and thinking, I am reasonably certain, of squirrels. But the arrival of the coffee (carried in by a coal-black gentleman named, I am glad to say, Ethelbert Gillmore) was apparently a signal. Anyway, Figaro came mysteriously to life and stared expectant at his master, who asked if he were feeling pious. It seems he was. Or at least fairly pious. He did rush to the wall and plant both forepaws on a chair which stood beneath a primitive Italian Madonna, but his mind was not really upon his devotions and he kept peering round at us as if more interested in earthly rewards. Reproved for such half-hearted orisons, he then buried his head deep, deep between his paws, so that he became—from the tip of his tail to the now invisible tip of his nose—a woolly arc of contrition. "Are you a miserable sinner?" Tarkington asked. A faint moan came from the woolly arc. "Are you"—much louder this time—"a miserable sinner?" A considerable groan from Figaro. *"Are you a miserable sinner?"* This final repetition elicited a very wail from an humble and a contrite heart. "Amen!" at which cue Figaro came bounding from church and was rewarded with a cracker.

Mr. Tarkington now writes me that he is teaching him to blush. It sounds like a stiff course. I shall drive over to the Maine coast in September to investigate the progress being made.

When next I pull myself together, it will be to do a piece

on "The Brotherhood of the French Poodle." There must be a place of honor in it for your Mouton, whose grave I have ceremoniously visited and whose portrait is part of a canvas which will again be one of my best reasons for a visit to London next spring.

But the main purpose of this letter is to report that I have heard from the Lunts all about their temerarious proposal that you visit America, of all places. From dependable spies I hear that their *Shrew* is a sumptuous delight. When it reopens in September for a trial flight before the New York premiere, I shall go out on the road to see it, so that I may tell the country all about it when I resume broadcasting in October. If and when you do come to America, I hope to have due notice, so that I may be on the dock when your ship comes in and help create the illusion that ours is an hospitable country.

Alexander Woollcott

To MRS. OTIS SKINNER

Bomoseen, Vt.
August 2, 1935

My dear Mrs. Skinner,

I think you would have enjoyed—or at least been struck by—the sight of me at breakfast Wednesday. I had come in from swimming and was at table alone, using bits of toast to scoop up that incomparable honey and weeping steadily because once again I had come to the great healing last chapter of *The Brothers Karamazov*. It always chokes me up and fills me with a love of mankind which sometimes lasts till noon of the following day.

Tell Mr. Skinner I enjoy having *The Fight* and that his signature has not changed an iota since he gave me his autograph when I was in school. That collection began with the signature of Anna Held, with whom I was infatuated. I used to write the most seductive letters to get them. I remember assuring Mary Mannering that I was her old admirer (at fifteen, to be exact) and well-wisher. I am not sure whence I got that archaic locution. Out of *Richard Carvel*, probably.

I enjoyed your visit to my dear island.

Alexander Woollcott

To D. G. KENNEDY

[This young Hamilton alumnus first caught Woollcott's attention through an amusing fan letter. Woollcott replied, and from this beginning a firm friendship evolved.]

Bomoseen, Vt.
August 16, 1935

Dear Gerry:

As for the island, I shall be here intermittently throughout September and perhaps you and Folley could stop off on your way back to school. If this should prove feasible you might telegraph on to find out if I am here. On receipt of such a telegram I would not leave unless I were going anyway.

I enjoyed your letter, with its familiar accent of hero worship faintly tinged with contempt. Even so, I could not be stirred out of my torpor to answer it were it not for the fact that I have news which I wish you would transmit to that Brazilian beauty who will run the Theta Delt house next year and whose name I cannot spell. Jerome Kern, made irrational by the broadcasts of the Hamilton Choir, has decided to send his favorite nephew to Hamilton. This nephew is a seventeen-year-old tot, six feet and one inch in height and reputed to be handsome, wholesome and sufficiently prepared to get into Hamilton. I should like to have the Theta Delts get first look at him. Will you see that that Rio rascal communicates with me on the subject?

Hoping that your yellow gloves have become somewhat dimmed with the passing of time, I beg to remain

Yours fraternally,
A. Woollcott

To *HAROLD K. GUINZBURG*

Bomoseen, Vt.
August 16, 1935

Dear David:

I enclose two letters. The one from Rebecca [West] I would like to have back by return mail. The other one can be thrown in the scrapbasket.

I am in receipt of your instructions (conveyed by postal card specifically transmitted by the S.S. *Bremen,* you dirty roscher) to report all matters to you on your return. I have no specific news beyond the fact that I have recklessly committed myself to another broadcast series beginning October 6th, and my entire day is now spent in dreading the necessity of quitting this island as soon as that.

The amiable [Marshall] Best seems to be taking *The Woollcott Reader* seriously. I wish I could have a talk with you or with him about it before I have to start work on my part of it, about which I feel some perplexity. What I am trying to do is to find some unity in the collection and I can't even begin to look for it until I know what the collection is.

All this discussion by mail will be unnecessary if you happen to be coming this way in the near future. I wish you could forget your mischpokah and business and come on the receipt of this letter. What looks like an entrancing aggregation will be coming and going throughout the week. But from the 24th on until Labor Day there is at least a threat of our being too crowded for comfort. Of course I could always make room for you in Beatrice's bed, and I suppose you won't mind eating in the men's toilet. You could defeat this ugly prospect by getting here first and helping me repel invaders, but between now and the 24th I can offer you Neysa, Harpo, Lederer, Beatrice, Irene Castle, Dr. [William] Mann (head of the Washington Zoo) and the Lunts. The Lunts will occupy my house on the top of the hill. Perhaps you could arrange a design for living with them.

Letters about "WRB" [*While Rome Burns*] continue to trickle in, including one this week from a reader in Berlin who took dignified exception to one incident in the chapter called "The Sacred Grove." Chap named Hanfstaengl. Incidentally, in a correspondence with Earle Walbridge of the Harvard Club Library, I had recourse to the abbreviation employed in the preceding anecdote and it only made matters worse because he thought I was talking about William Rose Benét.

My badminton has improved. Nothing to boast about yet. It's like the triumph of an idiot child finally learning to say boo.

A. W.

P.S. I am nuts in a quiet way about *The Circus of Doctor Lao*.

P.P.S. Harpo was caught by M.G.M. as he was getting into the plane today. He will be held up another ten days. This means the congestion will be less grievous and you can come any time, but the sooner the better for me.

To *FRODE JENSEN*

Beverly Hills, Calif.
November 20, 1935

Dear Frode:
 I should have written you after my agreeable visit in Winnetka, but there seems to be an incredible amount of business to do, and words from me on this trip will be few and

far between. I approve highly of the Leonards—I think the old man is a good deal of a darling. You will have to take an entire summer off each year to teach him how to pronounce Frode.

I am glad to think that you are keeping an eye on Eleanora [von Mendelssohn], who has had such lousy luck that I can't bear to think of it. Fortunately for me, I haven't time to think of anything. There are more old friends of mine in this corner of the world than I had suspected—more, in fact, than I like, because I want to spend my time, if possible, with Chaplin, Disney and a few others whom I came out to see. I have had a long dinner with Chaplin, an enchanting visit with Disney, a congested cocktail party at Dorothy Parker's (at the peak of which Marc Connelly decided to tell me in a loud voice that my article on him in the *Ladies' Home Journal* was the meanest, cruelest and most malicious thing that had been done to him in fifteen years). And now tonight I am off to dinner with Dashiell Hammett, who shares my ideas, if not my feelings, about the Lamson case. Commander Brown is off playing tennis with Harpo's Susan (I think Harpo would better hurry back), and we are all going off Sunday evening to attend divine services under the guidance of Aimee Semple McPherson.

What day do you leave for Chicago?

A. W.

To *PAUL HARPER*

[The agency Mr. Harper represented handled the Cream of Wheat account which sponsored Woollcott's radio program.]

New York City
November 22, 1935

My dear Harper:
               This is an answer to your official letter of November 22nd in which you announce that:

"The Cream of Wheat Corporation is unwilling to continue the broadcasts after December 29th unless you will agree to refrain from including in your broadcasts material of a controversial nature which, in our opinion, would be offensive to individuals or groups in the radio audience."

This paragraph would be unintelligible to anyone who had not previously read your letter of November 14th in which you transmitted this message from Mr. Thomson and Mr. Clifford of the Cream of Wheat Corporation:

"They went on to say that they preferred that you didn't make any more caustic references to people like Hitler and Mussolini as there are large racial groups who are apt to be antagonized by these references."

Now, in these broadcasts the Town Crier has for several years been freely reporting his likes and dislikes on the books, plays, pictures, prejudices, manners and customs of the day. In undertaking such an oral column, he could not with self-respect agree in advance never to take pot shots at such targets as Hitler or Mussolini. Or, for that matter, at any other bully, lyncher or jingo whose head happened to come within shooting distance. If he did embark upon a series thus hamstrung in advance, his own interest in the broadcasts would so dwindle that they would deteriorate in short order.

I am entirely in sympathy with the viewpoint of Mr. Bull and his Cream of Wheat associates. If they think an occasional glancing blow antagonizes old customers or drives away new ones it would be folly for them to address their advertising to such an audience as I might assemble. It is my own guess that the allusions complained of have no such effect. It would seem to me as reasonable to expect every crack at Hitler to send all the Jews in America rushing to the grocery stores to stack up with Cream of Wheat. It would be as reasonable to assume that the [Sir John] Buchan broadcast (which Mr. Bull so highly approved) with its hands-across-the-sea, England-and-America shoulder-to-shoulder theme, alienated from Cream of Wheat every Irish listener and all those whom Mr. Hearst and Father Coughlin have industriously filled with a distrust of the English. It would be as reasonable to fear that the November 10th broadcast, which you yourself loudly applauded, may have so infuriated the Scotch that they all reverted to oatmeal in a body. I have said enough to make clear what a blank check I would be signing if I recklessly promised to omit all controversial material. Before each broadcast, you see, there would be so much honest disagreement as to what material was controversial. The irony of this impasse lies in my own suspicion that it is these very elements which most promote interest in the series. The only reason I don't indulge in them oftener is because I believe they are more effective when infrequently used. They lend the series salt, provoke discussion, whip up attendance and enlarge the audience. The sponsor is therefore most worried by the broadcast which serves him best. At least, that is my guess, which may be as good as Mr. Bull's but need not be any better. And after all, it is his business and not mine.

I have overheard enough of the experiences of other broadcasters to suspect that it would be difficult to find anywhere among the big national advertisers a sponsor who would be as considerate, liberal and agreeable as the Cream of Wheat people have been throughout all our dealings. This would seem to indicate that the Town Crier is unlikely to find any other sponsor willing to meet the terms he must insist on so long as he uses the now established formula which inevitably represents him as one citizen leaning over the fence and talking freely to his neighbors. And since all the good time on the great networks has been pre-empted by advertisers, that in turn would mean I must drop out of national broadcasting altogether, which, as you know, would be a solution entirely acceptable to me. I would merely be driven back to the comparative privacy of the printed page where, in my own opinion, I belong and where, at long last, I might get some writing done.

Yours sincerely,
Alexander Woollcott

P.S. By the way, in your final paragraph you say that I have "declined to accept any restrictions made by the sponsor" in my choice of material. When you wrote that sentence you must have been either absent-minded or disingenuous. I told you yesterday that I had no objection whatever to letting your representative cut out of my script any joke, anecdote or phrase which, in his opinion, was either coarse or suggestive. If you still do not recall this promise, [Leggett] Brown may be able to refresh your memory.

One other point. You yourself asked why I should ever need to introduce controversial matter into a broadcast since I could so easily let off steam in the various publications to which I can always contribute. Unfortunately, this suggestion is impractical. I find the weekly preparation of the next broadcast and the consequences of the preceding one so time-consuming that when I am broadcasting I am unable to do any other kind of work. I haven't even time left to write a post card to the folks.

A. W.

To *THE EDITOR, WORLD HERALD,*
    OMAHA, NEBRASKA

San Mateo, Calif.
December 19, 1935

Dear Sir:

May I not, as the late Woodrow Wilson used to say, call your attention to an editorial which appeared in your issue of December 9th under the caption "The Woollcott Menace"? It has found its way out to me here in San Mateo, out in the great open spaces where men are menace. And as it reiterates a frequently repeated allegation, I am experimenting, for the first time in some years, in the luxury of answering it—for publication or not, as you see fit.

It is the substance of this editorial that as a recommender of books over the radio, I take advantage of a nation-wide network to further the sale of soft, sentimental works. "Marshmallows" was the term employed. Since this series of broadcasts began, I have cast my oral vote for the following works:

Paths of Glory, by Humphrey Cobb
Life with Father, by Clarence Day
North to the Orient, by Anne Morrow Lindbergh
Valiant Is the Word for Carrie, by Barry Benefield
I Write as I Please, by Walter Duranty
The Woollcott Reader, an anthology of seventeen authors ranging from J. M. Barrie to Evelyn Waugh.

In addition to these there have been brief parenthetical bursts of applause for

Death and General Putnam, by Arthur Guiterman
Mrs. Astor's Horse, by Stanley Walker

It is quite impossible for any literate adult to think that this list represents pink publications for pale people. If these be "marshmallows," then I am the Grand Duchess Marie.

What interests me in this instance is the apparent lack of journalistic conscience manifested by the editorial I complain of. If that editorial was written by someone who would think of that list as so many marshmallows, it was the work of a fool. If it was written by someone who was not even familiar with what books I had recommended, it was the work of a knave. Neither alternative is agreeable for a colleague to contemplate. Of course, there is always the third possibility that your editorial writer is a nicely balanced mixture of the two.

Yours sincerely,
Alexander Woollcott

VI

1936-1937

To *FRODE JENSEN*

Santa Fe, New Mexico
January 8, 1936

Dear Frode:

You might begin telephoning the apartment along about the 21st to see if I have come back. You will have to move fast if you want to catch me before I go away again.

As for the ceremonies planned for Winnetka on September 12th, I think you would do well to find someone else to stand up with you. Whether you can lure Hennessey and Brown to the midlands at that time of year you can discover only from them. I have no idea where they will be in September or by whom employed. I have no idea on what continent I will be in September.

Even if I were to be in or near Chicago on September 12th I would strongly advise against your engaging me as best man. I can tell you right now what poisonous thoughts I would be thinking all during the ceremony. I should be wondering whose love of display and whose servility to fashion had ordained a church wedding with flocks of ushers and bridesmaids for a young couple for whose life immediately thereafter such a parade would be a grotesquely inappropriate inaugural. I should be thinking how much better the money thus squandered could have been spent by any young couple upon their immediate necessities. I should be wondering whose interests were being consulted instead of those of the bride and groom, the only people whose interests ought to be consulted. I should be thinking that if you and Deb [Deborah Leonard] had slipped over to Middlebury and been married with the legal minimum of witnesses, how much more grace and dignity that wedding would have had. If you have read thus far even your slow Scandinavian mind must have taken in the fact that I think church weddings are vulgar and stupid. They seem to me as much out of date and as essentially useless as a banquet photograph.

Having thus brightened your day and suspecting that if I am the best man you could think of, your plight must be pretty desperate, I remain,

      Yours with deep affection,
      Alexander Woollcott

To *FRODE JENSEN*

Chicago, Ill.
January 15, 1936

Dear Frode:

  I doubt if my stern letter distressed you unduly. I did have the notion that you might show it to Deb and that she might show it to her father and that—possibly—a great light might then dawn on him. This would have extricated you young people from a burdensome mess and I still think it's worth trying—at least if Deb is with you and me in this matter. Maybe she herself wants to wallow in orange blossoms, rotogravures and sweaty ushers. However, I realize that there are factors involved in the problem of which I know nothing and which—from a distance—I cannot sufficiently take into account. So I will say no more.

After all, as you both must dimly suspect, you are my joy and pride and no good or ill fortune can come to you without my sharing it. I may even so far forget my preferences as to attend the repellent ceremonies you are planning, but I cannot possibly decide that question until you finally tell me when they are to be held.

I shall arrive in New York in false whiskers on the morning of Monday the 20th, but don't tell anyone.

Your affectionate uncle
A. Woollcott

To MRS. NEWTON D. BAKER

[Mr. Baker was Secretary of War under President Wilson.]

New York City
February 3, 1936

My dear Mrs. Baker:

When I first went abroad in the unsuspecting spring of 1914 I was a saucer-eyed young journalist sent by the New York *Times* and bent on storing up all kinds of impressions against the time when I should be old enough to sit in the sun and remember. Among my great occasions was an invitation to have tea with Barrie in his mullioned aerie in Adelphi Terrace. I went there intending to note Barrie's every syllable for subsequent relation to my grandchildren. I was so excited by the sheer eventfulness of meeting him that I talked a blue streak and in the two hours and a half I was there he never got a word in edgewise. I will say that once or twice he tried to interrupt, but I struck him down.

I suspect you will find something vaguely familiar in this episode. For a good many obscure reasons, at some of which you could not possibly guess, I was enormously exhilarated by the household in which I found myself on the 19th of the month just past. If I were a real neighbor and could come in once in a while this would subside to manageable proportions. The irony of it lies in the fact that, of the deficiencies in my life of which I am most acutely and hungrily aware, one is the need to have more contact with minds like Mr. Baker's. Such contact would give me the refreshment, correction and stimulation I am most desperately in need of. And what do I do when I get a chance to sit at his feet and listen? I know what I do. I drown him out. I drown him out and I shout him down and perform on trapezes and, like the man in his own very bad story, forget what I came for. By the way, you tell him the best variant of that is the helpless little boy who went to the druggist. "What's the matter?" asked the old apothecary. "Did you forget what you came for?"

"Oh, yes," said the boy, much relieved, "that's it. Camphor."

I often find myself thinking what fun it would be to live in a town of two hundred people provided I could name the two hundred—name the editor of the paper and the priest with whom I would talk over the affairs of the parish and the atheist with whom I would play cribbage at the corner saloon. Mr. Baker could have any job in that town he wants.

Will you tell him for me that in 1934 Ian Colvin wrote the second and final volume of the life of Lord Carson which had been left unfinished by the obnoxious and self-slain Eddie Marjoribanks. Tell him also, please, that among the jobs I hope to do when I go to London on the 20th is to persuade the publishers of the *Notable British Trials* to put out a volume which would contain the complete record of the Archer-Shee case. You might also tell Mr. Baker that I am counting on his sending me not only Mr. Wilson's commutation decisions in the four capital cases during the war, but, if possible, the memoranda on which he based those decisions.

I have had the translucent paper-cutter and ruler outfitted

with a new and unsullied glass. I now brandish it so effectively that I am more like Mrs. Fiske than ever.

Yours sincerely,
Alexander Woollcott

To LADY COLEFAX

[Lady Colefax's hospitality greatly increased Woollcott's enjoyment of his trips to England, as before the war she was hostess to many figures in the literary, political and artistic worlds. Now she has turned her salon into a canteen.]

On Board S.S. Manhattan
April 10, 1936

Dear Sibyl,

This shall be posted at Queenstown to tell you how kindly and how fondly I am aware of the part you play in making any visit of mine to London something to enjoy at the time and long afterwards when I am old and can only sit in the sun and remember. You have a great talent for friendship and I count myself fortunate in knowing you

Alexander W.

To LUCY CHRISTIE DRAGE

[Lucy Drage's daughter, Betty, with her husband, Fred Harvey, was killed in an airplane crash a few days after she disembarked from the *Manhattan* in New York.]

New York City
May 13, 1936

Dear Lucy:

It was only at the last minute that I decided to come back on the *Manhattan*, which left Southampton on the evening of the 9th. I had been planning to return on the *Aquitania* which left the day before, but my chief objective overseas was a meeting with J. W. Dunne. He lives down near Banbury in Oxfordshire but was staying with his mother at Montreux throughout the winter and was so late in returning to England that I could visit him at all only by staying over a day. I had rather counted on spending most of the return trip on the *Aquitania* in the company of Mrs. Belloc Lowndes, an enchanting old woman who is a great crony of mine. However, my friend, George Backer, would be returning on the *Manhattan*. He and I came down from London to Southampton together for the midnight sailing.

My eyes were hardly open next morning when the assistant to the Chief Steward popped in with the gracious announcement that I was to sit at the Captain's table. I am much too old a bird to be caught by that bait any more. Sometimes I have to work up the theory that I am hard at work on something and must be left undisturbed to read throughout dinner. Thereafter I always have to keep the title of my book out of sight for fear it will be discovered that my researches are in detective literature. But this time I had Backer for an excuse. We would be eating together, I explained. Much shocked, the assistant retired. When news of my recalcitrance reached the Chief Steward he came in personally to repeat the invitation and, as a special inducement, offered the information that I would be sitting next to a Mrs. Harvey, the daughter of an old friend of mine. I replied that Mrs. Harvey might desert the Captain and sit with us if she wanted to, but that I was much too irregular and unsocial a traveler ever to sit at the Captain's table. I was afraid this might seem a trifle churlish so I sent around a note to Betty's cabin asking her to have cocktails with me in the bar that evening.

I had seen her only once or twice and that so many years ago that I wasn't sure I would know her and kept inspecting every youngish woman who came into the bar. But when Betty herself arrived, there was no mistaking her—very lovely looking and radiantly healthy and particularly attractive to me because of her beautiful walk. She was being indulged by the line with a large, hideous sitting-room all to herself. And everywhere she carried her new dog, a tiny three-months-old Australian terrier, so small that it could stand on my cigarette case and so fierce that it repelled all invaders. Its name was Sophia. Poor Sophia; I see that the newspapers mistook her for a monkey.

Betty and I became great friends at once. She used to call me every morning and demand that I come around to her cabin for coffee and every evening I used to carry her away for coffee and liqueurs after dinner. This used to annoy the old Captain tremendously. He didn't like this at all because he liked Betty. He wrote me quite a desolate note about her. He had implored her not to fly.

Betty and I had long talks together. She told me so much about you and her father and Charley and Charley's wife and Charley's baby and David—not so much recent things as things long ago, her troubles with Charley and the cures she had taken him to, her close bond with David and the time when she went to Pomfret to see him and found him in trouble and got him out of it (he had been caught smoking, I believe, and was going to be expelled and Betty saw the headmaster and burst into a torrent of old Christie tears and got him forgiven). I take it she had no great respect for or confidence in Charley's marriage and was skeptical about his and its future. I gathered, too, that she had always adored her father and that everything he had ever said and done was the most tender memory to her. What she thought of Fred Harvey I have no notion. Not the faintest. But you were the great enthusiasm of her life. I gathered as much from a hundred things she said to me and from what she said to other people. I am not inventing this to comfort you. Indeed you must know I am not. You must know how much she admired you and how she felt about you.

She was a good deal of a surprise to me. I cannot remember now where in some past years I had picked up the notion that she was superficial and scatterbrained. Instead I found her wise and grave and realistic and extraordinarily perceptive. I did, however, get the impression that this was a new phase of her, that she was but recently matured, that if she had a real serenity it was something she had recently achieved. From things she told me and from things she didn't know she was telling me I gathered she had been through some storm, with tormented, twitching nerves and the like, but that she had come out of all that as a person comes at last out of fever. She was clear-eyed and composed and enormously in possession of herself, as if she knew just where she was going and how to get there. I found myself enjoying her company and admiring her profoundly. As you know, this is no polite afterthought. I am so glad I wrote you that note on her last Saturday. You must have found it in your mail on Monday morning if you saw your mail on Monday morning.

The last morning she and Backer and I loitered together in the sun of the open deck as the ship waited at Quarantine and then came slowly up the Bay. After we docked, I did not see her again because she was planning to leave her maid to pilot the luggage through the customs while she herself departed immediately with Fred to whatever hotel he had picked out. She went off with my telephone number in her purse and, just before she started West, she called me up. I was not in, but my maid took the message. Mrs. Harvey was leaving and wanted me to be sure and send her the address of my camp as she wanted to wire me and tell me when she was coming to the island. You see, it had been all fixed that she was to visit us this summer in Vermont.

Alexander W.

To LADY COLEFAX

New York City
May 14, 1936

Dear Sibyl:

Along with this same mail I am sending you a copy of a novel Charley Brackett wrote about the island. I can't for the life of me remember whether you ever saw it.

However, I am writing you now for quite another purpose. I am in some slight embarrassment because I happen to be privy to the secret of a Christmas present you are going to get. And it is my notion that it might be a convenience to you to know about it in advance. After some irresolution I decided to tip you off. But you need say nothing about it and must be as surprised as one o'clock when the time comes. In brief, a half-dozen of your American friends, fearfully annoyed at the prospect of not seeing you for a long time, have decided to give you for Christmas (instead of a pair of candlesticks or even book-ends) a trip to America with all expenses paid, including three weeks of debauchery in New York. It is our idea that you would best enjoy cashing this check some time after the Christmas holidays. January, perhaps, or something like that.

I would throw in as one detail the promise of a dinner party for you at my new house but I cannot at the moment of going to press tell you precisely where that will be. The offer for the house I want has been made and is now in the hands of the Surrogate and some sort of decision may be handed down even while this note to you is on the Atlantic. I find one is extremely vulnerable when, as rarely happens with me, one happens to want something a lot.

By the time this reaches you I will have shifted my base to the island for the summer. My address there, as you know, is Bomoseen, Vermont. I still think often and gratefully of the good times you gave me when I was last in London. I set great store by my friendship with you.

Alexander W.

P.S. I have gone onto a heroic diet in an effort to keep my weight from becoming a peril and an inconvenience so I couldn't munch on those chocolate pebbles of yours even if I were in London. But what about that enchanting aroma as of burning pinewood that greets the guests as they step across the threshold? How is that produced? Is it some kind of tea that you have smoldering in the umbrella stands? If so, how and where could I get some?

To *LADY COLEFAX*

Bomoseen, Vt.
July 8, 1936

Dear Sibyl:
            One of my favorite people in all the world seems likely to come to England for several months in the Fall. I am so anxious that his visit should be happy that I shall have to repress from motives of common sense and economy an impulse to go over and manage it for him. His name is Robert Barnes Rudd and you would be simply enchanted with him. He was a classmate of mine at school. While I was starting work on the *Times* to learn my trade he went to Merton for three years. Now he is a professor of English literature at our college and is the somewhat surprised father of five incredibly beautiful children. Being slightly insane, he and his wife and all five children are sailing for Marseilles in August and will stay with her brother who has a farm near Pau. Once they are all planted there, Bob will leave them flat and go on to London for the weeks between early September and Christmas. I suppose he will go down to Oxford for a while for old time's sake, but mostly he wants to stay in London and do some reading. His sole problem will

be financial. I assume he will have to live on next to nothing at all, but he is used to that. I know he will want to call on Graham Robertson for he too belongs to the brotherhood of the poodle, and you are just the person to see that he is in on one or two experiences that would provide pleasant memories for him to take home with him. I will have a greater notion of what these might be before the time comes and I will write you again.

Alexander W.

P.S. I have been having a debauch of reading, including a colossal life of Andrew Johnson, the wretched man who was shot into the presidency by the assassination of Lincoln and who was the chief victim of the post-war hate which always takes the naïve human race by surprise. In the persecution of Johnson, one of the chief villains was a corrupt and flagrant Congressman who was later Grant's running mate in the next election. And why am I telling all this to you? Because his name was Colfax—Schuyler Colfax. He was known as Smilar Colfax and appears to have been a good deal of a louse. I thought you would like to know.

To MARGARET MITCHELL

Bomoseen, Vt.
August 7, 1936

My dear Miss Mitchell:
I have just finished reading *Gone With the Wind* and found it completely absorbing. Its narrative has the directness and gusto of Dumas. I enjoyed it enormously. I was almost through it when I said to myself: "God's nightgown! This must be the Peg Mitchell who wrote me once about the little girl who swallowed a water moccasin and the tall man in

the wrinkled nurse's uniform who thronged the road from Atlanta to Miami." Is it?

If your royalties have begun to come in, kindly send a large share of them as per the enclosed instructions and oblige

A. Woollcott

To RALPH HAYES
[Secretary to Newton D. Baker during the first World War.]

Bomoseen, Vt.
August 8, 1936

Dear Ralph:

In the matter of the coming election, I will attempt here only to report that I, myself, intend to vote for Franklin Roosevelt. I was driven into his arms through the peculiar repulsiveness of his opponents. In 1918 I had some misgivings about the course Woodrow Wilson was taking, but at that time, and immediately thereafter, one had to go along with him in order to avoid even seeming to reinforce such swine as Henry Cabot Lodge. The crowd that has been grooming Landon seem to me indistinguishable from the element that gave us Warren Harding. As you know, I could have wished another than Franklin Roosevelt to have been nominated in 1932. Now I devoutly hope he will be re-elected.

A. Woollcott

To MRS. HENDRICK EUSTIS

Bomoseen, Vt.
August 10, 1936

Gruesome Grace:

The island is perfect now, and I can't help thinking that any time you spend flouncing around Hollywood will be just so much wear and tear. I am able to report that Beatrice's chairs will have arrived before the week is out and that the Duchess [A. W.'s black shepherd dog] has had a bath, a quasi-public affair in the shallows of the lake in the manner of the late Susannah. She appeared to enjoy it, and I must confess to a marked improvement. Her reputation on the mainland has advanced by leaps and bounds due to the decision of a boatload of assorted females to land at the point. The Duchess decided they shouldn't and attacked in so startling a manner that they were all half drowned trying to get into their boat and launch it at the same time. You never heard such shrieks. An arena full of edible early Christians must have sounded something like this.

Black Neysa is becoming a tough baby. She rackets around with the boys a good deal and has even developed a habit of charging down to the shore and mewing at passing motor boats in what she imagines is an intimidating manner.

I stopped off at chez MacLeish on my way back. Your health and whereabouts were publicly inquired after. I think they will be up here soon—perhaps this week, more probably during the week of the 17th.

Leggett Brown tells me he is devoting some of his time to preparing Hollywood for your arrival.

A. W.

To STEPHEN EARLY
[Woollcott's friendship with President Roosevelt's secretary began when they were on the *Stars and Stripes* together in 1918.]

Bomoseen, Vt.
September 10, 1936

Dear Steve:

This note is a sequel to our talk across the luncheon table (you paid the check) last February. I am now seeking your sober advice as to whether a Roosevelt broadcast by me—let us

[169]

say a fifteen minute declaration of my reasons for thinking the country would be best served by his re-election—would be so valuable a contribution that I ought to make it despite my several private reasons for wishing not to do any radio work this Fall at all.

And if you do think I should thus do my bit, please tell me how and through whom I should make the offer. Here is my perplexity. I am reluctant to seem fussy and self-important but after all the whole point of my letting out a peep is the fact that I am reputed to have a considerable radio following. I don't want to enter in at all unless the offer is considered important enough to insure some preliminary drum-beating in order to assemble at least a part of that audience.

I think if I'd been lost like Stefansson in the Arctic for several years and returning, had heard only the arguments against Mr. Roosevelt, I should have decided, on the strength of them alone, to vote for him. I had heard those same arguments before —the same words from the same people. Then they were launched against Theodore Roosevelt and later against Woodrow Wilson. The last time they were triumphant they ushered in normalcy and Warren Harding.

A. Woollcott

To RALPH HAYES

Bomoseen, Vt.
September 28, 1936

Dear Ralph:

You should have received ere now evidence aplenty that your letter posted to this address came to hand. I can't be pried loose from this hide-out before the middle of October. After that, I shall go into winter quarters at Sneden Landing, having sold my flat to Noel Coward in one of my recurrent spasms of dislike for New York.

I read Mr. Baker's piece in *Foreign Affairs* with tremendous satisfaction, plus considerable exhilaration. He has the best prose style of any living American and I doubt if he realizes it or cares much. I sent five copies of the issue to sundry friends, but I hope it will soon be available as a modestly priced book. This is so obvious a publishing project that I assume it is even now issuing from some press, but you never can tell and on the chance, I suggested to my own publishers that they try to get it. That's the way Little Brown got *Good-bye, Mr. Chips*. It had caused a small sensation in *The Atlantic* but no one had thought of making a book out of it.

Well, I must run now and look up "pixilated" in the dictionary.

A. Woollcott

P.S. On October 20th I'm going to do a broadcast telling why I'm voting for Roosevelt. The real reason is as persuasive, I should think, as any I could manufacture. I want to disassociate myself from the swine who, almost in a body, are out for Landon. Some good men are out for Landon. All the heels are.

To STEPHEN EARLY

New York City
October 20, 1936

Dear Steve:

Something—possibly your stepping on High—produced immediate action. At least I am now scheduled for WABC on Tuesday, the 27th, 10.45 P.M. Eastern Standard Time, and announcements to that effect are already going out over the air and will, I assume, be printed in the radio programs on Sunday.

I wish I might have spoken sooner only because I must now give the impression of one who took the precaution to wait and pick a winner. Judging from all I hear in this neck of the woods, anyone who rushes out now to declare himself for Roosevelt is a little like someone having the impertinence to "discover" a neglected little work like *Gone With the Wind*. Aside from that, I shall speak for your chief with the great enthusiasm I really feel.

After Election I shall be in Washington for a few days during the fortnight of Noel Coward's engagement. I have known him since he was a shabby youngster in his teens who either ate at the expense of some rich wage slave like himself or didn't eat at all. It is part of the ritual of the American theatre that old Uncle Woollcott should go down on these occasions and hold his hand during the tremors of a try-out. I shall also be there collecting a hundred dollars from Alice Longworth, who will owe me same after the returns are in on Election Day.

Good luck, and God bless you.

Alexander Woollcott

To *LILLY BONNER*

New York City
October 31, 1936

Dear Lilly:

My immense enjoyment of the new *Hamlet* here was complicated all during the first half of the performance by my agonized inability to think who it was [John] Gielgud looked like. It was about the middle of the Closet Scene that it came to me. In every detail of feature, walk, voice, manner and what not, he is the spitting image of you.

Then I must tell you about my tremendous enjoyment of

[172]

the hunting season this year in Vermont. It's the first time I've ever really enjoyed a hunting season. It was pretty bad when all the nimrods began arriving the last of September. The island was carpeted with pointers, and these Daniel Boones stood around hefting their guns in the familiar manner I find so fatiguing to watch. Then, when the first came, they went out each morning at dawn and came back late at sundown with not a Goddamn bird. It didn't lessen their discomfiture that I named them the Audubon Society. Finally, at the rate of about one a day, they did accumulate four partridges. These were hung high on the wall of the house outside the kitchen door against Thursday night's dinner. Thursday afternoon the cook went to pluck them and found that the Black Duchess, my shepherd dog, was just polishing off the third. She's now known all over Vermont as Woollcott's bird dog.

The Black Duchess and my cat, Black Neysa, will be coming down to live with me in New York this winter, as I have sublet Hope Williams' apartment in Gracie Square for three winters. This is part of a program which includes the purchase of half the island from the club, and the converting of my little stone shack into a big, nine-room, all-year-round house, from which I expect, in due time, to be buried.

But why, as they say in the kind of plays usually backed by Paul, am I telling all this to you? Because, obviously, I want you to write me the real lowdown about Wallis Simpson. Instinct tells me that the public guess is all wrong, that the real story is importantly different from the one surmised. I chiefly hope that the King will be happy. He has that in him which makes many people hope this. I saw him only twice, but I feel an immense good will for him. But tell me all about it as confidentially as you wish—what has happened, what is happening, and what is going to happen. Write me at 10 Gracie Square.

Alexander W.

To DR. A. P. SAUNDERS

[For many years Professor of Chemistry at Hamilton College.]

New York City
November 19, 1936

Dear Percy:

I have just sent a book to you called *Ferdinand*, but that is not the point of this note.

Eckstein, who is like no one in the world except Chaplin and who, though he will be forty-six on his next birthday, is a gnomelike and tiny creature suggesting a frost-bitten twenty-two, is, all told, as enchanting a fellow as ever I saw. I took him down to Washington so that I might see him at the zoo with Bill Mann. Some time I must tell you about how he and the birds began talking to one another at a tremendous rate the moment he crossed the threshold. However, I am going to try my luck luring him to Hamilton to get a degree and you shall have him in the garden in June.

But this is the point: I have it in mind to give a small dinner party for him in New York when he comes back from Cincinnati three weeks hence. The date will be the 10th. I would make it a dinner of no more than eight and in composing my list of guests I haven't got beyond him and Anne Parrish. I am writing to inquire what chance there is of your being able to get down here for it. I could, of course, give you lodging for the night, as I have a guest room here.

Alexander W.

P.S. Hennessey has gone up to Vermont to select stone for the new house. He is also under orders to bring back my cat, shepherd dog, music-box and binoculars.

A. W.

[Woollcott did not know Dr. Gustav Eckstein, Professor of Physiology at the University of Cincinnati and friend and biographer of the Japanese scientist Noguchi, until he read Eckstein's book, *Canary*. He was fascinated by the personal quality of the scientist's relationship to his birds, and wrote to him about it. A strong and continuing bond then developed between them.]

To LADY COLEFAX

New York City
November 23, 1936

Dear Sibyl,

As for independent sorties and projects while you are here, that's your own affair, but you mustn't expect me to be sympathetic with them. You know I think you do four times too much, not only for your own good but for the full enjoyment of the things you would do even if you did much less. As I have to struggle with the same deleterious tendency in myself, I am alert to all signs of such folly in others. I do deeply feel that you must need some rest while you are here. That's why I roared with enraged disapproval last night when Lynn timidly suggested that you might like a brief triumphal tour of Hollywood. It seems likely that we all will be here when you come, for I think even Alice Miller will be back from the Coast by then and that the Lunts will still be doing such business with *Idiot's Delight* as to have found no excuse to go on tour. I myself am certain to be here because on the 5th I start broadcasting again and will have to be in or near New York every Tuesday and Thursday for some time to come. You will be here in time for my fiftieth birthday on the 19th, although I think it likely that I shall actually spend that day or part of it in Washington, as it is the eve of the inauguration. Since Washington will be intolerably congested at the time and since our great public occasions are rigorously lacking in the spectacular, I shall resist with my last ounce of strength any proposal of yours to come along. Noel, of course, will be in a dither with his new plays, which open here tomorrow night, and even John Gielgud will, I think, still be playing Hamlet. His final weeks are announced, but that is all eye-wash. When Leslie Howard presented a competing Dane, the press for Gielgud was even better than when he had opened himself, and as vast multitudes had apparently waited to see which Hamlet was the better bet, they are now going in droves to see John's. Leslie's was embarrassingly bad —a monotonous and rather pretty schoolboy reciting pieces taught him by his governess.

As the time approaches and I shall have to act on some of your communications, I must insist that you typewrite them. I know you think that my comments on your handwriting are fretful and spoilsport, but some day I shall succeed in convincing you that I have never been able to do more than guess at what you were trying to say. It would be a pity if I guessed wrong on some crucial matter like a date or an address. As the time approaches I will let you know what your New York address is to be and you can always get in touch with me if you will remember that my cable address is ACKIE, New York.

A. W.

P.S. The sum and substance of the above, in case you forget, is that if you don't have a good time when you are here I shall be bitterly disappointed, and if you don't take it easy, I shall bash your head in.

To LAURA E. RICHARDS

New York City
December 12, 1936

My dear Mrs. Richards,

My delighted encounter with "Tom the Pigman" at breakfast yesterday morning also served as a reminder that I must report the collapse of all my plans to get to the State of Maine this year. All my notions of what I would do after the middle of October went awry in the excitement of the campaign. The Republican tactics drove me into Mr. Roosevelt's arms and I was in a lather until I could get on the air and ring my bell for him. I have since had withering comments from a neighbor

[176]

of yours [Booth Tarkington] in Kennebunkport who professes to sympathize with this rush of mine to the aid of an imperiled cause and ventures to hope I will come up in the spring unless the President gets into trouble again.

Meanwhile, I seem to be leading a sufficiently violent professional life to need a New York headquarters and its address you will find duly engraved at the top of this writing paper. I am busy now putting together the contents for the second *Woollcott Reader* and in general trying to clear my desk so that I can begin broadcasting in January. It is to be every Thursday and Tuesday evening at seven-thirty.

I went to Anne Sullivan Macy's funeral and as long as I live I shall remember the sight of Helen [Keller] coming up the church aisle after it was over. Her secretary, Polly Thompson, a Scotch woman and as fine a person as ever drew the breath of life, was weeping beyond all control, and as they passed the pew where I sat I saw the flutter of Helen's hands as she sought to comfort her. I had not seen any of them nor heard from them since spring. They sent me word at last only because just before she lost consciousness for good and all, Mrs. Macy tapped into Helen's hand, "You must send for Alexander. I want him to read to me." They were together forty-nine years. I cannot imagine them apart.

Under separate cover I am sending you a book called *Canary* which is the present apple of my roving eye. If you like it, I will write and tell you all about the astounding little man who wrote it. Also—because it's just your dish—a book called *Ferdinand*.

Alexander Woollcott

To *LAURA E. RICHARDS*

New York City
January 23, 1937

Dear Mrs. Richards,

My fiftieth birthday found me toiling in Washington, but after the broadcast there was a small birthday dinner (without cake) given by young Joe Alsop of the *Herald Tribune* staff. He is a grandson of the late Mrs. Douglas Robinson and, therefore, a cousin of Alice Longworth and of Mrs. Franklin Roosevelt. He looks like the late Count Fosco and, although he went through Groton and Harvard, he comes extraordinarily close to being what I should call an educated man. Anyway, he gave this dinner for me and Alice Longworth and Rebecca West and, to my delight, Mrs. Winthrop Chanler. We talked about you and she said she had had some of the sherry, and I found her delightful, but I am still faithful to you.

I did get the brochure. It's just up my alley. The song and dance I do on the subject is usually limited to attacks upon the people who nick the edge of a good word by trying to use it for something it was never intended for. It's the transpire-happen, prone-supine, imply-infer group that I have in my mind. Indeed, I am thinking of doing a broadcast about it, calling upon the people to rise and kill off all those who use flair under the impression that it means knack or talent or aptitude.

I meant to write you a long letter about Dr. Eckstein, but I have been discouraged by two things. First, I had really said my say in the magazine piece I sent on to you and, second, my best story on him needs too much pantomime to tell in a letter.

Alexander W.

To ARTHUR HOPKINS

New York City
February 15, 1937

Dear Arthur,

I think it was those two hundred banquets I had to attend during my novitiate as a reporter on the *Times* which gave me a neurosis about public dinners. I would not have believed that I could attend one in any capacity, even as a guest of honor, and have so pleasant an evening. This, I realize in retrospect, was all due to you. It also dawned on me that most of these people, from Henry Hull to Helen Hayes, came not because the dinner was for me but because you had asked them. As that was why I came, I can not quarrel with their motivation. I feel we have written another chapter in a long and still far from finished story about two neighbors—you and

Yours affectionately,

A. Woollcott

To DAVID McCORD
[Author, and editor of the *Harvard Alumni Bulletin*.]

New York City
February 15, 1937

My dear David,

This is a tardy acknowledgment of your *Notes on the Harvard Tercentenary* in which I did the required reading and some more. From afar I followed that observance with an envious and admiring eye.

I find I shall be in Boston on the 26th as I have promised to speak there for the Seeing Eye. I don't know where the meeting will be held, but I do know that I shall be lodged at the Ritz and after my show and theirs I am having the Lunts for supper. I would be glad to have you, too. If, as seems improbable, you want to go to the Seeing Eye meeting, let me know and I will have a seat sent to you. I think it's to be at Symphony Hall and I doubt if it is open to the public.

In a quiet way and on good but scanty evidence, I have a tremendous admiration for President Conant. This is based partly on what I hear about him, partly on things I know he has said and done, and partly on the glimpse I had of him that night when he rose superior to all ineffectual turmoil at The Signet dinner. Do you suppose that if I lingered over in Boston on Saturday the 27th and Sunday the 28th or even Monday the first, I might have a chance to call upon him and talk to him? My reasons are two. One is that I wish I knew him. The second is that as a trustee of Hamilton, where for use after next year we are going to need a new president, I should like to ask him to keep us in mind and to suggest one or two men whom the committee of trustees could interview and meditate upon.

A. W.

[The Seeing Eye, which trains dogs to help the blind attain physical independence, was the institution nearest to Woollcott's heart. He lectured about it, broadcast about it, and contributed to it generously from his own funds.]

To MRS. HENDRICK EUSTIS

New York City
February 23, 1937

Puss Eustis,

I wonder if it can be possible that, behind this poor mask of disgust and under a steady barrage of abuse, I have ever really succeeded in concealing from you the fact that I look on you as one of the most enjoyable companions and the most admirable human beings it is my good fortune to know.

Print *this* in the *Journal* and see what it gets you.

Your lovesick
Pickwick

To MARGARET MITCHELL

New York City
March 19, 1937

Dear Margaret Mitchell,

Well, that's the most tantalizing paragraph in your letter of March 4th—the one in which you said you were sending me the work of another Georgia author. I am driven to ask whether you did actually send it.

As you may suspect, the new books go squealing through here like pigs through a slaughter house. But I have elaborate devices for singling out the ones I'm going to want and I'm pretty sure that no such opus has gone through as the one which you make sound so alluring. I've been slightly hampered by the fact that you told me everything about it except the title and the name of the author. If, even so, you did send it and it has eluded me, I may kill myself. I can't begin to tell you how startled I was to learn that Atlanta isn't on Eastern Standard Time. This has thrown my whole sense of American geography into confusion. I'm still holding on pathetically to a conviction that it's in the South.

Speaking of the South, there came this week from Birmingham in Alabama the most gratifying letter my earnest efforts have ever elicited. A woman named Vance reports that her Negress cook asked permission to listen to one of my broadcasts. When it was over she said, "There's voodoo in his voice but glory in his tales." I'm arranging to have this embossed on my professional stationery. I've often thought of getting out a pink glazed professional stationery with photographs of me in various roles the way character actors do. In my time I've played Puck and Henry the Eighth, which is quite a range.

If you're reading anything at all these days let me recommend *Of Mice and Men*.

A. Woollcott

To HARPO MARX

New York City
March 24, 1937

Dear Harpo,

This is the reminder I promised about Helen Keller. She and Polly Thompson will sail April 1st from San Francisco on the *Asamu Maru*. For two days ahead of that they will be at the St. Francis Hotel. If you have it in mind to send flowers, remember that for a blind person one flower that smells like all get out is better than the most costly bouquet which may be merely something to look at.

[Charles] Lederer is here having his tooth pulled and pacifying MacArthur, who strikes me as being at the half way stage between Lederer and John Barrymore. I have pointed this out to Lederer. He didn't care for it.

Have you read *Of Mice and Men*? Just your dish. Just your length. Beatrice, as you probably know, has bought the dramatic rights. I'm in on it with her. One of the characters is an amiable and gigantic idiot, so tender that he has to fondle everything he likes and so clumsy that he eventually breaks their necks—mice, puppies, rabbits, tarts—whatever he happens to be petting at the moment. I tried to get Broun to take this part and he was very hurt.

I've forgotten what you look like. I guess that's a good break for you, at that.

The Prince Chap

P.S. Come to think of it, Helen would prefer a bottle of bourbon or scotch to a mere bouquet any day.

A. W.

To *MARGARET MITCHELL*

New York City
April 3, 1937

Dear Margaret Mitchell,

You're just goading me on to tell that story of the elevator. I wrote it years ago for *The New Yorker* and it was my first encounter with folklore. In that version the scene was an elegant Southern home with the scent of magnolias in the air and the crunch of wheels on gravel. It was a hearse that came by and the driver with the livid face took off his top hat and looked up at the window and said, "Room for one more." It was those words issuing from the selfsame face (but this time the face of the man operating the elevator) which, in a department store up North the following winter, led her to recoil in the nick of time.

I have since learned that that elevator has been crashing steadily since the late Eighties. It crashed at A. T. Stewart's in New York and the rescued girl was none other than Lucy C. Lillie. But you are too young to have known *Harper's Young People* when Mrs. Lillie was writing for it. So am I, for that matter, but I was the youngest of five and any kid knows best the books his older brothers left around the house.

More often than not there is a hearse, though I, too, have known the man to carry the coffin. There's always a hearse where, as it does periodically, the apparition visits the chaste precincts of Randolph-Macon. It is a hearse that's heard on the cobblestones at Dijon and the crash occurs afterwards at a hotel in Paris. In America the face is usually livid with a scar across it. As you get past the Rhine—the story has long had currency around Warsaw—the man is distinguished by a shock of scarlet hair, crowning a face the color of a fish's belly. Very pretty.

This past summer when you came roaring back into my quiet life, did I tell you my adventures with the legend of

[183]

Sherman's missing one fine house on his march to the sea because the family ingeniously succeeded in hiding it from him? I inquired about this in a broadcast a little more than a year ago and received volumes of assurance that the house stood near Chattanooga, Vicksburg and Atlanta, but suddenly from a most interesting source I got confirmation (once removed) from Sherman's own lips. Did I tell you about that? And even if I didn't, maybe you are a wee bit tired of William Tecumseh. You must tell Mr. Marsh [Margaret Mitchell's husband] of the bitter complaint I heard on the lips of Mrs. Lloyd Lewis. She said (with a snarl) that she had lost her husband in the Civil War.

A. Woollcott

To CYRIL CLEMENS

New York City
May 10, 1937

Dear Mr. Clemens:

I shall be very happy to receive the Mark Twain Medal and shall feel that I am in very good company.

After an examination of my credentials for a place in the Mark Twain Society, I can find only one item. Having always traveled light through this world, I still own, at fifty, only one object which I also owned when I was ten. That is my copy of *The Adventures of Tom Sawyer!*

With all good wishes,

Yours sincerely
Alexander Woollcott

To DR. GUSTAV ECKSTEIN
[See note on page 174.]

New York City
May 19, 1937

Dear Gus,

I expect to be at the island and visitable there by anyone proposing to convert it into one of the Canary Island group on the following dates:

May 28—31, inclusive
June 4—7, inclusive
June 18—21, inclusive

Elegant time in Canada. Plenty of exercise getting up to drink toasts to the King. General condition greatly improved. Lingering protests and portents from the alimentary tract. Sounds and signs of mutiny down there. Another yip out of that region and I'll give it something to worry about—a few Welsh rarebits and some strawberry shortcake.

Yesterday at two-thirty New York time frantic calls from Omaha where the Lunts had encountered a mayor who forbade their show unless they made some sixteen deletions from the text, which has since been referred to by some New York scrivener as "Idiot's Delete." Lynn had written a statement she wished to make to the public before the rise of the curtain but I denounced them both as poltroons not fit to be trusted with a play by Sherwood or anybody else if they didn't have the gumption not to play at all. This advice entranced them so they told the mayor to go to hell and he collapsed at once. The play was therefore given last night as written. I shall get the details by air mail. But you may have read all this in your funny little local newspaper.

Meanwhile, the Omaha *World Telegram*—a newspaper of which I know nothing beyond the fact that it once printed an editorial called "The Woollcott Menace"—has wired for permission to print the somewhat tedious and sententious broadcast I did last night. I refused, but offered to give them in its place a few opinions of my own on their mayor. That's the situation at present.

My love to your mother and "Big Gus" and Mrs. Wehner and "Wisdom Tooth."

A. W.

To SOPHIE ROSENBERGER

[Miss Rosenberger was Woollcott's teacher when he was in the second grade in public school in Kansas City.]

Bomoseen, Vt.
August 28, 1937

My dear Miss Rosenberger,
       Is this my Miss Smoot—the one who taught the first grade in the Franklin school when I matriculated there in 1892? I remember my Miss Smoot as a formidable woman who subjected me to my first public disgrace. And it was unmerited. At least I was innocent. "The woman tempted me." You remember when we were all made to sit at attention, each with his hands clasped in front of him on the desk. This was a way of keeping us out of mischief. Once Miss Smoot gave that order because she wanted to go out of the room. I never would have thought of relaxing if two little girls in the front row hadn't turned around and giggled at me. Then one of them thumbed her nose at me. I did not know the significance of this gesture but I felt that it called for a reply, so I unlocked my hands and was thumbing *my* nose just as Miss Smoot walked in the door. I was made to stand out in the hall for what seemed several years but I suppose was no more than half an hour. I remember my agony of apprehension that one of the grown-ups of twelve or thirteen from Aldine Place would pass up or

down the stairs at that time and report my outcast state at home.

Well, that was forty-five years ago and here is Miss Smoot taking baseball lessons in New York

Alexander W.

To FRANK SULLIVAN

Bomoseen, Vt.
September 1, 1937

Dear Frank,

Can you come up here some time this week and stay for a meal, a night, a week, or until October 20th, when the water will be shut off? At this time I can easily provide transportation. After September 9th, I shall still have a car but my chauffeur will have resumed his classical studies at Hamilton. I don't think you would enjoy having me drive you.

Alice Miller (with a small flock of satellites) is scheduled to arrive Wednesday, bringing (I believe) Dan Silberberg.

My piece on Jack Humphrey (very good) has gone in to *The New Yorker*. The reason I am telling all this to you is because I have decided I must start work today on a book and writing to you is as good a way as any of postponing parturition.

A. W.

P.S. I've ordered one of my ten privately bound two-volume editions of the Ackie Reader sent you. It will arrive shortly after the 10th.

A. W.

[*Woollcott's Second Reader* was published in November 1937. The nickname "Ackie" was also Woollcott's cable address.]

To LAURA E. RICHARDS

Bomoseen, Vt.
September 1, 1937

My dear friend,
          Yes—as you asked me on August 9th and here it is nearly a month later before I answer—I am still faithful but I see no prospect of my getting to Maine much before mid-November when you will be at Gardiner. For all I know, you may be there already but on the chance that you aren't, I am sending this to Indian Point. As I may have told you, I am in the throes of building me an all-year house here on the island, one fortified against the slings and arrows of a Vermont winter, and here I expect to make my base from now on, lingering this year until the end of December, but making one or two expeditions in October and November, including one that will take me to Mr. Tarkington's doorstep and yours.

I have sent for *A City of Bells* on your say-so, but have not so much as looked inside it yet. Indeed I have been reading only what I had to in preparation for *Woollcott's Second Reader* which is to come out in November and on which I am even now getting in my last licks. Some of the things in it you will like.

Earlier in the summer I did look inside *Harry in England* and, even though it was meant for the very young, found myself reading it all through with interest and pleasure. It was a happy idea to have Reginald Birch illustrate it.

Two or three years ago he came to call upon me, a figure of somewhat frayed elegance, very dapper, charming and gallant. On the fiftieth anniversary of *Fauntleroy*—it came out the same year as *Huckleberry Finn* which served as a happy corrective —I mentioned in a broadcast how all the little boys in America had to be rigged out by their mothers in Fauntleroy get-up. All except me, who had to importune my parents for a Fauntleroy costume. At the first sight of my huge bullet head with its five cowlicks rising out of that lace collar, the whole family went into gales of inconsiderate mirth and promptly ordered the entire regalia given to the laundress's little pickaninny. Whereupon, hearing this or hearing about it, Birch did a water-color sketch of Fauntleroy at Dorincourt Castle, golden curls, velvet pantaloons, huge mastiff and all, with only one variation—my face in the place of Cedric Erroll's. The effect was singularly sickening.

I shall be free in the Fall to come moseying along the road to Maine because, beginning on October 1st, I intend to blow myself to a year off—a year free, that is, from long-term contracts, radio programs, magazine commitments and the like. I expect to twiddle my thumbs and, in the good, old medieval phrase, make my soul. If, as I expect, I also write a book, I hope it will be a good one.

I am taking a huge interest in this house which is the first one I have ever had. I was two when my folks started their migrations and what with this and that I've never settled anywhere since. The house is stone with many fireplaces and bathrooms of such marble elegance that they are already the scandal of Vermont. I was in the midst of selecting a name for it when with one horrid accord all my friends started calling it Glamis, for reasons which I fear will not escape you.

My salutations to your husband and your daughter.

Old Faithful

To DR. GUSTAV ECKSTEIN

Bomoseen, Vt.
September 10, 1937

Dear Gus,

A most extraordinary thing has happened. Frank Lloyd Wright, filled with a noble grief because I had let Hennessey do my house for me instead of getting him to do it, sent me a letter of forgiveness together with a notice that he was at least sending me something to put in the house. In due course I began to get notices all along the line that a valuable package would be awaiting me at the express office in Castleton. It turned out to be a set of Hiroshige prints—fifty-three of them, starting at dawn from the bridge in Yedo and ending up at Kyoto in the sunset. Frank writes me thus: "When the series of views was made by Hiroshige, eternity was now. I think it is destined to endure longest of any graphic masterpiece whatsoever. In it a unique civilization lives for posterity. But for this record by a native son, that civilization will have vanished before long."

Frank says that there are only seven complete sets in the world and this is one of them. Such a gift embarrasses me. It seems to me this set should be given at once to someone equipped to enjoy it. Shall I leave it to you in my will?

Even now, even before the sugar-maples have begun to turn, each day is enchanting. Do you remember in *Tennessee's Pardner* how the newspaper accounts of the hanging told what the prisoner wore, what he had had for breakfast, and who was there to see him hanged? But none of them mentioned "the blessed amity of earth and air and sky."

Today there came a letter from Thornton Wilder, full of his adventures backstage at the Comédie Française and visiting Gertrude Stein in the Ain. Then he picked up Sibyl Colefax and carried her off to Salzburg for four of the Toscanini concerts. Much sitting around beer gardens with Erich Maria Remarque. Nightly dinners at Schloss Leopoldskron with Max Reinhardt and Fräulein Timmig. Great proposals that I join him for Christmas in Zurich. But I would rather be here. I would rather be here than anywhere in the world. I was never so sure of anything as that I want to lie back for a year and be quiet.

I suppose you will be coming here when it best fits in. I think if you can stay only one week I would like best to have you see that first or second week in October when the coloring is likely to be its most brilliant. Yet if you came earlier, you might find Noel here (he and Neysa come on the 22nd) or young Alsop returning. But then Anne Parrish is coming some time, too, and Percy Saunders will be driving over from Clinton and none of these would entertain you as much as the pup would. He's as big as Pip now and his four feet, which have thoughtfully anticipated the size he is going to be, make his tread sound like that of the stone-footed gods in Dunsany's *The Gods of the Mountain*. The other evening he patiently chewed his way through an electric insulation. His immediate reaction to the shock was to send out a whirling spray of urine and to fill the island air with banshee wails that could be heard as far as Rutland.

My furniture came last night at sundown. Odds and ends that I have picked up all over the world without ever meaning to at all. This will be their last resting-place as far as I am concerned. I may not stay but they will. They came across the lake after the wind had gone down with the sun—came on trip after trip of a barge made by putting a raft on three rowboats lashed together. Tomorrow and next day the floors will be waxed and all this duffle slips into place and by the end of next week your room will be ready. Are you bringing Pawley?

Alexander W.

To *FRANK LLOYD WRIGHT*
[Woollcott was an admirer of Mr. Wright, the leading exponent of modern architecture in America.]

Bomoseen, Vt.
September 15, 1937

Dear Frank,
    I don't know quite what to say, which is not a characteristic difficulty. It isn't enough to call the Hiroshige portfolio a handsome gift. I'd say that of a bowl of chrysanthemums or

[191]

a case of wine, which would both be gone before Christmas. So I'll just say that it is a gift drawn to the scale of the giver and let it go at that.

Since the prints came, I have already made the journey three times. I hope to make it next under the guidance of Dr. Gustav Eckstein of Cincinnati. He's the minute and astonishing teacher from the medical school there, who once wrote a play called *Hokusai* and is best known, I suppose, as the biographer of Noguchi. Are you ever in Cincinnati? You must go to his laboratory where a tribe of canaries has the run of the place. I wonder if you have read his book *Canary*. On the chance that you have not, I shall send it to you this week. Eckstein will be coming this way for a visit during one of these Fall weeks when the Vermont hills are in their glory.

The house has turned out to be one I would show you without embarrassment. It is a one-story house of stone, built on two levels and, like one I once saw in Wisconsin, running along the crest of a hill like a vine. It was built by an amateur—a crony of mine who engaged no architect and no contractor. The result is astonishingly right—right for me and right for its setting.

I was born in a frame house with eighty-five rooms in it. This belonged to my grandfather and at the time when I was born it hadn't been painted since before the Civil War. Come to think of it, it hasn't been painted yet. Vines kept it from falling apart—a protective outer coat of white-grape and trumpet and wistaria and crimson rambler. For a long time it was the only home I knew. I was homesick for its sloping green when as a kid I was exiled to the dust of a hot Kansas City street. All through my school days I hurried to it for every vacation. The returns which remain most vivid to this native were the ones which each year began the Christmas holidays. I would reach the station five miles away in the early dark of a winter afternoon, hire a smelly hack and drive home over the rutty roads. It would be too dark to see where I was at any time, but I would know by the hoof-beats on the bridges. Finally there was the last bridge but one and I would know that in another moment, through the leafless trees, I could see the house itself—the twelve French windows down the front all lamplit because the tribe would be homing for Christmas. Not since then have I had any feeling of attachment for any place until I found this island. I get something of the same sweet sense of homecoming when, two miles down the road, I take the left turn at Castleton Corners.

I began coming here seventeen years ago and have come more and more ever since. At last I realized that I was spending more time here than anywhere else, so it seemed sensible to make this my base instead of New York. Hence the house and Eckstein coming to see me and the Hiroshige prints to be kept in a place of honor.

I have decided that I can't thank you enough for the prints so I shan't even try. My obeisances to your wife.

A. Woollcott

To D. G. KENNEDY

Bomoseen, Vt.
September 15, 1937

Dear Gerry,

You're in some confusion of mind. It wasn't I who thought you ought to go and get a writing job; that was you. I was the one who thought that you might better practice law and write on the side—write something every day on the side —write something every day on the side for a year or two without necessarily any thought of its ever being printed. I have a distinct feeling about people who think of writing. It is this. If anything can stop them it is probably no great loss.

I'll be here without a break until the 20th of October and

then again all during the early part of November. If your present occupation leaves you any leisure days you will, of course, always be welcome here. This might go without saying and won't be said again.

  Al [Getman] is coming with Louise for the week-end of the 25th and 6th and then coming back again alone for the first week in October.

A. W.

To DR. GUSTAV ECKSTEIN

New York City
October 31, 1937

Dear Gus,

  On Thursday I was lunching with Alice Longworth in her suite at the Ritz when the desk phoned up that there was a telegram for me. It was your affable message from Cleveland. The only theory I can construct is that you had forgotten I was at the St. Regis and guessed I might be at the Ritz. It is a hotel I have never stopped at and seldom frequent; it was the first time I had lunched there in seven years. The telegram came during the hour I was there. Seen from your end, there may be some simple explanation of this, but on the face of it it looks like an instance of clairvoyance which might be filed for reference with the extrasensory boys at Duke University.

  I speak my piece for La Guardia early this evening and will be lunching on the island tomorrow. I am having Dick Wood send you two photographs he took while you and Kit [Cornell] were there. I was glad to hear that you had dropped off and visited the Saunders' household at Clinton. I will be expecting to hear how you found Ruth Gordon on and off.

A. W.

To DR. GUSTAV ECKSTEIN

Bomoseen, Vt.
November 22, 1937

Dear Gus,

I grieve for you about Polly [a macaw]. You will miss her beyond all telling.

On the chance that you may be eastward bound, I write to report that I will be at the St. Regis in New York from the 30th until the 4th—with one day's absence, the 2nd—when Jack Humphrey and one of the Seeing Eye dogs and I are to do our act at the old Academy of Music, the shabby cavern where I heard my first symphony (Fritz Scheel conducting the "Pathétique") and my first opera (*Faust* with Pol Plançon) and from a seat in the vertiginous topmost gallery caught my first glimpse of Mrs. Fiske. The play was *Mary of Magdala* and she wore high heels and stood on her toes because she was unhappy about being short.

I'm to eat my Thanksgiving turkey at Kennebunkport along with Booth Tarkington and Kenneth Roberts, who linger on the Maine coast long after every other house in their colony has been shut up until another June. And even as I set all this chatter down I keep thinking of Polly and remembering that Millay poem which begins "Listen, children. Your father is dead" and ends with the lines:

Life must go on.
I forget just why.

I can't believe I've known you less than thirteen months. It's ridiculous.

A. W.

To CHARLES LEDERER

Bomoseen, Vt.
December 6, 1937

Dear Master Charles:

I started to write this on a typewriter but these old fingers have lost their cunning. There are three things I hope you will do for me.

(1) Remember that you are to sign up Harpo and Irving [Berlin] for a radio benefit to be held some time in March or April. What I want to do is to nail them and the Lunts and Kit Cornell now. Then I can go ahead with my negotiations and round up the rest of the cast as the time approaches.

(2) What is the correct name and present address of that Riskin or Ryskin or whatever whom you brought to Gracie Square for a little gaming and to whom, on the eve of his sailing with you, I sent a charming check which he never cashed and may never have received?

(3) I have an idea I wish you would present to Harpo—but only if you yourself are sympathetic with it. It is based on my belief that we who know him have seen an even better show than the public has ever had a chance to see. I wish that just once he could appear in a picture all by himself and governed only by *his* taste and *his* imagination. As this would present many difficulties both personal, professional and financial, it is my idea that he should do a short—or three shorts—just for the hell of it. Just for himself, or for that matter, just for me. I can envisage it as a combination of Benchley and a Disney symphony. You or Benchley or MacArthur or all three could write it for him. Why not?

(4) Are you still interested in trying out that play with me? I advise you to answer candidly.

A. W.

To LAURA E. RICHARDS

Bomoseen, Vt.
December 6, 1937

My dear Mrs. Richards,
A wily dealer in second-hand books has just filled up the gaps which yawned in my old file of *St. Nicholas*, with the result that last evening when I should have been at work on a piece for *The Atlantic*, I sat reading a delightful serial called "When I Was Your Age," which escaped me at the time of its publication because I was brought up on *Harper's Young People*. I cannot begin to tell you how I enjoyed the picture of Laura reading poetry to old Margaret in the feather room.

Just about the time you were committing that account to paper, I was writing my first letter. Or rather dictating it. It was addressed to one Celeste, who was my first love. She never answered it but when next she came to see me (forty-two years later) she had it with her. It had been written on July 3, 1891, and contained, among other items, the vainglorious announcement that I had sixteen torpedoes, twenty-three cents and a verbena. Its other details brought suddenly to life a forgotten and uneventful day long ago in the house where I grew up and a resurrection so abrupt and so accidental had an effect on me as disquieting as if some dislocation had turned back time itself. The process of memory is pleasurable for me but here were things which I had altogether forgotten so that they came back like ghosts and left me feeling haunted.

I treasured the Binyon verses.

You won't hear from me at Christmas because I've sworn off Christmas. How about some sherry for your birthday?

My salutations to the Skipper and the resident daughter. I wish I lived in Gardiner.

Alexander W.

To FRANK SULLIVAN

Chicago, Ill.
December 17, 1937

Dear Frank,

  While you (or so they tell me) are being rheumy in Saratoga Springs, I am being weak-minded in Chicago—and will still be here on Christmas Day. I won't get back to the island until after the first of the year.

  I thought you would like to hear about the telegram just sent by the printers on a small-town Connecticut newspaper to the foreman of the composing room on the occasion of his marriage. It consisted of one word—"Stet."

A. Woollcott

VII

1938-1939

To PAUL BONNER

Philadelphia, Pa.
January 7, 1938

My dear Paul:
My first talk with your BBC men proved to be most unfortunate. In the first place, your letter did not come until the next day. A long distance telephone call woke me out of a sound sleep and an acutely English voice announced the speaker as representing the British Broadcasting Company. Being half asleep and very cross, I was immediately suspicious and puzzled to decide whether it was Benchley or Charlie Lederer calling. So when he said, "Mr. Woollcott, I represent the British Broadcasting Company in America," I answered, "And I am Marie of Rumania." Well, after that part, he told me he was arranging to have President Roosevelt and Mr. Hoover broadcast to England. I promptly suggested that twenty minutes of Mr. Hoover was a better reason for going to war than England had been known to act on in the past. Much discouraged, he then said he wanted me to broadcast on the future of American literature. I told him it had none; and more discouraged than ever, he asked when I would be in New York. I said I did not know, which is God's own truth. It is most unfortunate and due

to the fact that I was taken unawares and half asleep. There were some things said about his calling the next day, but as my telephone was busy with long distance calls from New York for more than three hours, I don't even know whether he tried or not. It is too bad because this is really something I would like to do. Of course I would not like to broadcast about the future of American literature but I would like to do them a good job in some field where I really was interested.

My love to Lilly. It may or may not have escaped your attention that I am acting again. In my opinion and in the opinion of all whose judgment I respect, the play [*Wine of Choice*] is in deplorable need of minor revision. The trouble is that we are playing to capacity and the audience are unmistakably enraptured.

Next week, Pittsburgh. Address me, if needs must, at the William Penn Hotel.

David Garrick

To *BEATRICE KAUFMAN*

Pittsburgh, Pa.
January 13, 1938

Dear Lamb Girl:
It is my fond expectation that I will be lodged all next week at the Gotham—much too busy to give you a present on your birthday or to receive one on mine. I might, however, have time for a kiss and in any event I enclose the improbable sum which Moss Hart tells me that even your aching ear did not prevent your reminding me of. I shall never cease to be surprised at the actuarial minds which spring from the clothing business.

It is only fair to add that I intend to revisit Beatrice-on-toast soon and often. You ought to have some kind of flag by which Ferber and others could be warned, just the way a passer-by at Buckingham Palace can tell at a glance whether the King is in town.

I must run now. Yours fondly

Mint Sauce

To THORNTON WILDER

Baltimore, Md.
January 28, 1938

Dear Thornton,

I understand. Good for you! Stick to your guns. But not to the last ditch. After all, what matters most is that the play [*Our Town*], as published, be the way you would have it. That is the form in which it will be read in years to come and from which, in years to come, revivals will be made. Too often playwrights have allowed themselves to be bustled into revision because a trial audience had been restive under some uncertain and half-articulated performance of the scenes as he had written them. Yet this, too, is true: all the great plays that we know—certainly *The Trojan Women* and *Hamlet* and perhaps even *The Cherry Orchard*—are not the plays as they were written, but the prompt-books after the actors had messed them up a bit. And because a play is and must always be a corporate endeavor in which one factor—the audience—changes with every sunset, the picking up of a certain alloy somehow turns what may be the pure gold of the original script into something that can be called—and used as—currency.

So here I am, counselling you to go in both directions at once. I might better say nothing and trust to that hard core you have—rock-ribbed and ancient as the sun—upon which the Jed Harrises and the Frank Cravens and the haute noblesse of Boston will break like spray.

However, I merely meant to make this letter a response to one sentence in yours. You spoke of our forgetting these unrests in Vermont. I must beg of you to meet me there some time for a week or so between now and Thanksgiving. Promise? And I am not entitled to be thought of as experiencing any unrest at all. I am engaged in a continuous frolic, with considerable sympathy for the author and director and the superb company, but with my own vitals unaffected. You will now say that I am always overcareful to keep my vitals uninvolved and that, I will admit, is almost true. Not quite, but almost. It is why I am still alive. Of course, that may be a pity.

From all reports, a broadcast I did on *A Doll's House* had the effect of adrenalin. It now remains to be seen how lasting the effect will be. Come to think of it, it can't be lasting. It can have been only a firm push in the right direction. The audience which would relish that play as now acted is, I am completely sure, enormous. Perhaps now it will get to it in time. I think it will.

This Behrman comedy [*Wine of Choice*] reopened here last night at Ford's Theatre. Pretty good performance. Very good audience. Rave notice, I understand, in the *Sun*. Much too good, according to Shumlin. I'm sure he's right.

Incidentally, you can have the island all to yourself right now if you want it. It is as silent and as snow-clad as a birthday cake. You can drive right from the mainland to my front door. Just wire Bill Eagan that you are coming. He and Alice will take care of you and there are now—God help me!—four black dogs to go walkee with you.

Coquelin

To REBECCA WEST

New York City
February 21, 1938

Dear Rebecca,

This letter is about a year late. I always have so many things I want to tell you that instead of dashing off a note to you now and then, I wait, in my incurable optimism, for some quiet time. There is none.

Let me begin by acknowledging that book review by Anthony [West—Miss West's son], which impressed me greatly and reminded me afresh how helpful it is for a journalist, in writing, to know what he's talking about. What I cannot possibly account for is the glow of avuncular pride I took in the piece. It would be difficult for me to construct any explanation that would justify my feeling avuncular about Anthony, but there it is. I do and that's that.

The review and the note with it trailed me to Chicago where, on Christmas Eve, to my own surprise—I'd gone out to Chicago about something else—I was rehearsing in a play. It is difficult for me now to recall just why I went into it but I did so lightheartedly in the not unreasonable conviction that the whole thing would blow up in two or three weeks. Instead, it has gone on and on, gathering strength as it went.

I am writing this as best I may on the train from Boston to New York. It is difficult for me to continue any longer pretending that we are not going to open there tomorrow night. If you and Henry [Andrews—Miss West's husband] should, after all, make that threatened visit to New York before April 10th, you could find me depicting like mad at the Guild Theatre, because with its subscription season, it takes that long for a Guild play to flop in New York.

I enclose documentary evidence of the mischief I've been up to. I also enclose a piece of Mrs. [Dorothy] Parker's which I think it probable you have already seen but which I send along just the same on the chance that you haven't. It is the first thing she's printed in *The New Yorker* in several years and as good a piece as she ever wrote. Certainly it comes nearer to telling the reader exactly what she is like than anything else she ever wrote.

I have enjoyed this barnstorming immensely. I wish we could go on right across country without lingering in the one city which is no treat to me. I think I must wind up by telling you the story of Leslie Banks' encounter with Jane Cowl. It was during that heady interlude when Jane, having got hold of a bank-roll, was going in for repertory in a big way. Banks was one of the many actors she sent for and at the end of a long day gave him a few minutes of her exhausted attention, explaining that they would all be a simple troupe of players together. She herself might be a stellar one night and play merely a bit the next. "Yes, Mr. Banks," she said. "On Monday I may be Lady Macbeth and Tuesday carry on a tray."

Leslie went home considerably impressed but Mrs. Banks proved more skeptical. "You watch out for that woman," she said. "I know that tray. It's got John the Baptist's head on it."

When shall we three meet again?

P.S. I am wondering if it is indelicate to report a story I heard only last night over my midnight cocoa at the Ritz in Boston. Mrs. Banks was telling me about a week-end hostess in England who recently felt alarmed when a too easily impressed young girl was led out into the moonlight by H.G. [Wells]. Later she went to the girl's room. "See here, my dear," she said, "if you're not careful you'll find yourself the shape of things to come."

P.P.S. Ten days later. This letter has hung fire because I wanted a moment to add another postscript.

When I was last in London, I felt out several people on a mystery to which I have never got the answer. It seems to me fantastic that the *Notable British Trials* should keep on publishing case after case and leave out the most notable piece of all—the Archer-Shee case. The only data I have on it except from memory is contained in a few pages of the first volume of the *Life of Lord Carson* by that dreadful young Marjoribanks who, as you may recall, shot himself when that work was but partly completed. There ought to be a book on the case. It could be a short one. I wish to God you would do it. If you won't and no one else will, I'll come over and do it—unless it turns out that there is none because, for some reason I cannot understand, the documentary evidence is missing. What we would have to have would be Carson's examination of the witnesses when, at long last, after the issue had been got into court on a petition of right, the witnesses against the boy were actually subjected to intelligent questioning. They were none of them in any sense hostile—merely stupid and stubborn. The moment they were shrewdly questioned, the whole case fell to pieces. Isaacs threw up the case for the Admiralty and the boy walked out of court completely exonerated only to be killed four years later for his King and Country.

    I once did a broadcast about the case and people still talk about it. The only reason it is so much on my mind now is that there is no better way of illustrating what it is we in America hope will survive in Europe. If you really want the perfect picture of the Germans, you have only to say that the Archer-Shee case simply couldn't have happened there.

    I started to write you last September when we finally assembled and shook down all the tentative ingredients for my second *Reader* and I decided after all that, separated from the Low cartoons, the magnificent Lynx word-portraits needed some sort of connective tissue or preface or container to give them body.

    Next I was going to write you about H.G.'s visit, some odds and ends of which I greatly enjoyed. We were both week-end guests at the [Theodore] Roosevelts down at Oyster Bay and enjoyed together a dinner to Dr. Hu Shih, who is, I assure you, quite a boy. A car was sent for H.G. and he was instructed to pick me up. We drove out together and I had a very good time with him. He had just been lecturing in Boston. As I was due to speak there the night before Thanksgiving at the Harvard Club, I asked him as one road star to another how he had found the Boston audiences. After some dejected thought, he answered plaintively, "The people of Boston lack the faculty of attention." Which led me to surmise he had not wowed the haute noblesse of Beacon Street.

The book-fair was in progress when he sailed and, on his last day, the *Times* printed a long interview with him in which he spoke angrily of the puzzling American appetite for large books. It was illustrated by a two-column photograph of Wells taken at the book-fair with an explanatory caption that it *was* Mr. Wells, photographed in the act of examining a display of his own works. To my delight, the photograph clearly revealed that what he was really examining was *Woollcott's Second Reader*—which is a very large book, indeed. Incidentally, if you would like a *Woollcott's Second Reader* let me know and I'll send you a copy. Everyone likes it better than my first one, but it isn't as good.

Have you any way of inquiring about the accessibility of the facts, the existence of stenographic notes, the verbatim report of Carson's arguments, etc. etc.?

P.P.P.S. I have an impression from a fairly faithful reading of Dorothy Thompson in the *Herald Tribune* that she may sail at any minute in order to strangle Neville Chamberlain with her own hands. Would this be a good thing?

A. W.

To W. GRAHAM ROBERTSON

New York City
March, 1938

Dear Graham,

Since last I wrote you, I have accumulated so many things to tell you about that it would really be a saving of time and strength if, instead of writing, I just jumped on a boat and came over in what is known—to put it mildly—as the flesh.

At the moment, however, I am otherwise engaged, as I can most compactly explain by the clipping hereto attached [announcement of the *Wine of Choice* engagement]. So instead, I am arranging to send over two legates who will report to you by word of mouth in a duet—the Lunts, who, on May 16th or thereabouts, will open in London, probably at the Lyric, in *Amphytryon 38,* an enchanting and iridescent piece which shows them at the top of their bent. Everyone is puzzled that they should be going to London to play this at this time—everyone, that is, except me. I know that they are really going over so that you can see it. This may sound bizarre and extravagant, but it's the God's truth.

The reason why such an excursion mystifies the local wiseacres can be traced to the prodigious success they are now enjoying—if that's the right participle for their present excruciating agony—in *The Sea Gull.* It opened on Thursday night of last week in Baltimore with the audience demanding twenty-eight curtain calls and then going home only by request. I saw a single rehearsal of it—the first complete run-through of the play. I have never seen anything better anywhere. They have never done anything so good. It can never be so good again, I expect, as it was in that stripped, unadorned, hair-trigger performance.

Just now they are playing a preliminary week in Boston and, though Alfred succeeded in sounding very depressed over it on the telephone this morning, this viewpoint was difficult to maintain in the light of the fact that every seat for the entire week has been sold. They come here Monday for five weeks, shut up shop, set sail and play *Amphytryon* for you in May—that is, unless you go to war or something. However, if I may judge from this week's headlines, the English seem at the moment disposed to exercise their national genius for flying into a great calm.

By the time the Lunts' curtain rises in London I shall be back once more upon my island. As you know, each glimpse of your place in Surrey reminded me that I must get me a place just like it. When this impulse finally found expression in stone and plaster, I could not help laughing because it is so little like it. I sometimes allow myself to think that some day when the ferryman comes across from the mainland he will have you as a passenger, but I am not sure that I could look you in the eye when you discover that in my primitive and rustic retreat I have four marble bathrooms and enough electric light to put your eye out.

The livestock there has been augmented by a Briard. He arrived last summer at the age of nine months. He was formally named Banco and on the first day he promptly fell off the pier into twenty feet of water. Now, for reasons which escape me, he is known as Mugwump and is roughly the size of the National Gallery.

The lady who gave him to me issued full instructions as to how one must treat and deserve a Briard. These included a stern injunction never to strike him. As I had no intention of striking him, I noticed this rule only in passing. But as summer turned to winter and the first snow made the island look like a birthday cake, it began to irk me when the Mugwump, after a morning romp, would come in with his whiskers covered with snow and nuzzle up to me while I was at breakfast. I began by pushing him gently away and, as this did not work, ventured,

[208]

despite all my instructions, to strike him. At this he was obviously entertained and it reached the point where I doubled up both fists and hit him in the face with all my might. This so entranced him he got right onto my breakfast tray. You would like Mugwump.

Dear Graham, I think of you often and with great affection and before you know it I shall come up the road and knock at your door.

Alexander Woollcott

To *WALTER LIPPMANN*

Bomoseen, Vt.
April, 1938

Dear Walter,

As I told you when I saw you in Washington earlier this month, I feel strongly that Ralph Hayes would write the most valuable and the most illuminating biography of Newton Baker that could be written at this time. His would be a labor of love. It would be offered as such. It would be read as such.

And as such, it would be a none-the-less useful source book for that "ideal detached historian" who may turn up later—who will indeed inevitably turn up if, in the long retrospect, the World War impresses those who come after us as having been important. How important it will seem fifty years from now depends entirely, I suppose, on what happens between now and then.

In the meantime, however, there is a book to be written by one who knew Mr. Baker as Nicolay and Hay knew Lincoln. I have never heard it suggested that their testimony was considered without value from the mere circumstance that they had known well and loved well the man they were writing about.

Another thing. Baker's own letters will tell the story—tell it without impairment from the emotional bias of the man editing them. I should be sorry to see these wait upon the leisurely judgment of posterity. I want to read them myself and I should relish the satisfaction of seeing them read by those who in his own lifetime never realized what manner of man Newton Baker was.

Alexander Woollcott

To *LAURA E. RICHARDS*

Bomoseen, Vt.
May 4, 1938

Dear Mrs. Richards,

Here I am back at my headquarters after a vagrant winter of unpremeditated wanderings. There I was traipsing around the country in a play, vastly enjoying my adventures, but considerably abashed now to realize how many things I let slip in my absorption. Your birthday was one of the many things I forgot all about.

It was in mid-December that I made a hurried trip to Chicago, picking the day when the new ice had already formed such a sheet over the lake that in another twenty-four hours we could neither have walked across nor gone by boat. I took duds enough for a three-day stay and was gone four months. My life in a nut-shell.

Just before I left I had been engrossed in reading "When I Was Your Age" in the 1892 *St. Nicholas*. I am trying now to recall whether I wrote you about this as I meant to.

In the course of my fitful researches into the life of the late Justice Holmes, I have been pausing to contemplate that interesting creature who was his Uncle Johnny. There has come to my hand a volume of Uncle Johnny's letters, published in the Nineties by the Cambridge Historical Society. They were edited by Alice Longfellow. What was she to Henry? I have been entranced by the opening sentence of her introduction to the volume. I wonder if it will entertain you as it does me. It begins this way: "Mr. John Holmes, or John Holmes, as he was always affectionately called." I cannot begin to tell you how I have enjoyed this flighty bit. I tried sundry paraphrases in the vain hope of sharpening the flavor. "Mr. John Holmes, or John Holmes, as he was always called in moments of abandon."

I should be glad to hear that you have forgiven me in the matter of the birthday or at least suspended judgment on my promise to make up for it next year. My plans for the next six months are necessarily vague. I shall probably be right here most of the time and, in any event, it will always be my best address.

A. Woollcott

To MRS. THEODORE ROOSEVELT, JR.

Bomoseen, Vt.
June 30, 1938

Dear Mistress Quickly:

Here's an odd coincidence. Yesterday morning, waking too early, and groping for something to read, I took down an early collection of Pearson's murder sketches and reread—for the first time in many years—the dimly remembered details of the Webster case. Later in the day there arrived by post the record of the trial.

However, what is on my mind to write you about is that lovely house of yours. My thoughts have revisited it so often that I think of many of its rooms as rooms I already know well.

At first—in telling someone about it—I tried summing it up as the final and most satisfying answer to the whole tribe of

[211]

decorators. To be any good, a house must be as self-sprung as a beard. Yours, I said, was as indisputably yours as your toothbrush.

But that really doesn't tell the story. It is so clearly a part of this house's quality and secret that all the family had hands in the making of it. For instance, so much of its color and character derives from what Ted has done and is. Then Cornelius busy lighting up the innards of goddesses and Grace being at such pains to marry an architect. But you must know a hundred instances for one that I know.

An analogy haunts me. All the Du Maurier manuscripts are in the Morgan Library. Affixed to one of them—*Peter Ibbetson,* perhaps—is an attestation that it is all in his own handwriting except for one passage, to the transcription of which his wife and all his children lent their hands, this as a ceremony of propitiation to their household gods.

Well there you are. I haven't really said my say because if I really set down here all the elements which, in my guess, had blessed this work of your hands, I would have to use such words as "love" and "goodness" and our generation has lost the trick of using such words without self-consciousness.

I declare, Mistress Q, that, from sheer force of habit, I've let this letter turn into a review of your work for all the world as though you'd written a new play. Yet why not? It's as authentic an art. And your example of it is certainly a cut above any new play I've seen in recent years—except *Our Town,* perhaps. Yes, except *Our Town.*

From all of which you might deduce that I hold you in great admiration. I might as well say so and get it over with.

The island is at its best. Alice Miller and Old Man Hennessey arrive today, the Iveses, I think, tomorrow, and the Kaufmans next week.

A bientôt
Wackford Squeers

To NOEL COWARD

Bomoseen, Vt.
August 1, 1938

Lamb of God:

Ever since you paused in Albuquerque on a day in March and wired me some of the verys which you had torn bleeding from the bosom of your memoirs, I have had no word of you—no word from you, none about you.

I am sending this word of affection and inquiry and am moved to do so by the notion that you might be susceptible to a suggestion that you come over and sample life on the island. I will be here until October and then intermittently through October while I make brief angry visits to New York for broadcasting purposes. The island is loveliest in October, gayest in August. In the latter part of August, Neysa and the Lunts and God knows who else will be here. I am glad Neysa is coming back. She was here in July and left a trifle the worse for wear. In one ill-starred badminton game, I was her zealous but unwieldy partner. In one behemothian lunge at a quill, my racket struck Neysa instead—hitting her on the head and laying her out stiffer than a plank. After she had been revived and the game resumed, I flung myself into the contest with all the old ardor, leaping about like a well-nourished gazelle and coming down with all my weight, such as it is, on the little lady's foot. Later I upset her out of the canoe into the cool, sweet waters of the lake. But only once. So she left in good humor and will be back on these shores on the 21st inst.

I have spoken of August and October. But September's a good month, too.

Anyway, write me and tell me how you are. And how Jeff [Amherst], whom I love, is. Come to think of it, I'd rather have Jeff come over to the island than you. So please send this letter on to him without reading it. And don't think I'll listen to any of this nonsense about your both coming. I can't have this pine-scented nook crawling with Englishmen.

My obeisances to Lady Vi.

A. Woollcott

To LAURA E. RICHARDS

Bomoseen, Vt.
November 29, 1938

My dear friend,

I am up to all manner of minor mischief, going one place to have a tooth pulled and another place to christen a baby and another place to do a broadcast. I have even resumed, rather awkwardly at first, the trade of writing, which I had put aside for nearly two years.

Speaking of broadcasts, I am in something of a dither because I have been asked to broadcast to the British Isles on the day after Christmas. That is Boxing Day, when the lords of the BBC assure me all England listens. This was a surprise to me because I had always understood that by nightfall on Boxing Day all England was practically unconscious. I shall have an orchestra and a quartet with me and I am going to tell them about Stephen Foster—tell them what manner of man it was who wrote so many of the songs they've known all their lives and how he died alone and in despair in a charity ward and how now, after many years, his memory is held dear throughout the land. I want to do the broadcast in the spirit of that dedication those two actors wrote who edited the First Folio: "to keepe the memory of so worthy a Friend, & Fellow alive, as was our SHAKESPEARE."

I've run across another story about Alice Longfellow that I think will amuse you. I'll come up and tell it to you some day. Is Grave Alice still living, do you happen to know, and whatever became of Laughing Allegra?

Old Faithful

To ROBERT MAYNARD HUTCHINS
[President of the University of Chicago.]

New York City
December 19, 1938

Dear Bob,

Yesterday when I read the report of your doings in the Stock Exchange matter, I was minded to send this telegram: "God bless you. Letter follows." But the evening became filled with the task of helping the sorely beset Wilder get tight at the Copley-Plaza. The new Academician—you may have noted that he has just succeeded to the chair left vacant by the belated death of Owen Wister, and all I have to say is, "What is this country coming to?"—the new Academician is having his troubles with the Boston try-out of his new play, a fine old-style farce rendered depressing to my notion by a humorless performance. So I was busy comforting him with strong drinks and the telegram never got written. Thus the letter arrives unheralded.

I have been meaning to write you ever since your piece in *The Saturday Evening Post* about football and the universities. I wanted to tell you then something that you may not yourself know—that you have reached that felicity in writing marked by the fact that your pieces sound like you, creating by the printed word the illusion that you are actually present and saying your say. This is all a writer can ask. He is not entitled to ask for more than this.

About my old project to come out and give some lectures on journalism at the University, is your capacity for candor equal to the task of letting me know whether this is something you would warmly like to have happen or something you merely wouldn't object to? I have in mind five or six lectures, for a small or large group as you prefer, and as many conference hours as you wanted. It occurs to me that this is something I might manage somewhere between the 20th of

January and the 10th of March or, perhaps better still, during the month of May. Will you think about it and let me know into how brief a time the visitation could be satisfactorily compressed—three weeks? a month? six weeks?—what form it should take and how much it would pay?

If you can also find time to tell me how long you yourself are going to stay at the University and whether your present wife is speaking to me, it would help me in making up what I sometimes effusively call my mind.

Alexander W.

P.S. And a Merry Xmas.

A. W.

To *BURNS MANTLE*

[In addition to editing his yearly anthologies, *Best Plays*, Mr. Mantle was the dramatic critic of the New York *Daily News*.]

Bomoseen, Vt.
February 21, 1939

Dear Burns,

I have passed your card of admission on to Joan Woollcott and I thank you for your trouble. It was just thirty years ago this spring that I came down to the *Times* office armed with a letter of introduction which Samuel Hopkins Adams had written to [Carr] Van Anda, with whom, by the way, I had lunch just the other day. I cannot see that he has altered in any particular in those thirty years.

The *Times* fought me off until September so that I had to get a job in the Chemical National Bank to sustain life in me while I was making my weekly calls on the *Times* office.

I hope I should hesitate to try to palm Joan off on a newspaper just because she was my niece but I do feel a strong twinge of avuncular interest and as far as I can judge she has a great deal more stuff than I had at the same age. Certainly she's much more masculine than I was.

Yours sincerely,
A. W.

To *HAROLD K. GUINZBURG*

Bomoseen, Vt.
February 22, 1939

Dear David,

I have just received the following letter from the chambers of Mr. Justice Frankfurter:

Dear Binkie,

The Archer-Shee papers should be made accessible to students of law and of the ways of man to man, and by Alec Woollcott.

Respectfully & warmly,
F.F.

This still leaves me in some doubt as to how to proceed if at all. It was Hamish Hamilton who spoke of publishing them in England. A couple of weeks ago I sent him *The Atlantic* article and could follow it now by news that I had returned the papers to the family, that the family might be addressed as follows, and that you would be interested to take over the English sheets or whatever the term is. I hesitate to do this for two reasons. The first derives from the fact that, once I have returned the documents it may be difficult for me to make them accessible to the Harvard or Yale Press, for instance. If I asked Weeks [editor of *The Atlantic*] to sound out the Harvard Press would you undertake to talk to the Yale people for me? I know no one in either outfit.

I am half way through *The Grapes of Wrath* which fills

me with astonishment and delight. It seems to me that in this book Steinbeck had done at last what Walt Whitman and Ernest Hemingway and Steinbeck himself and, in a way, Mark Twain tried to do. In fact, I suspect I am going to find that it is the great American book.

It is enchanting here and I am reluctant to depart even for a day or so but am subject to call because I have undertaken to do a broadcast in behalf of that bill now in Congress which proposes to raise the German quota for refugee children. Time on the air for the purpose is even now being arranged and I will have to go whenever the summons comes. Even so, you should write me here.

A. W.

To ALFRED LUNT

Bomoseen, Vt.
June 6, 1939

Dear Alfred,

Just before I got back here on Saturday a huge packing-case had arrived which Joe Hennessey tore open feverishly in the fond belief that it was a grand piano. It turned out to be my goblets which I greatly prefer to a grand piano. They are beautiful and most usefully replenish my devastated stock of glassware.

My Jensens have been here since the end of April with the flutter of diapers in the June sunlight imparting to the island the domestic note it has so long lacked and with Hennessey at last revealing his true talent. It is all too obvious that he has long suffered from a suppressed desire to be a nursemaid.

I have had an enchanting time with the Quints [the Dionnes] and could talk to you for hours about them. In fact I will talk to you for fourteen minutes about them if you can catch me on the Texaco program. I am scheduled for three Texaco broadcasts on the 14th, 21st, and 28th.

Some of the movies we took at Genesee are excellent and will be part of the record of that entire journey which I will show you when you come on here later in the summer. The more I think of your place the better I like it and after considerable gastric meditation I have come to the conclusion that you set the best table I know in America. The Charlie Bracketts, Joe Alsop in Washington, and the Ted Roosevelts on Long Island are the other entries for the benison of my approval.

On my way back from Callander to the frontier I discovered in Ontario a town called New Bliss. We know so many people who might like to go there.

A. W.

To JOAN WOOLLCOTT

Bomoseen, Vt.
June 17, 1939

Dear Joan,

This is just a line to wish you good luck in your new job. I think you have done wisely and I am sure you will do well.

I know of no trade that is as much fun as newspaper work and no job a newcomer finds so satisfactory as a reporter's. I am still a reporter, being merely one who has earned the right (or perhaps "craftily developed the technique" would be the better phrase) of assigning myself to various stories. In its simplest form and at its best it remains, I think, a young person's job. If I was glad to quit the city room after little more than four years and take over the easier job of a special department, it was partly because I did not know how in those days to make use of my spare time. There was plenty of this but it came at unpredictable times and I was never organized to take advantage of it but just sat vacuously on my can and waited. I could wish now that someone had effectively suggested then that I keep my hand in with just such a voluminous diary as I have recommended to you. I am not sure that I would have had the character to carry it on and I am not sure that you have, but if I could convince you of the importance of trying it would be the greatest single service I could do for you.

I know nothing about the *PM* project but I am inclined to think you might do worse than to stay where you are for a couple of years. I see so many young premedical men in anxious speculation as to what is the best medical school for them to attend when any good medical school could give them considerably more than they are able to take.

Let me know if there is anything I can do for you.

A. W.

To *LYNN FONTANNE*

Bomoseen, Vt.
July 3, 1939

Dear Lynn,

When you come to the island—when will that be?—I will be able to show you a movie containing some lovely bits of Genesee.

What I send along with this note is the script of the first broadcast to England—the half-hour with music—which I did last Wednesday in New York. Of the six Sunday broadcasts, which are shorter and simpler and without music, I did the first yesterday from Schenectady, compelled by the exigencies of the BBC to drop in with my distant chatter just as Mr. Chamberlain had finished his lugubrious communication to his constituents. About the longer broadcast, I think you can get some notion from the script. You will see where music was indicated and may guess that in the medley a tenor did some of the songs and I achieved the rest with recitative. It was enormously exciting and I was worked up into a kind of dervish tension, what with the timing so complicated, the audience so fantastically far away, and a mess of friends crowding all around me in the studio.

Tell Alfred that I, too, have not been idle. I, too, have had a tooth out and would like now to find out how novocaine affects him. It affects me strangely. I rose from a painless extraction, strode majestically out of the office, stopped at Holliday's [bookshop] and bought half his stock, went to Saks-Fifth Avenue and made many injudicious purchases of sporting-wear. These included a green straw hat. Through the fog I could hear the clerk protesting faintly, "I advise against it, sir," but I just brushed him aside. Then, before the effects wore off, I also bought a new Cadillac car and a French poodle pup. The next time I need a tooth out I shall tie a string to it with the other end on the doorknob. It is more painful but less expensive.

A. W.

To SOPHIE ROSENBERGER

Bomoseen, Vt.
July 10, 1939

My dear Miss Rosenberger,
    I am distressed about my namesake's [her dog's] blindness but the thing that really disturbs me is the thought of your retiring. You mustn't retire. Not altogether. Can't you make some deal with the school board that would let you meet pupils once a month or something like that?

While you ponder this suggestion, I want you to have before you a few words spoken one night a little more than eight years ago by that man who was, to my notion, the greatest master of prose this country has yet produced. I mean the younger Oliver Wendell Holmes. The editorial staffs of the Harvard and Yale law journals observed his ninetieth birthday with a tribute broadcast which he himself heard and to which in the last two minutes he himself contributed. Sitting at the desk in his library in Washington, the old man said this:

"The riders in a race do not stop short when they reach the goal. There is a little finishing canter before coming to a standstill. There is time to hear the kind voices of friends and to say to one's self: 'The work is done.'

"But just as one says that, the answer comes: 'The race is over, but the work never is done while the power to work remains.'

"The canter that brings you to a standstill need not be only coming to rest. It cannot be, while you still live. For to live is to function. That is all there is in living.

"And so I end with the line from a Latin poet who uttered the message more than fifteen hundred years ago: 'Death plucks my ear and says, "Live, I am coming."' "

A. Woollcott

To LAURA E. RICHARDS

Bomoseen, Vt.
October 15, 1939

My dear Mrs. Richards:
       I have read the small book with great pleasure. It is full of old friends of mine.

I know one member of this younger set whose agitated parents decided not to have him learn to read at the conventional age, feeling that he would need every encouragement to grow sturdy by an outdoor life. They were the more abashed when, at the age of five, by reading aloud an elaborate sentence from a menu in a restaurant, he betrayed the fact that some bootlegger had been stealthily supplying him with the education which his father and mother thought it best to withhold.

Later they tried to keep the more bloodthirsty fairy tales from him and once his father, finding the boy chuckling happily over a book, was relieved to find that it was a volume of short stories by Chekhov. But the story which had moved the child to such merriment was one in which the nursemaid cut the baby's head off.

At this point they sent him to school after all. His mother thought this was the best way to stupid him up.

However I merely wrote to ask if I could come to lunch with you at one o'clock on Monday, October 23rd?

Yours affectionately,
Old Faithful

To *LLOYD LEWIS*

[The biographer of Sherman and authority on the Civil War period is also sports editor and dramatic critic of the *Chicago Daily News*.]

Dallas, Texas
November 15, 1939

Dear Lloyd:

Here I have been sucking around you in preparation for my Chicago debut and it turns out that after all when I climb into that wheel chair as *The Man Who Came to Dinner*, it will not be in the Chicago company but in the one that opens in Santa Barbara on February 9th.

I am cavorting through the country now on a lecture tour which takes me through Texas, and up the coast as far as Vancouver. I shall have Christmas dinner in Seattle with Miss Kitty Cornell, and it is possible that I can sneak into Chicago on my way to Minneapolis for a glance at the Chicago troupe which by that time should be under way.

Just before I left Vermont I read that lecture on Lincoln by Infinitive-Splitter Lewis. I think it is a superb piece. In fact, I think you have as right an idiom for writing about Lincoln as, for example, Trevelyan had for writing about Charles James Fox. I tried to say this to Carl Sandburg when I ran into him at the NBC studios in New York the other night, and it occurred to me afterwards that he received my discourse with something less than rapture.

The advantage of playing in the Pacific Coast company is that it will close for the summer and let me go to Vermont, where I expect you and the little woman to come for something more than a fly-by-night visit. I see I am airily planning away as if we were not all sitting on a keg of dynamite, but that is the only thing one can do.

A. W.

VIII

1940

To *NOEL COWARD*

Laramie, Wyoming
January 4, 1940

Dear Noel,

You must have long since discovered (and probably could yourself have forseen) the peculiar paralysis which, since the 3rd of September, has numbed any American with English friends to whom he might wish to write. I find, if I try writing about the war which is now on our minds all the time, that what comes out on paper is either stale or pretentious or offensive. Or all three. When, on the other hand, I try reporting on our own doings, the most innocent and casual preoccupations suddenly sound as fatuous and shallow as a bit of iron merriment got up by Elsa Maxwell for Mrs. Hearst. Perhaps they are.

What now blasts me out of my resulting silence in your case is an obligation to say something about your book [*To Step Aside*]. I have had great difficulty in reading it. As I started on this lecture tour—I have already driven eight thousand miles in a car shared by Joe Hennessey and a French poodle pup—a copy of the English text was pressed into my hands by Grace Eustis. After I had read one story, I abstractedly left this copy in the automobile of the Canadian Minister in Washington and there-

[225]

after spent a small fortune in telegraph tolls vainly trying to get it back. Then I got an American copy which was stolen from me in Texas. It was a third copy, which I had read all through not once but twice, that I gave to Lynn and Alfred in Los Angeles. I think you have done nothing which has impressed me more. I suppose there are more people alive and functioning in the world who could have written this book than could have accomplished such a stupefying feat as *Tonight at 8:30*. But the stories are most of them superb and as pieces of prose they are several parasangs ahead of *Present Indicative*. I particularly relished "Aunt Tittie" and "The Kindness of Mrs. Radcliffe" (I am not sure of these spellings) and rolled in the latter, as I think you yourself must have done, like a cat in catnip. Writing it—like writing "Fumed Oak"—must have been a debauch of self-indulgence.

In early September I thought by this time to be up to my ass in the war and I suppose that before long it may yet take such a pattern that an unneutral American can see where his job is. In the meantime I traipse somnambulistically about the country and on February 9th open at Santa Barbara in the Pacific Coast company of *The Man Who Came to Dinner*, a contemporary dramatic work of which some account may have filtered to you, just as I cut out and sent to Lynn the Philip Gibbs dispatch reporting a show for soldiers he saw you and Maurice Chevalier give in some theatre in France.

I have heard with exquisite pleasure from Rebecca West that (a) the overworked censors are compelling Sibyl Colefax to use a typewriter, and (b) that the renegade Englishman broadcasting from Germany had become embittered with the British Empire through your refusing him a small part in *Hay Fever*.

In return you might like to hear the anecdote which Kathleen Norris thought appropriate to use when she introduced me at my lecture at the Opera House in San Francisco last week.

She told about the day long ago when a small niece reported that Charlotte was coming over to play. "That's nice. And who is Charlotte, dear?" "Oh," replied the niece. "She's that friend that I hate."

Alexander Woollcott

To *BEATRICE KAUFMAN*

Hollywood, Calif.
January 28, 1940

Dear Beatrice:

I think you must recall a certain trip we made once into the Alps when I snowballed you on July 4th and you rode grandly off into the valley, leaving your passport, jewels and incriminating documents on a garden table on a mountain peak. If you think back to some such drive you will recall how, as a car starts its winding ascent, you may see up near the clouds ahead of you, a village, a patch of cultivation, a church spire. It seems incredible that there could be human activity at so high a point. Then, before you know it, that village, that patch of cultivation, that church spire, lie not only behind but below you. I am nearing such a patch now. It was just two years ago this month that I bitterly complained to Moss [Hart] in Philadelphia—it was a few nights before that gracious week-end—about my life in art. I told him that just once before I died, I wanted to go on the road in a play where I played the central character so that I could belch without knocking the plot through the backdrop and sending Miriam Hopkins into hysterics. Dear Guv'nor, they is goin' to hang me Sat'day and here it is Tuesday.

From sundry sources I hear an echo of your reproaches about my shortcomings as a correspondent. On this subject I never want to hear a peep out of you again. In times like these it is quite impossible for me to write a letter to anyone to whom I have so much to say. So shut your trap, dear, and let me hear no more from you.

We seem to rehearse quite a lot, and in such intervals as are permitted, I am trying on suits, bathrobes, shirts and the like, and am wrestling silently with an attack of asthma which I hope to have on the run—that phrase unfortunately suggests a nasal engagement—before the week is out.

For news I have to report that when I lectured in Minneapolis (where the attendance was meager enough to have satisfied even Moss) I occupied such a gala suite of rooms at the Hotel Niccolet as must have been designed originally for Queen Marie of Rumania and subsequently used as a twenty-dollar house. Where all the other doors in the hotel are walnut in hue, this suite has a white door. Where all the other suites have numbers, this has only a name painted in gold on the door. The name is "Nordic Suite." If only they had thought to have that name printed on special stationery you would have heard from me before this.

I thought you would also like to know about my valet, a beaming Filipino who comes to work tomorrow. The point about him is that he comes to me from Walter Wanger and went to Walter from Gene Markey. It makes me quite nervous.

I asked George about Mr. Martin. He explained that this was one of your young protégés like Oscar [Levant], for example, on whose account he thought you should have several good marks in Heaven. "You know," he said with that affectionate note that gets into his voice in speaking of you when you are at least three thousand miles away, "Beatrice is always picking up these sensitive, ambitious young Jews." "Sometimes," I said, "she marries them." So we all went in to rehearsal.

Are you coming out? Moss imparted the improbable news that Alice Miller was coming along for the ride. Dan Silberberg is even now lolling at Floyd Odlum's ranch at Indio near

Palm Springs. The crowd seems to be gathering—like the pus in my right maxillary sinus. I must go now and get it washed out

Alexander W.

P.S. Of course, I would rather you came out for the San Francisco engagement, partly because I ought to be better then (in the part, I mean) and partly because I would have some time for general conversation. We could play croquet with the Norrises and I would get a motor-boat wherewith we could explore San Francisco Bay. This part of California seems to me completely loathsome, but I like San Francisco.

P.P.S. I wish I could be the first to tell you that I, too, am sometimes Woolley-witted. I have an unfortunate tendency in the second act to say: "Yes, yes, you are. At Christmas I always feel the needy." It makes rather a pretty picture—a good subject for Peter Arno—with an old gentleman from the Union Club, swathed in a fur coat and moving up and down a breadline.

A. W.

To *REBECCA WEST*

Los Angeles, Calif.
February 4, 1940

Dear Rebecca:
There are all kinds of fidelity in human relationships and I proffer you my kind. The other night in a hotel in Sioux Falls, South Dakota—I forget what I was doing there, but I suspect I was lecturing—I read your article in *The New Yorker* and paid it the involuntary tribute of a great roar of laughter. After all, my acquaintance with you began back in

1916 by a similar response wrung from these embarrassed lips on a Broadway trolley-car while I was reading your *New Republic* piece on Ellen Key. Such discreet attestations—spanning almost a quarter of a century, my girl—nourish my need for continuity. It is as though you had been declared venerable and are now beatified.

I relished the whole piece. It was one of those pieces of yours which I sit right down and read through two or three times. Only Evelyn Waugh at the top of his bent can give me that kind of delight. I thought the whole thing was artful propaganda, if I may use a word now so enfeebled and corrupted as to have lost all savor. (American to the last, dear.) But the point that elicited the great buffalo roar out of me was the Nightingale "Too kind, too kind."

All of which is so much chatter. But at this distance in space and time, these days, one must write irrelevantly, and, after all, I started out only to say that I think of you often and with deep affection. My best to Henry and Anthony.

A. Woollcott

To *LADY COLEFAX*

Hollywood, Calif.
February 19, 1940

Dear Sibyl:

You owe this holograph letter (and I have patiently told you again and again how angry I am when *I* get a letter that is *not* typewritten) to the fact that I celebrated the first week of *The Man Who Came to Dinner* in Los Angeles by a nasty little case of laryngitis and between performances for a while they are putting these frayed, old vocal chords into splints of silence so that I am not *allowed* to dictate a letter. I shall entrust this one to the sea-borne mails as I have found that letters sent by the Yankee Clipper take an unconscionable time in finding their way to England.

Laryngitis or no, the play has started off with a bang and in San Francisco next month we shall throw in an extra matinee for the Finns, which is the most popular present outlet for American feelings about the war. Henry Miller—Alice's Henry—is chairman of a committee that is being showered with money for Finnish munitions and, after a long tour in *The Taming of the Shrew,* the Lunts have just given eight performances for the Finns in New York and then retreated to their farm to study a new Sherwood play—or perhaps it is just our old friend *Acropolis* rewritten. So it goes—all very pleasant and remote from the shadow under which your days are spent and *nothing* you or anyone can say will convince me that you can hear of such comparatively carefree lives without a deep resentment—some such resentment, let us say, as the people of Prague must have felt when, after Munich, they read of week-end parties at Cliveden.

Now here is an item for you. [H.R.] Knickerbocker and I have both been lecturing all over the country, and our paths crossed in Kansas City. He is strongly an interventionist and had been warned by everybody in New York that it would be indiscreet of him to let that cloven hoof be visible to his audiences. But once he had taken to the road and felt his way, he discovered that his argument for our immediately contributing our navy and our air force was what his midland audiences really wanted to hear.

No more now. My love to you.

Alexander Woollcott

P.S. This singular haven is an odd place in which to sit in the sun and read about the boarding of the Altmark. Kaufman, Hart and Alice Miller, all of whom came out to see the opening, are quitting their villas here today. Rachmaninoff has the next one to mine and begins practicing every morning at dawn. Beyond him are the Charles Laughtons. Beyond them Robert Benchley. Beyond him is Dorothy Parker. It's the kind of village you might look for down the rabbit-hole. That muted mutter from across the way is just Dame May Whitty, rehearsing as the nurse to the impending Juliet of Vivien Leigh and the Romeo of Larry Olivier. Down one street is the charming home of a small Jewish screen-writer who used to be my office boy. He has just bought a Reynolds. It's a mad world, my masters! and always was.

A. W.

To *CORNELIA OTIS SKINNER*

[The actress, monologist, and co-author of *Our Hearts Were Young and Gay* is the daughter of one of Woollcott's boyhood heroes of the stage, the late Otis Skinner; her husband is Alden Blodgett.]

Hollywood, Calif.
February 19, 1940

Dear Cornelia:

This is to tell you (a trifle belatedly, for the news was late in catching up with me) how sorry I am about Alden's accident, to give my love to your father, to thank you both for the memorial booklet on Miss Durbin [Mrs. Otis Skinner] and to thank you also for that neighborly note from you which I found waiting for me in that aromatic hotel at Tyler, Texas. At every lecture thereafter, I read aloud the more indelicate passage from that note and it was always good if not for a belly laugh at least for an abdominal titter.

I read the pieces about your mother with the liveliest interest and there lingers with me most vividly that first clash of wills with her father. I realize now that it was that same iron will, always playing counterpoint to her gentleness and dearness, which imparted that piquant savor which was part of her charm.

I am having a high old time as a road star and unless I collapse or something, should be cavorting along this coast—I call the Atlantic littoral *the* Coast—until June. Will you visit me on the island then? I set great store on seeing you from time to time. I think you know that I hold you in great admiration and that I enjoy your company. I know no better basis as a relation between neighbors.

God bless you in 1940.

Alexander Woollcott

To *LADY COLEFAX*

San Francisco, Calif.
March 18, 1940

Dear Sibyl:

Bless you for the copies of the two letters from Max [Beerbohm], which will come to rest before the year is over in my files at the island—files as orderly as the British Museum, all ranged in a hideaway which might, I suppose, be called the Closet of Awful Joy.

Bless you, indeed, for many things. Indeed (aside from a not infrequent wish that you would use a typewriter) I hold it against you only that you never made it possible for me to see Winston plain. I am sending for that book of his speeches, but I do not need it to strengthen my admiration for him or deepen my regret that he was not made Prime Minister of England at least two years ago. Of the many factors tending to keep my country and yours from working in partnership, I think of Mr. Chamberlain as an important one. There is no estimating, of course, the deep lack of respect for him in millions of American minds, and the uncomfortable distrust of England because she has not divested herself of him.

Perhaps I have thought of Winston the oftener because, during the ghastly first week of last September when we on the island in Vermont hung round the radio every hour of the twenty-four, there were three among the guests who had known Winston and loved him well. Of these, two were Vincent Sheean and Diana Forbes-Robertson [Mrs. Sheean]. The third was Ethel Barrymore. I seem to recall that, back in the Nineties, when Ethel was playing at the Lyceum in London—young, slim, shy, gawky, lovely and disturbing—young Winston Churchill had a soft spot in his heart for her.

The Sheeans were lodged for the summer in a guest cottage across the mountains at Dorothy Thompson's. They were awaiting the advent of a baby who turned out to be something pretty special in the way of a daughter who, when I met her at the age of ten days, had already been named Gertrude Ellen in honor of Lady Forbes-Robertson and Ellen Terry. Well, that place of Dorothy Thompson's is only sixty miles away, and when Ethel came up for what little vacation she took last year, I sent for the Sheeans because I knew what glowing letters Dinah would write home to her mother after seeing Ethel as she is these days—Ethel, who has passed through the valley and come out on the other side—serene, genial and more beautiful, I think, than ever. The unforeseen by-product was that, whatever Dinah may have written home, Sheean himself was knocked right off his pins by her, and in no time was muttering to himself that he must write a play for her. Well, that was in September, and I'll be damned if the play [*International Incident*] isn't opening in Boston on Wednesday of this week. Since it was born—or shall we say conceived?—on the island, I have an avuncular interest, and shall be waiting eagerly for news of the accouchement. I will pass the reports on to you when they come, though those from the Boston try-out may be inconclusive.

My own theatrical venture [*The Man Who Came to Dinner*] is flourishing mightily. We are scheduled to remain on this Coast through the spring, to disband for the summer, and to open a long tour in Philadelphia at the end of September. Six weeks in Philadelphia, two in Baltimore, two in Washington—that sort of thing. Of course this is tentative, but for many reasons I hope it goes through, for I know I am more stimulated (and I suspect I am of more use) when I move up and down the country. Curiously enough, I never feel so much as a twinge of nostalgia for New York, although there have been times during the past five months when I have envied those who were in Washington. But such wandering as a tour like this enforces immerses me in America, and nothing goes on in New York that I would exchange for such adventures as visiting Frank Lloyd Wright in his studio on the mesa in Arizona, or sitting with Disney in a projection room watching the early and spontaneous stages of the masterpiece which the world may not see for another year. The playing time in the theatre uses up so few hours out of a man's day that I have more time for writing than I have things to say, and as much opportunity for broadcasting as I want.

In Hollywood I watched the preparation of *Our Town* for the screen. We shall see what we shall see. It is being directed by the man who directed *Good-bye, Mr. Chips,* which was, to my mind, the best picture I ever saw. In fact, if you don't count Chaplin, the only good picture I ever saw.

No news of Thornton. For months now, he has lapsed, as far as I am concerned, into moody silence.

In New York the Lunts are working like mad on the rehearsals of a play by Sherwood on Finland [*There Shall Be No Night*]. Whether it will be too late depends on what their purpose was, and how good the play is. Did you ever study the political background which inspired *The Trojan Women*? I would not say that was too late, even now.

A. Woollcott

To *CHARLES LEDERER*

San Francisco, Calif.
March 26, 1940

Dear Bosie:

Oscar [Levant] came and went like a tornado, accompanied by his pregnant bride, and staying here at the Fairmont because I had suggested it. As it is extremely expensive he grew more bitter with every check he had to sign. My major triumph was seeing to it that his telephone call to Harpo, which he made from my room, was charged to his. At the concert his performance was truly incandescent. After he had finished the "Rhapsody," Claudia Morgan and I joined him backstage and through the peep-hole we watched Monteux conduct the final Sibelius and Ravel numbers. With the concert finally over Oscar and I, heading for the green room, debouched into the corridor where a comely Miss with an autograph book was lying in wait. "Oh! Mr. Woollcott," she said, "may I have your autograph?" With a bellow of pain, Oscar left for New York.

A. W.

To *BEATRICE KAUFMAN*

San Francisco, Calif.
April 1, 1940

Dear Beatrice:

I suppose you know that your letters have not only been few but morose. As you know, I am myself so familiar with the states of mind you find afflicting that I have a sense of understanding you as I understand nobody else. You and I are more given than most to stewing in our own juice. I am pretty sure that you are troubled now, as often before, by a sense of staleness and futility from which I find escape by resolutely breaking the pattern of my life every year to prevent its hardening in any given form. To this practice I think I owe the fact that I have enjoyed the past twelve months rather more than any other year I can remember. I have, however, no idea to what to ascribe the fact that, ever since I started on this trek at the end of October, I have felt in better health than I have known in a dozen years. Of course I may be at death's door, but I feel elegant. It will startle you to learn that, after more than twenty years of fidelity to one cigarette, I now smoke another brand and that, for some unknown reason, I no longer belch. You would hardly know me. God knows I offer my life as a pattern to no one. It is merely the best adjustment I can make to my own familiar limitations. And of course I recognize my sundry antics as anodynes (a little superior, but not much, to backgammon, let us say) in a world where the Finns can go down to defeat and the Hitlers trample their way to success while you and I do nothing much about it. I take it that the job of work you're doing with this Mr. Martin, who has not yet been submitted to me for my approval, is just such a deliberate rearrangement of the pattern as I have been talking about. But I know it does you good to get up and get out from time to time, and I think it might be a refreshment if you would grab a plane one of these spring days and visit me if only for a week.

You can probably find out at the Sam Harris office how long they now think we will stay here, and where we are to put in the remaining weeks of the season. Here at the Fairmont I have rooms with a balcony that looks out over the bay and catches the morning sunlight at breakfast time. Larry Olivier and Vivien Leigh move today into the rooms below mine. They are here to rehearse *Romeo and Juliet*, which has its premiere at the Geary next Monday, and they are affably giving a Friday matinee so that I can see it. H. R. Knickerbocker passes this way on Tuesday of that week, and Margaret Webster a day or so later. For some unspecified time in April the Alan Campbells have bespoken the other bedroom that gives on my sitting-room. There is talk that the Marxes will come up then to try out their new stuff in vaudeville.

No one has ever been such a blessing to me as Joe [Hennessey] was throughout the lecture tour and the rehearsals of the play. Now he and Cocaud [the poodle] have departed on a Norwegian freighter and must, by this time, be nearing the Canal Zone, where they will shift to a Grace liner and come up by way of Havana to New York. This leaves me with my Cadillac and no one to drive it, so I have offered the chauffeur's job to Howard Bull for the balance of the season. At last reports he was working like mad on his boats in order to get them ready for the summer before he comes out. I really don't need him in San Francisco, but it would be a great comfort to have him once we start out on tour.

I don't know what you were told about my performances in this play in Santa Barbara and Los Angeles, but I am a far better judge in such matters than anyone who could have reported to you, and you may take it from me that I was pretty lousy. It was at Fresno that I began to be comparatively good, and by this time I am giving a performance I wouldn't mind your seeing. If I play it next season it will be still better or I'll eat my hat.

Porky

To *LAURA E. RICHARDS*

San Francisco, Calif.
April 2, 1940

My dear Mrs. Richards:

I once knew and liked a raffish old soubrette at the Music Box who, when the chorus all chipped in and gave her a birthday cake, swore there were so many candles on it that four of the chorus girls had to be taken to

Bellevue Hospital as sufferers from heat prostration. I will not actually swear that on February 27th we out here on the wrong coast saw a strange and lovely light in the East but I can truthfully tell you that the glow of your birthday cake has warmed my heart ever since I heard about it.

I am so proud to be one of those who received the card of acknowledgment. I think that in all your days your pen was never happier and that is saying much. I am torn between a reluctance to part with mine and a desire to have it seen in England by friends of mine and yours. Indeed I am writing chiefly to ask if you have any left over and can spare me as many as three. This hotel will serve as my address throughout April. This play, in which I am acting away like all get-out, is a great success in San Francisco, and as an erstwhile dramatic critic I can assure you that my performance in it is simply superb.

But my real job is to pass on any good word about books and let me urge you to keep an eye out for a collection of short stories by Geoffrey Household which is shortly to be published by Little Brown. It takes its title from the first one—*The Salvation of Pisco Gabar*—and that is a tale to be taken to the heart if ever I read one.

Yours to command.

Old Faithful

To *FRODE JENSEN*

San Francisco, Calif.
April 15, 1940

Dear Frode:

Just as it was inevitable for me to see the rise of Hitler in terms of my Jewish friends—Harpo, George Backer, George Kaufman, Irving Berlin, etc.—so I naturally read the news from Copenhagen in terms of you. With me that day were

H. R. Knickerbocker, the foreign correspondent, and his wife. She is a very pretty young woman from Montana whose father and mother were Norwegians and all of whose relatives are in Norway and whose income has always come from property in Norway. Last night I put her on the train for Los Angeles. Knickerbocker has been engaged for some months in a lecture tour, preaching the gospel that America should intervene. He thinks we should do this for our own sake, that it is a matter of vital national necessity that Hitler should not be victorious in his war.

I quite agree with him, and I believe that every day more and more Americans will come to this same conclusion. Of course the crucial question is whether they will reach it in time. A democracy of one hundred and thirty million people can never act as swiftly as one man can. That is one of the disadvantages —probably the only one—of not being governed by a dictator.

My love to all three of you. I'll be back on the island before the end of the first week in June. I might even see you at commencement if you can drive over to Clinton on Saturday or Sunday.

A. W.

To *MRS. LAWRENCE GILMAN*

Bomoseen, Vt.
May 25, 1940

My dear Mrs. Gilman:
You and my doctors tell me the same thing and I am obeying orders with a docility which must make me almost unrecognizable. There seems to be a good chance however that I will be up and about in the Fall unabated. I think I am glad of this for I do not seem to have picked the most appropriate moment in the history of mankind in which to start living the contemplative life.

I cannot begin to tell you how often, and with what a rueful mixture of pleasure and pain, I think of Lawrence. But I can tell you that though now a slightly damaged article, my heart can still be warmed by such a letter as yours.

God bless you,
A. Woollcott

P.S. I think I should like to tell you something else. Your letter came to me at a time when my mail was being read to me by an aide who had known Lawrence only through his writings for the *Herald Tribune*. I found myself saying, "Lawrence Gilman was one of the most charming men—" and then knew suddenly that that was inexact and inadequate. So I changed it to "He was *the* most charming man I ever knew." And had the satisfaction that comes from having said exactly what was in my mind.

A. W.

To *WILLIAM ALLEN WHITE*

Bomoseen, Vt.
June 7, 1940

Dear William Allen White:

Perhaps it is the doom, the obligation and the privilege of each generation to lay its own Hitler by the heels, and since England and France have put their hands to this task, the most that we can do to help them is the least we should do. I am one of those who believe that by such help, given now and without stint, we shall best defend all that we are and most of what we have. It seems to me that the isolationists are not only faithless to this country's tradition, but frivolously indifferent to the freedom and well-being of all Americans for a hundred years to come.

I am glad that yours is a rallying call which comes from the midlands, and I shall deem it an honor to be enrolled in your committee.

Yours to command,
A. Woollcott

[The committee of which Mr. White was chairman was the Committee to Defend America by Aiding the Allies.]

To *LUCY CHRISTIE DRAGE*

Bomoseen, Vt.
August 29, 1940

Dear Lucy:

All through May and June I was such a damaged piece of goods that the few wobbly letters I tried to write only served to convince the recipients that my end was near and since then my correspondence has run dry because I have not known what to say. I can only report that I've peeled off at least thirty-five pounds since last you saw me and that a week from today I am going to my doctor in Syracuse for an examination. He is then to tell the authors of that play whether I am a good enough risk for the tour to be resumed in the Fall. In any event it won't be resumed before November, until which time I shall stay here and brood. I have no serious doubt that I could do a lot of carefree dashing about right now but somehow, having attracted the attention of about fourteen specialists all of whom solemnly adjured me to sit still for at least six months, I have thought it wisest to do just that. Maybe, if I make the experiment of behaving myself, there will be a few years of work left in the old boy yet.

Late in May I was drenched with regret when there came my way a job after my own heart and at a time when I could not accept it. Indeed, it was a job that I had been guilefully angling for for several years. All the broadcasts I did to England last year were groundwork for it. When it came it took the form of an offer from the London *Telegraph* to fly me at once to London by Clipper where I would be shown the country at war under the auspices of the *Telegraph,* write ten pieces for them and also do a few broadcasts there and a few to America. It came along at a time when I could just about get from my bed to the steamer chair on the terrace and I had to say no. In my more candid moments I admit that I probably would have died of fright and the altitude before reaching the Azores but just the same I have a sense of having missed a boat that will never come my way again.

In politics I cannot see much further than the fact that our own interests and all our best instincts bid us give all the help to England we can. As Mr. Roosevelt seems to be the one person who can be counted on for that I am sticking to him. As for our friend Colonel Lindbergh, I must tell you—and for general circulation in Kansas City—a comment on him that was made here a little while ago. It was at the time when Laurence Olivier and Vivien Leigh were staying here and we were all out drifting on the lake under the midsummer moon and the talk in the launch fell on the Colonel's recent speech in Chicago. The most sagacious observation I have yet heard made on him or it or anything else came from the small native at the wheel. "It seems to me," he said, "as though that fellow Hauptmann kidnapped the wrong baby."

Please pass my love along to Sophie [Rosenberger] and tell her I expect to be doing her credit on the warpath in the Fall.

Alexander W.

P.S. The four Woollcott girls continue to entertain and astonish their incredulous uncle. Nancy, the prettiest and oldest, will be here in September with her young Ph.D. husband. He has been appointed to the faculty of the University of Vermont and they will be neighbors of mine before another month has gone.

Joan, the second, is a successful reporter on the *Bulletin* in Philadelphia, audibly trying to make up her mind which of two young Jews she will marry in the Fall.

Barbara, who is a stunning-looking girl—recently expelled from the University of Michigan at the end of her Freshman year—has got herself a job by sheer merit on the *Herald Tribune* in New York and wrote the signed review which held the front page of its Book Section a few Sundays ago. At nineteen or thereabouts, she has four or five times as much ability as I had at her age and considerably more courage. She, too, is planning to marry at once. Thus far it has done no good for her father to point out that the young man has no job and never has had one. "That," says Barbara, "doesn't matter because I shall support him."

Polly, who is still in school and must be about sixteen, has a reporter's job for the summer at Vineyard Haven and, from all accounts, is the best of the lot.

A. W.

To DR. GUSTAV ECKSTEIN

Bomoseen, Vt.
September 2, 1940

Dear Gus:

Because (when I last saw you swathed in Noguchi's kimono in the vestibule of a train in Syracuse) you talked of coming here some time in the Fall, I am writing to report that I shall be here at least until the 20th of October except for one expedition to New York on September 23rd. At that time I shall stay the greater part of the week, during which I want to see a good deal of [Edward] Sheldon and Gerald Murphy and, you will be delighted to know, a great deal of the dentist. Day after tomorrow I am driving up to Syracuse and staying there just long enough to be checked over by [Doctor] Al Getman. At that time he is supposed to tell me (and incidentally, Kaufman and Hart) how I am. I can only tell you that I have systematically peeled off between thirty and thirty-five pounds since I was laid low in San Francisco and, after a ghastly June, now feel so nearly well enough that I suspect I shall be all right as soon as I am allowed to be too busy to give any thought to the subject. Already I am cautiously and experimentally resuming the practice of doing some work.

The early part of the summer was a painful experience to a person who has had no training in the technique of being sick, and among the unexpected impasses that I think I could probably explain, is the fact that I found it difficult to the edge of impossibility to write letters or even brief notes to the very people who mean the most to me. Therefore I have accumulated so much that I want to talk to you about—about this monstrous world and how to live in it, about my own inner need to turn myself into another kind of person for the dubious purpose of survival, about *Christmas Eve* and its magnificent last act and wherein I suspect its weakness lay.

A. W.

To *THORNTON WILDER*

Bomoseen, Vt.
September 7, 1940

Dear Thornton:
Well! Well! When you come here you shall see your Cousin Bessie in the group photograph taken the morning after the Shakespeare tableaux that were held in the vestibule

of the Woollcott house in Aldine Place in the summer of 1891. That's when I was the Puck (in red cheesecloth tights) and my lovely sister (not yet twenty, then) was the Juliet, and Bessie Stone was, I think, the Miranda. I forgot to question Bessie on this point the last time I saw her (after a parting of more than forty-five years) when she came backstage at my lecture at the University of Kansas in January. It was the night of a blizzard but we sold out. The hall seats four thousand. My draw is better than it was in 1891.

That lecture tour flushed many a memory of those Shakespearean tableaux. When I spoke at the theatre in San Diego, the Titania sent a note to my dressing-room to say that she was in the audience and to ask if she could see me after the lecture. I replied that I would expect her wheel chair to come straight to the stage door. In Kansas City, where I lingered for five days, I stayed with the Cleopatra and the Desdemona. Why does the mere fact that I have known people for half a century make them dear to me as no wretched newcomers like you could be?

The oldest of my brothers [Harry Woollcott], who died some years ago, was betrothed to Mary Stone. She was the Lady Macbeth. But the Stone I can't recall without a lump in the throat was Waterman. The neighbors regarded him as evil incarnate but I admired him tremendously. He did without any hesitation all the things I was afraid to do. When a group of our elders was going by in party dresses on their way to some occasion, Waterman just leaned over the railing of the Stone's high front porch and spat on them. Magnificent! He had a passion for playing with my geography game which was a jigsaw puzzle of the states of the Union. "Aleck," he used to say, "cahn't I play with your geography game?" All the Stones talked that way which made them unique in Aldine Place, and I used to answer, "No, Waterman, you cahn't," because if I had said, "Yes, Waterman, you can," he would never have known that I could talk that way, too. I was six or seven at the time and became less precious later. Waterman, who was better made for living than I ever was, has been dust in the churchyard these many, many years.

I hope to God your reference to the lecture as one of the millstones of literary criticism was not a slip of the pen. I guess it wasn't. It was formally decided yesterday in Syracuse that I would better not go back to the play. I seem to be the only person in our common acquaintance who thinks it is a good idea and I was finally worn down by the opposition. Al Getman is now of the opinion that I am going to get back a good heart muscle which is more than he thought three months ago. But he also thinks that anyone who has had a heart lesion so recently as June should not take on, if it could be avoided, any unremitting task within a year, and I find it too difficult to convince him that unremitting tasks to a Puritan are a crutch and an arm sling and an arch support and that I have no doubt at all that I shall fill in the void with activities that will be much more of a strain on me. In fact, if the heart repair at the end of October is good I am going to try to get that London offer repeated.

A. W.

To *D. H. SILBERBERG*

Bomoseen, Vt.
September 7, 1940

Dear Danny:

My last letter was meant to tease you but I never dreamed it would be so successful as to sting you into replying in such a hurry that, for the first time, I've seen your tell-tale handwriting.

I am indebted to Miss D's father for a bit of medical advice easy to take. Al Getman has been embarrassed by riches of such advice from all over the country. Sometimes these have had the vantage of cancelling each other. Thus Gus Eckstein insists on my tonsils being taken out but Dr. Myerson says there isn't money enough in the world to pay him to do it. The opinion you were good enough to transmit, however, is apparently orthodox. I've been given ammonium chloride all summer as a dehydrant and have been kept, since late in June, on a ration of two quarts of liquids a day. That is why I've cut out fruit juices at breakfast and why I've had only two glasses of iced coffee all summer. Your reminiscent shuddering must have been based on one or both of them. Since the two quarts a day rule has left me with no craving for more it strikes me as being over-liberal, but since I have dropped from something over 230 in April to 193 as of Wednesday, it probably doesn't matter. That is, if anything, an injudiciously rapid decline but Al's preference is that I go to 185 and linger there until further notice. Incidentally, he decided officially in Syracuse on Thursday morning against my going back into the play. I regret this more than there's any point in my saying.

I, too, was glad to see that President Cowley felt he could come out for Willkie as this will strengthen his already strong hold on the confidence of his Board of Trustees. It is also in the tradition of Hamilton presidents. His predecessor, Dr. Ferry, always made a point of retching at the name of Franklin Roosevelt, and the man before *him*, Dr. Melancthon Woolsey Stryker (the father of Lloyd Stryker) was apoplectic at the mention of either Theodore Roosevelt or Woodrow Wilson in the order named. Dr. Stryker's idea of a real statesman was one of his trustees, the Honorable James Schoolcraft Sherman, who was Vice-President with Taft. And because Teddy Roosevelt came back from Africa and started criticizing that administration, Dr. Stryker was so indignant that when, in 1910, T.R. backed Stimson for the Governorship of New York, Prex actually campaigned for John A. Dix, a hollow, handsome and crooked Democrat, who, as his last act in office, pardoned

Albert Patrick. Dr. Stryker also had most of his trustees with him in his hostility to Wilson. You were probably too young to remember that when Wilson forced through and signed the act creating the Federal Reserve Bank, that proceeding was denounced at the next meeting of the American Bankers' Association as pure socialism. That attitude toward all of Wilson's work was characteristic of the Hamilton trustees of that day. Not all of them, to be sure. Samuel Hopkins Adams was a trustee then and it was he and I who rose and stamped noisily out of the alumni luncheon at Commencement when Dr. Stryker so far forgot himself as to speak sneeringly of Wilson in his postprandial discourse. But for the most part he had the Board with him. He certainly had Henry Harper Benedict, the bewhiskered ninny who was president of the Remington Typewriter Company. I can still see Benedict, across the years, shaking his fist and declaring that Wilson should be impeached because he had signed the income tax measure. And he had Elihu Root with him, of whom it must be sternly remembered that he signed the indignant protest when Wilson proposed to undermine the United States Supreme Court by nominating that dreadful Mr. Brandeis.

They're all gone now, the men on the Board who could not stomach T.R. and Wilson. Mais plus ça change, etc. I was most amused by the Cowley statement because it came out in the paper the day after I had mailed to an editor a political piece I had been drafted to write. In that piece I entertained myself by the ravings that went on when first T.R. and then Wilson was "that man in the White House." I spoke of how when T.R. sailed away to Africa all of those whom he had described as malefactors of great wealth gave a sigh of relief—"they and all their train—their biddable rectors, their servile editors and even their tame college presidents." It seems to me grossly improbable that Cowley (or you either, for that matter) will ever see that piece in print but on the bare chance of someone sending him a marked copy I am letting him have a carbon of this letter so that he will know that whereas I cannot share his wishful thinking about Mr. Willkie I was not indulging in a covert slur at his expense.

A. W.

To *CORNELIA OTIS SKINNER*

Bomoseen, Vt.
September 11, 1940

Dear Cornelia:

By this mail I am writing Otis to say how welcome you both will be here for luncheon any day next week and to urge you to come early in the day—we lunch at 1.30—because I have a horrid, senile habit of getting drowsy after luncheon and like to do my post-prandial conversation *before* lunch. I am writing you this private word to 7 Gracie Square to ask if you can't steal part of your Woodstock week for a night or two here. The dogs always remember tenderly the lady who not only took them for a walk but held them spellbound for hours at the back of the island with stentorian rehearsals of *Edna, His Wife*. Indeed, the Duchess has one wistful look which I translate as, "For God's sake, when is Cornelia Otis Skinner coming again?" And whether you manage this detour before or after your luncheon I shall come over to see you both in Woodstock because I enjoy you and admire you and have reached that stage, what with my heart being a little damaged and our world coming to an end anyway, that I see no further point in the old, nasty reticence.

You will be surprised to find me looking unusually spry. I've peeled off forty pounds and lissome is the word for

Yours with great affection,
A. Woollcott

To ARCHIBALD MACLEISH

[Woollcott and Mr. MacLeish were drawn together by mutual literary tastes, which constituted a firm foundation for a Woollcott friendship. In the years before the poet became Librarian of Congress, the MacLeishes were frequent island visitors.]

Bomoseen, Vt.
September 19, 1940

Dear Ambrose:

I have just caught by the tail an idea so large and rambunctious in its possibilities that I can hang on only long enough for you to grab hold if you are interested. Here is the history of the idea.

In my time I've done some wheezy and stertorous recordings for the Talking Books for the Blind and am, by the stern designation of Helen Keller whom I obey in all such matters, a member of the committee that recommends books to be recorded. In submitting this week a carefully considered list I added two special extras—Theodore Roosevelt's *Letters to His Children* to be recorded by young Ted, and the eighteen sonnets of Millay's *Epitaph for the Race of Man* (you must not be disaffected at this point by my enormous admiration for them) to be recorded by Helen Hayes, whom I have already half persuaded to do the job.

In acknowledging my list, Robert Irwin, the Director of the American Foundation for the Blind, mentions in a casual postscript the receipt of an official notice that the Foundation will shortly receive orders for the recording, by casts assembled for the purpose, of half a dozen recent plays. Among these are *Elizabeth the Queen, The Barretts of Wimpole Street,* and *Saturday's Children.* As an impresario, I was immediately tantalized by the notion that these should be recorded in the principal roles by those who had played them first—the Lunts, Miss Cornell and Ruth Gordon. I think they would be willing to do this and glad to do it for nothing.

But it occurs to me that this could be made into something

larger than the present limited purpose of the Talking Books. Why could not the Library of Congress invite any superb performance of a good play—there is no such thing as a good play unless the performance is also good—to go on record for the archives of the nation? For instance, if *There Shall Be No Night* is as good as I have heard it is, it might be so recorded, and if *Twelfth Night,* now in the throes of preparation with Helen Hayes, Maurice Evans and God knows who else, should prove to be as lovely as it may well be—a better *Twelfth Night* possibly than any of the twenty I have seen in my time—I think its management would be delighted and its cast honored to be invited by the Library of Congress to go on record, incidentally for the benefit of the blind but more importantly for the storehouse of the American spirit.

I've got hold of something here and will not let go until I hear from you.

      Yours to command
      (vintage formula which I never use without
      meaning it)
            A. Woollcott

To MRS. THEODORE ROOSEVELT, JR.

Bomoseen, Vt.
October 7, 1940

Dear Eleanor:

There is a paragraph in my morning's mail which I think Ted would enjoy but as I suspect he is barnstorming the midlands in behalf of the lost cause I send it to you and trust that you will see that it reaches him. The paragraph is plucked from a Tarkington letter. I shall be visiting Kennebunkport week after next and he writes me:

"*And as you suggest, we'll both be gentle with each other*

—even if mutual embarrassments caused by our candidates and their upholders shall have increased by then."

I've asked Quentin [Roosevelt] to attend the Helen Hayes-Maurice Evans production of *Twelfth Night* in Boston on the 21st, the day on which I happen to have an appointment for a check-up by the heart doctor. Family tradition compelled him to accept by Western Union in code. Turning to Noel Coward at breakfast I asked, "What is *The Tempest,* Act V, Scene I, line 215?" After some thought he said it was either "Prithee" or "Sweet, my coz." He turned out to be so near right that it made no difference.

Also I meant to tell you that Martha Cross has been and gone and will, I hope and believe, come again. Noel was here only for a day but he left us a manuscript of his new lyric, which runs as follows:

> *McNary had a little lamb*
> *He called it leg o' mutton*
> *And every time it wagged its tail*
> *It showed its Willkie button.*

Hoping you are the same, I remain

Yours affectionately,
A. W.

To *CORNELIA OTIS SKINNER*

New York City
October 28, 1940

Dear Cornelia:

On my way up to Kennebunkport the other day, I was interested to note that Beverly, Massachusetts, announces itself as the birthplace of the American Navy whereas Lynn, as you approach it, boasts with a huge sign that it is the Home of Marshmallow Fluff. This naturally reminded me of you.

You see, I still marvel at the social *sang froid* with which you passed over a little incident which might so easily have wrecked my last dinner party with your father at Woodstock. Here I had come across the mountains to dine with him who had been my first Charles Surface, my first Petruchio and my first Shylock. And just as I was dipping an abstracted spoon into a nasty little dessert which looked like a slightly soiled white of egg, the still sonorous voice boomed forth disconcertingly as follows: "Aleck, don't you want some goo on your fluff?"

I must also report that he came over to luncheon during my last week at the island when Thornton Wilder and your old college chum Lois Jessup and Senator Walcott were there. He leaped in and out of the boat with the tottering infirmity of a mountain goat.

This Fall the coloring in our part of Vermont reached a new high. During two days when the air was crystalline, Dick Wood caught it all in a moving picture which is the most beautiful I have ever seen. Night before last I showed this to a casually chosen few at Neysa's apartment. She lives at 131 East 66th Street, her doorway facing your old man's. We fetched him in and I think he was vastly entertained. Anyway, I am devoted to him and to you.

A. Woollcott

To *DR. GUSTAV ECKSTEIN*

New York City
November 7, 1940

Dear Gus:

I am off to the island tomorrow morning for twelve days of quiet. Then, on the 21st, I am due back for rehearsals of the "Battle Hymn" broadcast which has been postponed until

December 4th to give Deems Taylor time to arrange and score the music.

I am sorry you missed the November 1st broadcast which was, I think, as good a job as I've ever done. It was drafted on the train going to and from Utica and called for the kind of concentrated work which is the only anodyne I know or ever want.

Al [Getman's] funeral service was in the College Chapel, packed to the doors with men and women who had come from great distances. Life must have rhymed then for Frode Jensen whose room, during three years, in which he worked his way through college, was in the chapel spire because it was his job to toll the bell. It was Frode Al sent for when he had his first attack and after his final message to me, a paragraph dictated on the last day before he went into his final coma, he insisted, although his eyes would not focus, in scrawling something like this. "Frode has been a great help to me and I will tell you about it some time."

I wonder if you remember the chapel bell which has been flinging its notes down into the valley for a hundred and twenty years. It is so vibrant that when I go back to the hill for a visit it wakes me in the night until I get used to it. Hamilton men never forget it and the best poem ever written on the hill is all about it. I know that for me this business of finishing out the race without Al will be not unlike life on the hill if, quite suddenly, the bell were hushed forever.

I know from my only previous experience that I am a delayed-reaction boy and if some months from now you hear me howling like a dog you will know it is grief for the loss of my friend

A. W.

To SOPHIE ROSENBERGER

Bomoseen, Vt.
November 11, 1940

Dear Teacher:

Eyes can be guilty of infidelity and mine had been so unfaithful as to forget how beautiful a picture the "Praying Hands" is until I saw it again here on my own island when I got home on Friday.

I am here for a twelve-day sequestration after a stormy week in which I did two broadcasts in behalf of Mr. Roosevelt, a week turned into a nightmare by the death of my doctor. Now I am being maddened by letters which assure me that one never really loses anything one has ever had. Nonsense! I have just been irreparably impoverished. He had roomed with me while he was studying medicine. He had been my dear and sheltering friend for more than thirty years and I counted that friendship as an honor and a delight. He was one of the rocks on which my house was built and I know now just how England is going to feel when she loses Gibraltar.

He had turned me loose as a patient before he died—the lighter by fifty pounds and the more cautious for a nasty experience. I am under orders—his last injunction—to work intermittently. My next big job will be a nation-wide broadcast on an American theme, with music arranged and conducted by Deems Taylor. It is scheduled now for December 4th. After that, I am to speak—on the 10th—at Hampton Institute in Virginia, lingering between those engagements in Washington, where I shall see enough of Walter Lippmann and Felix Frankfurter and Archie MacLeish to get a fresh charging of my batteries.

This leaves only one of your questions unanswered. Do I love you? Yes, I do, indeed.

Alexander Woollcott

To REBECCA WEST

Bomoseen, Vt.
Armistice Day, 1940

Dear Rebecca:

I do not know why you should believe me when I begin by telling you that for the past four months I have thought of you many times daily.

For long weeks in the late spring and early summer I was down and out, the worse for a damaged heart, incapacitated for the first time in thirty years, "Incensed with the disgusting intricacy of life." It was on May 10th that the hospital shipped me here to the island with orders to lie quiet, do nothing, not even worry. May 10th. As H. G. [Wells] said to me once long ago, "My beautiful Rebecca picked a good day for it."

The first letters I tried to write, as the fog of morphine lifted, were feeble communications, emerging in a palsied script at the rate of a page a day. You will understand that creeping pace when I tell you that once I wanted to report (to my brother) that the doctors had found me guilty of a coronary occlusion and I spent an entire day trying to remember the word "coronary."

Then, as the stock of unanswered letters began to afflict me, the hardest to write were the ones to England—everyone has been staggered by the difficulty of finding words for what we would like to say to our friends in England—and of them I kept putting off till the next day the one to you as something special, so God-damned special that in the end I could not write it at all. I composed a hundred in my mind, even got a long, wordy one down on paper and tore it up. I suppose some nasty vanity was involved in this psychic block, but also involved was my old admiration and the delight I have always taken in you. Perversely this expressed itself in my dashing off glib letters to everyone else—like Hamlet lightly managing to kill everyone else in Denmark before he got around to doing in his uncle. And now I've given up the immodest project of writing you a masterpiece and have decided as more feasible to send you (in weekly installments, of which this is the first) the rough notes for the letter I'd like to write, all the while incurably oppressed, as any journalist would be, by the disadvantage of sending dispatches from the country where the news isn't to the country where it is. We all read and reread every scrap of testimony that comes from England and the letters we get pass from hand to hand.

(Which reminds me that Mrs. Vincent Sheean—Diana Forbes-Robertson as was—cabled without my knowledge for permission to print your letter of September 27th and though I let her have it, after deleting several paragraphs, I promise this will not happen again.)

I am writing from the island to which I have retreated for twelve days after my first week of hard work. The doctors let me out provisionally and I got back to the warpath in time to mix into the campaign, doing two broadcasts for Roosevelt and having the satisfaction of believing that one of them, at least, was as competent a job as I've ever done. And there was a mass-meeting in Carnegie Hall, with Dorothy Thompson and myself among the speakers, and I told the crowd how you and I at the past inauguration had watched the Roosevelts sharing the rain with us and what we said. Do you remember what we said?

It came in handy. Of course, as an Aid-to-Britain boy, I *had* to vote for Roosevelt.

It would surprise you to know how much you have been on this island this past summer. Represented by your letter of May 22nd, represented by *Lions and Lambs* which everyone took to rereading in their wisdom after the event and finding it so good that Ethel Barrymore damned near got away with my *second* copy, too. Represented by the faithful Emanie [Arling] exhorting me (at a time when I could not walk to the jetty) to cable affidavits to our Ambassador assuring him of my eagerness (and financial ability) to support Mr. and Mrs. Anthony West in the manner to which they have been accustomed. Represented by news of Lilly Bonner taking in the Lowinsky children, whose parents once gave me food and shelter because I was with you. Above all, represented by the first chapters of your book which came up for a week-end in the suitcase of Master Guinzburg. On this topic I must here write eloquently because *The Atlantic* has just telephoned for permission to quote, as an advance notice, my letter to George Bye. I have so much more to say on this subject that it must go over till next week— How long since *you* have read those compact pieces by Lynx? Read the one on Winston Churchill. And (to humble you) the one on the then Prince of Wales which, if memory serves, begins, "They will never let you go."

All of which I will now entrust to the airways, realizing that I have left you to guess at all that is in my heart. Give my love to Henry Andrews.

Alexander Woollcott

To *JOAN WOOLLCOTT*

Bomoseen, Vt.
November 18, 1940

Dear Joan:

Is it the Daughters of the American Revolution you are trying to get into? Even though I suspect you of intentions to bore from within I must pass on a word of warning about General Warren. He was a lively and public spirited medico who was appointed general overnight, arrayed himself gaudily to suit that rank, made himself conspicuous on a parapet at Bunker Hill and was therefore popped off in the first ten minutes of the battle. However, it is not because he was a bad general that you should avoid claiming descent from him. It is because he was a bachelor. Your descent is in the direct line from his brother, Stephen, who was properly married all right and to whom, as a wedding gift, Joseph Warren presented the bedroom furniture of which the chest of drawers in due time came to me. I gave it to your father because he seemed more likely to abound in descendants. Your great-great-grandmother was Lydia Warren. On my wall here I have a sampler of hers dated February 16, 1797. If you are interested in such things I will make a notation on the back that it should go to you when I depart this world. The news of Raymond Pearl's death reminds me afresh that this might happen at any moment. Your father will miss him.

Confidentially, the question of my touring in that play has come up again and will be settled before the week is out. The tour would involve a six or seven weeks' engagement in Philadelphia in the course of which I would expect to see something of you.

A. Woollcott

To ROSALIND RICHARDS

Bomoseen, Vt.
November 19, 1940

My dear Miss Richards:

One more question. That toast I myself heard your mother give. I find that it warms British hearts to tell them about it and I am not sure I have the wording right. Is it "Down with all dictators!" or "Death to all dictators!"?

I have just been thrown into confusion by an invitation from the BBC to broadcast to the British Isles on December 28th. Try to think what you yourself would say in an allotted fourteen and a half minute talk and you will see how impossible an assignment it is. I find the task of writing a letter to any friend in England one nicely calculated to paralyze the hand. But an American broadcast that will be addressed to besieged British homes—for that I find it hard to think of a single sentence that would not be either misleading or offensive.

But this broadcast I expect to do on the 4th I should like to have English people overhear and I am trying my best to arrange just that.

Do I seem to be taking myself au grand sérieux? Well, I do take my *work* seriously. And my life as a neighbor. And it is an incurably afflicting memory that on that disastrously telescoped day on which I visited Gardiner last month I should have passed through your mother's gentle house like a tasteless hurricane. I could wish she would write me and say, "Go out again and come in properly."

A. Woollcott

To W. GRAHAM ROBERTSON

Bomoseen, Vt.
November 20, 1940

Dear Graham:

Perhaps you heard last spring that, while touring the Pacific coast in that foolish play that was written for me, I collapsed ignobly with a heart attack, halting the season then and there and throwing a good company out of work. If you also heard that for many a leaden-footed week thereafter I was down and out, I beg to report that now once more I am up and out. I wish with all my heart that I could be with you tonight in Surrey.

Our friends the Lunts, on their way to Canada for the start of a triumphal tour in Sherwood's most moving and beautiful play, *There Shall Be No Night,* passed this way the other day, their train halting for ten minutes at the obscure railway station where we meet all guests headed for the island.

Waiting for them on the platform we had a goodly supply

of such right New England refreshments as cider and doughnuts—enough cider and doughnuts for the whole company. In such times we might have been more rationally occupied for if there is a troupe in the world that doesn't need feeding it's that one. Nor cheering, either. At least Lynn and Alfred feel as never before that they are engaged in something worth doing. This play lets them say every night what is in their hearts so that nightly they are refreshed and renewed.

I've often felt—I remember feeling it strongly at the first uncostumed run-through of *The Sea Gull*—that a performance can never recapture the clean perfection it has when it is first played barely, under the monastic pilot-light. There is that in the Sherwood play and the way they feel about it that somehow maintains that quality week after week, month after month, city after city.

It was late in the run when I was first able to see it, tottering to New York, a still shaky convalescent who was defenseless as the play unfolded. I had thought myself quite safe emotionally as it went along and was the more unprepared, on my way backstage, for the sudden and violent need of privacy. I bolted for the nearest covert which turned out to be Lynn's dressing-room. She tactfully shooed people out so that I might have a little decent quiet for a good cry. But if she counted on being allowed to stay and enjoy the spectacle herself she was in error. I threw her out and wept noisily amid her costumes.

I've seen them often since. One night after the play I took Charlie Chaplin up to supper and on the morning they left town I was down at the station to see them off.

Of course we never meet without speaking of you and wishing you were here with us—and knowing you would rather be where you are.

Alexander Woollcott

To *LESLIE BANKS*

[Mr. Banks, the English actor, played the leading role in *Wine of Choice* with Woollcott.]

Bomoseen, Vt.
November 20, 1940

Dear Leslie:
            Today I am sought out by a letter from the New York office of the BBC beginning with this paragraph:

"Would you care to broadcast a fourteen and a half minute talk to England on December 28th next, the fee being as previously, one hundred dollars? If so, would you agree not to stress the political angle, it being Christmas week, but deal with the more human and seasonable aspects of the United States at that time?"

This is a staggering proposal to me, who, ever since last May, have found it hard enough to write man-to-man to my friends in England.

After collapsing ignobly while on tour in that funny, foolish play, I was down and out for many weeks. But now, more or less on probation, I am up and out. In these times there can be no anodyne except work and no satisfaction except in work that contributes (or seems to do so) to the only thing in the world that matters just now. It seemed to me that the first job was to get Roosevelt re-elected and I am glad I got back onto the warpath in time to campaign for him.

I am up to my neck in preparations for an ambitious broadcast I am supposed to do on December 4th. It will be me performing in collaboration with an orchestra conducted by Deems Taylor. I am trying to make the BBC believe as I do that it would be better served if this broadcast—or a repetition of it or a recording of it—were overheard by British listeners. There are no words for what I would like to say to my friends in

England but any American with my viewpoint has got a whole lot to say to his fellow-countrymen.

Yet, while the world holds its breath, one becomes engaged in such foolish minor preoccupations. Here have I today been cleaning out my cubbyholes, engrossed with two fading photographs showing scenes from Galsworthy's *Justice* as it was done in New York back in the spring of 1916. It was then revealed for the first time that John Barrymore was a good actor. Cathleen Nesbitt played the girl and my momentous task last evening was ferreting among my papers for the address of one Jennifer Ramage who is at school somewhere in Providence, Rhode Island. I want to send her the photographs because she is Cathleen's daughter. Well, bustling about and looking for her address was my heroic occupation while, according to the radio news bulletins, the bombers were at work over Birmingham. Of such sickening discrepancies is each day made up.

My best to Gwen. I think of you both often and always with deep affection.

Alexander Woollcott

To *LAURA E. RICHARDS*

Washington, D. C.
December 9, 1940

Dear Mrs. Richards:

Yes, my mail, too, must be coming from all over but I had to be on my way before it could be collected at the various points and brought to me. It will be forwarded to me in batches here and I will go through it when I get back on Wednesday from Virginia. I am speaking there tomorrow night to the Negro students at Hampton Institute. Acceptance of the invitation to speak there was mysteriously obligatory. I haven't stopped to examine the reason.

But the very night of the broadcast and the next morning enough telegrams came in, including the most important one from Gardiner, to tell me what I wanted to know. A broadcaster is peculiarly dependent on such testimony. A speaker from a platform does not have to be told. He knows. Perhaps he even knows more than is good for him. I am always abashed by the anecdote about John Bunyan. A woman in his congregation once asked him if he knew what a wonderful sermon he had preached that morning. "Yes," he replied, "the devil whispered it in my ear just as I left the pulpit."

But a broadcaster is really in need of testimony for professional guidance. And this was particularly true in this instance because I was, though only the technically minded may have noticed it, trying out a new form. New, that is, for radio. I mean a musical score composed to accompany and sustain a prose narrative. Something like this had been tried by Richard Strauss, notably in the case of a score written for *Enoch Arden*. I could have only a dream of an idea, turn the script over to my betters and thereafter trust everything to them. When I saw the hours and hours of work this meant for others I had the decency to feel a little guilty. Then came the actual performance in one of the New York theatres which the National Broadcasting Company has converted into a studio. As 7.30 approached the house was packed, with people standing in the balcony and gallery. On the stage was the orchestra and chorus with Deems Taylor himself on the conductor's stand. The left-hand box, glass-enclosed and sound-proof, housed the engineers whose job it is, with dials and gadgets like the dashboard of an automobile, to control the volume and pitch of both voice and music as it goes out on to the air. In the right-hand box, also glass-enclosed and sound-proof, sat Mr. W., hideously visible under his desk lamp, himself seeing nothing but his script and hearing no note of music, completely dependent for his cues on an alert young man who sat beside him with a patiently annotated score on his lap and earphones clamped on his head. Through the ear-pieces he could hear the orchestra and his score had been so marked that he knew at exactly which note it would be time for Mr. W. to speak again. All I needed to see was his outstretched, uplifted hand. Whenever that hand pointed downward I spoke.

When thus described, does the whole mechanism seem damnably and preposterously intricate? Well, it is. But I think there is some merit—I am sure there is some fun—for any journalist to try to use each medium available in his time. That you heard the broadcast and were pleased is more than half my pay, which (I am not speaking boastfully) is saying a good deal.

I am due back in New York for a strange christening at the hearth in the house of the Irving Berlins. He was brought up as a Jew and she as a Catholic. Her mother was the lovely Katharine Duer. This time the youngest of their three daughters —an enchanting child named Elizabeth Irving Berlin—is to be started on her way by a ceremony at which Alice Duer Miller and I will stand as sponsors. Each of us brings her a wish and both of us join in a present to remember us by when she is grown up. I do not know Mrs. Miller's plans but I am wishing that all the days of her life the child may have courage. As a present, instead of bringing a silver mug or a napkin-ring, we are giving Elizabeth Irving a two-volume edition of the Oxford Dictionary bound in Morocco and stamped with her name in gold.

Once that chore is finished, I shall be off to the island, counting on staying there at least until the middle of January and hoping that the ice, already forming in the bays along the mainland, will be solid enough by the week before Christmas to let me drive all the way from the station to my front door.

My best to all your household. I fairly burst with affection every time I think of you. I hope you don't mind.

Pumblechook

To JOAN WOOLLCOTT JENNINGS

New York City
December 18, 1940

Dear Mrs. J:

    I hope that you like your marriage and that I, when our paths cross, shall like your husband.

    Let us dispose, for the time being, of your debt to me which, properly enough, is more on your mind than on mine. I should like to have you pay it back under one of two circumstances: (a) That you do it when, if ever, money is flowing freely in your direction and you can make the repayment without a wrench, or (b), that I myself am in difficulties in which case I should let out a squawk. If, as seems not unlikely, I should be gathered unto my fathers before either of these contingencies arises, I hope you will regard it as a bequest to you. And if there is any order in your life I wish you would file this letter away as evidence of these testamentary intentions. To this contingent request there is attached not a condition but a suggestion. If I should hurry to my grave before you settle our account I think you might keep it in mind that I would like to have you make your repayment take the form of putting some other youngster through college some day.

    From Washington, whence I have just returned, I went over on Sunday and had lunch with your father and mother in their strangely quiet house. I thought they both looked well and they seemed to have taken your nuptials with the greatest tranquillity. Of course this may have been only comparative.

A. W.

IX

1941

To *WALTER LIPPMANN*

Bomoseen, Vt.
January 1, 1941

Dear Walter:
      I've been meaning to write you and Mrs. Lippmann to say how agreeably I remember that dinner at your house two weeks ago and now another occasion to write you turns up. I remember your quoting the late Justice Holmes as telling you that he had not realized that Lincoln was a great man until he read the Nicolay and Hay life. I am wondering when he read it and can find no record that he ever laid eyes on it.

    This is odd because, as you may know, he kept a record of all his reading year by year from 1881 until the day of his death. I think the original of this notebook is in the Harvard Law School Library but a number of facsimiles were made in '35 and I have been poring over the one I borrowed from Felix Frankfurter. His own magnum opus, *The Common Law*, was published in 1881 and the record begins with the item "My book." Oddly enough it ends—during the last three years the entries were made in the handwriting of his current secretary—with Thornton Wilder's *Heaven's My Destination*. It was, if anybody's is, but I doubt if he thought so.

In 1902 he read Norman Hapgood's *Lincoln* and in 1918 he read Lord Charnwood's, but I can see no trace of his encountering the ten volumes of Nicolay and Hay. He could hardly have overlooked such a chunk of reading when he was so careful to note everything. Thus in 1914 he not only recorded his first encounter with Freud but such trivia as *Tobogganing on Parnassus* and *In Other Words* by F.P.A. and also, since I'm on the subject, *A Preface to Politics* and *Drift and Mastery*. Undiscouraged by this experience he read *The Stakes of Diplomacy* in 1915 and followed it immediately (there is probably some association with Fortinbras here) with *Hamlet*.

Well, what I would like to know is when he told you about Lincoln and if he left you with any impression as to when he read it.

A. Woollcott

To LYNN FONTANNE

Richmond, Va.
February 21, 1941

Dear Lynn:

As I see that you, too, plan to lay off for Holy Week, I am wondering whether you both intend to hot-foot it for Genesee Depot. Or do broadcasting commitments and medical attention require a week in New York? (In that connection I would like to know if Robin Hood is still the apple of what, for the sake of delicacy, we might call your eye.)

I ask about Genesee Depot because, laying off after a week in Columbus, we open Easter Monday in Chicago. There I shall be in the midlands with a car in my possession and a week of leisure. I had thought to drive over to the Tarkingtons if they are still in Indianapolis, to visit Gus in Cincinnati and then to hurry, buckety-buckety, for a night or two at Genesee.

Speaking of the Tarkingtons, a recent talk with him has stimulated afresh the already passionate conviction of *The Saturday Evening Post* that I should do a Profile of Gus [Eckstein] for them. This presents unique difficulties. Half of the things in the piece would have to be things he himself has already reported and reported better than I could. The difficulty about the other half derives from the fact that he is, in my considered opinion, a saint. I am embarrassed at the thought of Gus finding what I really think of him in type, wedged between brightly colored ads for Campbell's soup and Chrysler cars. And I think he would feel an embarrassment among his co-workers and neighbors in Cincinnati if I ever put the minimum truth about him in print while he is alive.

Not that I shall have a chance to afterwards. He will live for ever and ever. When he is an old, old man (looking roughly about thirty-six) I shall have been dust in the churchyard—and you and Alfred, too—for so many years that he will have only the dimmest recollection of us. He will still be driving his 1941 Ford but he will have forgotten who gave it to him.

However, the trouble with writing to you now is that I have waited too long. I waited under some mysterious compulsion not to acknowledge that cozy bathrobe until it was actually in my possession, which it now most satisfactorily is, replacing the one Leontovitch bought in Chicago for me to wear in *Wine of Choice* (no expense to the Guild) and which by now is not only as ragged as fringe but dotted with souvenirs of many and many a breakfast.

I have waited so long that I now have more to tell you than I could be bothered with. I will merely submit a few items.
A. Nancy Woollcott Smith is with child in Burlington, Vermont.
B. I got an enchanting letter last night from Graham [Robertson] and although it largely duplicates the information contained in yours I shall send you, before the week is out, a

copy for you and Alfred to read because, like me, you both savor every word he says.

C. Thornton is being dispatched by the State Department to South America where his name, thanks to "The Bridge" [*The Bridge of San Luis Rey*], is the most potent of all American writers. He already thinks in Spanish (he had read it for ten years) and is dashing off a play for production at the big theatre in Lima.

D. At a dinner at Edna Ferber's in New York last week George Kaufman spoke so candidly to Florence Eldridge that she left the table in tears. I like to think of my good work going on while I am away.

E. On Sunday I was enormously relieved to get a cable from Henry Andrews telling me that Rebecca West had that day come triumphantly through an operation at a nursing home in Reading. Only two days before I had received a long, luscious letter from her written at various times during December. Of this, too, I shall send you a copy.

F. I may not have told you that on the last Sunday of the year, largely at the instigation of Bob Sherwood, I went up to Montreal and did one of those Canadian broadcasts that go by short-wave to England. In it I happened to quote the same Longfellow poem into which the President dipped for the message which Willkie carried over to Churchill. I had hit upon another passage.

G. A word of warning about Hershey, Pennsylvania, where we played on Monday night and where I see you are scheduled to wind up the week before Holy Week. We sold out the nineteen hundred seats and had two hundred standees, all of whom listened in a kind of grieved, Lutheran silence to the coarser jocosities of this script. If you have never played there I think you should be warned that no Negro attendant can find lodging in the town and that at the great Hershey Hotel (where I had the suite that had previously been polluted only by Sonja Henie who must have found that it saved time to skate from her bed to the bathroom) they lock up the kitchen at 10 P.M. sharp and thereafter will give you nothing but chocolate drops. These, to be sure, are gratis but they are not on my diet.

H. Speaking of my diet I am, if anything, thinner than when we last met and feel robust as all get-out. The gain in strength since November 1st, when that campaign broadcast left me a quivering mass of cardiac spasms, is almost beyond belief.

I. Thinking to surprise everybody and steal a march on the Kaufmans, Moss Hart flew privily from Palm Beach to Washington on Monday greedily intent on responding to the first cry of "Author! Author!" which might be raised on the opening night. Unfortunately he got the wrong week and swept up to the National Theatre only to find it occupied by *Tobacco Road*.

As a matter of fact we go into Washington for two weeks on Monday the 24th and during that fortnight—or perhaps pending good behavior—I shall be lodged at the White House, where you might address me the only answer all this calls for. I mean the one to the question about Holy Week.

D. D.

[Woollcott was again on tour in *The Man Who Came to Dinner*.]

To *EDMUND WILSON*

Richmond, Va.
February 21, 1941

My dear Wilson:
If by any chance something will bring you to Washington during the two weeks beginning February 24th or to Philadelphia during the three weeks beginning March 10th

—in Philadelphia I could even put you up as I expect to have a house there—I can be spared the labor of writing you a long letter *re* Rudyard [Kipling] and the Balestiers. However, if you won't come to Mahomet I *will* write you.

In the meantime you might note that Arthur Waugh's book of memoirs was called *One Man's Road*. In it there is a good deal about Wolcott Balestier. My guess is that it was published in this country six or seven years ago, perhaps by Longmans, Green. You might also note that a Kipling story (as worthy of mention as any you do mention in the second article, of which Ted Weeks sent me the proof) is one that has not yet been published in this country. It was called "Proofs of Holy Writ" and appeared in the *Strand Magazine* for December 1934. I've reason to believe that John Buchan presented him with the idea for it. The result is one of the most saturated of his latter day concentrates yet is one of the best things he ever wrote.

I share your feeling about "The Gardener" which seems to me a masterpiece. There is this to be noted about Kipling's stories—that few of them lend themselves to oral retelling. One of the exceptions is "The Gardener" which, recasting it of course into words of my own, I used as a fireside tale in a broadcast I did from Chicago on Kipling's seventieth birthday. It seemed astonishing that he was only seventy—younger, for example, than Shaw and Pershing to take two wildly arbitrary examples, although he had seemed part of the landscape for as long as I could remember.

I don't care to discuss Dickens with you. I don't know what you mean by his "most successful book" to which I note you attach the weasel-word, "perhaps." Whatever you mean by it, *Bleak House* is topped either by *Pickwick, David Copperfield,* or *Great Expectations*.

You *would* have to listen to Information Please on the night when I must have given the impression of being not quite bright. The last time I appeared—it was less than a month ago—I was that snotty little teacher's pet whose hand is always up in the air and answers every question. As you may guess, they were none of them difficult.

Incidentally, I may be allergic to *Bleak House* because it was the only Dickens book I had not read before I was twelve, at which point I became more critical—though not much more. I never read it until I was in my thirties and then it seemed to me tremendously padded. You could hear him panting as he ground out the installments.

In letting me know whether I am to write you or talk to you, you can address me for the next two weeks at the National Theatre in Washington. But you can't get a seat. They are all sold. This is a much more successful play than *The Crime in the Whistler Room*.

A. Woollcott

To BEATRICE KAUFMAN

The White House
February 25, 1941

Lamb Girl:

I am looking forward with pleasure and apprehension to the impending invasion from New York. For me it will be three first nights in one week. Last evening's went as well as I had any right to ask. Tonight the President and Mrs. Roosevelt occupy the royal box while the whole house will be crawling with Secret Service men. They may make a good audience at that because, even with Taylor Holmes, this play must provide them with more fun than they usually get while on duty. The President has invited the entire company to the White House for supper afterward.

Any of your party could pay a morning call on me in our

quarters here on Saturday or Sunday or both. I have the big Pink Room that was occupied by Queen Elizabeth so that the small and rather chilly bedroom adjoining gives Hennessey the status of lady-in-waiting which he seems to enjoy. But, if you have any notion of visiting the tenants of this house, my local adviser in Washington etiquette—Joe Alsop has taken over this job since Alice Longworth has become such an isolationist that she no longer cares to meet me—tells me that one of you, Alice [Duer Miller] or Ruth Gordon or Moss or you yourself, should write Mrs. Roosevelt announcing that you are coming to town, reporting where you will be lodged and asking if there is any time when you can pay your respects.

A. W.

To *EDMUND WILSON*

Washington, D. C.
March, 3, 1941

Dear Wilson:

I find I have no time to write you what I could tell you if our paths should cross. I don't know how to compromise between a post card and something of novel length. This hasty note, dictated between chores, merely outlines one of the main points.

Old Balestier was a lawyer from Rochester who, oddly enough, was once counsel to the Mikado. He emigrated to Vermont, taking his children with him. As to Wolcott, you will find in Waugh's book the account of his whirlwind invasion of the publishing business in England during which he annexed Kipling and was actually planning to put Tauchnitz out of business on the Continent. But he was cut off long before his prime. In the interval his sister Carrie had come over to keep house for him somewhere along the Thames—at Marlowe or Maidenhead or somewhere like that. Kipling had started on a contractual journey around the world when, in Japan, he was halted by a cable from Henry James telling him that Wolcott had died. He turned in his tracks and in the emotion of his return to England, married the bereft Carrie. He then resumed the journey around the world as a honeymoon. You may remember that when he reached Japan the second time he got word that his bank had gone to the wall, wherefore the move to Vermont was dictated in part by thrift. But there was another consideration and that was Beatty Balestier. This younger brother was the problem child of the family. To keep an eye on him, Wolcott had brought him over to London several times and there are uneasy recollections of his striding through the Savoy, stewed to the gills, dragged by several leashed wolfhounds.

On Wolcott's deathbed he left Beatty in trust to Carrie and it was also to keep six eyes on him—her two and Rudyard's four—that they set up housekeeping in Vermont.

Now Beatty, whom I knew in his later years, was a charming and contentious rattle-pate and when he grew restive in Brattleboro it was natural for him to threaten to bust his brother-in-law in the nose. As he was twice as tall and four times as strong, Kipling had, I think, no recourse but to ask that he be put under bonds to keep peace. Up at my island in Vermont I have a photostat of the Brattleboro *Reformer* for the day after the order to show cause was heard in court. When Kipling took the stand, the little courtroom was crowded with forty newspaper men from all over the country. This was the climax and symbol of Kipling's vast discomfort in America.

What he fled from was the pressure of the mob which milled around him as it had never done, before or since, around any author except Dickens. The difference was that Dickens, being a born exhibitionist, enjoyed it. Kipling found it distasteful and frightening. During that siege of illness when his firstborn died and he himself hovered on the brink at the old Hotel

Grenoble in New York—in my day as a reporter this was a seedy old caravansary at Seventh Avenue and Fifty-Fifth Street and I seem to recall that the dazzling Della Fox of *Wang* and the cigarette-card era died in the gutter in front of it, shapely and stinko to the last—that pressure continued. I think you will find from contemporary newspapers that the club-women of that pre-Hokinson era knelt day and night around the hotel so that traffic was shut off for three blocks in all directions.

It was from this that the Kiplings fled to England and then again fled in turn from the enchanting cottage at Rottingdean where I myself have stayed because, in 1920, it was occupied by young friends of mine. It had been built by smugglers three hundred years before and it was sheltered by seven gardens. It seemed secluded enough when the Kiplings took it. But in time American tourists began to arrive in busloads, crawling under the hedges, trampling down the rose bushes and driving the Kiplings into still further retreat. What may have been a moderate protective instinct on Mrs. Kipling's part became an obsession with her and during the last thirty years of his life she succeeded in shutting the world away from him. But in the process she also shut him away from the world and this was disastrous because, after all, just as Shaw and Wells are primarily pedagogues, Kipling was primarily a reporter. *Captains Courageous*, written after only three weeks in Gloucester, was a work of reportorial genius. Just how he did it is told us by implication in a fanciful piece which you will not find in his collected works, although in telling you about it I may be teaching my grandmother how to suck eggs. That was a piece in which he described how Shakespeare got all his stuff for *The Tempest* out of a garrulous sailor who had escaped from the wreck of the expedition to the Bermoothes and whom Shakespeare had plied with drink in the tavern across the way from the Globe Theatre. The New York *Times* republished this bit in the several special supplements it issued at the time of the tercentenary in 1916.

Have I, despite my haste, indicated what *I* think was the chief source of the marked change Kipling's work underwent in the latter half of his life? His craftsmanship improved but he had been cut off, by circumstance, from his supply of fresh material.

Alexander Woollcott

P.S. During the heyday of the AEF, Kipling, momentarily placated by our having sent two million soldiers to France, gave the *Stars and Stripes* the privilege of being the first to publish one of his poems. In acknowledgment, we sent a courier, accompanied by a blushing young orderly, to deliver the first copy off the press. Kipling received them and it at Brown's Hotel. The courier acquitted himself as instructed and the incident was about to close when the private, whose name I've forgotten and who was breathing heavily and obviously bursting with excitement, suddenly stepped forward, shook the gifted hand and said, "My, Mr. Kipling, it will be a great day when my folks in Georgia hear that I actually met the man who wrote the *Rubaiyat of Omar Khayyam*."

A. W.

To LAURA E. RICHARDS

Columbus, Ohio
April 1, 1941

My dear Mrs. Richards:
            Since you tell me you would like to know where and how I am, I must, however skeptical, report that I seem to be in Columbus, Ohio, and that I feel better than I have in years.

Then you ask what I am doing. Well, among other things I am devoting four months of this year to completing that tour which was interrupted by my unseemly collapse in San Francisco last spring. After three weeks in Chicago, we go to Montreal to play an entire week as a benefit for the British and then work our way down through Springfield, Worcester, New Haven and the like to Boston.

And what do I think of *Random Harvest?* Not much. More specifically, I think the thing Hilton had to tell was a *short* story in the sense that *Ethan Frome* and *Dr. Jekyll and Mr. Hyde* are short stories and that he unwisely inflated it into something longer, spoiled it by telling it in too many words. I suspect he was hounded by the feeling that he'd let too many years go by without writing a book. Authors do get that way.

As to the other books you mentioned, I have not seen them because I have so much required reading to do for the Readers Club of which I am one of the four judges and which, month by month, will reclaim some good work from obscurity. I am urging Aksakov's *Years of Childhood,* Trevelyan's *Early History of Charles James Fox,* Chesterton's *Dickens,* and a delightful book of memoirs called *An Englishman in Paris* which caused a considerable stir when it was first published anonymously along about 1890.

During the two weeks we were in Baltimore I did take time off to wallow in the Holmes-Pollock correspondence which has just been issued by the Harvard Press. I first became acquainted with the mind of the Justice when, in Shanghai some years ago, there was published without sanction a collection of letters he had written to a young Chinese law student named Mr. Wu. This was an acquaintance he had made long after he was eighty and the letters were completely enchanting. If he wrote like that when he was in his eighties, I thought, what must his letters have been like when he was in his prime? Therefore I approached the Holmes-Pollock correspondence (which covered a span of sixty years) with the greater eagerness only to discover that the last decade of his life *was* his prime. His was a mind that grew in grace and charm after he was fifty. By the time he was seventy his letters took on a real lustre and from then on grew better and better every year. Indeed, while I was in Washington Justice Frankfurter dug up for me a note the Justice wrote when he was almost ninety-one. It was written in response to a letter of regret his fellow-judges sent him when he retired from the bench. It is buried now in the files of the Supreme Court. I send you a copy.

I have thought of a score of quite plausible explanations as to why I should be going buckety-buckety around the country in this play at such a time as this but I see no reason for trying to fob any of them off on you. I suppose it is because I enjoy it.

Yours affectionately,
Old Faithful

To *REBECCA WEST*

Columbus, Ohio
April 3, 1941

Dear Rebecca:

Here are some notes for the letter I would write you if my life were not at the moment so messy.

First two brief ones about your book [*Black Lamb and Grey Falcon*]. I shall begin by confessing (what I am sure most of the people who know you should confess) that when, some time ago, I heard you were at work on a book on Yugoslavia I said, "What a pity!", or more precisely, "Good God, why Yugoslavia do you suppose?" Of course I have long since eaten those words but this week they make a banquet. In Washington, where I spent some time in December and again in February and March, I saw a good deal of Mr. Constantin Fotitch. He is the plump, engaging and chucklesome creature who is the Yugoslavian Minister. From such observers as Joe Alsop, Felix Frankfurter and Walter

Lippmann, I hear he is generally regarded as the ablest man in the diplomatic service in Washington. His natural conservatism and preference for under-statement has made him modify my prediction in *The Atlantic* that you had written a timeless book. He merely tells everyone he sees that, according to me, you have written a book which will be a best-seller for three hundred years.

One more note on the subject of your work and then, because I think it must render my letters monotonous, I promise not to mention it again for a year. As a topic it nags at me because I cannot understand why, quite abruptly and after a long professional life, you should suddenly begin to write four times as well as you ever wrote before. In particular it is marked by that cool serenity which would seem to come from a mind composed and how you have managed that in these times is beyond me. I have in mind two recent magazine pieces of yours. God knows when you wrote them or under what title, but one of them came out in *The Saturday Evening Post* as "Around Us the Wail of the Sirens" and is the one which includes that obnoxious refugee. You succeeded in making the reader want to bash in her head as one wanted to bash in the head of that husband in *Vera* which Elizabeth wrote in order to relieve her feelings about Frank Russell.

Raffish old Elizabeth went to her problematical reward the other day in Charleston with only Pat Wallace—there's a tangled story for you—to hold her hand, Elizabeth dying far from her German garden but going down with the orchestra playing, her name still fresh from the best-seller lists and Hollywood in labor with the movie of *Mr. Skeffington*.

The other piece—I have switched authoresses now—was the Reporter-at-Large article in *The New Yorker*, the one that began with Pounce the ginger cat and ended with the sprung and blasted table. This, I think, was the most telling and illuminating piece of writing to come out of England since the war. This, at last, as E. B. White wrote me, is what it must be like. This is true genius in reporting and it's done in a style of such shining lucidity that it is like breathing Swiss air to read it.

I am still rattled by the time-lag in correspondence with England. Here was I on a Friday in February in Baltimore, revelling in a long rich letter from you written on sundry days in December, yet reading it with the intervening knowledge, gleaned from Henry [Andrews] through the Viking Press, that you were due for a serious operation. And also plucking out of the air (from [Wendell] Willkie himself and other sources) that it was you and Henry who had entertained him one night when he was in England. But what about the operation? Had you had it? Were you still going to have it? That was on a Friday. Two days later came Henry's cable from Reading. This was an immense relief to everybody. But in the interval I have heard that you have been wretched in the aftermath and I do not know whether this is written in love and sympathy to somebody flat on her back or in envy and admiration to somebody out raising the roof.

This damned time-lag! It is baffling to come guiltily upon your dutiful expressions of sympathy over my minute illness when that unique collapse in a working life of forty years (I've been on my own since I was fourteen) had bowled me over so many months before that it had long since lost its fascination as a subject even for me. Having had no previous experience with convalescence I did not know when I began to get about again in October whether I was but half recovered or should think of my tottering condition as part of the fixed routine of being fifty-four. As I now feel better than I have for some years it has begun to dawn on me that I may amount to something yet.

Here's a literary footnote for you. You may have noted in the press that when Willkie went to London he carried with him a note from President Roosevelt which turned out to be several lines from a poem by Longfellow about the ship of state. I was the more interested because in a broadcast I had done in Montreal for the Canadians on the last Sunday in December, I had extracted three other lines from the same poem:

> Our hearts, our hopes, our prayers, our tears
> Our faith triumphant o'er our fears
> Are all with thee—are all with thee.

It seems that Churchill read F.D.R.'s excerpt when Willkie handed it to him. "Who did you say wrote this?" "Longfellow," said Mr. Willkie. "Well," said the P.M., "it's a damned bad poem."

In Washington I was lodged at the White House and saw a good deal of Harry Hopkins who had the room across the hall. Mine was the vast pink bedroom occupied two years ago by Queen Elizabeth. It was more dear to me because it had more recently been occupied by Martha Gellhorn [Mrs. Ernest Hemingway], who, with Hemingway in tow (I find comfort in the fact that women do not stay married to Hemingway), is now somewhere between Hongkong and the Burma Road to which she has been assigned by *Collier's*. In Washington I also saw a good deal of Averell Harriman before his departure. He is an old and dear friend of mine. With Winant, Conant, Harriman and Ben Cohen in England I think we are more creditably represented than we have been since Dr. Franklin was our spokesman in London.

Into this air-mail letter—easy come, easy go—I shall tuck a piece which H.G. [Wells] seems to have written four years ago. The magazine recently reprinted it in leaflet form and sent it to a lot of us with the suggestion that we do likewise. I am still waiting for inspiration.

A. Woollcott

To *HERSCHEL V. WILLIAMS, JR.*

[Before Major Williams joined the army he was vice-president of the advertising firm of Ruthrauff and Ryan.]

*Boston, Mass.
May 26, 1941*

Dear Herschel:

You asked me to jot down on paper some of the ideas that occurred to me when we discussed this morning the possibility of my doing or sharing in a radio program for the General Electric Company.

A complete prospectus on such short notice would hardly be practical and, in any event, I think a client would be better served who, without any too precise blueprint, turned me loose for an experimental thirteen weeks with an option on the resulting program if they care to continue. What I would enjoy doing is a weekly half-hour of words and music which informed the young and reminded the old of the inexhaustible riches of courage and vitality and adventure in the American past and present. I don't know what such a program should be called but the underlying objective must be the instilling of a pride in this country. I can see myself throwing all my weight into such divers contributions as these for instance:

A. A biography (with music by Deems Taylor) of the oldest living American, i.e., one of the Redwood trees in California.

B. An eye-witness account (with music by Deems Taylor) of Washington crossing the Delaware.

C. A description of such a unique and fabulous spot as the great aigrette rookery near Charleston during the nesting season. Now obviously the first two call for an immense amount of preparation and work and their like could not be turned out by one person once a week for fifty-two weeks of the year. But they are high spots to be kept in mind as indicating the character of the program I propose. After all, my chief contribution should be the good story told by the fireside after dinner, whether it is the story of "The Juggler of Notre Dame" or "The Death of Stephen Foster."

Finally, if I were regularly or intermittently on any General Electric program, I think I should make a report at least once every five weeks from Schenectady, throwing each time into narrative form in language comprehensible to laymen, some of the wonders that are being accomplished there. For that company at Schenectady is just as much of a university as Harvard or Chicago and I think it might be said that the people have a right to hear what is going on there.

I am completely unwilling to shoulder all of the work of such a program in addition to appearing on it. I should have as a collaborator a first rate impresario working on it as a showman morning, noon and night, planning the features, arranging for special numbers six or eight weeks in advance, and, in cahoots with me, rounding up the guest stars whose recurrence ought to be part of the picture.

I am unwilling to sign up for exclusive use on any program at all unless that program seems to me of valuable contribution to American life. I have too many other alternative sources of revenue to be willing to give all my time and imagination to a project which does not command my own respect.

At the risk of sounding self-important (although you will know better) I am reluctant, in such times as these, to vanish into the depths of any project which does not seem to me a form of public service.

A. Woollcott

To ARCHIBALD MACLEISH

Bomoseen, Vt.
June 7, 1941

Dear Ambrose:
    This unavoidably tedious letter is conscientiously written as a final contribution to your radio series.

As one who within the past two years has lectured or played to a hundred American cities and has been descended upon in each by a swarm of reporters all sent out to get interviews, I know it has not dawned on the city editors of the country that the interview is the dullest and most fatuous form of journalism. As editor of a department in one or another New York paper for fourteen years I never allowed an interview to be printed. What would you say were the four most successful journalistic ventures of the past twenty years? *Life? The New Yorker?* Winchell's column? *Reader's Digest?* At least these four have this in common—none of them has ever printed an interview. Yet from sheer momentum the city editors of the country go right on with the silly practice as if no helpful hint had ever been given them.

Well, here's another hint meant to be helpful. I think that the radio practice of dramatizing incidents—the casting of them into dialogue form with a forlorn and doomed attempt at illusion—belongs in the same category. It is persisted in despite the fact that no programs using this device have ever been any good. If you were to suggest that Amos and Andy is an exception to the rule I might be able to persuade you that it is not. The good programs using dialogue—Jack Benny's, Fred Allen's, Information Please, We, the People, and so forth—all have this in common: that the setting of them is supposed to be a radio studio and the listeners are not asked, on too short notice and with too little help, to do any pretending.

You will probably discount all this as an opinion of your

scheme set down offhand by one who perhaps should have listened to half a dozen of your programs before making any comment. But as I seem unlikely to hear many of them this would probably mean that you would never hear my two cents' worth. Actually, I have read one script—the first—and heard part of another—the one I was on. Each of them seemed to me a confused and confusing mess. Well, think it over. And meanwhile show this to Master Cohen. This is not meant as a whisper behind his back but a shout in his ear from one who wants to make emphatic one man's doubt that his scheme is good.

Ilex

To W. *GRAHAM ROBERTSON*

London
October 8, 1941

Dear Graham:

You may have discovered from the papers that I have arrived in England. Last evening, when I came through the fog from Scotland and came to this hotel there were already swarms of reporters asking why I had come to England.

I invented various answers, telling them, at the caprice of the moment, that I had been sent over by the Columbia Broadcasting System to do a bit of oral journalism for them or that I had been commissioned by an American magazine to write some articles or that I was going to do a series of after-dinner talks on the BBC. I thought it might involve too much tedious explanation if I gave them the real reason—that I had come over to see you.

I come bearing gifts, one from Lynn for you and a few of my own selection. Some day early next week I will drive down to see you.

Dear Graham, when the war broke out I had not thought that you and I would ever meet again in this world and now I shall soon be with you.

        Yours affectionately,
          Alexander Woollcott

X

1942

To *COLONEL WILLIAM J. DONOVAN*

Bomoseen, Vt.
January 4, 1942

Dear Bill:

I have been to England and done my job there and come back and delivered twelve lectures in the midlands and retreated to my base here in order to catch my breath, of which my supply is less than in days of yore.

On January 15th I intend to arrive in Washington and loiter for a week or ten days, asking and listening and hoping thereby to find out what I can do in 1942, and what I might best attempt to do. I have accumulated so much to tell you and to ask you that I could wish we might have another midnight confab in Georgetown. This, however, is not a hint for bed and board, as two ladies, each more beautiful than you, have offered to provide me with the same during my Washington visit.

Did the publishers of *Black Lamb and Grey Falcon* ever send you the advance copy I asked them to? In any event, have you read it? So often during the past weeks I have had occasion to remember your prophecy that, in the long retrospect, the Yugoslav resistance might seem to have been the determining factor in the war.

I miss Father Duffy. Don't you?

A. Woollcott

To HOWARD DIETZ

Bomoseen, Vt.
January 4, 1942

My dear Howard:

On January 19th, Ethel Barrymore, by beginning her Chicago engagement in *The Corn Is Green*, and Kit Cornell, by launching the new Bernstein play in San Francisco, will fittingly observe my birthday. But so far I have not heard what you are going to do about it. Your plan to give a dinner party, to which, of course, I would wear my fur cap and red mittens, will be frustrated by the circumstance that I have to be in Washington that night. Instead, will you give the dinner on the night of January 13th, when I *shall* be in New York?

I leave the whole matter of place and menu to you, but in dread lest you fill the table up with Morrie Ryskind and the like, I must stipulate that you ask only Tanis [Dietz] unless you could manage to have Bob and Madeline Sherwood, Raymond Gram Swing and Vilhjalmur Stefansson, a foursome who admittedly have nothing in common beyond the fact that I would like to see them while I am in New York.

A. Woollcott

To LAURA E. RICHARDS

Bomoseen, Vt.
January 6, 1942

My dear, dear Mrs. Richards:

You sent me such a good packet of reading matter at Christmas—the Emerson extract is really breath-taking—that I will respond in kind. I have spent the last week going through the bales of letters written to me in November after my last English broadcast, and forwarded to

[290]

me by the BBC. The variety is fantastic. Thus, here is a letter from Elspeth Grahame, widow of the man who wrote a perfect book if ever there was one. I mean *The Golden Age*. Then next comes a letter from a Mrs. Wilkinson, writing me from Frognall and telling me how, long ago, at the request of the relatives of John Howard Payne in America, she had gone to Tunis and found his grave and cared for it. I can see her now, toiling away with knives and scissors for two days, cutting away the moss from the lettering on the tombstone. I relish the moderation of her closing paragraph. "Excuse writing and mistakes," she said. "I am very old now, eighty-four, and rather tired and wearied by this war." Then one charming letter from an old journalist in Fleet Street with this anecdote in it:

"When the first heavy raids started here my wife and I, before we knew better or learned worse, as time alone can prove, went to the basement of our lot of flats. A very heavy bomb fell not far away, one a lot nearer, shaking the whole place, and another nearer still. Great havoc was done around us. I sat holding my wife's hand and when silence came again I said to her: 'Not a tremor in your hand!' 'No!' she said. 'I was looking at yours!' Believe me, we had each forgotten ourselves. As an incident it is trivial—as an illuminant it is incandescent."

Next I include an anonymous letter from a docker. So many letters spoke of Mrs. Howe and the "Battle Hymn," letters from people who had heard her sing it, letters from people who had heard the song in odd parts of the world. I can't forward them all, but I do include two self-explanatory notes from Edmund Gosse's daughter, Teresa.

Finally, let me tell you one true story I heard and liked. The time was June 1940. The Danes, the Norwegians, the Dutch, the Belgians, the French had one by one caved in. The British had retreated to Dunkirk. A woman in Scotland got these tidings over the wireless. With their ancient distrust of the Sassenachs, she said: "Well, I suppose the English will give up next. In that case, it will be a long war."

After I got back, I did twelve lectures in the midlands. One of these was in Indianapolis, and I was most fortunate because the Tarkingtons left Maine early this year, and the Gentleman from Indiana was in residence. Then, as soon as the ice would bear my now inconsiderable weight, I came here to collect my wits. On Monday I sally forth again, speaking at the Academy of Music in Philadelphia, going to Washington to work on a national broadcast for the Red Cross, then reporting on February 1st at West Point. I am a great churning mass of legitimate pride and decent misgivings because the cadets themselves have asked me to come up and speak to them. After February 1st, deponent saith not, not knowing.

My love to everyone in the Yellow House, which of course means more than the three Richardses.

Alexander Woollcott

To *WALT DISNEY*

Bomoseen, Vt.
January 12, 1942

My dear Disney:

This is a letter of thanks from the bottom of my heart. Having been over to England, done a dozen broadcasts there, come back and delivered a dozen lectures here, I blew myself to a spot of rest. In fact, during the Christmas holidays, I did nothing but sleep, dine with Frank Sullivan, listen to Churchill, and go to see *Dumbo*. That's what I call a good life.

After seeing *Dumbo* for the third time, I suspect that if we could get far enough away to see it in its place, we would recognize it as the highest achievement yet reached in the Seven Arts since the first white man landed on this continent. This cautious tribute is paid by one who was several degrees short of nuts about *Snow White* and a little bored by *Pinocchio*. I was as afflicted by what went agley in *Fantasia* as anyone in this country, with the possible exception of yourself. But *Dumbo* is that once far-off divine event toward which your whole creation has moved.

After some thought, I have decided that you are the most valuable person alive, so for God's sake take care of yourself.

Yours to command,
Alexander Woollcott

To MRS. MARIAN STOLL

The White House
January 21, 1942

Dear Marian,

Under separate cover (which has always been our life in a nutshell) I have sent you two packs of playing cards because:

(a) you said you wanted some

(b) these, which were given me for Xmas, are not the kind I like and

(c) they can be washed with soap and water.

Personally I prefer washing my hands instead of the cards. I never soil cards because my hands are always pure, like my thoughts.

Your old playmate
Alexander Woollcott

To *LADY COLEFAX*

The White House
January 22, 1942

Dear Sibyl,

This is just an advance notice of a longer letter I'll be writing you within another ten days. If I have fallen behindhand in my correspondence it is in part because some days had to be spent in answering certain letters from England which could not in decency go unacknowledged. These were scattered through the bushel of mail elicited by the Postscript which you attended long, long ago. It took its own good time in reaching America and I found it accumulated on the island when I finally made my way across the ice on New Year's Eve. It was the total effect of that mail (it ranged from a letter written me by Mrs. Kenneth Grahame to a letter written me by a docker who did not sign his name) which made me sure for the first time that I did well to go to England. I am heartily glad now that I went and believe now for the first time that I am going again some time and that you are going to visit *my* island and see the recent additions to the screen, the Duse picture and the snapshot of Max and Thornton and me, so improbably and (by me) unforgettably assembled at Abinger Manor Cottage [Max Beerbohm's home].

While here in Washington, busy with some broadcasting preparations and doing a week of such intensive listening that my ears are lame with listening, I am lodged in the most comfortable room I know. Incidentally it is the one recently vacated by your Mr. Churchill. Of his great personal triumph here it would be difficult to give an adequate account. It was given to him to lay a spell on those at close range and also on all small decent people everywhere, the nameless and numberless people of good will who hold, I do proudly believe, the balance of power.

Well, of him and of others I will write you soon and, U-boats permitting, you should from time to time receive from me the makings of a snack.

A bientôt

Alexander Woollcott

P.S. I shall not be happy until Max has seen Walt Disney's *Dumbo* and I have heard, through you, how he liked it.

To W. GRAHAM ROBERTSON

Bomoseen, Vt.
February 6, 1942

Dear, dear Graham:

The first time I ever came to see you—I think it was in December of '32—I brought with me an American named Paul Bonner. He wanted to come because of his passion for William Blake. I wanted him to come because he had a Rolls Royce car. Well, after I got back from my latest visit to you (disguised as Government mission) I was lecturing in Dayton, Ohio, and Bonner, now a Major in the American Army, was sitting in the front row.

Therefore I threw an anecdote about you into the lecture and, as a result, some half-witted woman in the audience reported that I had come to Dayton and delivered an entire lecture about you.

Otherwise the Graham Robertson Society in this country is the finest group in America. I have just entered into correspondence with a member I had not known before and thereby hangs a tale.

The tale might begin anywhere, but I select for the purpose the kindergarten my mother attended back in 1851, clad in a plaid merino dress with lace pantalettes. The little girl who sat next her was a child of French parentage and they became friends for life. When the little French girl grew up, she married a Scottish engineer named Alexander Humphreys. My full name is Alexander Humphreys Woollcott. His next namesake was his own little boy who was drowned in the rapids of the Nile. His third namesake was his grandson, a young engineer from Harvard called Alexander Humphreys Loud.

You may be angrily asking at this point what all this has to do with you, but be patient and you will see.

I am always enough in touch with the Humphreys clan so that, some seven or eight years ago, I knew Aleck Loud was courting a Belgian girl who, for her sins, taught painting at a school in New York, and I shall never forget the day on the sands at Provincetown when old Mrs. Humphreys told me the story of that Belgian girl.

It seems that in 1914, she and her sister had been among the refugees driven before the German army as it advanced into France. In Paris they were eventually rejoined by their father who had made his way there through Switzerland and had got himself a job in an airplane factory.

The William Emersons from Cambridge were in Paris at the time and did what they could for the refugees, and on their eventual return to America, took one of the little Belgian girls with them.

Her desolate father wanted to give her a parting present, but had only about two francs to spend, so he haunted the book stalls in the shadow of the Odéon, found a shabby old French-English dictionary and gave her that.

On the boat, because she needed that dictionary every minute and because it was her last link with her father, the child carried it with her wherever she went. One day when Mr. Emerson was sitting in the next steamer chair, he noticed it was the same kind of dictionary he had used when he was at college, so he picked it up idly, flipped over the pages and came to a halt at the flyleaf. There, in the handwriting that had been his thirty-five years before, he read the legend: "William Emerson. Cambridge, 1880."

Whenever this kind of thing happens, I feel as if a star were dancing somewhere on the outer edge of space.

Well, Mr. Emerson, having heard somehow that I had been to see you, wrote to me the other day for a full report and we have since been in pleasant correspondence. So that's that.

My lecture tour wound up on December 19th at Cincinnati and I went off to spend that week-end with the Lunts. Their house at Genesee Depot is not only a comfort but an entertainment. The sight of Alfred making butter in the morning would rejoice you. They are still lying fallow there and I am doing the same at my own place in Vermont.

Alexander Woollcott

To WALT DISNEY

Bomoseen, Vt.
February 15, 1942

My dear Disney:

In a sense this is an answer to your note of January 30th. If *Dumbo* was just one of those little things that you knocked out between epics, it strikes me that the same could be said of *A Christmas Carol*. And as Thackeray said of *A Christmas Carol* so I would say of *Dumbo*, that it comes to every man and woman who sees it as a personal kindness.

I had seen the thing only four times before I was laid up for temporary repairs, but I got me the records which serve to bring it back before my eyes. Neysa McMein told me she would rather have signed her name to *Dumbo* than anything since the Parthenon. That infatuated woman saw *Dumbo* eleven times before that ghastly morning late in January when, while walking in her sleep, she pitched down a flight of stairs and broke her back. It was over two weeks ago. That blameless Lamb of God has had a bit of her hip grafted onto her spine and now lies in St. Luke's Hospital in New York, hourly blasted by pain no opiates can quite deaden. I thought you might not know and might want to. I thought you might also want to know that her official name is Mrs. J. G. Baragwanath.

The rest of this letter is meant for your publicity director and you might as well hand it right over. I am the lad who discovered *Three Little Pigs* in its eighteenth month and promptly went on the air about it. I would give several months of my life (a poorer and poorer offer as time goes on) if I had been on the air when *Dumbo* was first presented. I was not even in this country. Now I shall not be on the air before Fall at the earliest. But I am dimly aware that Disney pictures recur in tidal waves and it occurs to me that if *Dumbo* has a second coming an occasion might be found for me to do a broadcast about it. If I did so much as a fifteen minute spot, I would want to have the music of *The Big Bad Wolf* and all of the music from *Dumbo*. I have no means of knowing whether it would be possible or profitable for you to get me on the air for such a purpose. I hope it is needless for me to explain that my part in such procedure would be a labor of love.

Alexander Woollcott

To CHARLES LEE
[Literary editor of the Philadelphia *Record*.]

Bomoseen, Vt.
February 16, 1942

My dear Mr. Lee:
               Here is the piece I promised you. I am pretty sure that it is in time. I hope that I have got your name right. Will you acknowledge the receipt of this manuscript and will

you send me three copies of each page on which it is eventually published?

I must stop this expensive business of being sentimental about the newspaper business. I have taken this afternoon off to write this for you for no other reason than because, thirty-eight years ago or thereabouts, the Philadelphia *Record* paid me my first money for a piece of submitted copy. This makes five dollars that I got for the two pieces and it is not enough.

Alexander Woollcott

To *JANET FLANNER*

Bomoseen, Vt.
February 17, 1942

Dear Jan:

You revolt me. How would I see a column by Elsa Maxwell?

For your piece [in *The New Yorker*] on Bette Davis, who married a Rutland boy and was over there the other evening, I wish I could find a long cherished clipping in which she explains how she happened to spell her name that way. She said it was because her mother was English. Don't ask me to explain this.

I have an uneasy feeling that everybody variously scheduled to visit here this month will arrive at the same time. I do expect you and consider the fact that you cannot do your work up here as a characteristic sign of mismanagement.

I may have to take you over and run you myself. When you step out at night you may succeed in looking like Merry Del Val, but at close range your life looks like a pin-tray full of cigarette butts, stained with lip-rouge, and slightly dandruffical combings.

A. W.

To *SOPHIE ROSENBERGER*

Bomoseen, Vt.
February 19, 1942

Dear Sophie:
  In a month which I agreed to spend resting here in the snowy quiet of my Vermont house I am exhausting myself by stirring up some of the litter of my life, being vaguely disposed to give or throw away everything that cannot be drunk. Here, for instance, is a time-tinted decanter which, to my knowledge, stood on the sideboard of my great-great-grandfather, William Brown, two hundred and seven years ago. He was from Cheshire, Massachusetts, and served as a lieutenant in a Cheshire company that fought with Stark at Bennington. I thought I must give it to my brother Billy's eldest, who is pretty as a wild rose and who presented us in June with twin boys. But I have a notion that her generation and the next are going to be too streamlined and too constantly on the move to want any impedimenta at all.

  I'm sending *you* something which you can laugh at and throw away. It is the first manuscript I ever submitted for publication. I was eight at the time and took the precaution to send it to the editor by the hand of a friend, Rose Field. This precaution did me no good as it bounced right back and why, after all these years of wandering about, it is still in my possession I have no idea.

  Please telephone Lucy and tell her something she already knows—namely that I love and admire her.

            Alexander Woollcott

To JOHN PETER TOUHEY

Bomoseen, Vt.
April 12, 1942

Dear John:

This is to thank you for that letter you wrote me when I was laid low. I am up again and will be about in another two months.

I learned for the first time in Peggy Wood's volume of memoirs (a) that she was the first actress to sit at the Round Table and (b) that I *persuaded* her and Johnny to take a trip through France with me. Of course, it may be *my* memory that is failing.

I mention the matter at all only because the first discovery did lead me to pondering whether it would be fun to have one more reunion dinner of the old Algonquin Round Table. I think I should enjoy seeing just once more even those old chums that I still dislike with a waning intensity. Good luck to you.

A. Woollcott

To HELEN WARREN SEARS

[When Woollcott was at high school in Philadelphia, his cousin, Miss Sears, got him occasional jobs for the local papers.]

Bomoseen, Vt.
April 13, 1942

Dear Helen:

I am on the mend and back home and even attempting to tackle the mail that arrived when I was down and out. I am still down most of the day but it seems to be the general opinion, in which I concur, that I've got a lot of work left in me yet.

All is now quiet at the Phalanx. You must remember the cottage which Charles Taber used to call Staten Island Gothic. When it was the kindergarten, my mother attended in plaid merino with pantalettes. In those days it stood at the end of the big house and I think it was still there when Aunt Julie moved into it at the time of her marriage just after the Civil War. Later it was moved onto grounds of its own far off. It was there that Mr. Sauerwen came to spend the summer of 1880 with his two motherless children. He stayed thirty-eight years. Julie [A.W.'s sister] lived there during most of her late but tremendously happy marriage and only in January of last year, when Polly [A.W.'s cousin] took it back from her tenant, did Billy and I take Julie's ashes down and bury them in the narcissus bed. Polly threw her tenant out because she wanted the place for herself. She has done it all over—oil burner, electric icebox and what not—and is immensely contented there, too deaf for her own and anyone else's comfort, and sewing away like mad for the Red Cross.

In Baltimore, Billy Woollcott has a new grandson, presented to him by his second daughter. His first, whose husband is a young professor in the University of Vermont just up the road from here, presented him with twin grandsons last June.

Charlie Chaplin has made the experiment of reviving one of his masterpieces of the silent picture days—*The Gold Rush*— and there is a special reason why I wish you would go and see it.

Alexander W.

To MRS. W. PARMER FULLER, JR.

Bomoseen, Vt.
April 15, 1942

Dear Mrs. F:

I am going through the mail that arrived while I was in a state of coma. Now that I am back on the island, with my really strenuous activity limited for some months to come to moving from chair to chair, I am glad to have so much good reading matter.

In yours of March 10th, Mrs. Fuller, you said this: "I have a feeling that maybe it has been worth it—that you don't regret your trip to England or anything else." No one but you had the sense to say anything so true and so comforting as that.

Once upon a time, when my niece Joan Woollcott was a freshman at Swarthmore and *While Rome Burns* had just been published, one of her classmates said: "That uncle of yours is just a happy little extrovert." Joan, apparently in some confusion as to the meaning of that word, socked him in the jaw.

It is quite true that I have not the habit of introspection, but I can testify that even a happy little extrovert, when he knows that he has had a mighty close call and lies awake in hospital boozy with a kind of egocentric melancholy, does fall into the habit of taking account of stock. In hospital in Syracuse I came finally to the conclusion that I deeply regret nothing I have ever done. The several regrets which make me burst into cold sweat in the middle of the night are for things I didn't do, failures of courage and generosity and even common decency, for which I can never atone. To use a phrase of Bob Hutchins, I was denied the gift of faith and some time I would like to ask some devout Catholic what comfort they can get out of being forgiven by God when they cannot forgive themselves.

Where did you get the idea that I never read long letters? I do and, as you see, write them. Good luck to you now and always.

A. Woollcott

To *ARCHIBALD MACLEISH*

Bomoseen, Vt.
April 24, 1942

Ambrose-Son-of-Heaven:

I have resumed my seat at the listening-post and must report that I thought last Saturday's broadcast first rate. I feel less regret in having been of no use to [Norman] Corwin in this series. I had thought of myself as performing only on one which I had helped to write. I certainly could not have done any of the major vocal parts as well as they were done. I could have come nowhere near doing the Donald Crisp part as well as he did it, nor the one done by Claude Rains.

I liked enormously your speech to the publishers. I wish I might have heard it. Yet I thought Walter Lippmann's point about it well taken. I share your feeling that something drastic should be done about Colonel Bertie, but I have always felt that that something should be done by the citizens of Chicago. I see something like organized mass meetings and an organization of undergraduates at Chicago University to make morally and physically uncomfortable the lives of those who are so un-co-operative as to read the Chicago *Tribune*. I made a few libelous statements about him as a part of each of the twelve lectures I did in the midlands in December and found that there was no easier way to bring down the house.

Ambrose, I wish you would send me a notifying wire the next time you are going to do a broadcast yourself. I have heard you only twice, each time reading either a message from or a letter from the President. Your voice is a great asset, but on those two occasions I was troubled by the fact that you sounded noble, detached, and curiously dejected. Perhaps this latter note comes from a mere fall in the voice at the end of sentences, but I doubt it. I think the voice goes wrong only when one is somehow thinking it wrong.

I must lay low for some time to come, but I now feel sure inside me that I'm coming up to bat again. You haven't heard the last of me.

My love to Ambrosia.

Ilex

To LAURA E. RICHARDS

Bomoseen, Vt.
April 24, 1942

Dear Mrs. Richards:
             I have a story on my mind and I feel I must tell it to you. It warms my heart because I am romantic about my country and it's a part of the epic of America.

Let me begin at a point nearly twenty years ago when a very small thirteen-year-old Danish boy named Frode Jensen came home from his grandmother's to find that his widowed mother had married an oafish brute who not only beat her but insisted on being addressed as father. When the boy refused to give him this title the man knocked him down; whereat the boy jumped out of the window and those parts saw him no more.

Somehow he got a job as bell-hop on the Scandinavian Line and in two years made eighteen crossings of the Atlantic. It was at the end of the eighteenth that he lingered in New York while his boat sailed. He was fifteen now and, though he knew no English, thought he would try life in America for a while. I am not sure he even knew that there was a local prejudice in favor of people entering with passports and the like. In his first job, promised him by an alcoholic passenger who was also named Jensen and also Danish and had an elaborate house in Brooklyn, he was put to work as page-boy. In the meantime, this worthy had been investigated by Congress and was about to be deported. He told the boy that he must come home too and the boy said he wouldn't; so the man hit him over the head. His only resource those days was flinging himself out of the window and you must picture him running through the streets of Brooklyn. He must have had an engaging smile or something which served him in lieu of a passport. Anyway, an affable policeman took him to the YMCA and the YMCA got him a job as errand-boy for the *Daily News* in New York. For exercise he swam in the pool at the Y, where the physical instructor, who ran a boys' camp in New London, Connecticut, in the summer, offered him a job. All Danish boys swim well and Frode, who didn't understand much that was said to him, assumed he was being engaged as a swimming instructor. So he accepted. The *Daily News* promised him his job back in the Fall; so off he went, only to discover that he was to be used as handy-boy in the kitchen and breadcutter in the pantry.

One Sunday there came to the camp a young divinity student named Howard Kennedy from Troy, New York. It was his custom thus to make trial flights in preaching and he also said grace in the camp dining hall. As he rose to say grace, he was a little startled to have the bread-boy give a joyful shout as of recognition. So when dinner was over he investigated and discovered that he was recognized as a passenger on the Scandinavian Line the preceding summer who had given the bell-hop a memorably large tip. I don't know whether they needed an interpreter, but somehow he managed to find out that the boy wasn't going to school because he had no family, no money, and had to work.

On the day Jensen got back to work at the *Daily News*, he found a telegram which the motherly woman in charge of office personnel translated for him. It was signed Howard Kennedy and said that, if he could be at the railroad station at Troy the following Monday morning at eight, all school arrangements would be taken care of. His savings would manage the carfare to Troy and he was advised to take the plunge. He arrived in his Danish suit with all his possessions in a paper bag.

It seems that Howard Kennedy's grandfather was Chairman of the Board of the Green Mountain Academy in Poultney, Vermont, which is just eight miles from my house. A scholarship had been arranged and he would have lodgings in a Poultney household where he could work for his keep by chopping wood and doing the chores. From Poultney, under his own steam, he went on to Hamilton College, where he delivered laundry, waited on table, and slept in the white belfry of the Hamilton Chapel, which is the most beautiful college chapel in all of this country. The music of its bell can be heard far across the Oriskany Valley and the sound of it stays with every Hamilton man wandering across the world. Frode was allowed to sleep there because it was his job to toll the bell to wake the students in the morning, to summon them to services, and to sound the curfew. He rejected all fraternity offers as too expensive.

By this time the traces of his Danish accent were almost gone and he was able to understand the lectures almost as well as the next man. He had taken on stature, too, and was football captain his senior year. In Hamilton they have an intermittent custom of assembling the entire student body to name by secret ballot the squarest man in college, who is then presented with a carpenter's T square. When I first met Frode at the Elihu Root house across the road from the campus, this T square had just been presented to him.

How he went on from there to study medicine at the College of Physicians and Surgeons, which is the medical school of Columbia University; how, after a bad start, due to his effort to earn his living and study at the same time, he emerged as an interne of brilliant promise; how he fell in love and I represented him in the conference with her father, who held out for a church wedding, while I wanted them to get married before his last year at medical school; how at his wedding in Winnetka, near Chicago, I was not only best man but provided at least two ushers out of my hat, offering my personable young secretary as one and plucking Thornton Wilder out of the University of Chicago faculty as the other; how the baby was named Alexandra in my honor, thereby acquiring a good Danish name in the process; how she was christened in the Hamilton Chapel, beneath the belfry where he used to live, with Mrs. Root as godmother and me as godfather and the Reverend Howard Kennedy officiating—these are high lights in a long story.

Only the other day I was reminded of that summer we spent in the maddening and exhausting task of getting his illegal entry into this country corrected. It was managed in the nick of time for him to get his citizenship papers when he was ready to practice medicine after his internship at the Presbyterian Hospital in Chicago. There might have been an unfortunate delay because no court was sitting at the time, but Frode makes friends along the way. At the Presbyterian Hospital, one crosspatch patient who was also a Federal judge remembered the young interne with violent affection. When word of the difficulty reached him, he came to town, opened the court, and Frode took the oath of allegiance to this country in solitary grandeur. The day after Pearl Harbor he had occasion to write me about something and I remember his postscript. It was, "Oh God, it's good to be a citizen." The other day he was sworn in as a Captain in the American Army.

Well, when I was out in California in January 1940, I got a letter from Mrs. Howard Kennedy. She was a lovely girl from Belfast. By this time Howard was rector of a small church in Chatham, New York, and they had an eight-months-old daughter named Sally. One night when Howard had gone to Washington to see Mrs. Roosevelt about some benevolent hanky-panky they were both up to in the Hudson Valley, Sally was put to bed with a sniffy cold and woke next morning with a temperature of 107. It was characteristic that Mrs. Kennedy thought first of Frode, to whom she telephoned in Syracuse, one hundred and sixty miles away. After his internship, he had accepted the post of Assistant Pathologist at the University. Then she wrapped the baby in blankets and started driving to Hudson, the nearest town that had a hospital. As she walked up the steps of the entrance, she saw a young man coming out, carrying what looked like a doctor's bag. She halted him in his tracks, dragged him back with her, and in the very foyer of the hospital he performed a tracheotomy; for the baby was choking to death.

Meanwhile, up in Syracuse, Frode had consulted the authorities; learned who was the best man for such a case in Albany, forty miles from Hudson; and over the long distance telephone persuaded that man to start driving for Hudson as soon as he could. Then he himself, a fledgling doctor with only his experience as an interne behind him, jumped into his own car and broke all the speed laws getting to Hudson.

He is a quiet, mannerly fellow and was deferential to the older man he found in charge. He did ask a few questions. One of them was, "What did you find in the ears?" and the older man had to admit that he hadn't thought to examine them. Frode just gave him one look and with no more words the older man stepped back and the fledgling doctor took charge of the case. "Have you used sulfanilamide?" This was then a new drug about which the medical profession was nervous. The older man had brought it along but had been afraid to try it. I have never asked, but I can imagine the anguish of indecision that must have gone on in Frode's mind. Remember, this was Howard's baby. I suppose he crossed himself or whatever Danes do. Then he said, "We use it." The temperature dropped—106, 104, 103, 100, 99. Afterwards the old muddle-head in Hudson wrote to ask Frode's permission to report the case to the medical journal. Mrs. Kennedy wrote me that if Frode had any notion that he was indebted to the Kennedy family the debt was paid.

For eight years now I have acted for Frode *in loco parentis*. I think of him as the best investment I ever made. It was never a legal adoption, but that was the relationship as we both came to look upon it. I really shudder when I think how close I came to missing the chance. Mrs. Root had reminded me that he was studying at P and S and had asked me to look after him. It was a wild time for me, what with *The New Yorker* articles, two broadcasts a week, and the Hauptmann trial. I forgot all about him; in fact, I did nothing for him at all except invite him to a cocktail party. Then, in the spring of '34 when a book of mine called *While Rome Burns* had come off the press and the broadcast series was finished, I went through some fantastic treatment for overweight which required my spending a preliminary fortnight in hospital. It chanced to be the hospital attached to young Jensen's medical school. It chanced also to be the Easter vacation and, as he had no home to go to and no funds for carfare, he used to drop in every day for a talk about Hamilton. I have never recovered from being a reporter and I got it out of him that he was running the elevator, managing the cash register in the school restaurant, translating from Scandinavian documents for the Academy of Medicine, and coaching football, basketball and baseball at Riverdale Academy near by. I had thought of the studies in the first year at a first-rate medical school like Harvard or P and S as designed to consume about all the waking hours of a keen-witted youngster. I asked the internes and they told me this was true. Then how did young Jensen manage? The answer was that he wouldn't. He would be quietly dropped for good and all at the end of the first year.

I remember calling him in and telling him that I would take over his expenses for the rest of the year if he would give me his promise that he would do no more outside work and would spend every waking hour on his studies. I remember his asking, "Mayn't I even run the elevator?" and my telling him severely that it was out of the question. I never heard until just the other day that in his third year he cheated on me a little. He waited on table all year to pay for an engagement ring.

I can't boast of any prescience in this matter. I think I acted chiefly from a sense of guilt because I had done nothing but ask him to a cocktail party. Also there was the then unfulfilled promise I had made myself when the man after whom I was named would not let me pay any interest when in time I repaid him the money lent me to go to Hamilton. I swore I would put two boys and two girls through college, asking each not to repay me but to put some other kid through college when and if they could.

But pretty soon I began to realize that I was in luck. Frode was going to be a good doctor. People were going to begin to get well when he came into the room. It's no fond parental illusion of mine that he has an inner light. He is compact of sheer goodness. I had not foreseen what I think many people now think—that he would be a *great* doctor. A good deal of evidence has accumulated that he has a kind of genius in diagnosis and there was never anyone kinder.

When I accomplished my unseemly collapse early in March, it was Frode who flew from Syracuse and rode with me in the ambulance that carried me the two hundred miles to his hospital. From Dr. Levine, the great heart specialist from Boston who was called in consultation, I learned that I am now in existence because of young Jensen's swiftness of decision and his courage in applying drastic measures.

Well, I have been an unconscionable time telling the story. Of course, it's an unfinished story and *is* part of the American epic, isn't it? That too, please God, is also an unfinished story.

I am what is known as up and after a few more weeks hope to be about. One thing disturbs me. Shortly before I was laid low, the Secretary of the Treasury was arranging for a series of short American biographies to be syndicated in the newspapers. I believe a good many writers were asked to accept these assignments and that all of them did. I know that I was asked to do a piece about Mrs. Howe, at a moment when there was just time for me to dash off a hasty revision from memory of one of my broadcasting scripts. It was just while I was in a state of coma that my piece appeared in I know not how many newspapers and when I got out of hospital I learned with apprehension that the editors of the *Reader's Digest* had seen it in the St. Louis *Post-Dispatch* and were infatuated enough to buy it. Now it is on the newsstands in an edition of six million copies and in I know not what mutilated form. It's only when I write for them direct that they forego the condensations. If you see it and it strikes you as no great shakes, don't hold it against me—much.

I had thought that when I could take to the road I would head for Kennebunkport and Gardiner, but with the gasoline ration I do not know whether it can be managed.

The ricksha I have just acquired is intended only to get me back from the shore when I have progressed to the point when I can walk down to it. Such persons as come to visit me are openly voicing their apprehension that I expect them to play coolie between the shafts. They are so right.

Well, you can't say that when I finally got around to writing you I just dashed off a note. My best to all your household.

A. W.

To *EDWARD SHELDON*

[The author of such successful plays as *Romance*, *Miss Lulu Belle*, *Salvation Nell*, and *The Nigger*, Mr. Sheldon has held, during his long confinement at home, a unique place as friend and counselor of some of the foremost people of the American theatre. Woollcott never came to New York without carefully planning to see as much of him as Mr. Sheldon's health would permit.]

*Bomoseen, Vt.
April 24, 1942*

Dear Sheldon:

Joe Hennessey is busy constructing a dovecot according to your specifications. I must explain something about this island. It has several levels. On one of the high ones is built my own stout all-year-round house with stone walls two feet thick—a fortress successfully designed to defeat a Vermont winter. When it's 30 below outside—it was 18 below the day I went over the mountain to help bury Otis Skinner—this house is cozy and will be as long as it is possible to get oil. In the path of nothing, and therefore unlikely to be blown up, it will probably still be standing a thousand years hence and archaeologists will write speculative articles about it, musing in print about the vanished civilization which could have produced it. The original clubhouse is at the foot of a sharp declivity which brings its chimney-pot on a level with my living-room. On Decoration Day, when the official season opens, my kitchen staff moves down to the clubhouse and I go with it to avoid the now forbidden climb. There is a point to all these fascinating details. I would like to have the pigeon-coop first set up on the level of the upper house and then in June have it moved fifty yards away to the lower level so that I can visit it all summer long. Will such a move wreck their orientation?

Out of the store of Phalanx legends, a long forgotten one popped into my mind the other day when Frode was fetching me from New York. It led me to telling him that our family had engaged some quite notable doctors at one time or another, although I know of few periods when it would have been possible for any member of that family to raise a hundred dollars without straining its credit. First, of course, there was young Doctor Georges Clemenceau. I think I have told you of the time in the late Sixties when my Aunt Mary was going into what was then known as a decline. It was her suitor, a French painter named Rondel, who, with doubtless justified distrust of the local medical talent, dashed to New York, consulted the French colony, and came back with young Clemenceau, then fresh from the Sorbonne. I remember that they had to take a boat to Amboy and ride their horses into a lather in reaching the Phalanx.

The only single thing at the Phalanx now which I covet—it has been willed to me but I'll never get it—is Rondel's portrait of my grandmother. The photographs of me which people say are good look so like her. Her husband was president of the Phalanx when that was a functioning communist experiment and I can imagine the grimness of her comment when the New York *Times*—plus ça change—used to suggest that she wore trousers and practiced free love. A New England Sears by birth, she was a formidable and, to me, a frightening woman. My mother has told me how, when she was younger, my grandmother could take away pain by the stroke of her hand and that there would be a crackle of electricity when her fingers left the forehead of the person she was comforting. The wildest animals obeyed her slightest word. I saw this happen once myself when she was old and frail and helpless. It must have been when I was eight or thereabouts. We always had setters—English setters for the most part—and one autumn night we let two six-weeks-old puppies into the house who had never been in any house before. My uncle put two freshly shot partridges on a low rocking-chair in the long living-room to see which pup had the sharper nose. They rushed around as a team, for all the world as if they were being driven in harness, and came first to my grandmother's room. She was seated in a rocker with her gnarled, slippered feet resting on a pillow. The two pups flung themselves on this pillow as if it were a haven and before any of us could interfere she merely said in a low voice, "Get out of here." She might just as well have shot them. The next moment both of them were out in the kitchen, flinging themselves against the door and whimpering with terror.

It was years before this that she was visited by the symptoms of a palsy ascribed by the medical opinion of that day to a clot on the brain. Her youngest son took her to Philadephia to consult S. Weir Mitchell—a name forgotten in these days, I suppose, along with *Hugh Wynne: Free Quaker*. Gus would remember him. I think Noguchi and Weir Mitchell overlapped. Anyway, Dr. Mitchell said that my grandmother's malady was inoperable and incurable, but that no one had been known to live longer than two years under the blight of it. She lived eighteen. Once during those eighteen years it was recorded that some insensitive visitor made the mistake of mentioning her illness compassionately. I can hear her contralto voice replying: "One rises above such things." I forget what became of the visitor. I suppose he was removed to be treated for frostbite. If you could have heard the amount of caterwauling I did at the hospital in Syracuse, you would know how the stock has deteriorated.

Well, I was telling you about her effect on animals. Sometime back in the Eighties, her oldest son, my Uncle Charles, owned a devoted but surly Gordon setter named Mac. Everyone was so afraid of him that when he lolled on the sofa and would not get down they were all afraid to push him off; but if my grandmother came into the room and said quietly, "Get down off that sofa," he not only got down but could be seen a moment later leaving for the woods with what Portia's steward at Belmont used to call "all convenient speed."

But I was talking about doctors. One day, while they were all out hunting, one of the dogs went mad and in his frenzy bit Mac and my Cousin Ed, then a husky lad of fifteen. For weeks, in addition to his humiliation at having been bitten, Mac had to be sequestered until all danger of his having been infected had passed. The Charles Bucklin tribe were all hunters and he himself was out with a gun on his eighty-fourth birthday. Just about then Clemenceau had come over to lecture and I remember how surprised Uncle Charles and Aunt Julie were when the papers spoke of him as perhaps too old for such a venture. Too old? Good God, what was the human race coming to? Some years after Mac and Ed were bitten—it was while the Charles Bucklins were living in Keyport—the fear of Mac in the neighborhood had grown to such legendary dimensions that one man said he would shoot him if Uncle Charles didn't. So Uncle Charles did. Usually when he got his gun out Mac went into transports of happiness, filling the air with a kind of carillon of rapture. But this time he knew better. He just walked alongside with his tail drooping and when Uncle Charles lifted the gun looked at him with such sadness. I can't imagine C. S. ever shedding a tear, but I'll bet he had to tramp for many an hour in the woods before he went home that day.

But to get back to that hunting party when the dog went mad. My Uncle Charles wrapped Ed in a blanket, leaped into a buggy and drove to Newark, where the doctor he consulted said there was only one thing for him to do. The next morning he and Ed were on a liner sailing for France. I think of this as an act of magnificent decision, particularly for a man who probably had to borrow the passage money. Yes, they went to Pasteur himself, Ed going daily for treatments and Uncle Charles finding some bond of sympathy with the great man and having many a talk with him.

What I shall never succeed in making plausible to a new generation, if I ever write the Phalanx book in the sedentary days which have been ordered for me, is the America in which such a household as ours could exist. Here was a threadbare and unambitious family, no member of which had ever thought before my time of going to college and many of which had never even been to school, who nevertheless took in the Atlantic when they couldn't pay their coal bill, knew their Trollope and Jane Austen by heart and could speak French to Pasteur more readily than any boy coming out of Harvard these days. To understand them you must go to Concord and eavesdrop at the Bronson Alcotts.

Writing to my cousin Polly the other day about the Pasteur incident, I spoke of it as having occurred "in our palmy days" and she misunderstood me. I had been thinking of the time when every member of the tribe was as vivid and astonishing as any of the great Dickens characters. Let me quote from her letter:

"You said 'in our palmy days.' Were there ever any in this family? They just scraped enough together because it was a vital thing—these celebrated doctors—and did without other things. Poor Grandma—saving little by little for a piano for Aunt Mary, only to have to surrender it for something needed more—say fertilizer, or such."

"Well, there you are," I said to Frode on the train. "Clemenceau, Weir Mitchell, Pasteur—"

"— and Jensen," he added.

On the surface he was joking, but not deep down, I think, any more than Heifetz at fifteen would have thought it odd to couple his name with Kreisler's. People who are really virtuosos must know it deep down.

Did I ever send you a completely unsuccessful but brilliant novel called *Entirely Surrounded* which Charles Brackett wrote about the island? Brackett once abashed me by saying I never really liked anyone whose life story would not make a good Profile for *The New Yorker*. There is enough truth in this to make me uncomfortable and I suppose that any letter I write about Frode is really born of my immense frustration as being permanently barred from writing about him for publication. It could only embarrass him professionally and personally. I am in a similar difficulty about Gus [Eckstein]. For two years I have been bombarded with telegrams from *The Saturday Evening Post*, asking me to do an article about him. I would not know how or why I should write a piece about Gus that concealed his essential character or failed to present him as I see him; but, if I ever published the result in a magazine of such circulation, he would have to go round in false whiskers. It would be weeks before he could go on the street without having people point at him.

I hope you have taken the precaution to read this letter in installments.

A. Woollcott

P.S. Somebody—Anne Parrish, I think, or Gerald Murphy—has sent me some old theatrical post cards. One of them shows John Mason and Mrs. Fiske in the last act of *Leah Kleschna*. You must remember that Emily used to call it "Mrs. Fiske of the Lettuce Patch."

To DR. GUSTAV ECKSTEIN

Bomoseen, Vt.
April 26, 1942

Dear Gus:
        In the form of a letter to Sheldon I was telling a forgotten story for the first time and while I was dictating it, I thought it was a story for you, too, and bade my secretary make a copy. Here it is. You might read it some time when you have a week off.

When I was in England the most improbable people would come up to me to ask after Sheldon. One woman asked, "How does he always know just when to cable?" and I understood her when Edith Evans told me that once she was at the end of her tether during the Blitz and a cable arrived from Ned saying, "My hand in yours."

In hospital recently I had my first experience of being taken care of by Sheldon. There was a letter or telegram every day. It occurred to me that their chief effect on any trapped and temporarily afflicted mortal was to remind him that he had a nerve if he dared to indulge in one moment of self-pity. Indeed afterwards, in talking to Charlie MacArthur, I started to say that Sheldon could not have foreseen the real restorative value of his messages when I stopped short, remembering that it takes hardihood to say of Sheldon that he doesn't know what he is doing.

One of his telegrams offered me Ham and Eggs, a new-born pair of pigeons. Hennessey, who prowled the hospital while I was there, said I could accept them and now the coop is being built and soon eight young ones will arrive.

The Lunts are due here on May 6th. In New York, when all the sinews of my character were relaxed and flabby like an old garter, Lynn suggested that she wire for you to come at the same time and I objected on the grounds that I would rather have you (or anyone, for that matter, including Lynn) to myself. But of course there is no time when I would not rejoice at the sight of you coming up the path. Will you be free for that at any time this spring or summer?

I get stronger and clearer in the head every day, but a bit of letter writing, sitting up, and roaming about the house exhausts me as if I had been working all day in a chain gang. I expect to sit quiet for weeks to come, perhaps for months to come.

A fuse I lighted long ago exploded agreeably the other day when Captain Richard Carver Wood came up to show me himself in uniform. He looked not a day over eighteen. Jensen is a captain. I'm a mortified old non-combatant.

Morally, I'm in a poor position to mention it, but for the sake of me, Pavlov and others beyond counting, don't work too hard.

Bless you.

A. W.

To *LADY COLEFAX*

Bomoseen, Vt.
April 28, 1942

Dear Sibyl:

I got back to the island a month from the day I left it and could have come sooner if the lake had not been still too full of broken ice to make a crossing to the island practical for anyone less athletic than Eliza. Do you remember her in *Uncle Tom's Cabin*? I was then good for about a letter or two a day and there were many of these which had to be written. So instead I arranged to part with some of my hoard of the new maple syrup. Vermont is the state where it comes from and we dicker with the near-by farmers for their spring crop. I dispatched eight cans to friends of mine in England and I hope that you've already received yours.

My doctor was here over the week-end and reports that my heart is doing prodigies of recovery. I am still incredibly feeble but was promoted yesterday to the privilege of sitting out on the terrace in the sun. The whole convalescence from this sort of thing is maddeningly slow, as I have reason to remember; but all it kept me from last time was resuming the interrupted tour of that play. I hate having no war job, but I expect to have one and be working at it full steam by September.

The mail was so staggering when I was able to go through it because the first accounts of my illness on the radio and in the newspapers were spectacular and not only woke up friends long dormant but, since the hospital was named, provided an address for them. It seems that I elected to go slowly and gently into a coma just at the time when the question of the ice in these parts becomes critical. In the spring there does come a day when the ice gives way at the shores but elsewhere remains an impassable block, sometimes for a few days—but as it happened this year for three weeks—in which interval it's impossible to cross the lake. There was the nasty prospect of my not being able to get over. As it turned out, we had a grace of something like thirty-six hours in which the ambulance could have crossed.

It will warm your heart to know that the doctor who flew here in his own plane and took me for a two hundred mile ambulance ride to his hospital was one whose medical studies I had financed long ago. He's the best investment I ever made.

Perhaps if I had had my wits about me there was one aspect of my hospitalization I might have foreseen. The hospital was in Syracuse, N. Y., where I had played *The Man Who Came to Dinner* myself. More recently, the enormously successful movie of it has made it familiar to everybody. In consequence, each of the three nurses summoned to the job when I arrived went on duty most apprehensively, probably each with a dirk concealed in her stocking. I don't have to tell *you* that they were bewildered to find me practically indistinguishable from Saint Francis of Assisi.

By the way, Thornton tells me you were outraged by the aforesaid play and also puzzled that I should have permitted it and even endorsed it by playing it. It came about this way. I went on the stage as a nervous beginner at the age of forty-five. I played in two plays, both by S. N. Behrman, rewriting my parts in each from beginning to end because his dialogue simply cannot be spoken. In each case I succeeded only in throwing the play out of shape and the star into hysterics and on one occasion, between performances in Philadelphia, told Moss Hart that I yearned some time to tour the country in the central part, so that if I could succeed in being funny it wouldn't disturb the other actors. Perhaps there was nothing behind all this but a strong streak of exhibitionism, but I think there were other explanations. When I was twenty-seven, to the fury of everybody consulted on the subject, I was made dramatic critic on the New York *Times* and, since that was even then in the process of becoming the foremost newspaper in the country, I became extremely well known in that capacity. Well, I thought, it would be amusing to see a prominent dramatic critic end his days touring the country as a road star. None had ever done it before. Then, as you may not know, I have long sought every device to journey up and down this country. I invented lecture tours and the like to get me around. I have even had it in my broadcast contracts that I could speak from any city I wanted to. Against New York I have had a phobia since the first day I saw it. This has never changed. After one of my absences therefrom—I had been giving nine lectures on journalism at the University of Chicago and had then gone to Canada to make a movie with the Quints—I came back to find the boys [George S. Kaufman and Moss Hart] with an act and a half written and puzzlingly guilty-looking as they arranged to read it to me. It had been my parting instruction that my role should be as different from me as possible. I was considerably taken aback to find they had done a cartoon of me. They had found it so easy and entertaining that they could not resist. They did not wish even to go ahead with it without my consent. I said I would take a week to think it over, my hesitation being based solely on the effect my playing would have on the play. It struck me that it would be alienating and even offensive for me to come forward and say in effect, "See how rude and eccentric I can afford to be. Dear, dear, how amusing I am, to be sure." Besides, I had a sneaking notion that the play would be a success, in which case I might have to stay in New York for two years. I have managed to stay out of it, except for four or five weeks a year, since 1928. Indeed, that was my chief reason for resigning as a dramatic critic. However, I thought the play very funny and told George Kaufman that once the joke had been sprung I would not at all mind heading a second company.

The ideal person to have played it was John Barrymore, but we all knew that even then his mind was so far gone that he could never have remembered the lines. Curiously enough, my nomination for the part was Robert Morley. As for my objecting to the cartoon, it would have been against all my principles and, as a matter of fact, except in one or two minor particulars, I do not consider it an unflattering caricature. But if it were twice as unflattering I would never have lifted my voice in protest. I am always shocked by the silly sensitivity my friends show over undiscriminating criticism. I find indefensible the anger of an author at an unfavorable criticism from a reviewer whose opinion on any other book would not interest him. I have had an immense number of fulsome and fatuous tributes paid me by silly people, but I can give you my word of honor that they never pleased me.

I doubt if *The Man Who Came to Dinner* ever lowered me in the opinion of those whose respect I covet, and if that is true what does the rest matter?

As long ago as 1934 I began the process of reading plays aloud to Ned Sheldon. I was reluctant to read *The Man Who Came to Dinner* because I thought it would sound weird with all the characters coming to him in the voice of Sheridan Whiteside. However, he insisted and when I had finished Act I there was an appalling silence. Finally he asked, "Do you think you are like that?" I found it so embarrassing to explain to him that he saw only my best side.

After all, each of us has a totally different relationship with every other person in the world. One does a few jobs well and a few more not so well and many badly. Once upon a time I discovered that through a complete misunderstanding one of my good jobs was angry with me. I couldn't wait to get to him. I straightened out his misunderstanding and then got madder and madder, banging on the table and yelling that if *he* didn't like me there was no reason why anyone on earth should. He had seen the best side I had. It was Harpo Marx, if you want to know.

All this seems to be about me. Just now I don't feel equipped to talk about the things that matter. I feel I must tell you that the almost forgotten sound of America in production is now deafening. We're already producing at a rate far exceeding the dreams of the wildest optimists and we have only just begun. The only trouble is ships.

Alexander Woollcott

To *ALFRED LUNT*

Bomoseen, Vt.
May 26, 1942

Dear Alfred:
In a nightmare last night I found myself arriving at a handsome, elegant, old-fashioned summer hotel somewhere in the White Mountains. A war benefit was to be staged in the big dining-room as soon as the waitresses could clear away the tables. I discovered with progressive discomfort that, under the management of John Mason Brown, all of us would be expected

not only to attend the performance but to partake in it—that, in fact, each of us was expected to do one of Ruth Draper's monologues. My own distress derived from the fact that I not only had less than an hour in which to learn mine but that no one could tell me which one it was. They could only say it was the one with which I always made Alfred Lunt laugh so. At this point I woke screaming and was discovered to be in an appalling state of nervous indigestion.

I want to tell you that seldom has anything I have heard stayed with me like your reading of that first poem in the *Spoon River Anthology*. I am now past the point of knowing whether you read it well. I only know that I cannot get it out of my ears and that I want you to come back and read the whole book to me.

I will always remember this theatrical season as the one in which Ethel Barrymore wrote me twice. The second time was to tell me that, in her penultimate week at the Colonial in Boston, she twisted her ankle and the show was closed for three performances. Also a letter from Sibyl, who has been given a preview at Denham and gives such a report on what she saw that I am sure Noel has made a great picture. I have suffered through the experience of taking her to the theatre when she twirled in her seat like a teetotum, giving the play what Thornton has called "her intermittent rapid attention." Yet I uneasily suspect that, in the course of those occasional glances, she sees more of the play than anyone else in the audience.

I have just had a lovely week with Alice Miller and today the Alan Campbells arrive and tomorrow, wonder of wonders, unprecedented in my life, my brother Billy is arriving for a week's visit. I hope to God I don't keep going into my embarrassing doldrums. I have my ups and downs and am constantly wasting away, with the result that I weigh less now than I have any time since the opening night of *The Scarlet Pimpernel*. Even so, I have a kind of irrational expectation of getting well again, based on nothing more substantial than that I always have. I think I can promise you that, when you come back in July, I shall be able to recite an entire limerick with only the slightest quaver in the voice.

Alexander Woollcott

To *CAPTAIN THORNTON WILDER*

Bomoseen, Vt.
June 4, 1942

Dear Thornton-As-Ever-Was:

It was way back in the early part of May that I was set upon writing a letter to you and only this evening am I putting key to ribbon. I was too full of things that were hard to say; but then, too, during most of that time, I was a most wretched creature, a groggy and drizzling old piece of misery, with day-to-day postponements of the question as to whether I might not better be shipped to Boston and have done with it. Certainly I am not out of the woods yet, but I will tell you in deep confidence that now, for the first time, I myself expect to be back on the warpath once more—perhaps as soon as September.

As for the letter I meant to write you, it will probably never be written or said. It was going to be an attempt to tell you what your exit into the Service had done to my thoughts. That news, when it reached me, told me again what I had known when Joe Alsop was taken prisoner—in what manner this war was going to wrench my life out of shape.

There has been a coming and going of people all along and all this past week I have enjoyed the Alan Campbells and my brother Billy from Baltimore. Long after I had been put to bed by the implacable Hennessey, I have heard filtering down the hallway the buzz of talk around the fireplace going on till all hours in the morning.

My brother is getting on—sixty-six if he's a day—but he changes in no way that I can detect five minutes after he has come into the room. Did I tell you about the letter he got from me when he ran away from home and ended up at the Phalanx? All I remember about it was the word of farewell at the end and that only because it was correctively jeered at by everybody. It was signed "Your favorite brother, Aleck." This was in 1894.

I am writing tonight rather than tomorrow to ask you one question and present one duty for you to adore and be afflicted by. I have gone over and over the letters written just before you went West to see if there was a date set for your return to the island. But I could find nothing and am wondering now if it was part of the fog in which I was moving that I ever thought you were coming here again. Straighten me out about this.

Second, drop a line to Paul C. Harper, Jr., 1615 Judson Avenue, Evanston, Illinois, telling him whether you can give him an appointment in Chicago on your way East. You may identify him as the present stage of that small, owlish thirteen-year-old boy from military school, who, when I dined with his pop and mom in Evanston many years ago, joined them in escorting me woodenly to the station, where I was boarding the train for Minneapolis. On the very platform, to the great astonishment of everyone except himself, he drew from the bosom of his tunic a typewritten manuscript, pressed it into my hands, and said, "I'd like your opinion on this some day, sir." I was too taken aback to protect myself and, when finally I had adjusted my bulk to the berth and settled down, curled like a porpoise under the grudging light, I broke one of my rules and actually inspected his effort. It was a typewritten manuscript which I have stupidly misplaced and it was called "A History of the Boy Scout Movement in Evanston."

Ever since, he has reported from time to time and I do my best to conceal the gratification I always feel when youngsters elect me as an uncle. He has been here a good many times on his way home from Yale and I last saw him when I was playing New Haven just two years ago. Since then, he has come on tremendously. He has won some prize for his thesis on state labor legislation and in another month will take his examinations as an officer in the Marine Corps. He wants so much and perhaps so uselessly to talk with all kinds of elders before he goes, so that he will be better oriented when the war is over. I told him that you were better at that than I was and he said, "I wish to God I had known that when I saw him at a party in New Haven a little while ago." So, if on your way back you can spare an hour from the Hutchinses and Bobbsie Goodspeed, send him a wire. You will thereby greatly oblige

Yours affectionately,
A. Woollcott

P.S. I've had four letters in quick succession from Sibyl, all pointing out that Thornton's quite *wrong* in thinking she didn't like The Man Who Came to Dinner.

To SAMUEL HOPKINS ADAMS
[It was Mr. Adams, newspaper man, novelist, and biographer, who helped Woollcott to get his first job as reporter on the New York *Times*.]

Bomoseen, Vt.
June 7, 1942

Dear Sam:

This letter to you has been accumulatin' forty-seven year, but I have only this week felt up to writing letters that just did not *have* to be written. I am being docile as hell and take my orders from Hennessey to the letter. You can't accept the tireless care of such a one and then dishonor it by going off on a toot. The trouble is that I spent my first fifty years ignoring all symptoms. If there was a twinge of indigestion, I went out and gave the rebellious tract something to worry about, such as four Welsh rarebits which I ate one night as a cure for the colic. It worked.

Wherefore I have acquired no technique for living on the shelf. When people stand around me in a bright, idiotic chorus, telling me to take everything very easy, I feel like making the response Max Beerbohm made privately to Queen Mary during the last war when she asked him to be one of a group of English poets to read from his works at Albert Hall, as a Benefit for the Seamen. He replied that he would be glad to accede to her request but that he was too busy: Admiral Beatty had just asked him to take command of one of the battleships in the North Sea.

Nor am I altogether comfortable in the hands of doctors. I know, but find it useless to say, that, whereas we are not precisely at cross-purposes, we have different objectives. I could make myself clear by quoting from the substitute I have found for Holy Writ; since I was not brought up in what could possibly be called a Christian family, I have always been in need of one and have found myself drawing heavily on the speeches, opinions, and letters of the late Justice Holmes. Did you hear his broadcast on his ninetieth birthday? He said, "To live is to function; that is all there is to living."

I saw a good deal of Max on the trip to England I made last Fall. I suppose that that unbelievably exhausting endeavor was the root cause of my recent crack-up. But if you think I wish I hadn't gone, you're crazy.

I am glad you and Jane [Mrs. Adams] have not been part of the trickle of visitors that have passed this way during the two months since I got back from hospital, for I have been a mass of misery most of the time and most atrocious company, being given to interminable and rather melancholy anecdotes. However, I am clapped into bed pretty early and then the visitors have been able to enjoy each other. My brother Billy had the time of his life with Dorothy Parker. Did you ever meet my brother Billy in Baltimore? I have always liked him, which is more than I could say of my other brothers. He is still the most charming person I have ever met. His twin grandsons called on me the other day and are unbelievably beautiful.

When I left for England in September, it never occurred to me that we would keep the island functioning this summer; but there has been such grave illness among the members—Neysa McMein, Alice Duer Miller, George Backer, and I are all at least temporarily useless—that it may justify itself this year as a convalescent camp. As you may not know, the island, since long before I came here (it was not, as Thornton Wilder insisted, a result of my Fourierite inheritance), has been a co-operative with ten shareholding members, a small flock of associate members, and many miscellaneous casuals, all going Dutch treat. It was I who, a few years ago, broke the rule by inviting people lavishly and paying their bills. This grew out of the fact that by that time I had bought half the island and built my own house on it and naturally did not collect from guests during the eight months here when the Club is not in operation. So you and Jane are hereby declared associate members, and this is fair warning that, if you come to see me prior to October 15th, you will each be soaked $7.50 a day. I tell you these actuarial details without embarrassment because I assume that they are academic. With rubber and gas having cut down on all our indulgences, I doubt if we can hope to see either of you here this summer. Of course, our return to first principles is part of the experiment by which we hope to find out whether the island is really useful to enough people to justify the effort to continue it in war time. I should doubt it.

Without reading this back, I know that it has a kind of sickroom smell to it and this would be genuinely misleading. I am much better and I myself feel for the first time that I am going to have another go at things.

My best love to Jane.

Alexander Woollcott

To *D. G. KENNEDY*

*Peter Bent Brigham Hospital,
Boston, Mass.
June 19, 1942*

Dear Gerry:

Once upon a time my old friend Paul Robeson, returning after an absence of several years in Europe, discovered that in the interval I had become a celebrity. At last he found me out in Hollywood surrounded by autograph hunters and I still remember his turning to his wife and saying, "My gawd, Aleck's a mess, ain't he?"

Yes, by all means write to Sheldon. I do not remember whether I had time to explain that in sending you to him I was paying you the greatest compliment that I can pay anybody and I will go so far as to tell you now that the telegram he sent me after your visit was the best notice any of my candidates got from him. I may leave it to you in my will or even send it to you some time if you ever get low in your mind.

As for my effort to persuade you to take the trade of writing seriously, I feel strongly on the subject and fortunately can straighten out Sheldon's confusion. What I told him was what I have told others—that when I saw you underfoot at Hamilton you made no impression on me whatever and I should not now know that there was such a person if it had not been for a correspondence that got started when I was broadcasting and you were at law school. You must remember that this began at a time when I was getting literally thousands of letters a week and if, as you now remind me, I stopped to engage in a brawl with you about Hamilton Armstrong's pamphlet you will realize that whatever letter you wrote me must have knocked me for a loop.

The reason I write a great many letters is because I like to receive many. Incidentally, I can't waste much time on you today as I have two honeys to answer, one from Thornton Wilder and the other from Felix Frankfurter, yet speaking of Hamilton

[330]

Armstrong, here's an odd thing about him. I am prone, for some obscure reason, to boast that my grandfather was born in 1807—that is, before Dickens or Lincoln or Offenbach or Oliver Wendell Holmes the Elder. Once Rebecca West countered by telling me that her maternal grandfather was smuggled out of Paris in time of stress by the assistance of a provincial lawyer named Robespierre. But Hamilton Armstrong topped her. He is considerably younger than I am yet all four of his grandparents were born in the eighteenth century.

All of which leaves me time to say only that on Monday of this week I abruptly began to feel better and this morning, at the persuasion of the x-ray, my gall-bladder came clean and confessed to having been the source of all my recent troubles. Eight lovely stones showed up in the picture and the operation is scheduled for tomorrow morning, which means most of July and all of August spent in convalescence at the island, and also means that for the first time I see a prospect of going back into circulation, not merely as well as ever, but considerably better than I have been for some years past.

A. Woollcott

To RUTH GORDON

[Woollcott first became acquainted with Miss Gordon back in the days when she played the part of Lola Pratt in Booth Tarkington's *Seventeen*. She has recently added writing to her acting career and has starred in her own play, *Over Twenty-one*. Their nicknames for each other, "Louisa" and "Joe," alluded to the two actors of an earlier day in the American theatre, Louisa Lane Drew and Joseph Jefferson.]

Boston, Mass.
June 19, 1942

Dear Louisa—

Back in the early Algonquin days, when everyone was so whimsical it was almost impossible to get any work done, there was the institution known as the going away present and

I remember sailing for Europe one fine June day with my cabin packed with drawing slates, toy trains, teddy bears, gollywogs and the like. Such fun! As for the friends of Charlie Towne's, it was difficult for one of them to go even as far as Chicago without finding in his drawing-room a bowl replete with goldfish. Well, after examining the enclosed, you can't say I never sent you a going-away present. I wish I could have it waiting for you at the Grand Central on Monday but there are legal reasons why you must cash it Saturday morning bright and early.

To my immense relief, my long-suspect gall-bladder was caught in the act yesterday with as pretty a set of stones—in the x-ray plate they look like moonstones—as one could wish and I am writing this under the impression that the guilty part is to be plucked out tomorrow morning. While waiting for the development of the plates, I attended the lecture being given by the roentgenologist in the next room and had the novel experience of seeing my own unpleasing internals thrown on the screen for comment. The students did not fail to appreciate the fact that I came in a wheel chair. The professor rose to the occasion by getting off a joke out of *Hamlet* and I came right back at him with one out of the *Aeneid*.

I am being allowed out this afternoon to see *The Gold Rush*.

A bientôt
Joe

To DR. GUSTAV ECKSTEIN

Boston, Mass.
June 25, 1942

Dear Gus:

It seems that the able gent who eviscerated me Saturday morning—it was Elliott Cutler, Professor of Surgery here at Harvard—drops in every morning for a rest and inspection and yesterday with no cue from me fell to talking about a conversation he once had with Noguchi. Then he told me about some journalist of his acquaintance calling up and asking for a fact he needed about Noguchi for an article in *Life* or *Fortune* or some such magazine. Where was he buried? Startled to find that he didn't know, Cutler bade his friend hold the phone while he looked it up. Reaching trustfully for your work on the subject he turned to the final pages and found himself frustrated. Hastily consulting eight men whom he would have expected to know he found that all looked blank.

He still doesn't know. I told him not to give it another thought. I might not be able to take a sip of water without assistance but I would let him know the answer to his question in forty-eight hours. Will you wire me at once? Where *was* Noguchi buried?

A. W.

[Noguchi was buried in Woodlawn Cemetery in New York City.]

To *EDWARD SHELDON*

Boston, Mass.
June 29, 1942

Dear Sheldon:

I am using the return envelope, which brings the Farrar letter back into your possession, as an excuse to sneak you an ad interim note about other matters.

I never sent the wire to Julia Marlowe, because I have no security that she remembers me at all, or, if she does, that the memory is pleasant.

Recently I have been approached by two editors to intercede in their behalf in bidding for Thornton's biography of me. I am not sure who started the rumor that such a work was contemplated, which of course it isn't. But he has been drawing up genealogical tables and poring over photographs of the Phalanx which would be the kind of objectless homework that *would* engage him, just another device to seem busy without actually doing the work he ought to be doing. I was amused when he denounced me for sending him one 1885 Phalanx photograph of which I was particularly fond without identifying one lovely young girl in it. It happens that she was the daughter of a French model by a painter from Baltimore. How she came to be playing governess to the young folk at the Phalanx in 1885 is one of my stories. "Who," wrote Thornton, "is this Duse-like beauty with her lovely hand shielding her eyes from the sun?" I mention the matter only because if the print had not been so old and faded he would have seen that she really was the Marlowe-like beauty. The likeness was really extraordinary. Indeed there was a legend in the family that Marlowe once stopped Amelie on the street and spoke to her about it. But Amelie was a great liar and this may not have been true. But Miss Marlowe may remember her because she married a man named Eustace Sumner and they all had friends in common at Greens Farms in Connecticut.

As for your knowing Hennessey, I've long felt a special frustration in my desire that you should. You see, he never says anything. At least he never says anything to me and for the life of me I've been unable to imagine how you would ever get to know him. Perhaps I have been of too little faith in this matter, in which case I will deliver him at your door. And if you do succeed in unlocking his lips there are some things about him I would like you to find out for me.

About the pigeons. I must sadly report that Ham died quietly the week before I left for Boston. He had been poorly from the first—kinda peakid, really, and was never meant for the rough life ahead of him. I loved the sound of them outside my window—a sound which Hennessey could reproduce to perfection. He *can* talk to pigeons.

As for James, I have read him with interest but do not share your enthusiasm. If you like detective stories at all I think you would be interested in two companion pieces by a man named Heard; one called "A Taste for Honey" and the other "Reply Paid." Both mighty special. As for Trollope, I had already clasped him to my now somewhat withered bosom, having brought along several short miscellaneous Trollopes which were unfamiliar to me. I've just finished *Cousin Henry* which I found engrossing and *An Old Man's Love* which I enjoyed none the less for discovering that he nobly stepped aside in favor of a mate of more suitable age. The old man was, I might explain, a grisled dotard of fifty.

My dear Sheldon, I have been knocked down by a wave several times the last few years. Each time I've climbed wearily to my feet with a chorus of medicos and friends all saying how well I was going to get. I always knew better. This time there is the same chorus but with a difference. This time I agree with them. Indeed, I think that by Fall I shall be well—or well enough for all practical purposes.

This has turned out to be more than the note I meant it to be, but then I always have so many things to tell you about. I need not tell you that I fairly burst with pride when my hastily improvised Sheldon-Kennedy meeting turned out to be such a success.

I hope that after another week you can address me at Bomoseen, Vermont.

Ethel [Barrymore] just telephoned from Mamaroneck. When I first came to here in Boston and collected my wits many things made me realize that for weeks I had been only half myself. Surely I was no more than half myself when Jack [Barrymore] died and my only thought was to write and telephone Ethel. The half of my mind which would have written you was not functioning.

A. Woollcott

To RUTH GORDON

Boston, Mass.
June 30, 1942

Dear Ruth:

The secret of my whereabouts lasted until Winchell confided it to his listeners Sunday night. There has been considerable commotion ever since but far less than it would have been if the story had broken earlier. From the ensuing spate of telegrams I plucked the enclosed voice from the past.

In my capricious fashion I was reminded by it of the fact that twenty-five years ago next month I went off to the wars. I refer to the time when two thousand of us sailed stealthily from Hoboken one July dawn in 1917 and got as far as Staten Island before we were sunk. Most of my friends bade me godspeed with varying degrees of heartiness and approval, pressing trench-mirrors upon me and other equipment which did not foresee (and no more did I) how much of my soldiering would be done in Paris. Among those who had no kind or good word to say to me in parting—in fact almost no word at all—was Arthur Hopkins. Our farewell luncheon was characterized by a wordless gloom. Finally he did break down and say that he considered my enlistment equivalent to desertion. I might be rallying to the flag but I was betraying the theatre which he considered much more important. This really meant, when I came to think about it on the transport, that I was deserting him. He felt he could no longer count on the literate and enhancing accounts in the *Times* of his productions.

It is thirteen years ago last month that I quit being a dramatic critic once and for all. But I still seem to be the actresses' friend. Winchell had hardly spoken before Ethel [Barrymore] was on the wire, and that voice still affects me as it did when I first heard it in *Carrots* at the Garrick in Philadelphia long ago. Then Kit [Cornell] is spending tomorrow morning with me and Lynn

[336]

[Fontanne] is coming Thursday for the day. Lynn is making a special trip only because Alfred has a broadcast to do in which she isn't appearing. But Kit is just stopping in on her way to the Cape. She telephoned this morning at a crucial moment in my hospital routine but, with television not yet perfected, I was able to talk to her just the same. She gets in at eight and leaves at one-something for the Cape and I assumed she would go to the Ritz because I would in her place; taking a bath, having some coffee, and enjoying whatever women do instead of having the barber shave them. But not at all. I take it she means to sit on a stool in the station, swig some coffee, and be right over—and if I were not here to entertain her she would probably just bum the streets from eight till one.

I expect that a week from today I shall be lying on the dock at the island in converse with Cocaud and the Duchess and waiting for the arrival of Neysa [McMein] and George Backer. I shall be starting the business of convalescence all over again but with considerably improved chances.

Alexander W.

To *HELEN KELLER*

Bomoseen, Vt.
July 15, 1942

Dear Helen:

I also want to know who owns the Jo Davidson portrait and where, in the reasonably early future, it may be seen by the likes of me. I am delighted that you had it made, but then of course I would be. Nothing is more oppressive than to have one's advice taken. If you had followed mine in this matter I should have been weighted down with doubts of my own wisdom. Now I can wallow in the comfort of irresponsibility.

Few things have brought home to me more vividly the

monstrous upheaval of our times than the casual way we all take the simple fact that Wilhelmina is living in a small cottage in Lee, Massachusetts. She was a bright star in the firmament of my childhood. I wonder if all bookish children are as fascinated by (and envious of) the famous youngsters of their time as I was when, as a small boy with an enormous head, I pored over the copies of *Harper's Young People* and *St. Nicholas* in the early Nineties. There were five such wunderkinder for me—Elsie Leslie the child actress who was a little older than I but who looked young enough to be my daughter when I took her to lunch a year or so ago in New York; Josef Hofmann, the boy pianist; Alfonso, the boy King of Spain; Wilhelmina, the girl Queen of Holland—and, in my doubtless immature judgment, the most enthralling of them all, Helen Keller. Well, it has taken a world war to bring my three girl friends all together in the same country. If I weren't still enfeebled by a long illness I would try to give a dinner party for the lot—perhaps with incidental music by Josef Hofmann.

I have strong personal reasons for wanting to see some old friends who are scattered along the road which leads down through the Berkshires past Stockbridge into Connecticut. Perhaps if I hoard all the gas which should be my portion for July and August I can get as far as Westport.

In the meantime my dear love to Polly [Thompson] and to you.

Alexander W.

To DOROTHY THOMPSON

Bomoseen, Vt.
July 16, 1942

Dear Dorothy:

In answer to yours of Bastille Day, let me take up the points seriatim:

1. Fair Haven 230 W 2 is the number of a telephone on the mainland over which you can transmit messages to me and learn at any time whether I am in residence. The invitation to come and see me is now in your hand and you do not need to accumulate any gas for the purpose. The White River Junction bus goes through Woodstock to Rutland whence you can get another bus to Castleton Corners. Given due notice we can meet you there and bring you the remaining two miles.

2. The same information goes for your farmhands who should be instructed, however, to hitch-hike or walk that two miles from Castleton Corners to the lake and once there to ask for the Bull family who will attend to their delivery on the island by boat. Send them here any Sunday you like with the reservation that they take a rain-check for the following Sunday in case it turns out to be bad weather. Send them in any number with the reservation that we could not easily provide lunch for more than twenty-five. Send them about eleven o'clock so that they can get in an hour or two of swimming before lunch. Tell them to bring bathing trunks if they are modest. There will also be sailboat, motor launch and canoe entertainment liberally provided. I suggest that you give me a chance to OK your selected date because, as soon as I am a little steadier on my pins after a drastic gall-bladder operation now only three weeks behind me, I must make one flying trip to New York and it is conceivable that you would hit upon the only Sunday I shall be away from the island between now and Labor Day.

3. I will post you five hundred words of Green Mountain prose so that you will get it not later than Monday.

4. You inquire if I have any money and I must confess that after years of improvidence and months of enforced unemployment, I am completely bankrupt. As this condition always induces in me a giddy state of financial irresponsibility I enclose my check for $50 leaving you to fill in the name of the payee. Presumably I shall learn from the cancelled voucher whether you were able to make it payable to any organization which would permit me to deduct the gift from my income tax. It seems to me this is information you ought to furnish at the time you solicit funds. What do you think?

I believe I told you that the ironmonger in Rutland got a great kick out of the news that you had divorced me. He is telling everybody.

Alexander W.

[Dorothy Thompson's "farmhands" were a group of young people from the Volunteer Land Army, for whom Woollcott planned a pinic on the island.]

To KATHARINE CORNELL

Bomoseen, Vermont
July 19, 1942

Dear Miss Kitty:

In the midst of that mass meeting which was inspired by your visit to the Peter Bent Brigham, I hope you felt one-half the frustration I experienced at being cheated out of the long, uninterrupted, relaxed talk I so wanted to have with you. I suppose it was my fault in that I had mentioned to one of the nurses that you were coming. I was craftier the following day when, all at loose ends because Alfred was going to do a radio program without her, Lynn took the Wednesday evening train to Boston, spent the night at the Ritz and came over to spend the following afternoon with me, looking very lovely and, at a rough guess, about twenty-seven. At last we had quite a talk about *The Three Sisters*.

In a lather of impatience to get out of hospital and onto the island I tottered forth on July 5th just two weeks and a day after I had been hacked into on a grand scale. Pretty good, I think, for a somewhat backward boy now going on fifty-six. Since then my convalescence has progressed a little more slowly than I had foreseen and a good deal faster than I probably have any right to expect. Yesterday I actually went in swimming which would suggest an entirely rugged condition to anyone who had never seen me swim and therefore could not know that I have contrived to make that sport almost indistinguishable from immobility. But then you might guess as much because you have seen my skating for which the only word is massive. I am certainly the only athlete of your acquaintance who succeeds, while on skates, in giving the impression of a slow motion-picture.

I may go down to New York on Thursday for three or four days to see Alice Miller who has been so gravely ill. But otherwise I foresee that I shall stay put here until Labor Day at the earliest. You spoke of paying the island a visit and I would greatly enjoy that but in your behalf I am appalled at the thought of that long, awkward, hot trip from Vineyard Haven to Rutland. You might, however, write and let me know if you are seriously considering it and will you at the same time give me Margalo's [Gillmore] address? I believe she is in your vicinity because she wrote from that general territory suggesting that she and the present Mrs. Romney Brent might attempt a joint expedition to this retreat. I wanted to write and tell her that I wish they would come separately because one of the alarming changes brought about by the war is the heavy preponderance on the distaff side among the people planning to visit us. Indeed I would have written Margalo to that effect already but I have mislaid her letter and cannot recall her improbable address.

Have you heard in detail from or about Ruth [Gordon]? I have.

Have you, in casting *The Three Sisters*, considered the possibility of getting Charles Laughton for any one of several parts?

Have you told Guthrie [McClintic] that I wish he would come up and entertain me at the modest cost to himself of $7.50 a day which Hennessey will try to collect from him?

Alexander W.
July 20th

P.S. If, as I suspect, the foregoing sounds pompous and polysyllabic put it down to the fact that it was dictated at the top of my lungs during a combination hurricane and electrical storm which tossed boats and docks around as if they were autumn leaves, littered the island with tree-limbs which should keep us in firewood when we run out of oil and during which the Duchess was in such abject terror that I was surprised when it was all over to find that her hair had not turned white.

The morning's mail brought me one of the most engaging letters I have ever received. It was written from the Hotel Bossert in Brooklyn and signed Gaby Delys. As it was in a handwriting I have seen too seldom to recognize at sight it took me some little time to figure out it was from Ethel [Barrymore]. She says she will be here on the 12th in time to celebrate her ninety-third birthday

To MARSHALL A. BEST
[Of The Viking Press.]

Bomoseen, Vt.
July 19, 1942

My dear Best:
As for the book, already too long delayed, I think it improbable that it will be ready for publication before February or March because my convalescence seems likely to take a little

longer than I had, in my incorrigible optimism, foreseen. As to its title, I am wavering between two choices: *I Sometimes Think* and *Long, Long Ago*. I have never given serious consideration to any other.

Here, in a nutshell, is the difficulty. I already have ample material to make a good clip-book but as I think it unlikely that I will ever do another I would prefer to include in it two, and possibly three, pieces which I have not yet written. I am reluctant to do these at a time when I am still perceptibly below par. There is the further complication that once I am in shape to do my best work I could be, and therefore should be, devoting that new lease on life to an activity more urgent.

In any event please send me at your leisure the two manila folders of pre-*While Rome Burns* material, *Lessons in English* and the crime stories from *Look*. None of the last two are worth reprinting but there *are* a few real jewels that you haven't seen and presumably don't know about.

A. W.

To *HELEN HAYES*

Bomoseen, Vt.
July 20, 1942

Dear Helen:

This is a line to tell you that on the chance of a few bedside visits to Alice Miller who is so gravely ill, I shall try to go to New York Thursday and stay (at the Gotham) until Tuesday morning. You might telephone me there to confer about your impending visit to these parts.

If you and Charles arrive on or about the 30th you are likely to find the Kaufmans and Moss Hart here. If you were to linger through the second week in August you would certainly share the island with the Lunts and be in time to welcome Ethel

Barrymore on her arrival. Other visitors are probable but less predictable.

Meanwhile I have found myself wondering if you have ever read *Salvation Nell* and given a thought to reviving it or a revision of it. As I have never read it I cannot even guess how much it shows its years. But, all the way from the Christmas vacation of 1908, I remember vividly every moment of its first and last acts. The second act is vaguer. I seem to recall that its scene is a tenement bedroom and shows Nell crooning implausibly over the cradle of her unsanctioned child. What I remember best about that act is the great speech in it which Sheldon never wrote and which was delivered on one night only. You may have heard that when the play was new there were great mirations in the press about the scrupulous actuality of the saloon in Act I. Real beer came foaming from the taps, probably because no substitute was cheaper. God knows how many kegs of it the company put away in the course of a season. One night it was so hot that even Mrs. Fiske felt like a good draught and sent word to the stage manager that she saw no reason why she should be the only member of the company never to sample that prop. The agitated old stage manager drew a mugful, went looking for her everywhere and found her at last down on the stage, neglecting to notice only that the curtain was up. Cousin Minnie was half way through her best lullaby when she saw the old fool in his shirt sleeves come mooning toward her with the outstretched refreshment. She sprang forward to bar the path of this monster as he moved toward the cradle of her little one and drove him into the night with one of the most devastating temperance speeches that ever issued from human lips. I never heard what became of the stage manager but I suppose he dropped dead in the wings. Or was that John Flood?

Alexander W.

To CAPTAIN THORNTON WILDER

Bomoseen, Vt.
July 20, 1942

Captain, O My Captain:
                        On the 5th inst., gaunt and troubled by a certain fluidity in my underpinnings, I wobbled and tottered my way out of the Peter Bent Brigham and drove back to Bomoseen, lavishly escorted by a brilliant, successful and strange young physician of my acquaintance [Ethan Allan Brown] who, after several Jack-Londonish years before the mast and an impulsive two years spent in the company of Edmund Spenser and Dante at Oxford, ran into Sir Almroth Wright one summer while the latter was on the loose in Italy. He decided on the spur of the moment to become a physician and, having put himself through the Medical School of the London University, is one.

Ever since he delivered me here, with the odds lengthening on the wager that I shall be in full working trim by Fall, I have been limbering up by writing a very freshet of correspondence. The only person I can't write to at all is you, partly because I have far too much to say and to ask and to hear, partly because I am too acutely conscious of the widening gulf between us. I remember too well from the summer and Fall of 1917 how dim and, when brought to my attention at all, how distasteful all my civilian friends seemed. When compared with the men who slept in the adjoining bunks on the transport or stood in front of or behind me in mess line, the oldest and dearest friends I had back home seemed like paper dolls.

A widely circulated newspaper photograph of that exit from the Peter Bent Brigham elicited a good many voices from the past, including a note of inquiry from one woman in East Cleveland who looked like a buxom Ina Claire in the days when, a quarter of a century ago next month, she was an army nurse stationed at Savenay in the department of the lower Loire and we used to make clandestine visits together to the back-room of Madame Cocaud's buvette. Now she writes to ask if I am *touring* the hospitals.

I relished your blurred and almost indecipherable post card even if my own memories of close-order drill had no kindred emotion in them. In that respect all of us at Savenay were unfortunate. All of our officers were doctors, some of them good doctors but none of them good drillmasters. The job of putting us through our paces in a near-by meadow was usually assigned to some officer of such low rank that he had not a chance to protest. One of them, whose other functions included the care of all teeth in the vicinity, was a foggy fellow named Applegate. He used to carry the manual with him, select a sentence at random, read it aloud at the top of his lungs and then look up to see what was happening. I remember the terror of a blameless French cow as we would swing toward her after "Right front into line." It was for her sake as much as mine that I risked court-martial by leaving a memorandum for the adjutant reminding him how painful it always was to be drilled by a dentist.

There are two things I want to tell you and one I want to ask.

First I pass on, without comment, a paragraph from a letter Helen Hayes wrote me on July 2nd:

"*I am very fogged at this point in my career and I want to help. Have you read Thornton's play,* The Skin of Our Teeth? *I think it is one of the great plays of our time. His mysterious producer, Mr. Meyerberg, sent it to me with a suggestion that I play Sabina. Of course there's only one person to play that part—the person for whom I suspect it was written —Ruth [Gordon]. I wouldn't dare attempt it, since I'd be haunted by the thought of the way she'd speak every line. It's very distracting, though, to have to turn down a good play.*"

Now for my question. When I spoke to you over the telephone from Boston I was still pretty groggy from sundry opiates and my memory of things said at that time is blurred. I forget the precise date of the four-day visit you predicted (I'm not foul enough to say promised) you would spend at the island. I attach great importance to those days for reasons innumerable, including the fact that I have been presented with my first clean break since 1928. All available evidence tends to suggest that I have been vouchsafed a new lease on life and I have from now until Labor Day at the earliest to think what use I might make of it. As the burden of choice is always heavy I would welcome some compulsion but, failing that, I would rather talk it over with you than anyone I know.

I would feel satisfied if you answered this letter by a telegram addressed to me here or by a postal addressed to the Gotham.
Alexander W.

To SAMUEL HOPKINS ADAMS

Bomoseen, Vt.
July 21, 1942

Dear Sam:

The trouble with your letters is not that they drive me to hospital but provoke me to immediate reply.

I must disown one viewpoint you ascribe to me. If, in the thirty-six years of our acquaintance, you had seen more of me you would have known that even in my most buoyant moments I never quite admitted that this business of living was worth the candle. I am entirely sympathetic with Bill's reluctance to prolong his stay here. Among the odds and ends of good reading I ran across in *City Lawyer,* the recent autobiography by Arthur Garfield Hays, I particularly relished his quotation from a funeral oration which Clarence Darrow once made at the bier of a friend of his who had committed suicide. This friend, Darrow said, in a moment of temporary sanity had decided that life was not worth living.

As for Brigham Young, his birthplace was a bleak mountain farm near Whitingham in Vermont. I enclose a snapshot of the stone tablet which still marks the spot, or did, at least, when I saw it two or three years ago, standing weatherbeaten and askew and half covered with brambles. It is the local tradition that it was placed there by some pious and humorless Mormon pilgrims from Connecticut but I have heard testimony to the effect that it was the facetious work of a mordant wag from somewhere down in the Berkshires. You might send the photograph back to me.

Joe sends his love to Jane [Adams] and so do I. Of course ours cannot match yours. You speak of her as turning handsprings all over the place and only a uxorious, infatuated old man could imagine her doing that.

A. W.

To MRS. EDWARD ROOT

[Another member of the large Root family with whom Woollcott was in frequent contact.]

Bomoseen, Vt.
July 22, 1942

Dear Grace:

In the empty, silly, noisy years which immediately preceded the Wall Street crash of 1929, I used to get hot tips on the market from big shots. I suppose they rather fancied themselves in the role of Maecenas, giving a genial lift to someone more literate and intellectual (and therefore presumably more incompetent and idiotic) than themselves. No good ever accrued from these tips except the potential benefit which anyone can experience by merely losing all his money. Indeed, I have made only one investment in my life which has brought me rich dividends, and because it was made on a tip given by you, I shall embarrass you with my gratitude all the days of my life, of which, by the way, it is now generally predicted that there are going to be more than I had foreseen.

You may remember that in June 1937, the young Jensens went to Denmark for their delayed honeymoon. Its high point was their visit to his grandmother who died shortly thereafter. She and the navy brother who was drowned appear to have been the only two persons fondly remembered from his childhood. From the first money he saved out of his *Daily News* earnings there was enough left over, after he bought a new suit, to have his picture taken in it by a Fourteenth Street photographer— this so he could let his grandmother know how well he was getting on. She had cherished that picture for a dozen years but she gave it to Deb and I saw it for the first time when Deb brought it over to the hospital in Syracuse. She offered to have a copy made for me and I asked her to have two copies made. Here's yours.

As for the remaining days of my life (see above), I shall spend the next few weeks of enforced repose meditating on what use I can make of them. I am always surprised whenever I discover that what everyone tells you is, as often as not, quite true. For example, that after a drastic operation the patient's strength flows back slowly. But day by day it does flow back. I am hoping you will verify this by that predicted August visit.

A. Woollcott

To *ALAN CAMPBELL*

Bomoseen, Vt.
August 11, 1942

Dear Robert Strange:

(I just *had* to top Felix Krembs. Don't ask me to do it again. The effort has exhausted me.)

Tell Dotty that I hope she will come here as soon as she can and stay as long as she will.

There is always this disadvantage about any island (including Manhattan), that one can get trapped on it with someone uncongenial or, more probably, just embarrassing. I can think of several people in our common acquaintance whom Dorothy would prefer to avoid. Even if she were to rush here this very week she would find that all of these had already come and gone. Tomorrow Ethel Barrymore and Eleanora von Mendelssohn arrive from New York, Dr. Levine from Boston and, I hope, Frode Jensen (angry father of a new second daughter) from Syracuse. Lou Calhern and Dorothy Gish are due Monday. Joe Alsop, now speeding from Rio on the *Gripsholm*, looms in the distance.

I doubt if I could be of any help in encouraging her to work which, of course, she wants to do. A life-saving project, in my own case, was wrecked on the morning of December 7th. Thornton Wilder, who is a born gadfly, gets his work done by going away into a semi-solitude for two and a half months at a clip. His plan was to go into partnership with me after my return from England, the two of us to work together, each at his own stint, but each being a pacemaker and disciplinarian for the other. But I am afraid that Dotty and I would be as mutually helpful as Leopold and Loeb.

I hope, at least, that beginning Saturday morning of this week she will keep me supplied with an address where I can reach her. And speaking of addresses, I predict a time when you would find a package of books not unwelcome. When that time comes let me know.

Finally I must tell you about the time when I found that *The Man Who Came to Dinner* was booked to play in Montreal. As Canada was then at war and we were not, I naturally felt uncomfortable at the prospect of our raiding Canada and carrying off some of their money. Therefore I offered my salary and percentage to the British War Relief and before Sam Harris,

George Kaufman and Moss Hart had time to think, they had donated their take as well. I remember vomiting quietly all over a well-intentioned letter from Rachel Crothers cheering me to the echo for this magnificent behavior of mine for which she could find no other apt adjective except "glorious." With you I have sought to avoid the same note but I will not be denied the privilege of saying that I think you have done the only thing which, were I in your place, would give me peace of mind.

A. W.

To DR. A. P. SAUNDERS

Bomoseen, Vt.
August 12, 1942

Dear Percy:

One Arthur J. Derbyshire, whose stationery describes him as Director of the Community Arts Program of the Munson-Williams-Proctor Institute, seems to be readying a needlework exhibition for November and wants to borrow the embroidered waistcoat that Mrs. Theodore Roosevelt made me, to be shown at that time. This seems to me an idiotic activity for such times as these, worthy of a group of twittery Hokinson women, but maybe I am merely inventing an excuse for avoiding the infernal nuisance of lending anything valuable to anybody. Can you give me a confidential report?

Eleanora [von Mendelssohn], recently summoned to New York for the birthday of Mrs. Toscanini (Ned Sheldon maintains that I am much better for her than Toscanini), returns with Ethel Barrymore this afternoon and will resume her efficient practice of massaging my useless foot. She does this every night before I go to bed, her costume for the purpose being a black and gold evening gown of Fortuny silk, the while she dips her expert fingers into a pot of cold cream called, I am afraid, Modern Charm.

Frode Jensen arrives by plane today. He has a new daughter named Karen and is a Captain in the medical corps and goes on duty in Louisiana on September 1st.

A. W.

To *JOSEPHINE WOOLLCOTT ELLINGTON*

Bomoseen, Vt.
August 13, 1942

My dear Josephine:
　　　　　　　I usually make no attempt to answer the letter of anyone so depraved and monstrous that she fails to furnish her address either at the beginning or the end. I am having to guess at yours from the one which was rendered indecipherable in tearing open the envelope.

You pose a question which I never know how to answer. It would be easy to supply you with the names of several literary agents in New York but my guess is that they are all lazy and haphazard and would be of no use to you. Anyone intent on following writing as a trade would naturally study each publication in her potential market and thereby become so familiar with the appetite of each editor that in submitting manuscripts she could pick her shots.

She would, of course, enclose a stamped and self-addressed envelope for the possible return of each manuscript, she would never send one out without keeping a copy, and she would never be so base and lost to all sense of human decency as to leave her address off the accompanying note.

It is a fair picture of my family life that I have no idea who my aunt Maude Woollcott is. Your cousin Phil has sent me from

Asheville a picture of his two boys on whose fertility rests the sole prospect of the name being continued in this country.

A. Woollcott

August 14, 1942

P.S. I had signed and dispatched that waspish but honestly instructive reply to your question before I recalled there was one thing I wanted to say. My once famous memory suffered some damage during my recent illnesses but it is still pretty good. It tells me that your mother has a birthday in the offing. With no records to consult I shall have to make a stab at it. My guess is August 19th. If I am right about that please prop the enclosed card against her breakfast coffee-cup on that morning.

A. W.

To RUTH GORDON

Bomoseen, Vt.
August 21, 1942

Dear Louisa:

Herewith some first-class reading matter: one is that obituary of the blind cocker spaniel written for the private comfort of Mrs. Tarkington; the other a letter from an English friend of ours. You might send the letter back.

ISLAND SOCIAL NOTES

Louis Calhern and Dorothy Gish will leave for New York on Monday, where, after a week of rehearsals, they will take over the principal roles in the New York company of *Life with Father* for six weeks.

Miss Ethel Barrymore left last night for Mamaroneck, New York.

Mr. and Mrs. Harpo Marx and Mrs. Paul Bonner arrive this afternoon.

Poupee Parker, a French poodle ingénue owned by the Alan Campbells, was shipped here just before Mr. Campbell left for camp. She was deflowered by Cocaud two minutes after her arrival and, with the tranquility born of inexperience, is awaiting nine blessed events. Then Sally, a four-months-old English sheep dog presented to the island by Moss Hart, is considered to be charming but weak in the head. The dope began her social career here by trying to bite the Duchess.

Now about Master Kanin [Garson Kanin—Miss Gordon's husband]. In the days when it used to be important to me to be reassured from time to time that I *was* a connoisseur of acting, it was always a satisfaction, on a second visit to a play, to discover that my enthusiasm for this or that performance had not been born of the mood of a moment. Damn it, it *was* good! This week a letter from Pvt. Kanin brought me similar reassurance. My meeting with Garson had refreshed me with evidence that after all I still possessed my once famous appetite for human society. Then came his letter. Anyone who can spell cat and count above four would know it was a good one. But for me it had the extra value of proving I had been right about him in the first place.

You might give my love to Charles Lederer, Charles Brackett, and Frank and Mary Craven. I cannot, at the moment, think of anyone else who is both dear to me and in California—except you, Louisa.

A. W.

To *LADY COLEFAX*

Bomoseen, Vt.
September 1, 1942

Dear Sibyl:

Well then, here's a report on some friends of ours. Was Joe Alsop one of these? He's the young American journalist with Roosevelt blood in him, his mother being a first cousin of Alice Longworth, Brigadier General Ted Roosevelt (now in England) and Mrs. F.D.R. Joe is the only person of my acquaintance to pass through the Groton-Harvard tunnel and come out educated. With his partner, Robert Kintner, he was writing a political column until a year ago and at his house in Washington you ate the best food and met the most interesting people in that city. Just before I left for England last September, he had joined up with the Navy and departed for Bombay as an observer, but en route he wriggled loose and joined Chennault (pronounced, if you do not want to infuriate him, Shuh-nawlt, with the accent on the second syllable), the soldier of fortune who commands the American fliers in China. On a mission for his chief he was flying back from Manila to Chungking at the time of Pearl Harbor and was among those caught and interned at Hongkong. I spent Friday night at the Alsop farm in Connecticut, listening to Joe's placid tale of his adventures. For a time they all herded into several hastily evacuated brothels but by late January these internees, three thousand of them, mostly British, were sent to a camp out on the Stanley Peninsula where the British remain and on such short rations that Joe thinks they will die of starvation. He himself was one of the few who had a little cash on him and this, if judiciously expended among the Sikh guards, could produce some supplementary groceries from the black market in Hongkong. Furtive foraging, ingenious cooking on an electric-heater, and endless plots for escape were the major distractions of each endless day. But characteristically, Joe hit upon the reason-saving scheme of studying Chinese. A woman among his fellow-prisoners was available as a teacher and he put in eight hours a day with her to such effect that on the boat which brought him from Portuguese East Africa to New York, he translated the *Book of Rites* which I take to be a classic of the Confucian era. Joe spent all of Friday afternoon down the road at the village where Justice Frankfurter is spending the summer with Alfred Cohn of the Rockefeller Institute. It was as good a way as any of finding out just what had happened in Washington during the year of his absence. Yesterday Joe left for Washington to find out how he stood and what chance he had of rejoining his outfit in China.

My next topic is Captain Thornton Niven Wilder, U.S.A. (Air Corps Intelligence). I wish I knew, in making my report on him, how much he has already reported to you about himself. At the risk of telling you things you already know, I will give you the whole story in outline. I gather that among the felt wants of the air service is someone on each raid with enough leisure and spare attention to note what happens and tell about it afterwards. For this special service a few men have been and are being trained and Thornton is one of them. On September 19th, at a camp in Pennsylvania, he will have finished his second course of sprouts. Thus it is conceivable that some day, when next American bombers go over Tokyo in force, you will be able to read Captain Wilder's description of what happened. For this service Thornton volunteered through Archie MacLeish. The call to training came in June at a time when Hitchcock in Hollywood was also summoning him to a profitable job in the writing of a new picture. As there was only about three weeks leeway, he would not undertake to write a story but did agree to go out and tell them one and as the plot was still unfolding when the time ran out, Hitchcock returned to New York with him, listening and taking notes all the way across the continent. I do not know what the picture will be called [*The Shadow of a Doubt*] but it is all about a black-sheep returning at last to his native village at a time when the whole world is joining a man-hunt for a certain Jack the Ripper. You watch the protagonist settling into the quiet ways of his boyhood home, working as of old in his sister's vegetable garden, going with her to prayer meeting at the village church, swapping yarns with the neighbors around the cracker barrel in the village store, until the man-hunt closes in on that village and lays its hands on him as the guilty man. Captain Wilder arrived breathless in New York on Saturday, June 27th, telephoned a word to me at the Boston hospital where I lay trussed up after my operation, and flew that evening by plane to Miami where he was scheduled for six weeks of basic military training. In no time he had been swallowed up, body and soul, by his new world. And now, if he ever thinks at all of those he left behind on the other side of the sundering gulf, we must seem to him as thin and unsubstantial as paper dolls. Meanwhile, on this side of the gulf, preparations go ahead for the autumn production of his new play for which Frederic March and Tallulah Bankhead have been signed [*The Skin of Our Teeth*]. I have not read that play nor heard from him anything more about it than I could help but Edward Sheldon tells me it is a work of indisputable genius and Helen Hayes thinks of it as the finest script she ever read. It occurs to me that I might have let Thornton tell you all this himself and on a separate sheet of paper I shall copy, in chronological order, telltale and characteristic excerpts from letters and postal cards he has written me in the past three months.

Here we are still trying to adjust ourselves to the bleak fact that there is now no such person in our world as Alice Duer Miller. I have never realized more forcibly that for anyone so injudicious as to live after fifty, life consists largely of such forlorn efforts to close ranks.

Alexander W.

To *LYNN FONTANNE*

Bomoseen, Vt.
September 9, 1942

Dear Lynn:

A gay, acute, and charming young papist [D. G. Kennedy] to whom both Joe and I are deeply attached—next to Thornton he is the most articulate and luminous friend I have in the armed forces—was married last Saturday morning in New York, and despite the obvious lunacy of going down and coming back in the midst of the Labor Day migrations, we planned to dig up some city clothes and attend the ceremony. But at the last minute it seemed better not to go. I was sorry to miss the meeting with you two, but perhaps all three of us would have been too weary to get much out of it. I think of it as only a brief postponement and will do my best to see that our paths cross before long. To help me plot this out—I shall have to come to New York at least once in September anyway—please send me, when you know it, the date and place of the opening [of *The Pirates*] and the tour for the first few weeks. I'll show up somewhere along the line.

Alice Miller used to say that no one gave presents with more generosity and imagination than I did and that no one received presents with less grace. When I protested she pointed out coldly that she had made me handsome presents at each of the three preceding Christmases and I had yet to acknowledge a single one of them. If I have been as remiss with you it is high time that I expressed my appreciation of that watch you gave me. The reason I had none worth mentioning was because my profession had made me hard on watches. In my nights as a dramatic critic I used to prop mine beside the typewriter as I wrote and about once a month would knock it off onto the concrete floor. My bill for repairs at Tiffany's took about all my income. I decided I must get something cheaper and less fragile and picked out a nice plain one, in a Fifth Avenue shop, that seemed to be encased in gun metal. Obviously it was better than a mere Ingersoll dollar watch but what if it cost $5 or even $10? They told me the price was $1,500. So I went out on the sidewalk, did some figuring on the back of an envelope and decided it would be cheaper to give up being a dramatic critic. Then I could afford to have a good one, especially if someone else paid for it. This was where you came in. It being a Christmas present from you I got it along about May. What year was that? 1929, I think. It was while you were still living in that triplex on Thirty-sixth Street. Indeed, it was presented to me just before one of your less successful dinner parties—the one when you thought you could insure a relaxed and digestive evening by limiting the guest list to me and Edna [Ferber]. In fact it was the watch that started the brawl. I mention it only because I think I should report every thirteen years that I still have it and it still keeps perfect time.

I've had a wonderful dinner and breakfast with Joe Alsop, just back from seven months of internment by the Japanese at Hongkong. Tonight Howard Bull departs for induction into the navy. He will be a chief bosun's mate and will be assigned, he thinks, to drive a motorboat in the inshore patrol. Captain Wilder keeps me posted from his training camp in Pennsylvania.

Dear Lynn, I have by no means forgotten that there is a long story I must tell to you—and to Alfred, too, I think. Whether it is a good story I would not know and can find out only by telling it to you.

A. W.

To *CHARLES BRACKETT*

[Mr. Brackett, whom Woollcott often mentions in his letters as the author of *Entirely Surrounded*, is now a motion picture producer.]

Bomoseen, Vt.
September 12, 1942

My dear Charles:

You must feel that your world is being depopulated. I warn you that it is one of the penalties of lingering on this scene after fifty.

Late at night on the next to the last Saturday in August, my dear Lilly Bonner and I were out on the terrace here relishing a fabulous moon. Through the windows, from inside, there came the muttering and card slappings of a gin rummy game with Dorothy Gish and Lou Calhern involved. The quiet of the lake was disturbed by the sound of Howard Bull's motor launch chugging toward the island. At such an hour this could mean only one thing—a telegram and an important one, too, or he would have let it go until morning. The Bulls sit in judgment on our telegrams and decide among themselves if there is any rush about our seeing them. So while Howard moored his launch at the dock, I told Lilly that Alice Miller was dead. It was on just such another August Saturday night fifteen years ago that the same messenger brought the same news about Gregory Kelly. I remember how he found all lights out and, calling through the window of the ground-floor bedroom in front, awakened Neysa. She came in and got me up and we put on bathrobes and put a log on the fire and sat until all hours talking about Gregory.

The impulse to say something to somebody about Alice has brought me cables and telegrams and letters from all over. And now I am summoned to appear before Mr. Justice Frankfurter to hear a story about her he wants to tell.

I think you may guess with what courtesy and grace of spirit Alice made her exit. She had written me confidentially early in June telling me that the jig was up and thereafter our exchanges were on that basis. It was precisely as though she regretted having to leave early but whispered it behind her fan so as not to disturb the party. Finally I decided that Lederer and Harpo ought to be told. I am glad I did for Harpo came East ahead of schedule and was in time by forty-eight hours to be welcomed by her. The second day she could not speak but held his hand while he talked to her, squeezing it when she was most interested. I am proud to report that out of the topics in his repertory, she squeezed hardest for Charlie Lederer, myself, and the Giants. I've found it an enriching experience to read over the letters I've had from her in the more than twenty-two years of our association. The file began with a hand-painted Christmas card. As the accompanying verse addresses me as a Cribbage Pimp I assume that a check came with it but apparently I was not sentimental enough to file that, too. The letters were fewer and less intimately communicative than they would have been if, throughout those years, we had not been so much together or were not always either just parting or about to meet. They evoke many an agreeable day and bristle, of course, with references to you. I wish you might sit here by the fire some day and read through it. Among my many regrets is my failure to obey an impulse which has visited me a dozen times in the past three years. I wanted to write and sharpen your sense of the value of time by reminding you that the sands were running out for all of us and that you might do well by insisting on another week here with Neysa and Alice and me before it was too late. I could see all of the reasons for your days in Hollywood but there were these things, too, and you might have had them.

 I feel bereft by Alice's going because I knew her so well. The news of [John] Mosher's death saddened me because I didn't, and, thanks to your accounts and Janet Flanner's, I always meant to do something about it. I think I have never read any letter with greater interest than the one Dorothy Parker wrote me after she had seen Private Alan Campbell off to the wars.

You would be ravished by the sight of Edmund Devol who will be seventy-one this month unless he is an even greater liar than I think. Now he has become extraordinarily sprightly in appearance as if he entertained the hope of entering Princeton next year. With so many of the medical fraternity called into the service he is busier than all get out.

I expect to be here pretty steadily until mid-October and then, at odd times, in Washington and New York and here until Christmas. If anything brings you East you might wire me ahead and let me see if I cannot arrange a meeting.

A. Woollcott

To *LUCY CHRISTIE DRAGE*

*Bomoseen, Vt.
September 14, 1942*

Dear Lucy:

It was fourteen years ago that I took over from Julie the annual chore of remembering your birthday. I think I have not failed at it once, though at the time back in 1928 it would have seemed to me improbable that I would still be doing it in a year so unimaginably remote as 1942. Surely something would happen in the meanwhile. The world might come to an end. Or at least one of us would.

I am wondering now if it was the birthday letter which I so well remember writing you from Antibes. That was a gaudy summer, with the world already full of portents that an era was coming to an end—and high time too. Alice Duer Miller, Harpo Marx, Beatrice Kaufman and I shared a sumptuous villa, with a butler named Guy, an insane but excellent cook, and a whole retinue of servants. A stream of incredible people came and went at our luncheons—Bernard Shaw and Elsa Maxwell, Cornelia and Otis Skinner, Mary Garden and Grace Moore, Somerset Maugham and Irene Castle, Lady Mendl and Daisy Fellowes, Ruth Gordon and Frank Harris, etc., etc. I remember Daisy Fellowes, with her ghost of a French accent, looking at me, rolling her eyes and saying: "You are all so talented. You write or dance or act or sing. But I can do nossing." I said I had heard different.

Perhaps you remember the Rapallos with whom Julie lived during those first years in New York before I came down from college. I think it must have been to you I was talking about them recently and saying that I had never known more than one side of the tangled and difficult story which came to an end when Julie married Charles. How they sent word of the marriage I never knew. I know only that from that day neither Julie nor Charles ever saw or heard from Constance Rapallo again. Then just thirty years later—it was while I was on tour in that play last year—Edna Rapallo wrote and asked me to come and have cocktails with her and her mother. Edna had been a little girl at the time of the break. She practiced law and never married. I wrote to say I hoped they would repeat the invitation some time when I was in New York. Well, since then I have been either on tour or in England or in hospital and the other day I read in the *Times* a press notice that Edna Rapallo had died—an admiralty lawyer in her late forties. I have written Constance and may hear from her. You never can tell. A third of a century's a long time.

Of course, a third of a century is no time at all to old neighbors like you and me. Next year will be the one-hundredth anniversary of *A Christmas Carol* and the fiftieth anniversary of my entering Miss Rosenberger's class. I hope to celebrate both milestones.

Happy birthday.

Alexander W.

To *WALTER LIPPMANN*

Bomoseen, Vt.
September 29, 1942

Dear Walter:

Welcome home! Only one who has discovered how difficult and rare a thing it is to state in a few words the very core of a case will know how magnificent a journalistic job you did in this morning's *Herald Tribune*. Perhaps I was the more impressed because those few words voiced what has been for three years my central misgiving.

The same boat from the mainland brought me letters from England, including one from Sibyl Colefax. In one long sentence of hers only four words could be deciphered by anybody. However, as the four words were Walter, Louis, Lippmann and Mountbatten, I guessed she had managed to bring you and the head of the Commandos together, which is probably all she wished to convey. Once in London I got even with her by sending around from the Carlton a four-page scrawl all designed to look like a mass of illegible words but really they were just meaningless pen-strokes—with a few exceptions. Here and there I did plant an actual word. I now remember only three of them —"adultery," "mayhem," and "Rebecca." By God, it worked! Sibyl knew I would be dining that night with Marie Belloc Lowndes at Boulestin's and on the way to her own dinner party, stopped off to see what the hell it was all about.

However, I intended only to greet you, to tell you that my allotted period of post-operative sequestration is approaching its close and that on October 13th I go back humbly and anxiously and gladly into circulation. This portentous notice calls for no answer. I merely wanted you to know that I expect to add to the congestion of Washington during the last ten days in October and that if I do, I shall ask you and Helen [Lippmann] and Brioche [their poodle] if I may have an evening with you.

A. Woollcott

To CHARLES BRACKETT

Bomoseen, Vt.
September 29, 1942

Dear Charles:

If I seem to be responding with suspect promptness to so tentative and subjunctive a paragraph as the one which wound up your recent letter, you will find a sufficient corrective in the coyness I would develop if the occasion ever arose to talk turkey. I merely want to clear up one doubt before I forget it. Were you by any chance thinking of me as making a trailer for your picture?

If so, there is an inherent difficulty in the time element. It seems I made a trailer once. I had gone to New York to attend Alice Miller's dinner for Marie Belloc Lowndes and as the first print of *Good-bye, Mr. Chips* had that day reached this country, Howard Dietz asked if I would like to show it to some friends in a projection room the next evening. I did and was puzzled by the ensuing silence all around me. I tried to dissipate this by an airy remark and found, to my surprise, that it was difficult for me to speak. Therefore, I tried again and instead of speech gave vent to a great, astonishing sob. In natural embarrassment I rose and started to leave the projection room in the still-enveloping darkness and nicely covered my confusion by falling down a flight of stairs. Howard Dietz, who knows audience reaction when he sees it, promptly engaged me to make a trailer and this was actually accomplished the next day, for reasons which escape me, in Marion Davies' own suite at the Warwick. I never saw the result and I gravely doubt if there is any evidence that it induced a single person to see *Good-bye, Mr. Chips*. That would seem to me an important question, but disregarding it utterly, all the producers immediately behaved as though getting a trailer by me was equivalent to getting an Oscar. The trouble was that I would not (and, indeed, could not) make one without seeing the picture first. My annoying punctilio on this point brought most negotiations to an end but it was managed in the case of *The Grapes of Wrath* which, on my way from San Diego to San Francisco, I stopped off to see. The result was one of the funniest nights of my life about which I shall tell you some time, the cast of characters being, besides myself, Harpo and Susan, Alan Campbell and Dorothy Parker, Gregory Ratoff and (heard only as on offstage voice) Joe Schenck. Of course I could not make the trailer.

Speaking of Marie Belloc Lowndes, you would relish a long letter I've just had from her about Alice Miller—a French grandmother's comment on so mystifying but dazzling a phenomenon as Harry Miller and on Denning's [Mrs. Miller's son] marriage to a girl with no dot whatever, my dear.

I shall be in New York, either at the Gotham or chez McMein, from the 13th to the 20th. I assume there is no chance that you will be.

A. W.

To MARIE BELLOC LOWNDES

Bomoseen, Vt.
September 29, 1942

My dear Marie:

This is really nonsense. A censored letter from you crosses three thousand miles of perilous seas and I sit down and reply to it half an hour after its arrival for all the world as if a messenger had just brought it from your cottage down the road and were drinking beer in the kitchen while I scribbled off an answer. I wish, by the way, that this were true. I could easily fix up for you the cottage Kipling had at Dummerton. He did some pretty good work in it—*The Jungle Book* and *Captains Courageous*. Years later I came to know the difficult but much misunderstood brother-in-law who made America uninhabitable for him—a violent, warm-hearted, disorderly creature, Beatty Balestier, worth ten of his sister and five of his brother. Did you know his brother? I think he must have been a good deal like Brendan Bracken. One of the good things I got out of my last trip to London was a talk with Arthur Waugh about him. You probably remember that when Wolcott Balestier commenced publishing in London (he rented quarters from the Curates' Augmentation Fund at No. 2, Dean's Court, Westminster) he asked Edmund Gosse to find him a willing and inexpensive office boy who might be content with a pound a week, and Gosse, out of his hat, produced young Arthur Waugh, just down (or up, I never can remember which) from Oxford.

But I can't be rushing off an answer to you just to give you the latest word about Wolcott Balestier, What I have in mind is to stop your looking for that bad book published about the Agra double murder. I take it you refer to the one by Sir Cecil Walsh, K.C., published in London by Ernest Benn Ltd., in 1929. Since I first encountered it eight years ago I have been picking up all the stray copies that have come to light in second-hand bookshops here. His is an artless narrative but at least he gets out of the way of the story which tells itself well enough. He quotes liberally from the letters of Mrs. Fullam. For this case, along with the Madeleine Smith case and the Bywaters-Thompson case, derives its fascination from the letters. I do not want the book. What I want is the letters. Do you suppose the full file exists anywhere? If so, could you start in motion such wheels as would bring a transcript of them to me, at my expense, three months from now, a year from now, three years from now?

By the time this reaches you I will have come to the end of the time allotted for sequestration after that operation and will have gone back into circulation. I depart on the 13th of October for New York and Washington and this odd invention, my island home, will close—for the duration of the war, I should think, and possibly for the duration of me. In times when it is difficult to get petrol and rubber and indecent to waste them, this island is an impractical home for one who can, must, and wishes to take part in the day's work. Now it could house only someone dedicated to and spiritually equipped for the contemplative life. I am certainly not the latter. Present and pending American shortages will doubtless be good for us all. Of those to which I have already been subjected I mind only the acute shortage of Thornton Wilder.

I am going to try sending you some maple syrup. From the newspapers I gather contradictory impressions about the possibility of shipping gifts to friends in England. The only thing I can do is try, which I shall do this week. Let me know if it reaches you. If a quart of Vermont nectar should arrive in Barton Street it will be from

Yours affectionately,

Alexander Woollcott

P.S. Will you accept another assignment? I am hungry for news of Rebecca West. Will you go out like a good reporter and get some and send me every scrap of it?

To *JO RANSON*

Rutland, Vt.
October 3, 1942

Dear Ranson:

I count it a great honor to be allowed to serve as master of ceremonies on the night when the air will be cleared by and for the murder of Lidice. The fact that the poets of the country might care to use the radio as an instrument is the best reason for not throwing it into the scrap heap along with the rest of the junk of our time. And I agree with the National Broadcasting Company in its belief that such a script as this one by Edna St. Vincent Millay has the right of eminent domain. Let me suggest that all of us who will participate in its first performance should meet ahead of time to rehearse the pronunciation of the word Lidice.

Only a wild optimist would expect us to pronounce it correctly but at least it should be humanly possible for us all to pronounce it alike.

Alexander Woollcott

To KATHARINE CORNELL

New York City
October 15, 1942

Dear Miss Kitty,

This is a love letter, so you can put it aside and read it when you feel like one.

Of course I might let its substance go unsaid until our next meeting but there's always the chance of my being run over by a truck. So this is what I had in mind.

You had gone and I was looking at the rhododendrons and day-dreaming about *The Three Sisters* which I think of now not only as a play I want to see but as the only play I ever want to see, over and over again, and my thoughts then fell into some such pattern as this—Miss Kitty is someone I love and admire and enjoy and trust. In our relation as neighbors I find great comfort and take deep pride. If I were really to tell Miss Kitty how great and how deep, she would turn to stone from sheer embarrassment.

Well, goodbye. See you at rehearsal.

A. Woollcott

To *CAPTAIN THORNTON WILDER*

New York City
October 22, 1942

Dear Captain:
            I am writing this in haste in my panic at the thought of your running up the steps between Helen's [Hayes] parrots to have a word with me. To begin with, Helen gave me the flower-pots. The parrots were given me, in obedience to a now regretted impulse, by Dorothy Backer who will soon, I understand, be leaving for Reno. Then lovely as the terrace of Glamis must be this week, you would have to have your word with Joe and his doxie.

    I departed on the 13th for a month of exploring—trying my legs. Since I left the island, with consequent loss of all leisure time and freedom from interruption, I have written three magazine articles—I couldn't write them at the island because I had nothing else to do—which will be in the December issues of the *Reader's Digest*, *The Atlantic* and *Good Housekeeping*, respectively. Now I am off to Washington for a week or ten days, during which I shall be lodged at the White House with a reasonable certainty of having some time with Felix Frankfurter, Elmer Davis, Bill Donovan, Archie MacLeish and others. In Philadelphia, on my way back to New York at the end of next week, I shall see "The Long Christmas Journey from Yonkers to Our Teeth" and report on it. Then back to the Gotham for at least two weeks. I speak to twelve thousand women in St. Paul on December 2nd and go from there to Chicago for a stay with Lloyd Lewis. After that I think of three months in Louisville as a possibility. How it will all end knows God.

    Ernest Hemingway is publishing this week a thousand-page anthology called *Men at War*. I first heard of it from Gerald Murphy who had received an announcement from Scribner's which described it as a book written by Julius Caesar, Alexander

Woollcott, U. S. Grant and others. I found I actually have two pieces in it and am thereby mysteriously gratified.

I got *The Atlantic* piece done in time to go off to dinner with Charlie Chaplin. The two of us sat at Le Pavillon until midnight. He lavishly acted out every scene of his coming Landru picture which, as you may know, is going to be called *Lady Killer.* The procession of victims will, each in her own little way, be so obnoxious that he expects to murder each one with the enthusiastic approval of every man in the audience and go to the guillotine, at last, as a fastidious hero. I suppose the picture, when released, will inspire a few throat-cuttings here and there but on the whole its effect should be beneficial and it will improve the home life of several million Americans.

A. W.

To *LADY COLEFAX*

The White House
October 26, 1942

Dear Sibyl,

Speaking of Alice Miller, Felix Frankfurter told me a story Saturday evening about the last war when he was Chairman of the War Labor Policies Board and there arose the again familiar chaos with each agency—the army, the navy, the factories, the shipyards—raiding the personnel of the others, and how a policy was planned which Woodrow Wilson was to approve and announce to the nation. A ghost-writer was first filled with the facts and then soaked in all Wilson's speeches. The result was a White House statement so masterly and so Wilsonian that, for once in a way, the President issued it as his own, without altering a syllable. In one press comment the New York *Times* referred to the inimitable Wilson style and the *Manchester Guardian* cried out in envy of a republic which could have at its head a man who was a master of English prose. These comments were relished in sparkling and enigmatic silence by one aforesaid ghost-writer who was, as you must have guessed, Alice Miller—as ever was.

I came back into the world, two weeks ago tomorrow, after eight months' absence, and so am only half way through an experimental month during which I hope to learn by trial and error how much work I can undertake and which of the many tasks I would better attempt. I am lodged in Mr. Lincoln's room and am writing you on his desk. There is a good deal of minor royalty coming to dinner here tonight but I am bid to the Walter Lippmanns and so shall slip away after the cocktails, which the President himself will make and much too strong they'll be, I know. I'll add a postscript to this before I post it tomorrow.

October 27th

At Lippmann's last night your name came up (this time not confused with that of Lady Halifax) and I would have been content to have you eaves-dropping.

Day after tomorrow I go to Philadelphia, where, on my way back to New York, I shall see Irving Berlin and attend Thornton's play, promptly forwarding my report to him in California where he is on duty with his squadron with new preoccupations so absorbing that I doubt if he will have much interest in my account of his play's performance. Indeed I can well believe that he has forgotten what it is about.

Give my love to my friends.

A. Woollcott

To CAPTAIN THORNTON WILDER

New York City
November 4, 1942

Dear Thornton:

This will probably cross a letter from you. If the one threatened in your telegram arrives before I get to the bottom of the page I will so indicate.

I haven't written to Rebecca West in more than a year. I know no other way to earn a letter from her and there is no one whose letters I more relish and treasure. If, in that intervening year, I have scrofulously cast off letters which now lie thick as thieves at Vallombrosa, yet written none to her, it is because I feel as if a letter to Rebecca ought to be something pretty Goddamned special, something I would always be up to writing not that day but the next.

I know there is some analogy between this sterile but gratifying procrastination and my disinclination to sit down and write you at once about that play of yours. It has suddenly occurred to me that I am under no mysterious obligation to match the stature of the play with the staure of my comment. There lies upon me no sudden duty to be profound, concise and illuminating. Suppose I do rattle off a lot of notions which, a week later, I might be glad to disown. What, if you will allow me the expression, of it? So here goes.

Having seen *The Skin of Our Teeth* and thought about it and read it, I know what I think about it. I think no American play has ever come anywhere near it. I think it might have been written by Plato and Lewis Carroll in collaboration, or better still by any noble pedagogue with a little poltergeist blood in him. I had not foreseen that you could write a play that would be both topical and timeless, though I might have remembered from *The Trojan Women* that it could be done. What I do not know now and will not know until I have seen it again, which

I am both eager and determined to do, is how completely the present production realizes the script.

One thing I *am* sure of. Tallulah does not know how to play Sabina and cannot be taught to. She has some assets as an actress but she is without any comic gift. Kit is not a comedienne and is ruefully aware of the fact. Tallulah is not a comedienne and thinks she's a wonderful one. When she comes to a line which she thinks should be read amusingly she manages it with a throaty vocal trick suitable for inferior wisecracks tossed around Sardi's in 1924. It's the vocal equivalent of a flirt of the fanny. She's like the little daughter of the hostess who feels an obligation to be entertaining. One can describe the product only as embarrassing. In the first act I found her afflicting. In the second and third acts I was quite reconciled to her. It was not until I read the play that I saw how in every scene and every line it aches for Ruth Gordon. It will be played many times and by many women. It will never be really played until Ruth plays it. March is good. Florence Reed is surprisingly good. Florence Eldridge is simply superb. Tallulah is, I think, a misfortune—how great a misfortune only those can say who know the play.

Thinking, on the way back, how tough a job it would be to review that play in the little time vouchsafed a critic of a morning paper and remembering what a good job Brooks Atkinson did on *Our Town* because he had been to a rehearsal and had had time to think it over, I called him up and suggested that he see *The Skin of Our Teeth* either in Philadelphia or Washington. He has just telephoned to say that he and his wife are going down to Philadelphia on Thursday.

When I wired that the play would profit by your proximity during these trial weeks, I was saying something that was generally true. I was not suggesting that I thought you ought to come on. I don't. Far from it. Specifically, I thought it would be handy to have you around to deal with the slight muddle caused, perhaps, by the introduction of Homer, Moses, and Company.

As matters stand it seems to me that they are impressively introduced and then given nothing to do. The result is clutter. My notion at the moment was that they should do more or not come on at all. However, you know, if I thought I were at all good at that sort of thing I would go out with that play for two weeks and not at all because you wrote it. I would do just the same if Channing Pollock had written it and I can't say fairer than that.

I have just received a V-letter from Lt. Quentin Roosevelt and also a post card (dated August 17th and, for reasons which escape me, addressed to me at 3 East Seventeenth Street) which reads as follows:

"Sir, I have just read, for the third time, your *While Rome Burns*. It is superb. But that is not what I want to tell you. This is the only work of yours that we have in our little camp library. A great pity, sir, a great pity. And there is not much we can do about it. Ours is the naval camp, all merry and bright, and hope for happy ending not too distant future. John Lavender."

Master Lavender is a Sub. Lieutenant in our navy and what interests me is that this is a post card from a Kriegsgefangenenlager and has been dispatched to me by Luftpost. When you pinched and nudged me into publishing *While Rome Burns*, you did not tell me that eight years later I would get an appreciative comment upon it sent to me by air mail from an American named Lavender in a German prison camp.

It has been suggested to me by others (and it strikes me as distinctly possible) that this post card is an elaborate German fraud. That is as easy to believe as it is to believe that our prisoners of war in Germany are in a position to write fan mail par avion.

Letter follows.

A. W.

To FELIX FRANKFURTER

New York City
November 9, 1942

My dear Watson:

You know my methods. I thought you would have detected from the script of that appreciative post card (and particularly from the numerals) that it was written by a German. I had studied it suspiciously because I could not believe that among the luxuries provided the men in German prison camps would be the privilege of writing fan letters, addressed (however incorrectly) to strangers in America and dispatched, not to the Red Cross in Switzerland, but directly by air mail.

Did Alice Duer Miller ever tell you about her cook who retired, went to live in California, and after some time sent back a post card with the following unpunctuated sentiment: "It is very beautiful here I don't like it." When I mentioned the misgivings I always feel about my kindred coldness to the orthodox classics in literature, I was making an honest self-examination. It has always disquieted me and I find no comfort in the familiar practice of such complacent fellows as, let us say, Noel Coward. (By the way, his navy movie, *In Which We Serve*, is one of the perfect jobs of our time. Only one print has thus far arrived in this country and because that man in the White House grabbed it for Thursday night, I did not see it until Friday when a wiggling handful of us—Somerset Maugham, Ben Hecht, Grace Eustis, and so forth—saw it here in an airless projection room. I wept throughout because it is of courage all compact and courage is the only thing that makes me cry—courage and, oddly enough, miracles. But then Al Jolson used to say of Sam Bernard that he cried at card tricks.) Well, Noel has hardly read anything. The great picture collections have been open to him and he couldn't tell a Vermeer from a Disney. He has never willingly listened to good music. He would bite and scratch if you took him to *Hamlet* or *King Lear*. When he finds me abject before the genius of Chekhov, who is for me the only playwright, Noel just assumes that I am showing off, that my admiration is faddish and bogus and designed to impress.

In so assuming, he is no more perceptive than you were in classifying the aforesaid misgivings as "meretricious modesty." When you used those words you were, in my judgment, as profound and mature as Martha Hemingway—every bit. The foregoing sentence was written with painstaking precision and without humorous intent. I think you have handed down one of your less creditable opinions.

Also, by the way, the new Thornton Wilder play, *The Skin of Our Teeth,* is being tried out in Washington this week, with a production that realizes, at a rough estimate, about 65 per cent of its possibilities which is a good deal. It is, in my opinion, the best American play to date, with no close runner-up.

Binkie

To *HARRY HOPKINS*

New York City
November 10, 1942

Dear Harry:

I should think you must be much too busy to read this letter. I can imagine none more uncomfortable to write nor duller to read. Let's go.

As you may know, when our paths crossed recently in Washington, I told you I was half way through an experimental month by which I hoped to gauge how much work I was going to be good for in the immediate future. It was my first month of being up and about since January. While I was still at the White House, and increasingly since, there have been disquieting symptoms (vertigo, loss of vision and the like) which will land me back in a Boston hospital next week for some days of re-examination. Whatever the verdict, I intend to go right on working.

One thing, however, I must not do and guiltily knew as much even when we were talking together a week ago. I must not pledge myself to any undertaking which I cannot honorably desert on twenty-four hours notice whenever I get the inner signal that I ought to go to bed. I cannot pledge myself to any sponsor for a six-months radio program when there is more than a fifty-fifty chance that I would not be able to stick with it that long.

What I can and should tell you is this. The form of radio program I suggested to you has, in my judgment, greater possibilities of public service than any yet devised. To such a program, if you can get it set up, I will devote all of my working time for the first half of 1943. I could plan and engage talent for many of the programs. I could appear on many of them. I would be willing and glad to. But I must not be pledged to the sponsor as dependable throughout. I must not be the cornerstone or the master of ceremonies. For instance, if you were to get Clifton Fadiman and make him the boss and constant factor, I could do three-quarters of his job for him and would prefer to do it without compensation.

I did a honey of a broadcast last Sunday night. I am going to do a honey on the Stage Door Canteen program this Thursday at 9.30. I shall be lecturing soon at Amherst and in St. Paul. I shall undertake an endless series of such short-time commitments, but it would be dishonorable to fool any radio network or sponsor into thinking I could be counted on for unbroken service for as long as six months.

I have just one message for the Big White Father. Give him my love.

Alexander Woollcott

To *NOEL COWARD*

New York City
November 12, 1942

Dear Noel:

There isn't a particle of you that I know, remember, or want. But my hat is off to you after seeing *In Which We Serve*. I've seen three or four good movies in my time. This is one of them. I saw it the other night in an airless projection room along with the oddest assembly of people. As we got into the elevator we found it was occupied by an elderly gentleman to whom I immediately knelt. Not to be outdone he knelt too. Grace [Eustis] was puzzled until I introduced him. "This," I said, "is Mr. Somerset Maugham." Howard Dietz sat in front of me. In the middle distance was Ben Hecht and I thought afterwards how paltry he must have considered the little puddle of water *he* had thrown you into.

My dear Noel, this job you have done seems to me a really perfect thing. There was no moment of it from which I drew back or dissented. I went away marveling at its sure-footedness and realizing that all the ups and downs of your life (in particular the downs) had taught you to be unerring for your great occasion. All your years were a kind of preparation for this. If you had done nothing else and were never again to do anything else they would have been well spent.

Of course I have thought of all these things afterwards. At the time I just sat and cried quietly. For, after all, this picture is of courage all compact and courage is the only thing that brings the honorable moisture to these eyes.

Work as good as this, even if it were not work to such good purpose, always has commanded me. I have got in touch with the United Artists people and volunteered to go on some national broadcast program and do a spot of drum-beating for the picture just before it is released, the fee to go to the British War Relief.

I do not know whether you are aware that during the greater part of the time since last we met I have been on a bed of pain. For some time in the spring I was at death's door but the old fool was out. Now I am up again and, after a fashion, about. I tell you these details in case you are torn with anxiety.

The rest of this letter is intended for Lorn [Lorraine] whom I love. A. Will she please note that, until further notice, the most dependable address for me will be the one at the head of this letter? B. Will she keep me in mind as one to whom she might pass on all tidings of Jeff [Amherst]? I will make it my business to circulate such among the considerable number here who hold him in fond remembrance. My last word from him was in early May.

If on receipt of this, you could find it in your heart to cable me the latest news of him, I would be indebted to you. Unfortunately, I believe you are no longer allowed to use my cable address.

A. W.

To *CAPTAIN THORNTON WILDER*

New York City
November 13, 1942

Dear Thornton:

I was staying at the White House for a week, living in the Lincoln Room but sleeping in a little ante-chamber because, unlike Edna Ferber (a previous occupant), I felt unequal to the strain of lying in his bed. Walter Lippmann, in order to illustrate a point we had been discussing, had just sent around by messenger the new *Yale Review* anthology and there was a brief New Orleans play of yours which I had never read and which I sat down and read at once. Well, I was going to write you about *that* but—

Then on Monday of this week I was free for a few hours and went around to sup with Dr. Kommer and that ineffably beautiful Paget girl who married Raimund von Hoffmannstahl. En route Kommer had picked up Harry Luce. So there was much talk of your reading Horace at Chefoo and I worked him up into a dither about *The Skin of Our Teeth*. He wanted *Life* to do a photographic blast about it (their photographers are on their way to Washington tonight for the purpose) and for me to write the accompanying text. I said I couldn't do this without seeing the play again and couldn't—physically couldn't—go down to Washington. So in the way of these great typhoons, or whatever you call them, he passed the word along to a chain of underlings with the result that yesterday Dan Longwell wrote me about *my* notion of going to Washington to cover the play for *Life*.

I am dictating this on a train bearing me toward Whitehall and the island where Dorothy Parker will join me tomorrow. I will have four days in which to sort out the books and files that must go with me when the island is closed as it will be, sine die, in another fortnight. On Wednesday I go back to the Peter Bent Brigham Hospital for a week of tinkering. I assured the heart specialist that I will no longer undertake to do the work of ten men. I must ingloriously do the work of only five.

Then a lecture to twelve thousand women in St. Paul on a new book, a new play and a new movie. (The book is Hesketh Pearson's *G.B.S.*) Then two days in Chicago largely with Lloyd Lewis but a little with Bob Hutchins. Then back to New York for quite some time.

A. W.

P.S. In the course of a discussion about my dubious equipment for editing an anthology for service men Felix Frankfurter sends me this anecdote about Holmes:

"*I don't suppose in our time there has been anyone more*

truly well read than the Justice. But it is a fact that some of the most famous among the orthodox classics in literature he did not get around to reading until late in life. Indeed it was a favorite belief of his that the great classics should be read late and not early. It was when he was about eighty that he began to read a lot of books that most people would be ashamed to deny they had not read. He said he was reading for Judgment Day—that when he appeared for examination Mon Dieu might say, 'Holmes, what do you think of the Odyssey?' or 'Holmes, what do you think of Thucydides?' And he would feel rather naked to have to reply, 'I am sorry, Sir, but I haven't read them.' So he would ask from time to time about books to read. I remember on one occasion saying to him, 'Mon Dieu might ask you what you think about Moneypenny and Buckles Life of Disraeli.' And he said, 'I don't care for biography, and if Mon Dieu is interested in such trivial things then I don't care much for him.'"

A. W.

To *FELIX FRANKFURTER*

New York City
November 23, 1942

Dear Felix:

You may be right. In any event, plans for *As You Were* are going great guns with invaluable suggestions coming in from people like Carl Sandburg and David McCord at Cambridge and with Tarkington picking out the James Whitcomb Riley stuff. The last copy must be in the printer's hands before the end of December.

I say you may be right noncommittally, not knowing where the truth lies. Perhaps I am overliteral and imperceptive. Perhaps irony is, after all, not your instrument. Perhaps in this you are like Emanuel Libman of whom Alexis Carrel says that he knows more medicine than anyone who ever lived and that medical science has no task before it so urgent as the need of getting down on paper what Libman knows before he dies. But, disastrously, Libman fancies himself as a raconteur and spends hours telling me funny stories, most of them about gefülte fish. He happens not to be a good storyteller.

However, I learned from H. L. Mencken a happy formula for answering all controversial letters. He invented one which is final, courteous and can be employed without reading the letter to which it replies. He merely says: "Dear Sir (or Madam): You may be right."

I am grateful for the anecdote about Justice Holmes and have passed it on intact to Thornton Wilder. I am low in my mind about the piece written for *The Atlantic*. I had pledged it for the anniversary issue and Weeks relied on me so ingenuously that it was announced in the November issue before I had put key to ribbon. I had not foreseen so prolonged a convalescence with the result that when at last I did get to work we were on the very brink of the deadline and there was no time to have the piece vetted. I shall be sad if, in print, it seems to do the Justice's memory a disservice.

I would have written you sooner but I have been back in the Peter Bent Brigham undergoing further hocus-pocus by the medicos.

A. Woollcott

To *SOPHIE ROSENBERGER*

New York City
November 24, 1942

Dear Teacher:
    Last night I came out of the Voisin Restaurant with Charlie MacArthur and stood in the rain on Park Avenue trying to interest a passing taxi. Charlie is an old and dear friend

of mine who is married to Helen Hayes and their lovely child Mary is my god-daughter. He has just been made a major and is leaving for parts unknown and this was our farewell dinner.

Already New York is dimmed down past recognition although it has not yet achieved that strange, luminous dusk which makes London in a blackout so ironically peaceful. Cabs are hard to get because even the eager empty cab cannot see the potential passenger signalling from the darkling curb. Out of one cab, halted for a moment by a traffic light and only a foot away from us, a stranger to me stuck his head and said: "I suppose that as a fellow-pupil of Sophie Rosenberger's, I ought to share this cab with you." At this moment the traffic light changed and the driver, with no sympathy for this new form of communism, started off up Park Avenue. That's all there is to the story.

I am bounding around, seeking to discover by trial and error how much work I am good for. At the moment I am snowed under in the preparations for an anthology designed (without profit or royalties to anyone) for the pocket of the American soldier. By the use of thin paper we can get in quite a lot and our hope and our limitations will be clear to you from the title-page which reads as follows: *As You Were: A Portable Library of American Prose and Poetry Assembled for Members of the Armed Forces and the Merchant Marine.*

I must stipulate, if convenient, that you arrange to live until next September and I, for my part, will try to do the same. We must celebrate the fiftieth anniversary of my entering your class.

Alexander Woollcott

To *ALAN CAMPBELL*

New York City
December 14, 1942

Dear Acton Davies:
You know God-damned well that that letter of yours was one of the best ever written. People are *so* tired of having me read it aloud and by now they behave as if it were my "Railroad Station on the Western Plains." So I am leaving for Washington day after tomorrow, and before the week is out, I shall read it to the President. He may have other plans but that is the way it is going to be.

I learn from June Walker, whom I have merrily but firmly dissuaded from calling on me, that Dottie is still in Florida and judging from the fact that she is pledged to several radio programs this week and that her house guest does not replace Margalo in *Life with Father* until early in January, I assume she will not be back here for Christmas.

I will send you a bulky packet of news next week but will let you off now with only two items, both true. On my return from the midlands last week, I was careless enough to tell Frank Sullivan that in St. Paul I had spoken to ten thousand women. "And what did you tell them?" he asked. "No?"

I will now tune off, abashed as I am by a mission from Wilder in which he says: "Nothing so lifts a soldier's morale as getting a letter from home and nothing so depresses him as reading it."

Eugene Cowles

P.S. I rather expect to spend the winter at *The Three Sisters*. Ruth [Gordon] appears to have made the hit of her life in it, despite a bad cold and the slight distraction of getting married.

A. W.

To *MARK S. WATSON*

[Woollcott was thanking Mr. Watson, one of the editors of the Baltimore *Evening Sun*, for the gift of some coffee.]

New York City
December 28, 1942

Dear Mark:
        This is, among other things, a word of thanks to you and Mrs. W. for that stomacher of emeralds you gave me for Christmas. Oddly enough, there survived in my trunk from that tour of the country I made when I was the Guy Bates Post of yesterday, an electric percolator, and you can easily envisage the secret vice that is going to be practiced in Room 1921 at the Gotham.
    Did Colonel Winty [J. T. Winterich] send you his pamphlet, "Clio and My Aunt Bertha"? He comes God-damned near being my favorite author.
    Will you, at your leisure, send me a secret report on why my niece Barbara did not last on *The Sun?* I know she had hardly arrived there before she got pneumonia. I also know she is astoundingly gifted. I suspect, however, that she is undisciplined, and, perhaps, undependable, characteristics which her sainted uncle never manifested until he got his hooks into a job. A good many opportunities to get work for her will come my way from time to time and I really want to know what's the matter with her. My favorite of the lot is Number One who married a first-rate Ph.D. from Johns Hopkins and precisely nine months later gave birth to twin boys of ravishing beauty. However, I was knocked for a loop by Number Four when she breezed in from Swarthmore to have dinner with me and the Berlins in Philadelphia. While I was engrossed with Ellin Berlin, Irving asked her in a stage whisper what she thought of me. She

replied, sotto voce: "Christ Almighty! Magnificent!" I have reached the age where I enjoy these restrained tributes.

Tell your bride that in *As You Were* I have the Civil War covered in a fashion I think she would like. I hope to hear that I am right.

A. Woollcott

XI

1943

To *LIEUTENANT FRANCIS ROBINSON*
[Ol Katharine Cornell's business office.]

New York City
January 4, 1943

Dear Francis:

   I scarcely know how to express my sense of indebtedness to you for that Lautrec drawing, which is with me now, can go with me on my unchartered wanderings and add much to the pleasure of my declining years. It is with me here at the Gotham and shares the wall space of my sitting-room with a photograph which I shall tell you about hereinafter, and the *Daily News* color print of Judith [Anderson] and Kit and Ruth in that play, which in the general state of Chekhov confusion, I found myself calling *The Cherry Sisters*. I attended a rehearsal of it, without scenery or costumes, on the Tuesday before they opened in Washington and now I am seeing it full-bloom this evening and will write you a full report before I seal this letter.

  As to the aforesaid photograph, it was sent me at Christmas time by someone I knew so slightly and so long ago that I have no idea now where to find him or how to acknowledge it. It shows a soldier of the last war apparently pacing in front of his tent, gun on shoulder, for the benefit of some photographer.

It could have been taken only in this country because he is wearing the canvas leggings and old campaign hat of the kind we never saw in France. I remember the first photographs of him I had seen were some taken with his father when he was a little boy, shortly after the turn of the century. Then in 1915, when I was the fledgling dramatic critic of the *Times*, I remember being moved by some sentiment for the memory of his father to go down, on a summer's night, to Christadora House on Avenue B, where this boy would be playing Robin Hood in a production of *Sherwood Forest* by Alfred Noyes, which they were staging with a cast of school children for no other purpose, I suspect, than to let him try his wings. In this picture which has just come to me he must have been nineteen or thereabouts, short like his father, spectacularly handsome as his father never was and with something of the gypsy outlaw about him that reminds one of Heathcliff.

It must have been shortly after this picture was taken that he died of spinal meningitis. I got the news from his mother who came over to France to work in the Red Cross. I remember having supper with her one night in a little apartment in the Rue Soufflot on the other side of the Luxembourg Gardens. Gentle and frail she was and sad beyond all healing.

I am not sure that she knew then or ever knew the circumstances of the boy's death which I learned later from the medical corps captain who happened to be in charge of the hospital at the camp near San Antonio. You may know him. His name is Logan Clendening.

One evening Captain Clendening was puzzled when his orderly reported that among the batch of patients which had just arrived was a kid who had given his name as Richard Mansfield. To men of Clendening's age and mine, that was still a name to conjure with. In the America in which we grew up, Mansfield was the equivalent of Henry Irving. He was born out of wedlock to some middle-Europe singer or actress who had retreated to the island of Heligoland for a discreet period of confinement. I am beginning to forget such details. As an actor, Mansfield had done everything in the grand manner. With his first success as Baron Chevrial to go on and his father's money to back him, he had produced things like *Monsieur Beaucaire* and *Cyrano de Bergerac* and *Peer Gynt*. He was, I think, the first one anywhere to produce Shaw and if you want some instructive reading you should go to the public library some time and dig up the first reviews of *Arms and the Man* which was denounced as a monstrous insult to all sacred feelings. You probably know that, eight years before Arnold Daly produced *Candida*, Mansfield went so far as to put it into rehearsal. When he discontinued these, he tried to spread the impression that he had found the play too talky. But I think he lost his nerve when, in the third act, as Marchbanks, he realized he had to say: "I was eighteen this morning."

Mansfield never had or sought any leading woman of a stature to share honors with him. The chance to be his leading woman was looked upon as a doubtful blessing. One season this post was held by a lovely young Jewess from your own state who afterwards went to England and married Max Beerbohm. She cooked such a good lunch for me and Thornton Wilder when we drove down in Surrey to see her a year ago last October. Another of his leading women was Beatrice Cameron who married him and bore him a son.

Much of all this must have been in Clendening's mind when he made the rounds of the new patients. He found the boy mortally sick. According to the Sick and Wounded card tied to the foot of his bed, his name *was* Richard Mansfield. The doctor began to ask questions which the boy answered in a haughty and thunderous baritone. Where had he got that name? From his father. Who was his father? Richard Mansfield. What Richard Mansfield? Richard Mansfield, the actor.

"But," said Clendening, "I remember Richard Mansfield as having had only one son whose name was not Richard." To this the boy replied proudly, "They called me Gibbs Mansfield but after my father died I took the name of Richard."

The doctor saw how things were and wired to Mrs. Mansfield in New London that she would better come down. After sending that desolating telegram, he used to go to the ward at all hours to keep an eye on the boy for whom there was no help then known in medicine. Mostly he was out of his mind. The dim-lit hush of the ward at night would be broken by his mutterings. From these one night there suddenly emerged, clear and resonant, these words: "Once more into the breach, dear friends, once more," and there followed the whole speech before Harfleur. Next, one by one, came all the notable speeches from Mansfield's repertory—Brutus, Richard III, Cyrano. Then the boy died.

January 5th

Well, I saw *The Three Orchards* last night and it was, as I had thought it would be, superb. I have seldom seen Kit as good in anything and never better in anything, Guthrie [McClintic], I think, has never done so good a job, fusing that great succession of bravura scenes into one glowing whole.

One of the things people can honorably do in time of war is to take a piece of the world's truth off into a corner and serve it with all their might and main. It seems to me that that is what this company is doing. Ruth is brilliant—you would think Chekhov had known her for years before he wrote the part—and Judith's performance is like a great tent-pole holding up the bellying canvas of the play. The only weak point in the cast is Tom Powers and that is incurable.

Edmund Gwenn had returned to his role after a week's illness. Guthrie had leaped into the breach as a trout leaps for a fly. Toward the end of the week I wrote him that I knew just how bored he must be, having to play it every night and offered, if Gwenn *didn't* get better, to take it over myself, agreeing to do so on a few hours' notice as the part was nothing, really. Of course I would add a wheel chair to brighten it up.

I thought you would be interested in Kit's solution of the dressing-room problem. She is building one on the stage for old Alice Belmore Cliffe, who is *my* favorite actress. The two connecting stage dressing-rooms, which Lynn and Alfred used when they played this theatre, she has given to Judith and Ruth. She dresses upstairs.

Good luck to you in 1943.

A. Woollcott

To *CAPTAIN THORNTON WILDER*

New York City
January 11, 1943

Dear Thornton:

You know that old, deaf and stertorous Arthur Waugh, who started in as errand boy for Wolcott Balestier, has been, these many years, chairman of the board of Chapman and Hall, Ltd., a firm which got quite a good start publishing the works of Mr. Dickens. It seems they have just put out, in a limited edition of five hundred copies selling at 8s. 6d. each, a work by his son Captain Waugh—"Dear Mr. Woollcott," the old man asked me when I went out to Highgate to see him in November 1941, "do you find Evelyn arrogant?"—a book called *Work Suspended: Two Chapters of an Unfinished Novel*.

And why, as you and Pinero make your characters say, am I telling all this to you? Answer: because Captain Waugh— he's a Commando officer and no longer pudgy—has inscribed a copy and sent it to me. It is dedicated to me and after the dedication page comes one in which this letter is printed:

Dear Mr. Woollcott:

This is the book on which I was at work in September 1939. It is now clear to me that even if I were again to have the leisure and will to finish it, the work would be vain, for the world in which and for which it was designed, has ceased to exist.

So far as it went, this was my best writing. Will you, who, in the past, have been so prodigal of encouragement, accept this fragment of what, complete, might have come within measurable distance of justifying your interest?

Yours sincerely,
Summer, 1942
Evelyn Waugh

When this arrived two days ago I detected on Hennessey's face the weary look of one who foresaw that he would have to spend the next six months taking me down a bit.

Yesterday I got up at seven and wrote a piece for the [Reader's] Digest and it's already on its way to the compositors for the March issue (print order 9,450,000) and it was in the hope of doing this kind of piece that I tied up with the Digest in the first place.

The other day I was showing to the elevator a fair visitor with whom I had been in momentous confab for an hour and a half. At the elevator she said: "I do not see how you have the time and energy to accomplish all you do." At this I let out a laugh of such honest surprise that I almost knocked her down the elevator shaft. For you see the visitor was Mrs. Roosevelt.

I need and miss you.

A. Woollcott

To CAPTAIN QUENTIN ROOSEVELT

New York City
January 13, 1943

Son of Heaven:

If you have not heard from me before this, it is not because some letter from me went to the bottom of the sea. It is because I wrote none. I wrote none for various reasons, chief among them my sense of that unbridgable gulf between soldiers and civilians. I remember so well from twenty-five years ago that I got no letter from America which didn't sound silly. This inhibition was scarcely dissipated by one paragraph in a recent letter from Thornton Wilder (Captain Wilder, Air Force Intelligence to you) which read as follows: "Nothing so lifts a soldier's morale as getting a letter from home, and nothing so depresses him as reading it."

This will be made up largely of oddments. Perhaps you know that I spent six months of last year in bed. In April it was decided by everybody, the doctors and me included, that I was about to shuffle off this mortal coil. Having adjusted my mind to that idea, I was faintly annoyed to find myself in October under a mysterious obligation to begin functioning again. I now work from seven till midnight. This is true. It sounds silly but I do.

Recently I tottered to Washington on sundry pieces of mischief, and was kindly lodged by such of your relatives as now live at the White House. My host and hostess were hardly cold on the train to Hyde Park when I invited an out-of-season Roosevelt over to breakfast. I found the ensign in tip-top shape. I had always known that he was the sport of the family, no Roosevelt at all really, but a throw-back. Well, Cornelius is a throw-back all the way to your mother. He is so like her in every mannerism and gesture and look that I would have thought she was sitting there telling me where I got off.

Two more little items. The first concerns my dear Harpo. He spends all his time traveling from army camp to army camp,

[394]

with wig and harp. I may have told you once that his entire academic career was limited to the five years he spent in the first grade of the public school around the corner from the grimy tenement at Ninetieth Street and Third Avenue where the Marx boys grew up. This truncated education has left him with a sense of geography as fluid as J. W. Dunne's sense of time. Well, night before last he telephoned me from Watertown, New York, where the snow was eight feet deep and he was arranging to proceed by horse and sledge. His next engagement was in Boston, and he was quite untroubled as he was laboring under the impression that Watertown was on the outskirts of Boston. I did not have the heart to undeceive him.

My second item is about a book. It is a book I shall publish in March, dedicated, incidentally, to Frode Jensen who is, as you know, the pride of my declining years. He is, at the moment of writing, on the high seas, bound, I think, for your vicinity. We look for publication late in March, but it is part of the nonsense of the book trade that advance copies are available several weeks ahead of publication date. The first one of these I can get my hands on will start on its way to you, as I had you in mind all the time.

Of course you are always in my thoughts, and so's your old man.

A. W.

To *BRIGADIER GENERAL THEODORE ROOSEVELT, JR.*

New York City
January 14, 1943

Dear Ted:

I was raring back to write you at great length but I have just written Little Benjamin and since the fifteen-mile gap between you (mentioned in your letter of December 22nd) may since have widened, I will just send along a copy of my letter to him for such news as may be in it and go on from there. At the head of this letter is a permanent forwarding address set up when, in November, the island was silenced and sealed sine die. The question presented by the island answered itself. Even if there were enough fuel for the furnace and transportation to Whitehall it would be impractical. So long as I am well enough to work, I must do the kind that cannot be managed from any such fastness and if I am not well enough to work then I must not whimsically sequester myself in a spot so inaccessible to medical attention, with the nearest doctor sixteen miles away.

Speaking of doctors, my beloved Frode Jensen (a Captain in General Hospital Number 52) has departed from these shores and must, I think, be headed in your direction. Take him to your bosom. Still speaking of doctors, it was your erstwhile roommate, Elliott Cutler, who knifed me at the Peter Bent Brigham in Boston last June, laying me open like a melon and removing such entrails as may well have been my bane all along. I know only that I seem to get better with each passing month and can now work long and hard, provided I sit tight. Not get tight, mind you. Sit tight.

Well, maybe in another few months I can get about and see things. Perhaps get over to London and broadcast. There is some talk of my broadcasting regularly—from my room here at the Gotham if necessary. But I feel about as up-to-date and equipped for the purpose as some smelly old English dowager of the kind whose family gave her enough to live in Monte Carlo so long as she promised to stay there and not come home.

Speaking of broadcasts, I was scheduled, two weeks in advance, to do a sister-act with Jeannette MacDonald on the Stage Door Canteen program for November 12th. The point of it was that "Home Sweet Home" was the salvage from a failure, a disastrous operatta called *Clari, the Maid of Milan,* written for Covent Garden by an American youth who, in later years, was appointed, after the affable fashion of those days, to a snug berth in our consular service. As you will see if you note the date of the broadcast, it became unexpectedly topical, for you probably know (although I would bet against anybody else's knowing it) that John Howard Payne was our consul at Tunis. Tyler appointed him. He moved into the consulate, which he bitterly described as a "Yahoo of a house," in May 1843.

I miss not having Signorina at Oyster Bay. I believe she has gone South to take care of the new Theodore Roosevelt. I hope I live to see him, if only to complete my set. It was a pleasure to hear Signorina's voice all warm with pride in her American family. I wish you could have heard her voice when she told me that Cornelius had spent his furlough with her. But then you would not have to have heard it to know just what it sounded like.

Nor do I have to tell you that I am fond, proud and envious of you and wish to God that I, too, were in North Africa. In my prime I was never much of a soldier but I do like to see things and nothing in this world ever did me so much good as being underfoot in the army.

Alexander Woollcott

P.S. In May of '19 at least one transport started back to Brooklyn from Marseilles. Aboard it were sundry very recent civilians, including ex-Private Harold W. Ross, ex-Private C. Leroy Baldridge, ex-Private J. T. Winterich (now Lieutenant-Colonel) and Sergeant Alexander Woollcott (Ret.) En route, where it stopped for coal, it was delayed for five days by a longshoremen's strike. This port was Oran. Did you know that part of the last AEF strayed as far as Oran? Curious one-piece bathing suits in wide alternate stripes of shell-pink and baby-blue were available at five francs each. Clad in these, both Ross and I aroused unfavorable comment as we sported in the waves of the gulf of Mers el Kebir.

A. W.

To SERGEANT LEGGETT BROWN
[Woollcott's secretary for several years.]

New York City
January 13, 1943

My dear Flight Chief (whatever that is)

Under separate cover —which will be one title of my autobiography—I am sending you a copy of *The Last Time I Saw Paris* which is a big hunk of as good reading matter as I have encountered in a long while. Enclosed is a hint of more which will be sent to you as soon as the advance copies come in. If this still leaves you with an empty feeling, watch for every copy of *Reader's Digest* and *Good Housekeeping* for I'm in them all for months ahead. God knows why I've started getting up every day at seven and working until midnight. It has been so ever since I passed under the aegis of my new agent. In the not improbable case of your being unsure just what aegis means, I hereby confide to you my suspicion that it means *lash*.

Alison Smith [Mrs. Russel Crouse] died last week. At the services Monday Crouse spoke for a few minutes, introducing the minister who was thereby put in a tough spot. I would as soon have followed Lincoln at Gettysburg. Now, after his six-months vigil at that bedside, Crouse has gone away to Hot Springs for a week with Frank Sullivan on whom he leans heavily but calls his Pillar of Jello.

With radio proposals, the air has never been so thick. I will let you know when I light somewhere as I think it fairly probable I shall. Meanwhile my life retains some of its familiar color. For example my breakfast guest on Wednesday was Sergeant Heywood Broun and I went out to lunch with Marian Anderson. I'm dining tomorrow night with Irving Bacheller, who is eighty-five if he's a day, which he certainly is.

If I reiterate wearisomely that I find you have a warm place in my chilling and slightly damaged heart, it is because it surprises me.

Your friend Captain Wilder is morose at the Mayfair in Washington.

Albert

To *HELEN KELLER*

*New York City
January 18, 1943*

Dear, dear Helen:

I still hug the delusion that some day I will get myself out to Westport and somehow get transported to your house. But not just now. At the moment I am like some of those very delicate and little known French wines—not transportable.

Anyway, there was nothing in the original contract which bound you to avoid me until I *did* come out to Connecticut. I keep hearing from this person and that how you have been racketing around New York like a mad thing and venture to suggest that it would be pleasant for me if, on your next visit, you stopped off at the Gotham where I am lodged at present and whence I seldom venture forth. To conserve my waning strength I now work only sixteen hours a day which leaves a lot of time on my hands.

I want you to join with me in urging on a project which popped into my head yesterday afternoon and on which I already have several people working. The time had come for me to send in my annual list of nominations for the Talking Book Library. This morning I sent off a list of seventeen headed by *The Three Sisters* to be recorded by Miss Cornell and her company. Miss Kitty was in to see me yesterday afternoon and it seemed to me that she would not only be willing to do it but glad. More than most playwrights, Chekhov can be enjoyed by those who must get their plays by the ear and it seems to me improbable that as good a company to record it will be available again in our lifetime.

My love to Polly [Thompson].

A. Woollcott

To *ROSALIND RICHARDS*

New York City
January 20, 1943

Dear, dear Miss Rosalind: (A great-aunt can be so addressed by a great-uncle who, even if he is one of comparatively recent standing, is doing nicely. I wish you could see my comely and well-nourished twin grandnephews who dwell in another Northern Countryside—Burlington, Vermont, to be exact.)

The book came and I am proud and pleased to have it. I have been dipping into it and it shall stay on my bedside shelf until I have read it all.

L.E.R. will be in my thoughts as long as I have any and off and on I shall be writing and telling the tale of her as long as I function. But this word of explanation is just for you. I am a lethargic person, really, and I have traveled far and traveled often always with a homesickness inside me. Never did a ship put out to sea with me aboard it that I did not come to like a sleepwalker and suppress with difficulty an impulse to jump overboard and swim ashore, wondering wildly why I should have embarked at all. I would have been glad had I been born into a village of two hundred souls and more than content never once in my life to leave it—provided I could pick the two hundred. This modest stipulation of mine never having been met, I have had to do a good deal of traveling because my two hundred were all over the earth. Thus I went to Moscow in 1932 not to inspect the Soviet experiment (having come of good Fourierite stock I was naturally sympathetic with it) but to visit an exhilarating companion of my youth, Walter Duranty. I had gone to Peking the year before to visit two old friends who were wantonly inconveniencing me by living so far away. If I would sometimes throw nineteen lecture invitations into the scrapbasket and then accept the twentieth, it was probably because the twentieth called for a speech in Indianapolis and, before or after, I could stop off and have a talk with Mr. Tarkington. Last year was the first year in twenty years when I was defeated in my wise plan to seek renewal at least once a year by visiting Mr. Tarkington.

Well, of course Laura Richards dwelt in my village. What a delight, what a refreshment, what a nourishment it was to see her and to hear her and to think about her I have no words to tell even you. Now I can only think about her. I do that a great deal. I always shall.

Of course it is my trade and my habit to do a good deal of my thinking in words. When the news came from Gardiner I had to suppress a strong impulse to go right down to the *Times* office—I have not been on its staff for more than twenty years—and push away from his typewriter whatever young man was writing the obituary notice. Now I have it firmly in mind to write a memorial piece about her for *Good Housekeeping*. I want to find my way to all those matrons who, when they were young, read and loved the Hildegarde stories. I am telling you of this project because perhaps the editor should illustrate it with a photograph. He can be trusted to dig up no end of pictures of her but perhaps there is one you would *rather* have used. If so will you send it to me or advise me how to get it? But if this is a bother instead of being a chore you welcome, I beg you to forget it.

There's one memory of my last visit to Gardiner which is so etched into my mind that nothing will ever efface it. It was L.E.R. going in to lunch on the Skipper's arm. What a triumphant life!

Alexander Woollcott

Index

Names of persons to whom letters were written are indicated in page references set in Roman figures (347).

Names of persons mentioned within letters are indicated in page references set in Italic figures (*97*).

Pages on which explanatory notes appear are indicated with an asterisk (327*).

Abbott, George, *97*
Adams, Franklin P., *xi, xii, 58, 61, 68, 75, 94, 95*
Adams, Mrs. Franklin P., *95*
Adams, Maude, *102*
Adams, Samuel Hopkins, *x, 216, 249,* 327*, 347
Adams, Mrs. Samuel Hopkins, *328, 348*
Agnew, George Smyser, *viii,* 2*, 3, 4, 5, 6, 7, 8, 10, 12, 15, 16, 18, 19, *54*
Alsop, Joseph, Jr., *178, 191, 219, 275, 280, 325, 350, 355, 359*
Amherst, Earl (Jeffrey Holmesdale), *86, 104, 114, 134, 213, 380*
Anderson, Judith, *388, 391, 392*
Anderson, Marian, *399*
Andrews, Henry, *203, 230, 259, 271, 282*
Andrews, Mrs. Henry, *see* West, Rebecca
Arling, Emanie, *258*
Armstrong, Hamilton Fish, *331*
Astaire, Adele, *see* Cavendish, Lady
Atherton, Gertrude, *107*
Atkinson, Brooks, *374*

Bacheller, Irving, *399*
Backer, Dorothy, *370*
Backer, George, *86,* 87*, *93, 97, 101, 122, 123, 162, 164, 239, 329, 337*
Bailey, H. C., *115*
Baker, Courtland, *3, 17*
Baker, Newton D., *145,* 159*, *160, 168, 171, 209, 210*
Baker, Mrs. Newton D., *159*

Baldridge, C. Leroy, *64, 397*
Baldwin, Mrs. Stanley, *134*
Balestier, Beatty, *276, 366*
Balestier, Carrie, *see* Kipling, Mrs. Rudyard
Balestier, Wolcott, *273, 275, 276, 367, 392*
Bankhead, Tallulah, *357, 374*
Banks, Leslie, *204,* 263*
Banks, Mrs. Leslie, *204, 264*
Baragwaneth, Mrs. J. G., *see* McMein, Neysa
Barbour, Joyce, *86, 87*
Barrie, Sir James M., *159*
Barrymore, Ethel, *xvi, xxv, 234, 258, 290, 324, 335, 336, 342, 344, 350, 351, 353*
Barrymore, John, *182, 264, 322, 335*
Barton, Ralph, *97*
Beer, Thomas, *110*
Beerbohm, Max, *232, 294, 295, 328*
Beerbohm, Mrs. Max, *390*
Behrman, S. N., *xv, xix, 98, 123, 321*
Belasco, David, *49, 97*
Bell, Clive, *115*
Benchley, Robert, *xii, xix, 78, 196, 232*
Benedict, Henry Harper, *249*
Benét, William Rose, *151*
Bentley, John, *10*
Berlin, Elizabeth Irving, *266*
Berlin, Irving, *77, 118, 123, 138, 196, 239, 266, 372, 386*
Berlin, Mrs. Irving, *266, 386*

[403]

Best, Marshall, *150*, 342*
Birch, Reginald, *188*
Bird, Richard, *86*, *87*, *114*, *115*
Bird, Mrs. Richard, *see* Barbour, Joyce
Blake, Henry, *89*
Bledsoe, Jules, *120*
Blodgett, Alden, *232*
Bonner, Henry, *92*
Bonner, Lilly (Mrs. Paul), *86*, *87*, *91**, *93*, *95*, *97*, *99*, *101*, *105*, *114*, *122*, *133*, *172*, *200*, *259*, *354*, *360*
Bonner, Paul, *91**, *92*, *94*, *95*, *100*, *101*, *103*, *114*, *115*, *125*, *130*, *173*, *199*, *295*
Brackett, Charles, *97*, *135*, *165*, *219*, *317*, *354*, 360*, *365*
Brady, Father, *75*
Brandeis, Louis D., *249*
Brent, Romney, *131*
Brent, Mrs. Romney, *341*
Brooks, Gerald, *123*
Broun, Heywood, *xi*, *xii*, *22*, *31*, *37*, *39*, *40*, *43*, *46*, *49*, *50*, *53*, *56*, *58*, *70*, *95*, *98*, *182*
Broun, Mrs. Heywood, *see* Hale, Ruth
Broun, Heywood II, *399*
Brown, Ethan Allan, *345*
Brown, John Mason, *323*
Brown, Leggett, *152*, *155*, *157*, *169*, 398*
Buchan, John (Lord Tweedsmuir), *273*
Bucklin, Anne, *1*, *14*, *82*, *83*
Bucklin, Charles, *315*, *316*
Bucklin, Edward, *315-16*
Bucklin, Eliza (A. W.'s grandmother), *81*, *313*
Bucklin, John, *14*
Bucklin, John (A. W.'s grandfather), *109*, *313*
Bucklin, Julie, *19*, *26*, *28*, *39*, *50*, *53*, *81*, *302*, *315*
Bucklin, Lillian, *18*
Bucklin, Mary, *313*
Bucklin, Polly, *302*, *316*
Bucklin, Tod, *2*
Bucklin, William S., *20*, *82*
Bull, Howard, *238*, *359*, *360*
Burlen, Robert, *42*
Burrows, Fritz, *25*
Burton, Richard, *51*
Bye, George, *259*

Calder, Jack, *59*
Calhern, Louis, *123*, *350*, *353*, *360*

Campbell, Alan, *xx*, *237*, *324*, *325*, *349*, *354*, *361*, *366*, *385*
Campbell, Mrs. Alan, *see* Parker, Dorothy
Campbell, Mrs. Patrick, *121*, *124*
Carrel, Alexis, *382*
Carson, Lord, *160*, *205*
Castle, Irene, *151*, *363*
Cavendish, Lady (Adele Astaire), *86*, *116*
Cavendish, Lord, *86*
Cazalet, Victor, *115*
Chamberlain, Neville, *206*, *233*
Chanler, Mrs. Winthrop, *178*
Chaplain, Charles S., *xix*, *138*, *152*, *174*, *262*, *302*, *371*
Churchill, Winston, *145*, *233*, *234*, *271*, *283*
Ciannelli, Eduardo, *102*
Clemenceau, Georges, *313*, *315*, *317*
Clemens, Cyril, 184
Clendening, Logan, *xxv*, *389*, *390*, *391*
Cliffe, Alice Belmore, *392*
Cocaud, Mère, *52*, *54*, *346*
Cohn, Alfred, *356*
Colefax, Sibyl, Lady, *96*, *115*, *124*, *128*, *129*, 161*, *165*, *166*, *175*, *190*, *226*, *230*, *233*, *294*, *319*, *324*, *327*, *355*, *364*, 371
Colfax, Schuyler, *167*
Collier, Constance, *103*
Colvin, Ian, *160*
Conant, James Bryant, *180*
Connelly, Marc, *xii*, *76*, *152*
Copeland, Charles Townsend, *113*
Corbin, John, *35*, *39*, 40*, *46*
Cornell, Katharine, *xvii*, *98*, *130*, *133*, *194*, *196*, *224*, *251*, *290*, *336*, *337*, *340*, *369*, *388*, *391*, *392*, *400*
Corwin, Norman, *304*
Coward, Noel, *xvi*, *85*, *86*, *104*, *128*, *133*, *134*, *142*, *171*, *172*, *175*, *191*, 213, *225*, *253*, *324*, *376*, *377*, *379*
Cowl, Jane, *204*
Cowley, Malcolm, *141**
Cowley, W. H., *248-49*
Craig, Gordon, *103*, *112*
Craven, Frank, *xix*, *354*
Craven, Mrs. Frank, *354*
Cross, Martha, *253*
Crothers, Rachel, *351*
Crouse, Russel, *398*
Cushing, Charles P., *65*, *70*
Cutler, Elliott, *332*, *333*, *396*

[404]

Dale, Margaret, *123*
Daly, Arnold, *39*
Davies, Marion, *118*
Davis, Elmer, *370*
Davis, Owen, *143*
Devol, Edmund, *49-50*, 71, 73, *362*
Devonshire, Duchess of, *116*
De Wolfe, Elsie (Lady Mendl), *100, 101*, *363*
Dietz, Howard, *xv*, *97*, *133*, 290, *365*, *379*
Dietz, Mrs. Howard, *290*
Disney, Walt, *xvi*, *xix*, *138*, *152*, *235*, *292*, *297*
Dix, John A., *248*
Dodd, Lee, *68*
Donovan, William J., *124*, 145*, 289, *370*
Douglas, Robert, *115*
Drage, Lucy Christie, *viii*, *24**, *46*, 79*, 161, *242*, *300*, *362*
Duchin, Eddy, *117*
Duffy, The Rev. Francis, *289*
Dunne, J. W., *162*
Duranty, Walter, *xxv*, *xxvi*, *37*, *40*, *47*, *68*, *401*
Durstine, Roy, *65*

Eagan, William, *202*
Early, Stephen, *xi*, 169*, 171
Eckstein, Gustav, *174**, *178*, 185*, 189, *192*, *193*, 194, 195, *244*, *248*, 254, *269*, *270*, *314*, *317*, 332, 381
Eldridge, Florence, *271*, *374*
Elizabeth, *see* Russell, Mrs. F.
Ellington, Josephine W., *352*
Emerson, William, *296-97*
Engs, Baba, *59*, *65*
Engs, Russell, *59*
Eustis, Mrs. Hendrick, *xv*, 168, 180, *225*, *376*, *379*
Evans, Edith, 318
Evans, Maurice, *252*

Fadiman, Clifton, *378*
Farrar, John, *121*
Fatio, Maurice, *94*, *123*
Fatio, Mrs. Maurice, *94*
Fellowes, Daisy, *363*
Ferber, Edna, 76, 77, 83, *115*, 120, *130*, *133*, *201*, *271*, *359*, *380*
Ferber, Julia, *83*
Ferry, Frederick C., *248*
Field, Roswell (Rose), *viii*, *81*, *300*

Fiske, Minnie Maddern, *ix*, *32*, *35*, *39*, *53*, *61*, *112*, *161*, *195*, *317*, *344*
Flandrau, Charles Macomb, 113*
Flanner, Janet, *299*, *361*
Fleischmann, Raoul, *xv*, *78*, *97*
Fleischmann, Ruth, 97
Fleming, Susan, *see* Marx, Mrs. Harpo
Folley, Jarrett, *149*
Fontanne, Lynn, *xvi*, *xvii*, *88*, *103*, *124*, 128, 131, *134*, 135, *151*, *175*, *179*, *185*, *196*, *207*, *208*, *213*, 220, *226*, *231*, *235*, *251*, *261*, *262*, 269, *287*, *297*, *318*, *336*, *337*, *340*, *343*, 358, *392*
Foster, Maximilian, *65*
Foster, Stephen, *214*
Fotitch, Constantin, *280*
Fox, Della, *277*
F.P.A., *see* Adams, Franklin P.
Frankfurter, Felix, *217*, *256*, *268*, *280*, *330*, *356*, *360*, *370*, *371*, 376, *381*, 382
Freddie, *67*, *70*
Fuller, Mrs. W. Parmer, Jr., *302*

Garden, Mary, *362*
Gellhorn, Martha, *283*
Gershwin, Ira, 138
Getman, Albert A., *194*, *245*, *247*, *248*, *255*
Getman, Mrs. Albert A., *194*
Gielgud, John, *172*, *175*, *176*
Giles, Frances, *20*
Gillette, William, *124*
Gillmore, Margalo, *123*, *132*, *341*, *385*
Gilman, Lawrence, *22*, *23**, *241*
Gilman, Mrs. Lawrence, 240
Gish, Dorothy, *350*, *353*, *360*
Gordon, Ruth, *xvii*, *121*, *122*, *126*, *194*, *251*, *275*, *331**, *336*, *342*, *346*, *353*, *363*, *374*, *385*, *388*, *391*, *392*
Gosse, Edmund, *367*
Grahame, Mrs. Kenneth, *291*, *294*
Grant, Jane, *xii*, *xiii*, *56*
Guedalla, Philip, *84*
Guinzburg, Harold K., *xv*, *95*, *97*, 140*, 144, 150, 217, *259*
Guinzburg, Mrs. Harold K., *97*
Gwenn, Edmund, *391-92*

Hackett, Peter, 84*
Hale, Ruth, *22*, *31*, *32*, *37*, *39*, *40*, *43*, *44*, *46*, *47*, *48*, *53*, *55*, 65, *74*
Hamilton, Hamish, *217*
Hammett, Dashiell, *152*

[405]

Hanfstaengl, Ernest F., *151*
Harding, Warren G., *168, 170*
Harper, Paul, *152**
Harper, Paul, Jr., *326*
Harriman, Mrs. J. Borden, *54*
Harriman, W. Averell, *283*
Harris, Frank, 363
Harris, Jed, *139*
Harris, Sam, *350*
Hart, Moss, *xix, 200, 227, 228, 231, 245, 272, 275, 321, 343, 351, 354*
Harvey, Fred, *161*, 163*
Harvey, Mrs. Fred (Betty Drage), *161*, 162-64*
Hawley, Hudson, 79
Hayes, Helen, *xvii, 126, 132, 179, 251, 252,* 343, *346, 357, 370, 384*
Hayes, Ralph, *168*, 170, 209*
Hecht, Ben, *126, 133, 139, 142, 376, 379*
Held, Anna, *149*
Hemingway, Ernest, *283, 370*
Hennessey, Joseph, *xvii, xix, 123, 157, 174, 189, 212, 218, 225, 238, 275, 312, 318, 325, 327, 334, 342, 348, 358, 393*
Hilton, James, *133*
Hitchcock, Alfred, *356*
Holliday, Terence, *96, 221*
Holmes, John, *210-11*
Holmes, Myra, *35*
Holmes, Justice Oliver Wendell, *210, 222, 268, 279, 328, 381, 382*
Holt, Mrs. Henry, *54*
Hood, Robin, *269*
Hopkins, Arthur, *50, 74, 120, 121, 179, 336*
Hopkins, Harry, *283, 377*
Howard, Leslie, *175-76*
Hoyt, Philip, *32, 65*
Hull, Henry, *179*
Hull, Robert, *25*
Humphrey, Elliot (Jack), *187, 195*
Humphreys, Alexander, *82, 296*
Humphreys, Mrs. Alexander (Eva), *82, 296*
Hu Shih, *206*
Hutchins, Robert Maynard, *215*, 381*

Iddesleigh, Lady, *115*
Irwin, Robert, *251*
Ives, Raymond, *xv, 97, 212*
Ives, Mrs. Raymond, *xv, 97, 212*

Jacques, *66, 74*
Janis, Elsie, *67*

Jennings, Mrs. Fritz, *see* Woollcott, Joan
Jensen, Frode, *127*, 151, 157, 158, 218, 239, 255, 305, 306, 307, 308, 309, 310, 311, 313, 317, 319, 349, 350, 352, 395, 396*
Jensen, Mrs. Frode, *158, 218*
Jessup, Lois, *254*

Kanin, Garson, *354*
Kaufman, Beatrice (Mrs. George S.), *xv, 79,* 85, 87, *97,* 114, *122, 123, 133, 150, 151, 169, 182,* 200, *212, 227,* 236, *274, 343, 362*
Kaufman, George S., *xii, xiv, xvi, xix, 114, 123, 129, 136, 212, 228, 231, 239, 245, 271, 272, 321, 322, 343, 351*
Keller, Helen, *177, 182, 251,* 337, *399*
Kelly, Gregory, *360*
Kennedy, D. G., *140*, 193, 330, 335, 358*
Kennedy, The Rev. Howard, *306-309*
Kennedy, Mrs. Howard, *308-309*
Kern, Jerome, *xvi, 77,* 117, *149*
Kikugoro, *88*
Kimball, W. S., *81*
Kinney, Selden Talcott, *9*
Kintner, Robert, *355*
Kipling, Rudyard, *273, 275, 276, 277, 278*
Kipling, Mrs. Rudyard, *275-77*
Klauber, Adolph, *x*
Knickerbocker, H. R., *231, 237, 240*
Kommer, Rudolf, *129, 381*
Krock, Arthur, *121*

Ladd, Schuyler, *37, 38, 42, 47, 72*
Landon, Alfred M., *168, 171*
Larrimore, Francine, *98*
Laughton, Charles, *xix, 232, 342*
Lawford, Ernest, *123*
Lederer, Charles, *116*, 126, 130, 132, 151, 182, 196, 236, 354, 361*
Lee, Charles, *298**
Lee, Thomas, *56*
Leigh, Vivien, *232, 237, 243*
Leonard, Deborah, *see* Jensen, Mrs. Frode
Leonard, John, *152*
Leontovitch, Eugenie, *270*
Levant, Oscar, *228, 236*
Levine, Samuel A., *311, 350*
Lewis, Lloyd, *223*, 370, 381*

[406]

Lewis, Mrs. Lloyd, *184*
Libman, Emanuel, *382*
Lillie, Lucy C., *183*
Lindbergh, Charles A., *243*
Lippmann, Walter, *xi, 209, 256,* 268, *281, 304,* 364, *372, 380*
Lippmann, Mrs. Walter, *268, 364*
Lloyd, Samuel, *55*
Longfellow, Alice, *211, 214*
Longwell, Daniel, *381*
Longworth, Alice, *121, 124, 172, 178, 194, 275, 355*
Lorraine, Lorn, *380*
Loud, Alexander Humphreys, *296*
Lowndes, Mrs. Marie Belloc, *86, 105, 114, 162, 364, 365,* 366
Luce, Henry, *381*
Lunt, Alfred, *xvi, xvii,* 88, 102, *104, 124, 125,* 128, 131, *134, 151, 175, 179, 185, 196, 207, 208, 213,* 218, *221, 226, 231, 235, 251, 261, 262, 270, 271, 297, 318, 323, 337, 340, 343, 359, 392*
Lunt, Mrs. Alfred, *see* Fontanne, Lynn
Lunt, Cornelia, *130*

MacArthur, Charles, *78, 116, 126, 133, 142, 143, 182, 196, 318, 343, 383, 384*
MacArthur, Mrs. Charles, *see* Hayes, Helen
MacArthur, Mary, *384*
MacDonald, Jeannette, *396*
MacLeish, Archibald, *145, 169,* 251*, *256,* 286, 303, *356, 370*
Macy, Anne Sullivan, *177*
Mann, William, *151, 174*
Mannering, Mary, *149*
Mansfield, Richard, *390, 391*
Mansfield, Mrs. Richard, *390, 391*
Mansfield, Richard (Gibbs), *389, 390, 391*
Mantle, Burns, 216*
March, Frederic, *357, 374*
Marjoribanks, Edward, *160, 205*
Markey, Gene, *228*
Marlowe, Julia, *333-34*
Marsh, John R., *184*
Martin, Charles, *228, 23.*
Marx, Groucho, *98*
Marx, Harpo, *xii, xv, xix, 79, 94, 97, 98, 113, 116, 125, 130, 151, 152,* 182, *196, 236, 239, 323, 354, 361, 362, 366, 394*
Marx, Mrs. Harpo, *125, 152, 354, 366*
Marx, Mrs. Minnie, *119*

Mason, John, *317*
Massey, Raymond, *114*
Maugham, Somerset, *363, 376, 379*
Maxwell, Elsa, *362*
McAdoo, Eva, *55,* 65
McClintic, Guthrie, *133, 342, 391*
McClintic, Mrs. Guthrie, *see* Cornell, Katharine
McCord, David, 179*, *382*
McMein, Neysa, *xv, 97,* 99, *135, 151, 191, 213, 254, 297, 329, 337, 360, 361*
Mencken, H. L., *383*
Mendl, Sir Charles, 100
Mendl, Lady, *see* De Wolfe, Elsie
Mestayer, Harry, *118,* 119
Miller, Alice Duer (Mrs. Henry W.), *xiv, xv, xvii, 79, 97, 105, 125, 126, 130, 136, 175, 187, 212, 228, 231, 266, 275, 324, 329, 341, 343, 357, 358, 360, 361, 362, 365, 366, 371, 372, 376*
Miller, Denning, *366*
Miller, Gilbert, *129*
Miller, Henry Wise, *231, 366*
Millis, Walter, *145*
Mitchell, Margaret, *167,* 181, 183
Mitchell, S. Weir, *314, 317*
Montgomery, Miss, *18, 141*
Moore, Grace, *362*
Moore, Red, *72*
Morgan, Charles, *115*
Morgan, Claudia, *236*
Morley, Robert, *322*
Mosher, John, *361*
Murphy, Gerald, *245, 317, 370*
Myerson, Dr. M. C., *248*

Nazimova, Alla, *45*
Nesbitt, Cathleen, *264*
Noguchi, Hideyo, *314, 333**
Norris, Charles G., *94,* 229
Norris, Kathleen (Mrs. Charles G.), *94, 130, 226*

Odlum, Floyd, *228*
Oglebay, Kate, *xii*
Olivier, Laurence, *232, 237, 243*
Orr, Thomas, *28*
Osland-Hill, Marie, *126**
Owen, Russell, *121*

Parker, Dorothy, *135, 142, 152, 203, 232, 324, 325, 328, 349, 354, 361, 366, 381, 385*

[407]

Irish, Anne, *108, 174, 191, 317*
Iteur, Louis, *316-17*
Iriarche, Marie Louise, 75*
Irick, Albert, *249*
Iterson, Cissy, *121*
Ine, John Howard, *397*
Ivl, Raymond, *260*
Ine, Marshall, *71*
Toberton, Brock, *xii, 51, 74*
Toberton, Murdoch, *xii*
Ivell, Bruce, *91*
Ivell, Phyllis Blake, *89*
Ivell, William, *xii*
Pvers, Tom, *391*
Pttzer, Margaret Leech, *xii, 133*

Rahmaninoff, Sergei, *231*
Rainge, Jennifer, *264*
Ransom, Jo, *368*
Reallo, Constance, *363*
Reallo, Edna, *363*
Ratliff, Gregory, *366*
Ramsdale, Lady, *115*
Reed, Florence, *374*
Reinhardt, Max, *190*
Remarque, Erich Maria, *190*
Rice, Grantland, *68*
Richards, Laura E., 105*, *107, 138, 139, 140, 141, 176, 178, 188, 197, 210, 214, 232, 238, 260, 264, 278, 290, 305, 400, 401, 402*
Richards, Rosalind, *137, 139,* 260, 400
Richdalc, Arthur, *8*
Richdale, Ella, *14*
Richdale, Guy, *14*
Richdale, June, *14*
Roberts, Kenneth, *195*
Robertson, W. Graham, *135, 136, 146*, 167, 207, 261, 270, 287, 288, 296*
Robeson, Paul, *330*
Robinson, Mrs. Douglas, *178*
Robinson, Francis, 388*
Roosevelt, Cornelius, *212, 394, 397*
Roosevelt, Franklin D., *168, 170, 171, 271, 274, 282, 283, 378*
Roosevelt, Mrs. Franklin D., *178, 274, 275, 308, 355, 393*
Roosevelt, Grace, *212*
Roosevelt, Quentin, *253, 375,* 394
Roosevelt, Theodore, *170, 248*
Roosevelt, Theodore, Jr., *206, 219, 251, 252, 355, 395*

Roosevelt, Mrs. Theodore, Jr., 211, 252, *351*
Root, Mrs. Edward W. (Grace), *127, 307, 309,* 348*
Root, Edwin B., *ix, 6*
Root, Mrs. Edwin B., *6, 12*
Root, Elihu, *249*
Root, Nancy, *14*
Root family, 10*
Rosenberger, Sophie, *viii,* 186*, 221, *243, 256, 300, 363, 383*
Ross, Harold W., *x, xii, xiii, 94, 397, 398*
Rudd, Alethea, *44, 53*
Rudd, Robert Barnes, 110, *143, 166*
Russell, Frank, *281*
Russell, Mrs. Frank, *281*
Ruth, George Herman (Babe), *89*

Sackett, Mrs. Anna Benson, *26, 51*
Sackett, Nelson, *26, 39, 45, 51*
Sandburg, Carl, *224, 382*
Sanderson, Julia, *118*
Sassoon, Siegfried, *105*
Sauerwen, Frank, *81*
Sauerwen, Mailie, *81*
Sauerwen, Mr., *302*
Saunders, A. P., *174*, 191, 194,* 351
Schenck, Joseph, *366*
Schoenberg, Lafey, *118*
Sears, Helen Warren, *ix, 20,* 301*
Sergeant, Elizabeth, *54*
Shaw, George Bernard, *103, 109, 121, 362*
Shaw, Mrs. George Bernard, *121*
Shean, Al, *118-19*
Sheehan, Gertrude Ellen, *234*
Sheean, Vincent, *234*
Sheean, Mrs. Vincent, *234, 258*
Sheldon, Edward, *112, 245,* 312*, *318, 322, 330, 333, 344, 351, 357*
Shepard, William P., *41, 51*
Sherman, James Schoolcraft, *248*
Sherwood, Mary Brandon, *130*
Sherwood, Robert E., *130, 185, 271, 290*
Sherwood, Mrs. Robert E., *290*
Shumlin, Herman, *202*
Silberberg, Daniel H., *187, 228,* 247
Siler, Joseph, *56*
Simpson, Wallis, *173*
Skinner, Cornelia Otis, 232*, *250, 253, 362*

[408]

Skinner, Otis, *ix, 148, 232*, 250, 254, 312, 362*
Skinner, Mrs. Otis, *148, 232*
Slezak, Walter, *118*
Smith, Alison, *398*
Smith, Mrs. Henry, *see* Woollcott, Nancy
Smith, Henry Clapp, *123*
Smith, Nora, *106*
Smith, Tom, *40*
Smoot, Miss, *186, 187*
Sorber, Miss K. R., *viii,* 1*, **2**, *141**
Stefansson, Vilhjalmur, *290*
Stehli, Henry, *105*
Stein, Gertrude, *144, 190*
Steinbeck, John, *218*
Stevens, Emily, *317*
Stewart, Donald Ogden, *xiii*
Stimson, Henry L., *248*
Stoll, Marian, *17, 293*
Stone, Don, *59*
Stone, Elizabeth, *246*
Stone, Mary, *246*
Stone, Waterman, *246-47*
Stryker, Lloyd Paul, *21*, 28, 44, 65, 248*
Stryker, Mrs. Lloyd P. (Katharine), *21*, 24, 28, 44, 65*
Stryker, Melancthon W., *9, 30, 248, 249*
Sturhahn, Pat, *121*
Sullivan, Frank, *xi, 128*, 187, 198, 292, 385, 398*
Swing, Raymond Gram, *290*
Swope, Herbert Bayard, *xi, 76*, 102, 123, 124*
Swope, Mrs. Herbert Bayard, *76*
Swope, Herbert Bayard, Jr., *89*, 102*

Taber, Charles, *32, 51, 53, 80, 301, 363*
Taber, Julie Woollcott (Mrs. Charles), *viii, 7, 19, 20, 22, 24*, 28, 31, 35, 41, 44, 50, 54, 73, 79, 80, 81, 82, 83, 246, 302, 363*
Taft, William Howard, *248*
Talcott, Carolyn, *45*
Tarkington, Booth, *97, 132, 138, 146, 147, 177, 188, 195, 252, 269, 270, 292, 382, 401*
Tarkington, Mrs. Booth, *353*
Taylor, Deems, *xi, xii, 76, 255, 263*
Terry, Ellen, *103*
Thomason, John W., Jr., *92*
Thompson, Dorothy, *206, 234, 258, 339*
Thompson, Polly, *177, 182, 338, 400*

Timming, Helene, *190*
Touhey, John Peter, *xii,* 301
Travers, Henry, *102*
Trexler, Samuel, *71, 72*
Truax, Mrs. Alice Hawley, *21*,* **23,** *24, 26, 35, 39, 40, 47, 53, 55, 57, 62, 73*
Traux, Chauncey, *21**
Traux, R. Hawley, *xii, 12, 21*, 22, 24, 28, 37, 40, 42, 44, 56, 97, 112*
Turnbull, Eva Humphreys, *82*

Van Anda, Carr V., *x, 50, 216*
Von Hoffmannstahl, Mrs. Raimund, *381*
Von Mendelssohn, Eleanora, *xxv, 152, 350, 351*

Walbridge, Earle F., *151*
Walcott, Frederic, *254*
Walker, June, *385*
Wallace, Pat (Mrs. A. S. Frere Reeves), *281*
Wallgren, A. A., *xi, 61*, 75, 99*
Waln, Nora, *see* Osland-Hill, Marie
Wanger, Walter, *42, 45, 228*
Watson, Leonard, *15*
Watson, Mark S., *xi, 386**
Waugh, Arthur, *367, 392*
Waugh, Evelyn, *230, 392, 393*
Weaver, John V. A., *301*
Webster, Margaret, *237*
Weeks, Edward, *217, 273*
Wehner, Mrs. Peter, *186*
Welch, Philip, *17, 19*
Welles, Orson, *130*
Wellman, Frances, *86*
Wells, H. G., *204-206, 257*
West, Anthony, *203, 230, 258*
West, Mrs. Anthony, *258*
West, Paul, *68*
West, Rebecca, *86, 104, 114, 115, 150, 178, 203, 226, 229, 257, 271, 280, 331, 368, 373*
Westley, Helen, *104*
Whitcombe, Wilcox L., *28*
White, E. B., *282*
White, William Allen, *241, 242**
Whitty, Dame May, *232*
Wiggin, Kate Douglas, *106, 113*
Wilcox, Miss, *18*
Wilder, Thornton, *xvii, 121, 124, 126, 144, 190, 201, 215, 235, 245, 254, 271, 294, 307, 320, 324,* **325,** *329, 330, 333,*

334, 345, *350*, *356*, *357*, *358*, *359*, *368*, *370*, 373, 380, *383*, *385*, *390*, 392, *394*, *399*
Williams, Herschel V., Jr., 284*
Williams, Hope, *173*
Williams, John, *39*
Williams, Wythe, *37*, *47*, *68*
Williams, Mrs. Wythe, *47*
Willkie, Wendell, *250*, *271*, *282*, *283*
Wilson, Edmund, *272*, *275*
Wilson, John C., *133*
Wilson, Woodrow, *74*, *160*, *168*, *170*, *371*
Winterich, John T., *xi*, *74*, *386*, *397*
Wood, Peggy, *xii*, *301*
Wood, Richard Carver, *194*, *254*, *319*
Woollcott, Barbara, *244*, *386*
Woollcott, Frances Bucklin (Bam), *vii*, *viii*, *7*, *14*, *15*, *19*, *20*, *32*, *48*, *51*, *54*, *81*, *314*
Woollcott, Harry, *246*

Woollcott, Joan, *216*, *219*, *244*, *259*, *267*, *302*, *303*
Woollcott, Julie, *see* Taber, Julie Woollcott
Woollcott, Maude, *352*
Woollcott, Nancy, *77*, *78*, *243*, *270*, *300*, *386*
Woollcott, Philip, *2*
Woollcott, Philip (A. W.'s cousin), *352*
Woollcott, Polly, *244*, *386*
Woollcott, Walter, *vii*, *viii*, *54*, *109*
Woollcott, Mrs. Walter, *see* Woollcott, Frances B.
Woollcott, William W., *79*, *260*, *302*, *324*, *325*, *326*, *328*
Wright, Frank Lloyd, *189*, *190*, *191**, *235*

Yamada, Osamu, *113*
Young, Stark, *55*
Yuan, Henry, *88*, *89**, *92*